The Great
Kitchen

The
Cellarer's
Office

The
Buttery
called
the Loft

The Dormitory
under which
is the song
schoole and
treasury and
other Offices

THE ART OF COOKERY

This facsimile of the Art of Cookery by John Thacker is published by kind permission of Leeds University Library. The publisher is grateful to Dr Oliver Pickering of the Special Collections Department for his time and trouble.

This edition first published in 2004 by
SOUTHOVER PRESS,
2 Cockshut Road, Lewes, East Sussex BN7 1JH
Copyright © Introduction, bibliography
and notes, Ivan Day

ISBN 1 870962 20 6

Typeset in Garamond 11pt
by Saxon Graphics Ltd, Derby
Printed in England on wood-free paper
by Woolnough Bookbinding Ltd,
Irthlingborough, Northants NN9 5SE

CONTENTS

Introduction by Ivan Day v

Bibliography xxiv

Notes xxvi

The Art of Cookery xxix

Preface by John Thacker xxxi

Original index xxxv

Recipes 1

Menus 323

Glossary 357

One or two pages in the original text are wrongly numbered.

INTRODUCTION

A SIGNIFICANT number of important continental recipe books have been written by cooks who worked for high-ranking religious dignitaries. John Thacker's *The Art of Cookery* is the only one to emanate from an English religious community. Although on a much smaller scale than its European equivalents, this delightful work opens a window into a remarkable world of ecclesiastical hospitality and entertainment which survived at Durham Cathedral for more than eight hundred years. [1]

Until the Reformation, Durham Priory was the third richest monastery in England. Its shrine to St Cuthbert had made it the chief pilgrimage site of the North and for many centuries it had been the seat of the powerful Prince Bishops. Since their arrival in 1093, the resident Benedictine monks had provided food for pilgrims and other guests from the priory kitchen.[2] Their code of hospitality was based on Christ's words 'I was a stranger and you took me in'. After the priory was suppressed during the Dissolution, a statute issued by Henry VIII in 1541 set up a new cathedral foundation. Its establishment was a dean with a chapter of twelve major and twelve minor canons. These changes went ahead relatively painlessly, as the prior willingly converted his post to that of dean. Likewise his twelve senior monks quietly became the major canons or prebendaries[3].

The Dissolution also brought changes to the domestic life of the community. In addition to the dean and canons, the new foundation stipulated a small body of inferior household ministers. These were to replace the Benedictine hosteller, cellarer and yeomen of the kitchen. Among their numbers were to be a *cuquo* (cook) and a *subcuquo* (under-cook). Both were to be elected by the dean and were to be 'industrious men of good report and upright life, who shall faithfully prepare all victuals and eatables for the table, that have their living in common.' The statute also directs that 'the minor canons, the deacon and sub deacon, and as many of the clerks as have no wives, shall mess and feast in the common hall. And let him who sits at the head rebuke and bring into order the others, if they be unruly, that all things may be done with decorum.' Communal life of this kind survived for about fifty years, but gradually the canons took wives and set up their own households. The cook and his assistant continued to use the great monastic kitchen complex, which had served the priory since 1374, but their duties became lighter as the community ceased to mess and feast in hall.[4] By 1663 the old Benedictine refectory had been converted into a library. The building which had been the prior's lodging became the deanery and the great kitchen was used mainly for preparing meals for the dean and his guests.

According to Henry's statute, the *cuquo* was to receive an annual stipend of 58 shillings and his *subcuquo* 38 shillings. In addition they were both allowed a length of 'raiment cloth' for their livery. As time went on these

INTRODUCTION

payments slowly went up to keep pace with rising living expenses. Records of wages to statute kitchen staff survive from the sixteenth through to the nineteenth century in the Cathedral Treasurer's Books. These reveal that the cooks always received their stipends in quarterly instalments, which they signed for on the feast days of Christmas, the Annunciation, St. John the Baptist and Michaelmas. Although their signatures survive in the accounts, nothing else is recorded about the activities of these men.

John Thacker, the author of this book, took up the ancient post of statute *cuquo* in 1739 and remained on the payroll until 1758. He was elected to the post by Dean Henry Bland (also Canon of Windsor and Provost of Eton College), whom he was to serve until the dean's death in 1746. He continued his tenure as cook under Dean Spencer Cowper (the cousin of William Cowper the poet) for a further twelve years. His immediate predecessor had been Thomas Johnson, who had cooked for the Dean and Chapter since 1729 for an annual wage of £6.00 – Johnson's *subcuquo* Jonathan Burly received a stipend of £2.8s. In the year before Thacker took over, Burly's wife Elizabeth filled in briefly as a temporary cook, probably because Johnson had fallen ill or had died. When Thacker started the job in December 1739, the annual salary was increased to £10.00. The dean and chapter may have been desperate to find a new cook and as a consequence raised the salary. However, at the time of Thacker's appointment the post of *subcuquo* was purged from the Cathedral statute. So it is possible that Thacker's rise was to help him to pay the wages of an assistant from his own pocket.[5]

A £6 salary was on the low side for a high-status cook of this period. According to R. Campbell, the author of

The London Tradesman (1747), an English cook could expect to receive between £5 and £50 a year, while one trained in the French system could be rewarded with as much as £100.⁶ In reality, wages of this calibre were extremely rare, but we do know that in the year that Thacker joined the payroll at Durham, the Duke of Newcastle was paying his celebrated French *cuisinier* Pierre Clouet an annual salary of £105.⁷

There were opportunities for extra earnings when special entertainments were held. For instance Thacker was paid an additional 10 shillings for preparing the installation feast of Dean Cowper in July 1746.⁸ In Cowper's personal account book there are also a number of payments made to Thacker for 'work in the garden'. These include one for a bill of £4.19s.9d. The industrious cook seems to have been growing the Dean's vegetables as well as dressing them for his table. However, it turns out that it was his wife who was actually doing the work! From 1748, these payments for tending the garden were paid directly to Mrs Thacker in the form of a private annual salary of £6.6s. She kept this position until 1754.⁹

Thacker had identified other ways of augmenting the family income. A cathedral cook was poorly paid, but his status was impressive enough to give credibility to a new enterprise. He decided to open a school of cookery. In early July of 1745 he entered a lengthy advertisement in the local weekly newspaper, the *Newcastle Courant*, in which he described himself as *'the Cook to the Right Worshipful the Dean and Chapter of Durham'*. This notice, which appeared in two successive editions of the periodical, was to inform the public of his recently opened cookery school. We learn that he ran the school in his own house at

INTRODUCTION ix

'the Upper-end of Old Elvet, where he teaches young Ladies and Gentlewomen the Art of Pastry, Confectionary, Pickling, Preserving and any Thing that is required in Cookery. His Prices are Half a Crown Entrance, and Half a Guinea per Quarter; or a Crown Entrance, and one Guinea by the Great'.[10]

Thacker's cookery school was well situated for patronage by 'the Great', since it was in one of the most fashionable districts of the city. There were a number of titled neighbours, including the Earl of Strathmore. However, no records of Thacker's occupation of a house in Old Elvet have yet been found. It was not a grace and favour dwelling that went with his job at the Cathedral and its exact identity remains unknown. It is curious that a mere cook on £10 a year could afford to live in such a prestigious location. We can only assume that his cookery school must have thrived.

Schools of cookery and housekeeping aimed at young ladies and gentlewomen had started to become a feature of English town life in the second half of the seventeenth century. The earliest known appear to have sprung up in Restoration London as a result of changing social conditions after the Civil War. The cookery author Hannah Woolley, writing in 1670, explains, 'I find so many Gentlewomen forced to serve, whose Parents and Friends have been impoverished by the late Calamities, viz. the late Wars, Plague and Fire, and to see what mean Places they are forced to be in, because they want Accomplishments for better.' Woolley taught some of these dispossessed gentlewomen and other aspiring servants at her own house, where, 'If any Gentlewomen, or other Maids, who desire to go forth to Service, and do want Accomplishment for the same: for a reasonable

Gratuity I shall informe them what I am able'.[11] A number of other food professionals, like the comfit maker Mary Tillinghast and the pastry cook Nathanial Meystnor, also ran cookery schools for gentlewomen in late Stuart London. In the following century the most celebrated establishment of this kind was that of the 'Pastry-master' Edward Kidder, which flourished in the 1720s. Kidder at first provided his scholars with manuscript copies of his recipes, but eventually released them in the form of a printed book.[12]

Thacker, who may have modelled his cookery school on that of Susannah Kellet in nearby Newcastle, felt a similar need to publish his recipes in a printed collection.[13] Like Kidder, he had made extra money by providing many of his scholars with a laboriously handwritten version. In the 1745 advertisement, he reveals *'And whereas it has been requir'd by most of his Scholars to have a Book of Receipts written for them, the Price of which was Five Shillings; he now proposes to print a Book.'* What was unusual about Thacker's plans to publish his recipes was his idea of releasing them in monthly instalments, rather like a magazine:

> *'. . . every Thing will be adapted according to the Twelve Months in the Year, mentioning every Thing as it comes in Season, with Bills of Fare for every Month, and instructions for furnishing a Table in its Courses; also proper Directions how to dress every Dish, and Deserts of all Kinds, suitable to the said several Months.'*

Some early works on gardening and horticulture had started life in this way, but this was the first time a book of cookery was to appear in magazine form. Perhaps

INTRODUCTION

Thacker got the idea for its calendar-like structure from Richard Bradley's *A General Treatise of Husbandry and Gardening*, which first saw life as a series of monthly periodicals published between 1721 and 1723. Books printed in this way were popular in the provinces at this time, as the cost of purchase could be spread over time. For many Northern readers a complete bound volume would have been prohibitively expensive. For instance, if Jonathan Burly, the last statute under-cook at Durham, had wanted to buy a popular recipe book in the 1730s, it would have cost him 2s 6d, more than two week's wages. A decade later, cookery books had become even more expensive – in 1747 a bound copy of Hannah Glasse's recipe book cost 5s. Thacker seems to have understood the provincial book market and decided to issue his monthly numbers at the manageable price of 6d each. However, before he could go to press he needed to build up a list of subscribers:

> 'In order that the Publick may come easily at this Work, the Author makes the following Proposals, first, That it shall be Printed in Twelve Numbers in Quarto, one of which shall be delivered each Month, stitched in Blue Paper. Price Six-pence. Secondly, That it shall be done on good Paper, and the same Letter with the Proposals. Thirdly, That the first number shall be published as soon as a competent Number of Subscriptions are come in to defray the Expence: No Money to be paid till Delivery and no more shall be printed than what are subscribed for'.

The advertisement goes on to give a list of booksellers, upholsterers and hardware men in twelve northern towns and cities where subscriptions could be registered.

INTRODUCTION

Although some authorities have stated that this magazine version of Thacker's book was published during the course of 1746, I have been unable to trace any surviving copies.[14]

A gap of thirteen years was to pass before The Art of Cookery was published as a fully bound volume. In the Newcastle Courant for Saturday January 7th 1758, the following advertisement appeared:

This Day is Published
And sold by all the Booksellers in Newcastle; and J Richardson,
and
P. Sanderson, Booksellers in Durham,
Price six shillings, neatly bound in Calf,

THE ART OF COOKERY
CONTAINING

Above six Hundred and fifty of the most approved RECEIPTS heretofore published, under the following Heads, viz. Roasting, Boiling, Frying, Broiling, Baking, Fricasees, Puddings, Custards, Cakes, Cheese-cakes, Tarts, Pyes, Soops, Made-wines, Jellies, Candying, Pickling, Preserving, Pastry, Collering, Confectionary, Creams, Ragoos, Brasing &c. &c.

Also, a BILL OF FARE for every Month in the Year. With an Alphabetical INDEX to the Whole: Being a BOOK necessary for all Families, having the Grounds of Cookery fully displayed therein.

By JOHN THACKER,
Cook to the Hon. and Rev. the Dean and Chapter of
Durham

The book appeared as a small quarto of 322 pages. It seems to have been successful, as a second edition was published in 1762.[15] In his preface, dated Dec. 24th 1757, Thacker makes no mention of the earlier periodical version.

Thacker also issued a small 24-page pamphlet containing a selection of 32 recipes from his larger book. This was printed and sold in Durham by the bookseller G. Sowler. It was also called *The Art of Cookery*. A single copy of this tiny undated chapbook has survived at the Brotherton Library.[16] It is a very crudely printed duodecimo containing a selection of simple homely recipes. These are more or less identical to their equivalents in the larger book, but lack French names. This simple compilation was probably aimed at servant maids. It is likely that it predates the 1758 book, suggesting that it was abstracted from the original periodical version of the work.

The Treasurer's Book reveals that Thacker's long career at the cathedral came to an end in 1758, seven months after *The Art of Cookery* was published. He signed for his last quarterly stipend of £2.10s on 15th July. This was two months earlier than the usual Michaelmas payment, so he must have resigned. Dean Cowper was left without a cook until the following March, when one John Duffield took up the position.[17]

How did Thacker ever find time to write this book, teach in his cookery school and run the dean's kitchen? The answer probably lies in the fact that the dean was frequently away for much of the year. His prolonged absences were rooted in a curious aspect of Durham ecclesiastical life that had its origin in a statute issued by Queen Mary in 1555. This ruled that the dean and every canon with an income of over £40 a year was required to keep what was called a 'residence' for a period of twenty-one consecutive days of the year. Whichever member of the chapter held the residence had a duty to provide hospitality and to 'keep more sumptuous entertainment than they are wont at the other periods of the year, giving meat to the Choir and inviting the citizens or strangers'.[18] This was to ensure that the old monastic tradition of hospitality continued at Durham. Residences could not overlap, so only one was ever held at any one time. The chapter members each took it in turn during their twenty-one days to give feasts to other members of the cathedral foundation and their wives, the gentry of the county, the mayor and corporation, the justices of the peace and military officers. They also provided meals for local tradesmen, shopkeepers, artisans, cathedral tenants, the poor and even on some occasions the felons in the local gaol. Strangers were frequently invited by the cathedral vergers from the city streets to partake in these meals. For over two hundred days of the year, the citizens of Durham could literally enjoy a gravy train at the dean and chapter's expense.[19]

In order to defray the expenses of entertaining, Mary's statute assigned an additional payment of £40.1s.3d to the dean and an extra £8.4.9½d for a canon. If any member of the chapter failed to hold his hospitality residence he could forfeit his entire year's stipend. As a result the tradition was taken very seriously. During the sixteenth century, the dean was allowed 100 days annual leave and the canons 80 days. If they were absent for longer than this they were subjected to a fine – 12s.5d for a dean and 1s.4½d for a canon.[20] However, by the middle of the eighteenth century, the income of the chapter had increased so much – an additional allowance of £50 just for hospitality was awarded to all members in 1675 – these fines were not high enough to act as a deterrent. The result was that many of the deans and canons took much longer periods of leave. Some attended College for little more than the duration of their compulsory hospitality residence.[21] Cowper, for instance, was frequently only at the cathedral for three months out of twelve. He spent the rest of his year at his family estates in Hertfordshire and Kent. Although Thacker helped prepare meals for other chapter members during their hospitality residences, most employed their own cooks, so his duties were frequently quite light when the dean was away for these long periods. This could explain how he found the time to manage his other enterprises.[22]

A few members of the chapter found the ancient duty of residence feasting and hospitality wasteful. Canon William Warburton wrote in 1757, 'I have done feasting and leave this place tomorrow. This luxury is not only opprobrious to us, but hurtful to the place, as only making a number of idle beggars. By that I spend, I reckon there is spent yearly by the Chapter £1000 a year in this unedifying way'.[23] Dean Cowper was also not fond of the custom and saw it as a chore. In the autumn of 1754, he wrote 'Thank God, I am now enter'd into the last week of my Residence, the Noble Mayor and Corporation were to have been my Guests today, but they have excused themselves, and my table is now open to all the riff-raff Corny (a cathedral verger) can pick up'.[24]

Cowper, who was the youngest son of Earl Cowper, the last Lord High Chancellor of England, generally found Durham life provincial and dull. When he arrived in 1746, he described his first impressions of the city. 'The town itself is nasty and disagreeable, the streets narrow and wretchedly paved, and the houses dirty and black, as if they had no inhabitants, but colliers.' The deanery was also not to his liking. He found 'the rooms so bad, it deserves an apology to lay a footman in them'. He was even critical of the ancient cathedral church: 'The inside is very clumsy. The Great Aisle is fill'd with heavy massy pillars all out of proportion.'[25] What then did this hard-to-please man make of his new cook? In his extensive correspondence, Cowper never mentions Thacker directly, but he seems to have been impressed from the start with his efforts. On October 31st 1746, Thacker prepared a very large dinner for the new dean's first major entertainment, which was to celebrate the birthday of George II. Cowper wrote to a friend, 'I had all the Gentry in or near Durham at dinner to drink his [the king's] health, both men and women. I think our numbers were three and forty, but the ladies were the majority by five or six. A most splendid show of Durham Beauties, and would have been welcome had not their hoops [hoop petticoats] been too large. My Feast was most magnificent, but I won't send you its Bill of Fare'. In his usual choleric fashion, Cowper then goes on to explain how much he disliked feasting and large companies. Rather worryingly for Thacker, he also adds how he felt terribly ill the day after the feast and had to resort to a dose of 'asafoetida, hartshorn and spa water'![26] The fussy new dean was a hypochondriac. However, his dissatisfaction with his medieval house and kitchen did have some benefits for his cook. During the 1750s he made some important improvements to the 400 year old kitchen by plastering the interior, repairing the chimneys and lowering the medieval roof lantern to prevent it leaking.[27]

Although Cowper did not record the menus for his entertainments, Thacker does include important examples in this book, giving us a very clear picture of the nature of cathedral close dinners at all levels. Among them is a full set of twenty-one bills of fare, one for each day of a residence held by Cowper, which began on September 29th 1753. Fifteen of these dinners are fairly everyday affairs of two courses, consisting of seven dishes in each

INTRODUCTION xvii

course. They were probably the meals prepared during the residence for the lesser guests, such as the beadsmen, merchants and tradesmen. Others are much grander affairs, that being served on the eighth day of the residence being particularly ambitious in scope (p.337). This was almost certainly a meal prepared for one of the two so-called 'prebendary days' of the residence. These were the most important repasts, when the canons (prebendaries) were invited, though it is unlikely that many actually attended, since only a few were ever at the College at any one time. The numbers were usually made up with local gentry and other dignitaries. This sumptuous entertainment comprised twenty-seven dishes in the first course, (including two soups and their removes) and twenty-five items in the second course. Apart from some woodcocks and capons roasted before the fire while the first course was being consumed, the second course consisted entirely of an elegant dessert with a spectacular centrepiece of pyramids of syllabubs and sweetmeats. The dean and his canons certainly knew how to entertain in the most fashionable style.

Nevertheless, the nature of the food prepared by Thacker for these Durham residence dinners is strongly English in character. Unlike the fashionable French cookery favoured by the Whig aristocracy, cathedral close dining seems to have been conservative and patriotic. A small number of French dishes however, do creep into Thacker's bill of fare for 'Dr. Sterne's first Dinner for the Prependaries' (p.345). Jacques Sterne was instituted as a canon of the second stall by royal nomination on 17th May 1755, and this particular dinner took place during his first residence later that year. Sterne was a learned man and his choice of a few classic French dishes, such as Fricandeaux of Veal, Eggs in Crampine, Beef Tromblance and Pulpotoon with Brochlets (Thacker's spelling), betrays a level of gastronomic sophistication, which Thacker would probably have liked to cater for more frequently. In the twelve seasonal bills of fare at the end of his book, which are suggestions for family meals, Thacker also includes a few more French dishes (pp.349, 351 & 352).

In the early days of residence hospitality, no chapter member was allowed to entertain more than six guests at a time, though an exception was made for Christmas feasts. In 1744 this was changed to twelve guests.[28] Important meals were held in the chapter members' own family dining rooms. Those for chapter servants, poor widows, tradesmen and others of modest status were given in the servants' halls in the dean's or canons' houses. The numbers of guests at these more modest entertainments could also be much larger. During his residence in January 1796, Canon Reynold Gideon Bouyer held a dinner for 14 debtors and 12 felons in the local gaol. They dined on two large rounds of beef, two plum puddings, a peck of peas, a peck of boiled potatoes and a 2d loaf each.[29] The dean and canons were also permitted to give dinners outside their residence periods if the local Assizes or Sessions were sitting, though again they were usually only allowed twelve guests. Thacker gives a bill of fare for a 'session dinner' of this kind, for 'the Grand Jury, when there was no residence'.[30] For the three hundred years of its existence, this extraordinary tradition of ecclesiastical hospitality catered for every level of Durham society, but it was far too archaic to survive the changing mores of nineteenth-century life and it faded away during the 1840s.

Unlike some of the popular cookery compilations of the mid-eighteenth century, *The Art of Cookery* is an original work, written by a professional.[31] It lives up to its author's claim that it was 'form'd on the Result of many Years' Experience'. Detailed and careful comparison with recipes in other English and French cookery texts published in the previous forty years have revealed no obvious instances of borrowing or plagiarism. This unusual honesty indicated that he indeed fulfilled that ancient requirement of the cathedral statutes, that he should be 'an industrious man of good report and upright life'. His clear and unassuming instructions frequently offer details that clearly bring the kitchen procedures of the period to life. His directions for roasting a sirloin of beef give meticulous butchery instructions and then explain how to balance the joint on the spit, before telling us 'to set the Jack a-going' (p.10).[32] English long spit roasting is now a lost art. Its techniques were once everyday kitchen procedures, so familiar to every cook that none would have thought of committing them to paper. Indeed few cookery writers of this period offer more than general directions for roasting. Thacker is an exception. His instructions 'To order and roast a Chine of Mutton' (p.105) are exhaustive and give us the clearest insight into the remarkable skills required by a roasting cook to have survived in English culinary literature. He tells us about the weighted 'balance Skewer' that was put on the spit to help the chine turn evenly, as well as the complex procedure for attaching the joint to the spit with iron skewers tied with pack-thread. In his directions for roasting a carp, he lets us into the secret of supporting the fish on the spit with laths made of hazel 'or other sweet wood' (pp.190 & 191). Thacker knew all of the tricks of the trade, but unlike a lot of other professional cooks, was willing to share them with his readers.

We know nothing of Thacker's origins, but he does give us a few tantalising clues about his employment history.

These reveal that when he arrived at Durham, he was already a 'professed cook' with considerable experience of working in great houses. In one of his recipes he discloses that he had once served Lord Exeter (p.112). This would have been Brownlow Cecil (1701–1754), the 8th Earl of Exeter, whose seat was the magnificent Burghley House, near Stamford in Lincolnshire.[33] He had also cooked for George Treby (ca.1684–1742), the Secretary of State for War to George II, probably at his London house (p.232).[34] In these important establishments he had rubbed shoulders with cooks 'of different Nations; but I cannot say I ever met with a foreigner who had so sound and good a Way of working as an Old English Cook'. This old-fashioned approach made him highly suited to running a kitchen in an ecclesiastical institution with an ancient tradition of communal hospitality.

Thacker's bill of fare for a Christmas dinner clearly reveals this conservative aspect of cathedral close gastronomy (p.356). With its Plum Broth, Collared Brawn, Swan pie, Roast Ling (a type of stockfish) and Minc'd Pyes, it differs little from Christmas meals served at the cathedral in earlier periods. The Benedictines had fattened up their Christmas cygnets at a swannery at Ferryhill and there are two stockfish hammers for breaking up the dried cod and ling listed in the Cellarer's Account Rolls for 1438–9. Thacker is also the only English cookery author of the eighteenth century who explains in detail how to decorate a peacock pie with its plumage (pp.278 & 279), a practice which the antiquarian Richard Warner illustrates a few decades later as a medieval curiosity.[35] Another survival from the medieval kitchen is his remarkable 'double' salmon pie (pp.264 & 265). It consists of an inedible outer crust in the form of a realistically-coloured pastry fish enclosing another pie.

The other woodcut illustrations of pastry designs in *The Art of Cookery* are elegant, but also rather old-fashioned. Some are similar to patterns published in Robert May's *The Accomplisht Cook* (London: 1660) and others to engravings in Conrad Hagger's *Neues Saltzburgerisches Kochbuch* (Augsburg:1719).[36] Hagger, like Thacker, had been a cathedral cook, having worked for the Bishop of Salzburg in the early eighteenth century. His book is also characterized by rather dated, highly decorative baroque food. In contrast to the fashion-conscious households of princes and nobles, ecclesiastical communities were probably more resistant to the new culinary developments of the Enlightenment. Thacker's design for garnishing a soup plate with triangular lozenges of parboiled carrot, turnip and spinach, is also more typical of an earlier period (p.7).

Although the dean and chapter seem to have preferred English food, many of Thacker's recipes show a strong French influence. In fact, his book indicates a mastery of French cookery methods and he gives his readers clear explanations of French terms.[37] He advocates the use of a 'brown' (*roux*) to thicken both sauces and cullis (*coulis*). He was also well aware of the preference among contemporary French cooks for simplified recipes, a trend he must have become aware of in the kitchens of the Earl of Exeter and Secretary Treby. For instance, his *Soup de Sante the French way* (p.75) is a much more 'trimmed down' recipe than that given in Hannah Glasse's book (1747), which is derived from the complex court cookery style of the earlier eighteenth century. He does give directions for making Olios and Bisques, two of the showpiece dishes of this old court style, but tells us that they 'were much in Fashion formerly, but are not so now' (pp.288 & 289). He was also well able to devise his own variations on French classics. His range of pulpatoons (from *poupeton* – a kind of meat loaf with a crust made of forcemeat) is ultimately derived from French baroque cookery, but some, like his excellent pulpatoon of lobsters, seem to be of his own invention.[38] Morels, a favourite ingredient of French *ragouts*, are frequently included in Thacker's recipes. He even offers brief notes on their natural history, telling us that they are 'Excrement of the Earth that grow near the Water and Foot of Trees' and were to be sought for in the spring (p.67). There are no modern records for morels (*Morchella esculenta*) in County Durham. They may have occurred before the Industrial Revolution, but could never have been common this far north.

Despite their impressive French names, the majority of Thacker's recipes are fairly English in character. Those that are of definite French origin, such as a number of meat and poultry dishes cooked *à la braize*, or *à la daube*, had become part of the English repertoire through adoption half a century earlier. Thacker's use of culinary French is frequently tenuous. He invents high-sounding names for British foods that were unknown in France. For instance, he calls wiggs *Petites Gateaux*, syllabub *Boisson refraichissante* and Welsh Flummery *Flomerée à la manière Galles*. Some of his dishes have very puzzling names. For instance there are eight instances of made dishes dressed *à la Smithergall*. He may have once worked for a family called Smithergall, or perhaps these delicacies were named after a long forgotten cook of that name. In his preface he comments on the use of French names,

INTRODUCTION   xxiii

'The Names of Dishes that have French Terms to them are supposed to be the Names of the Cooks that invented them, or the Names of the Persons that first took a Liking to them; though I believe, there are many of them invented by the English; and the French Names have, I believe, been given to excite Curiosity, and make them by that Artifice better liked.'

Perhaps Thacker's true reason for giving French synonyms to all his dishes (as well as his explanations of French culinary terms) was related to the fact that a cook with a mastery of French cookery could command a high salary. It is possible that Thacker was open to offers from more generous employers than the dean and chapter. His elegant book would have certainly broadcast his prowess as a cook throughout Northern England. It is interesting that he left his post at the cathedral six months after its publication. Whether he found more lucrative employment or just retired is not known. With nineteen years at the cathedral and an unknown number spent in the service of others before that, he must have been getting on in years, so I suspect the latter. Nothing more is heard of his activities from this time onwards. His death in not recorded in any of the Durham parish records, so he may have moved on to another part of the country.

The Art of Cookery is a rare book and deserves to be better known. Its clearly written recipes and charming illustrations make it one of the most original cookery texts of the Georgian period. A curious mixture of both up-to-date and ancient, it not only advocates the 'lighter' nouvelle cuisine of the mid-eighteenth century, but is also firmly embedded in a tradition of ecclesiastical hospitality that stretches back as far as the eleventh century.

I would like to thank the staff of Special Collections at the Library of the University of Durham and the staff of Special Collections at the Brotherton Library, University of Leeds. I am also indebted to Colin Higgins, C. Anne Wilson, Lynne Newall and Gill Whitehead for their invaluable assistance.

Ivan Day

Select Bibliography

Manuscripts from the Durham Cathedral Muniments (DCD) used in the preparation of this essay are cited in the Notes and References.

Anon., *The Whole Duty of a Woman* (London: 1737)
Richard Bradley, *A General Treatise of Husbandry and Gardening* (London: 1721 to 1723)
R. Campbell, *The London Tradesman* (London: 1747)
Charles Carter, *The London and Country Cook* London: 1749)
Vincent La Chapelle, *The Modern Cook* (3rd edition, London: 1744)
Ivan Day, 'From Murrel to Jarrin. Illustrations in British Cookery Books 1621–1820[prime], in Eileen White (editor) *The English Cookery Book* (Totnes: 2004).
J. Feather, *A History of British Publishing* (London: 1988)
Hannah Glasse, *The Art of Cookery made Plain and Easy* (London: 1747)
Conrad Hagger, *Neues Saltzburgerisches Kochbuch* (1719)
E. Hughes (editor), *Letters of Spencer Cowper*, Surtees Society, 165 (Durham: 1956)

BIBLIOGRAPHY

R. Hurd (editor), *Letters of a Late Eminent Prelate*. (London: 1809)

Margot Johnson, *Durham Priory Kitchen*. Turnstone Ventures (Durham: 2000)

Ray A. Kelch, *Newcastle. A Duke without Money* (London: 1974)

Susanna, Elizabeth and Mary Kellet, *A Complete Collection of Cookery Receipts* (Newcastle: 1780)

Edward Kidder, Receipts of Pastry and Cookery (London: nd, *ca*.1720s)

G.W. Kitchin, *The Story of the Deanery* (Durham: 1912)

Patrick Lamb, *Royal Cookery* (London 1710)

Virginia Maclean, *A Catalogue of Household and Cookery Books 1701–1800* (London: 1981)

Robert May, *The Accomplisht Cook* (London: 1660)

Patrick Mussett, 'Hospitality Residence at Durham Cathedral' in *Transactions of the Architectural and Archeological Society of Durham and Northumberland*, New Series 6, (Durham: 1982)

David Pearson, *Cathedral Cookery* (Durham 1985)

F.J.G. Robinson, *Trends in Education in Northern England during the Eighteenth Century:A Biographical Study*, 3 vols., University of Newcastle Ph.D. thesis (1972)

A.H. Thompson (editor), *The Statutes of the Cathedral Church of Durham*, Surtees Society, 143 (London: 1929)

Mary Tillinghast, *Rare and Excellent Receipts* (London; 1678)

The True Way of Preserving and Candying (London: 1681)

Richard Warner, *Antiquitates Culinariae* (London: 1791)

C. Anne Wilson (editor), *Traditional Food East and West of the Pennines* (Edinburgh:1991)

Hannah Woolley, *The Queen-like Closet* (London: 1670)

Notes and References

1   The papal cook Bartolomeo Scappi was responsible for producing the most beautifully illustrated recipe collection of the Italian Renaissance, the magnificent *Opera* of 1570. Across the Alps, Scappi's contemporary Marx Rumpolt, cook to the Archbishop of Mainz, authored the encyclopaedic *Ein Neues Kochbuch* (1581). Less well known, but on an equally lavish scale, is the baroque classic *Neues Saltzburgerisches Kochbuch* (1719), written by Conrad Hagger, cook to the Archbishop of Salzburg.
2   The magnificent priory kitchen, which survives at Durham, was designed and built between 1366 and 1374 by the master mason John Lewyne. It replaced a much earlier kitchen and has the distinction of being in continuous use from 1374 until 1940. For a full history of this remarkable building see Margot Johnson's *Durham Priory Kitchen*. Turnstone Ventures (Durham: 2000).
3   DCD/MS.C.iv, 33. See also *The Statutes of the Cathedral Church of Durham,* Surtees Society, ed. A.H. Thompson, 143, (London: 1929). Henry's original *Statuta Ecclesiae Dunelmensis* was issued in a letter patent dated 12 May 1541.
4   Johnson, p.16.
5   *Durham Cathedral Treasurer's Books.* DCD/L/BB/52 and DCD/L/BB/53
6   R. Campbell, *The London Tradesman* (London: 1747).
7   Ray A. Kelch, Newcastle, *A Duke without Money.* (London 1974).
8   Deanery Rental and Accounts 1746–74. DCD/H/DRA/17.
9   DCD/H/DRA/17.
10 *The Newcastle Courant,* May 1745. Virginia Maclean, *A Catalogue of Household and Cookery Books 1701–1800* (London: 1981) (p.141) states that Thacker's school was started in 1742. Although it was obviously running before the 1745 advertisement, it is not known exactly when it started. Maclean has based this date on some mistaken information in Robinson (p.221).
11 Hannah Woolley, *The Queen-like Closet* (London: 1670)
12 Mary Tillinghast, *Rare and Excellent Receipts* (London; 1678) and Mary Tillinghast, *The True Way of Preserving and Candying*

NOTES   xxvii

(London: 1681). The evidence for the existence of Nathanial Meystnor's cookery school is an illustrated trade card (nd. ca 1690s in the collection of the author of this introduction). Edward Kidder, Receipts of Pastry and Cookery (London nd. ca 1720s).
13 Susanna, Elizabeth and Mary Kellet, *A Complete Collection of Cookery Receipts* (Newcastle:1780). Susanna Kellet started a cookery school in Newcastle upon Tyne in the late 1720s or early 1730s.
14 J. Feather, *A History of British Publishing* (London:1988). Lynette Hunter, 'Printing in the Pennines' in C. Anne Wilson (editor), *Traditional Food East and West of the Pennines* (Edinburgh 1991).
15 Maclean lists a 3rd edition (1765), but this appears to be another error. I have been unable to trace a copy of this work in any British or American library.
16 This little pamphlet, described on the title page, as 'Being a Book very necessary for all Families' is not arranged on a seasonal basis, so it is unlikely to be a surviving copy of one of Thacker's monthly numbers. It is also in duodecimo format – Thacker intended his periodical to be printed in quarto.
17 *Durham Cathedral Treasurer's Book.* DCD/L/BB/53
18 Surtees Society 143.
19 Patrick Mussett, *Hospitality Residence at Durham Cathedral* in *Transactions of the Architectural and Archeological Society of Durham and Northumberland*, New Series 6, (Durham:1982), pp. 67–70. G.W. Kitchin, *The Story of the Deanery*, (Durham; 1912).
20 Surtees Society 143.
21 Mussett (1982).
22 E. Hughes (editor), *Letters of Spencer Cowper*, Surtees Society, 165. (Durham; 1956).
23 R. Hurd (editor), *Letters of a Late Eminent Prelate* (London: 1809).
24 Surtees Society, 165, p.130.
25 Surtees Society, 165. pp.61–2
26 Surtees Society, 165. pp.71–72.
27 DCD/H/DRA/17.
28 DCD Chapter Acts 20th July 1744.
29 Mussett (1982). One of Canon Bouyer's servants kept a residence account book, which lists the guests, table layouts, expenses and menus for residences for 1793, 1794, 1795 and 1796.

This remarkable document is preserved in Northumberland County Record Office, ZAN M13/B/7.

30 The Durham Grand Jury consisted of twenty-four members of the local nobility and gentry.

31 Among the compilations with recipes 'lifted' from other books popular in Thacker's period were *The Whole Duty of a Woman* (London: 1737), Hannah Glasse, *The Art of Cookery made Plain and Easy* (London 1747) and Charles Carter, *The London and Country Cook* (London: 1749). The latter was a spurious work which falsely gave Carter's name to a collection of recipes, some of which were pirated from the previous two books.

32 There are still the remains of an eighteenth-century smoke jack on one of the chimney breasts in the Durham cathedral kitchen. It could very well be the jack that Thacker actually used for roasting the dean's sirloin. It was annually maintained by a Mr Bartholomew Sykes, who in 1746 received 2s 6d 'for Cleaning the Kitchen Chimney and Jack to Lady Day'. *Deanery Rental and accounts*. DCD/H/DRA/16.

33 Unfortunately, there are no records of Thacker's employment at Burghley, as servants' names were not recorded in the Cecil family wages books during the eighteenth century.

34 The Treby family seat was in Plympton, Devon, until the nineteenth century. The fine house built by Treby's father Sir George Treby (judge and Recorder for London) is now a nursing home. It is possible that Thacker may have originally come from this area, as Thacker and Thackery are common Devon surnames. He gives a number of Devon recipes in his book.

35 Richard Warner, *Antiquitates Culinariae* (London: 1791).

36 For a discussion of pie designs of this kind see Ivan Day, 'From Murrel to Jarrin. Illustrations in British Cookery Books 1621–1820', in Eileen White (editor) *The English Cookery Book* (Totnes 2004).

37 Thacker's explanations of French culinary terms are very similar to those in the preface to Patrick Lamb's *Royal Cookery* (London:1710) and are almost certainly modelled on them.

38 Vincent La Chapelle, *The Modern Cook* (3rd edition London: 1744).

THE ART OF COOKERY.

CONTAINING

Above Six Hundred and Fifty of the most approv'd RECEIPTS heretofore published, under the following Heads, viz.

ROASTING,	CAKES,	PICKLING,
BOILING,	CHEESE-CAKES,	PRESERVING,
FRYING,	TARTS,	PASTRY,
BROILING,	PYES,	COLLERING,
BAKING,	SOOPS,	CONFCTIONARY,
FRICASEES,	MADE-WINES,	CREAMS,
PUDDINGS,	JELLIES,	RAGOOS,
CUSTARDS,	CANDYING,	BRASING, &c. &c.

ALSO, A

BILL OF FARE

For every MONTH in the YEAR.

WITH AN

Alphabetical INDEX to the Whole:

BEING

A BOOK highly necessary for all FAMILIES, having the GROUNDS of COOKERY fully display'd therein.

By JOHN THACKER, COOK to the Honourable and Reverend the DEAN and CHAPTER in DURHAM.

NEWCASTLE UPON TYNE:
Printed by I. THOMPSON and COMPANY.
MDCCLVIII.

THE
PREFACE.

AT the Request of my Friends, especially my Scholars, I have publish'd this Book. I know it will be said, that any Thing of this Kind is needless, there being so many Books already extant; but this Objection will be fully answer'd when it is consider'd, that all of them, or at least all that I have seen, are far short of being generally useful, especially in these Northern Parts, where the Seasons occasion such Alterations in the Bills of Fare for each Month, from those calculated for the Southern Parts; some being fill'd with Receipts quite foreign to the Purpose, as for beautifying Washes, &c. others stuff'd with Ragoos, and other Dishes a-la-mode de France, as they call them; in which the Mixture of Spices is so great, and the Expence so extravagant, that it frightens most People from using them; or, if any be so curious as to try them, and follow their Rules punctually, instead of Meats that are healthful, and agreeable to the Palate, they will find a Hotch-potch, destructive to an English Constitution. I would not have it thought that I am an Enemy to made Dishes, or ignorant in making them, as will be seen in the Book where Occasion offers: I have dissected the French Dishes, and given their Names in English, as well as French; and have shewn how they may be made to Advantage, by taking such Ingredients as are healthful and pleasant to the Stomach.——And in my Receipts for Pickling and Preserving, I have made Choice of such Fruits, &c. as are of our own Growth, and easy to come at. In short, through the whole, I have

endea-

PREFACE.

endeavour'd to make every Thing as plain as possible, so as to be understood by every Capacity. The candid Reader, I hope, will pardon the Plainness of the Style, and accept the Work as a Thing design'd for the Good of my Country, to which I am a hearty Well-wisher.

The Term *a-la-braise*, as the French call it, is a particular Way of stewing Flesh, Fowls, or Fish, as you will find in the Receipts. You must order the particular Ingredients as to Quantity of Herbs, Spices, &c. according to the Bigness of the Thing you want to dress that Way, and the flower you do it the better; the Cover or Lid of the Thing you braise any Thing in, must have a Rim to it to turn up to hold lighted Charcoal, and the Fire below must be very little at first, or you may cause it to burn to the Bottom before the Liquid is drawn out of the Ingredients. The Meaning of a Brown is a Piece of Butter put into a Stew pan, and Flour dusted in, stirring it, with a wooden Ladle till it is brown, then put in Gravey enough to make it the Thickness you would have it, considering the Time you have to keep it stewing.

Farces are a Sort of Forc'd-meats that we make use of in stuffing the Bodies of Fowls, &c. or putting them betwixt the Flesh and the Skin; the particular Ways you will find in the several Receipts.

Bards of Bacon are Slices of the Flitch cut the broad Way. See how used in the Receipts.

Court Bouillon, is a Pickle or Marinade, we make use of to give Fish a good Relish before boiling. See the Receipts.

Bisques are Soops, with Ragoos in them, as you will find in their proper Places.

Entremets are small Dishes or Plates of Sauces, or other Things to fill up your Table, and to complete the Course, as you will see in the Bills of Fare.

Blanc-Manger is a Term the French give to what we call Flummery; which is, in their Meaning, something white to eat.

Hors d'Oeuvres are little Dishes compos'd of choice little light

PREFACE.

light Things, to be set betwixt the other Dishes to complete your Table.

Lardouns are little Bits of Bacon, cut square, to lard your Flesh with, that is to say, Veal, Beef, Mutton, or any Sort of Fowls, as you like; sometimes we lard Fish with Eels, they being reckon'd one of the most suitable Fish to lard any other Sort of Fish with.

The Names of Dishes that have French Terms to them are supposed to be the Names of the Cooks that invented them, or the Names of the Persons that first took a Liking to them; though, I believe, there are a great many of them invented by the English; and the French Names have, I believe, been given them to excite Curiosity, and make them by that Artifice better liked. I have seen as good English Cooks as the World can produce, and I have had also the Opportunity of working with several of different Nations; but I cannot say I ever met with a Foreigner who had so sound and good a Way of working as an old English Cook; and I never have found their Ways of dressing much better than a deal of profess'd Hotch-Potch, &c.

I hope there is no Occasion for further Explanation of my Book, especially to an ingenious Practiser, or even to those who want to improve themselves in the Art, at least I have endeavoured to make the whole as plain and intelligible as I cou'd to all Capacities, and shall chearfully satisfy any of my Friends and Purchasers, on Application, either personally, or by Letter, who may meet with any Particulars in it they cannot comprehend.

As this Book is form'd on the Result of many Years Experience, I presume no Body will dispute its Practicability, the great Excellence of all Works of this Kind.—Good Manners forbid me to make invidious Comparisons with any particular Book, or Books on this Subject, intitled Practical Cookery, &c. and I doubt not but the Unprejudiced and Impartial, especially ingenious Practisers, will do me Justice on that Head.—As I am well assured, what we call

PREFACE.

call the Ground Work or Fundamentals of Cookery, together with all the approv'd Receipts and valuable modern Improvements, are therein fully exhibited and explained; I beg Leave to recommend the Book to the Public in general, and to my Friends and Benefactors in this City (to whom I return due Acknowledgments) in particular, as one of the most Useful as well as most Practical extant.

DURHAM,
Dec. 24, 1757.　　　　JOHN THACKER.

INDEX

INDEX to the RECEIPTS.

A

Almond Torte, for a China Dish, to dress 287
——— Custards, to make 41
——— Snow, to make 79
——— Butter, to make 82
——— to perch 140
——— Milk, to make 155
——— Cheese, to make 287
——— Cakes 99
Amulet of Sweet-meats, to make 268
——— of Ham, to make 120
Anchovey Sauce, to make 200
Andoulians, to make 83
Andouillets, to make 83
Angelica, to candy 94
Apples, to bake red 159
——— Cream, to make 288
——— Pye, to make 27
——— Fritters, to make 159
——— Tanzey, to make 96
Apricots, to preserve 160
——— to preserve green 169
——— Paste, to make 317
——— Tart, green, to make 108
Artichokes, to make to keep all the Year 145
Asparagus, with brown Sauce 52
——— to boil 51
——— à la Cream 52
——— in Amblit 53
——— to preserve 94
——— to pickle 97

B

Bacon Froyce, to make 81
Bak'd Plumb-pudding, to make 48
Barbels, Pike, or Salmon, in Bouillon, to dress 85
Barbel, to stew 136
——— to broil 163
——— to pickle 163
Barberries, to pickle 235
——— to preserve 236
Beef, Directions for salting 1
——— Surloin, to roast 9
——— to coller 30
——— Dish of, like Beef A-la-mode, to make 82
——— a la Braise 61
——— Stakes coller'd 116
——— to pot 138
——— to farce 163
——— a la mode 183
——— a la mode, to eat cold 186
——— tromblance, to dress 217
——— Stakes, to dress the Italian Way 221
——— Stakes, to stew 223
——— Stake Pye, to make 284
——— dress'd to eat cold 288
Beets to fry 116
Birch Wine, to make 101
Biscuit-Cake, to make 42
——— another Way 43
——— for Chocolate, to make 82
——— to garnish with 83
Bisques and Olios, to dress 288
Bisque of Fish, to dress 286
Black Puddings, to make 270
——— Puddings, another Way 272
——— Caps, to make 162
——— Heath-Cock, to roast 296
Breast of Veal, to stew white 46
——— of Veal a la Smithergall, to dress 279
——— of Veal fricasey'd 301
——— of Veal coller'd 305

Brit,

INDEX.

Brit, commonly called Turbat, with Lobster Sauce, to dress   104
Blawmange, to make   16
Boil'd Bread Pudding, to make, with baked ones round it.   11
Bonum Magnum Plumbs, to preserve   250
Boulogne Sausages, to make   226

C

Cabbage Soop, to make   196
——— a la Smithergall, to farce   223
Cakes for Breakfast, to make   204
——— to stew   165
Calf's Head, to hash   10
——— Head, to roast   90
——— Head sweet Pye, to make   199
——— Liver, to roast   114
——— Liver a-la-braise   117
——— Feet, to make a Florentine of   12
Capon, Turkey, &c. to cram   208
Carbonade of Mutton, to make   202
Cardoons, to dress   187
——— ——— Parmasan   188
Carp au Court Bouillon, to dress   188
——— to broil   188
——— to roast   190
Carrot Pudding, to make   18
——— to boil and order   171
Cheese-Cakes, to make   42
Cherries, to preserve   119
Cherry Brandy Ratifie, to make   166
——— Wine, to make   168
Chickens Chiningras, to dress   302
——— to roast   51
——— to fricasey   56
——— to brown   56
——— the Polish Way, to dress   91
——— à la Chirigrate   124
——— to force   106

Chickens drest a-la-braise   114
——— Bullio blanc, with Endive, &c.   123
——— and Rice, to dress   133
——— the Barbary Way, to dress   161
——— with Sweet Herbs and Bards of Bacon, to farce   258
——— a la Smithergall, to roast   260
——— Pye, the French Way, to make   290
China-Orange Chips, to make   44
China-Oranges, to ice   110
Chine of Veal a la Smithergall, to roast   544
Chocolate Cream, to make   123
Chocolate Almonds, to make   315
Clear Fritters, to make   176
Clear Cakes of Currants or Raspberries, to make   316
——— Cakes of any Sort, to make   205
Clouted Cream, to make   136
Cocks' Combs, to preserve   259
Cockle Soop, to make   252
Cocks' Combs, to farce   259
Cod's Head, to dress, with fry'd Fish round it   8
Codlins, to preserve green   136
College Puddings, new, to make   192
Colliflowers, to ragoo   63
——— to fricasey brown   223
——— to pickle   238
Compote of Mushrooms, to make   254
Cowslips, to candy   314
——— Wine, to make   99
Crabs, to dress   151
——— to butter   152
——— to butter   191
Craw-fish Soop, to make   182
make   260
Cream Foul, to make   80
——— to fry   152
——— Tarts, to make   152

Cream

INDEX.

Cream Toasts, to make 197
—— Veloute with Pistachos, to make 322
Crow-Fish, to stew 260
——————— to ragoo 192
——————— Soop, to make 281
——————— in Jelly, to dress 274
Cucumbers, like Mangos, to pickle 285
——————— to stew 63
——————— to preserve 137
——————— to farce 164
Cullis of Veal and Ham, 60
—— of Mushrooms, 261
—— of Crow-Fish, to make 260
Currants, to pickle 140
——————— to preserve 147
——————— Jelly, to make 148
Custard, to make 40
make 60

D

Damsins, to dry 317
——— Pudding, to make 229
——— Wine, to make 232
——— to preserve all the Year 230
——— Cheese, or Cullis, to make 233
——— or any Sort of Plumbs, to dry 237
Dish of Soles a la Saute 309
Duck, to hash 30
—— young ones, to dress 77
—— a la Braise, with Onions 127
—— a la Braise, with Turnips, to dress 263
—— to dress with Claret 125
—— and Onions, to dress 135
—— and Morels, to dress 267
—— and stew'd Cellery, to dress 267
Dutch White Herrings, to dress 119
—— Beef, to make 95

E

Eels a la Doube, to dress 86
—— to coller 86
—— a large one, to roast 87
—— Spitch-cockt, to dress 87
—— to boil 83
—— Pye, to make 88
—— to stew 88
—— a la Braise, to dress 89
—— in Cramp pine, for a Side Dish 92
—— in Gravey, to poach 93
—— with Verjuice, to dress 93
—— in Butter, to dress 93
—— in Crampine, to dress 264
—— and stew'd Cucumbers, to dress 267
—— with Sorrel, to dress 304
Elder Vinegar, to make 225
Eringo Roots, to preserve 225

F

Fish, to preserve 3
—— Sauce, to make 8
—— to marinade 31
—— Pye, Shape of 35
—— of several Sorts, to dress the French Way 68
Fillet of Beef in Ragoo, to dress 280
—— of Veal, to stuff and roast 220
Fitters, to make of Turkey 243
Flounders, to boil 73
Florentine of Apples and other Fruit, to make 198
Flour Pudding, to make light 164
Forc'd Meat, to make 26
————— of the Flesh of Fish 66
Fowls, to order and feed 4
—— to boil 14
—— Capon, or Turkey in Balneomariae, to dress 84
Fruit Bisucits, to make 320
French Biscuits, to make 257

Gal-

INDEX

G

Gallanted Goose, to dress	298
Giblets, to order and stew	268
———— Pye, to make	293
Gilliflowers, to make Syrrup	207
Golden Pippens, or Jennitons, to make green	159
———————— &c. to preserve	393
Gooseberries, to preserve	315
———————— Cream, to make	108
———————— to bottle	143
———————— to preserve	144
———————— to pickle	144
———————— Cream, to make	143
———————— Tarts, to make	143
———————— Wine, to make	144
———————— Jelly, to make	144
———————— Acid, to make fit for Punch	144
Goose Pye, to make	292
———— to boil	213
———— to coller	213
———— to roast	214
———— a la Braise	214
Grapes, to preserve	245
Gravey, to draw	5
———— Soop	6
Green Sauce, to make	115
———— Sprouts, to boil	170
———— Sauce, to make	201
———— Figs, to pickle	225
———— Figs, to preserve	238
———— Sauce, to make	301
———— Apricots, to preserve	314
Gudgeons, to dress	212
Gurnets, to bake or fry	243

H

Haddocks, to dress the Dutch Way	67
———————— to dress the Dutch Way	115
———————— to dress the Swiss Way	215
———————— to stew	216
Hams, to salt the Westphalia Way	
Ham to salt the common Way	2
——— to boil	9
——— Pye, to make	113
——— to roast	212
——— a la Braise, to dress	211
——— to roast	279
——— to roast	14
——— how to make a Pudding for	15
——— in Collops, to dress	133
——— to pot	138
——— to dress the Swiss Way	216
——— with Peas, to dress	229
——— Pye, the French Way, to make	296
——— to jug	297
——— or Leveret a la braise, to dress	313
——— to stew	25
Hartshorn Jelly, to make	244
Haunch of Venison, to roast	132
Herrico of Mutton, to make	49
Herrings, to broil	294
———— to bake	294
Hot Butter Paste for Standing Pies	20
Hog's Liver, to fry	84
——— Feet and Ears a la Grandvell, to dress	293
——— Haslet, to order and roast	81
Hotch-Potch of Fowls, to make	306
Hotch-Pot, to make	121

I

Italian Cream, to make	91
Italian Biscuit, to make	246

J

Jacobine Soop, the Italian Way, to make	227
Jellies, to make	28
———— of Grapes, to preserve	318
———— of Quinces, to make red	235

Kid,

INDEX.

K

Kid, to dress	295
Kidney Beans, to boil	193
———— to pickle	194
———— to preserve	194
———— to preserve in Salt	289

L

Lamb, to roast the French Way	55
——— to ragoo	55
——— to fricasey	55
——— Head with its Appurtenances, to dress	89
——— Trotters, to marinade and dress	107
——— Pye, to make	200
Lampreys, to pot	244
———— to stew	245
Larks, to dress	250
——— to roast	293
——— Sparrows, or any small Birds, to make a Pye of	276
Leg of Lamb, to boil	23
—— of Lamb, to force	47
—— of Veal, to boil the English Way	218
—— of Pork, to stuff and roast	297
—— of Mutton accommode	305
Lemonade, to make	139
Lemon Puffs, to make	319
——— to preserve	43
——— in Knots, to dry	44
——— Pudding, to make	18
——— or Oranges, to make a Jelly of	172
——— Cream, to make	209
Lettice, to farce	119
Ling, to boil	157
Lisbon Biscuits, to make	283
Liver Pudding to make	154
Lobsters, to ragoo	64
——— Soop, to make	64
——— to pot	71
——— to roast	72
——— to cream	72
Lobsters in Jelly	113
——— to order and keep a Month for Fish Sauce	261
——— Patty, to make	266
——— Craw-Fish, or Shrimps, in Jelly, to dress	273
Lumber Pye, to make	175
Lyng Pye, to make	283

M

Mackroncy for present Use, to make	269
Mackrael, to dress	228
——— to broil	228
——— to souse	228
——— to bake	228
——— to make a Pye of	228
——— to salt and dry	229
Macaroons, to make	247
Marmalade of Cherries, to make	316
——— of Warden Pears, to make	176
——— of Quinces, to make red	234
——— of Quinces, to make white	234
——— of Currants, to make	284
——— of Roses and Almonds, to make	144
Marrow Loaves, to make	177
——— Pudding, to make	20
Minc'd Pyes of Calves Hearts, to make	219
——— of Eggs, to make	220
Meagre Soop, to make	64
Moor Game Pye, to make	283
——— by some called Heath Pouts, to roast	135
Morels, to dress	67
Mould Fitters, to make	245
Mullets, to dress	244
Mulberries, to preserve	176
Muscles, to dress	247
——— to fricasey	248
——— to scallop like Oysters	248

Mutt．

INDEX.

Mushrooms, to make Catchup of 141
———— to preserve for any Use 141
———— to pickle 142
———— to fricasey 142
———— to a delicacy brown 143
———— to dry 143
———— to make Loaves of 143
Mutton, a Pigeroom of 38
———— Cutlets, to farce 263
———— à la Royal, to make 160
———— to dress the Turkish Way 177
———— Cutlets in Batter, to dress 190
———— to order and roast a Chane of 105
———— cuchob'd, to dress 302
———— Rumps farc'd 305
———— Cutlets, to dress 11

N

Naples Biscuit, to make 101
Natural Gravey, of Beef or Mutton, to make 129
Neat's Tongue, to boil 106
——— Tongue, to roast 24
——— Foot Pudding, to make 153
——— Feet Pye, to make 178
Neat's Feet, to bake 178
——— Tongue, to make a sweet Pye of 179
——— Tongue à la Braise 187
——— Tongue, to pickle 187
——— Tongue Pye, to make 200
——— Tongue, with Claret Sauce, to dress 222
——— Tongue à la Smithergall, to roast 222
Neck of Veal, to daub 77

O

Oatmeal Pudding, to make 308
Onions, to ragoo 195
——— to pickle 258

Orange Pudding, to make 17
———— Tart, to make 303
———— to preserve 43
———— in Knots, to dry 44
———— Drops, to make 45
———— Paste, to make 45
———— to preserve whole 313
———— Cakes, to make 314
———— Marmalade, to make 315
———— Clear Cake, to make 318
———— Puffs, to make 319
Oysters, to pickle 33
———— to scallop 34
———— Loaves, to make 70
———— to fry 71
———— in Jelly 192
———— to ragoo 241
———— to broil in their Shells 141
———— to farce 242
———— Pancakes, to make 242
———— Pye the Dutch Way, to make 307
Ox Palates, to ragoo 64

P

Pancakes of Apple Fitters, to make 160
Partridge Pye, to make 253
Pasty-Paste 20
Patty of Oysters, to make 254
——— of Cockles or Muscles, to make 268
——— of Lamb Stones, to make 275
——— of Calves Brains, to make 114
——— of Spinage, to make 207
——— Devo, to make 48
Peacock Pye, to make 278
Peaches in Brandy, to preserve 204
——— green, to preserve 206
Peas, to stew 303
——— Soup, to make 23
——— Soup, green, to make 103
——— to boil 110
——— to stew 111
——— to keep green all the Year 290

INDEX.

Pears, to stew	16
—— or Apples, to dry	206
—— to preserve	239
Perch, to dress	248
Petty Patties of Fish, to make	71
Pheasant, to roast	203
Pig, the best Way to roast and dress	26
—— to coller	49
—— Pye, to make	53
—— a la Smithergall, to dress	148
—— a la Grand vell, to roast	150
—— to make a white Fricasey of	150
—— to dress the French Way	151
—— to coller like Brawn	183
Pigeons, to farce and roast	165
—————— to fricandeaux	111
—————— Compote	54
—————— a la Smethergall, to broil	211
—————— a la Tartare, to dress	248
—————— en compote, to dress	209
—————— a la Sante Menehout to dress	210
—————— to broil whole	207
—————— like Cypress Birds, to dress	269
—————— a la Basilic, to dress	266
—————— Pye, to make the French Way	273
—————— to stew	296
—————— Surtout	313
—————— Dumplins, to make	266
Pike in Jelly, to dress	298
—— to dress the Dutch Way	112
—— to roast	131
Pippins, to make a Jelly of	173
Pistacho Amulet, to make	312
Plumb-Cake, to make, with the Iceing	37
———— Broth, to make	300
Plovers, to roast	234
Pork Pye, to make	297
—— to pickle	3
—— Chops, to dress	249
Portugal Cakes, to make	205

Potatoe-Apples, to pickle	237
—————— Pudding, to make	134
Poultry, Distempers of	208
Poupeton of a Leg of Lamb a la Cream to make	306
Pudding Cake, to make	154
—————— of Herbs, to make	75
Puff-Paste, Directions for making	19
Pulpotoon of Quails, to make	310
—————— of Patridges and and Chickens, to make	311
—————— of Woodcocks, to make	311
Pullets with Mushrooms, to dress	281
—————— a la Smithergall, with Oysters, to dress	186
—————— a la Braise, to dress	76
Pupton of Lobsters, to make	76
—————— of Rabbits, to make	153
—————— of Apples, to make	158
Pye of Mutton Olives, to make	229

Q

Quails a la Braise, to dress	119
Quails, to fricasey	219
Quails, to farce and roast	219
Quaking Pudding, to make	276
Quails, to roast	165
Queen's Biscuit, to make	308
Quinces, to preserve whole	320

R

Rabbits, to stew the French Way	308
—————— Pye, to make	257
—————— to roast	78
—————— a la Saingaraz, to dress	162
—————— a la braise, to dress	212
—————— to boil the French Way	203
—————— boil'd with Asparagus A la cream	106
—————— Surprize	124

Rab

INDEX.

Rabbits to boil the English Way 216
——— Pye, to make 122
Ragoo of Truffles for Fish, to make 59
——— of Morels, to make 60
——— of Turnips, to make 62
——— to use with Neat's Tongue, to make 156
Ramkins, to make 108
Rais'd Pigeon Pye, to make 21
Raspberry Cream, to make 16
——— Paste, to make 316
——— Jelly, to make 179
——— whole, or Strawberries, to preserve 168
Rasp Jame, to make 192
Rasberry Clear-Cakes, to make 193
Red Marmalade of Quinces, to make 317
——— Cabbage, to pickle 237
——— Quince Clear Cake, to make 318
Rhenish Wine Cream, to make 94
Rice-Pudding, to make 104
——— Cream, to make 79
——— Fitters, to make 129
Roach and Dare, to bake 295
Rock Candy, to make 321
Rosa-solis of Spinage, to make 81
Roses, to dry 145
Rose Water, to make 145
Roofs and Reeves, to feed and dress 231
Round of Beef, to stuff and boil 47
Rump of Beef, to roll 221

S

Sagoe Soop, to make 97
——— Pudding, to make 98
——— Cream, to make 98
Salamagundy, to make 119
Salmon Pye, to make 264
——— like Ham, to dress 310
——— à la Braise, to dress 57
——— to broil 58

Salmon au Court Bouillon, to dress 58
——— Meagre, to dress 59
——— to pickle 73
——— like Sturgeon, to pickle 74
——— to boil 9
Salpicon for Roast Meats, as Beef, Mutton, Veal, or Lamb, to make 115
Salt Fish, to fry 69
—— Fish Pye, to make 70
Samphir, to pickle 285
Sauce, called Poiverade, to make 171
——— Robert, to make 171
——— with Westphalia Ham, for roasted Chickens, Turkey, or Lamb, to make 201
——— for Capers, to make 201
——— for Ducks and Teel, to make 201
——— for Woodcocks, to make 202
——— for Truffles, to make 202
——— for roast Mutton, to make 202
Sausages, to make 255
——— stew'd a la braise 295
Scate, or Thornback, to dress 158
Seed-Cake, to make 38
Semey of Venison, to make 166
Sheep Trotters, to farce 128
——— Tongues to farce 155
——— Tongues, to pickle and dry 220
——— Tongues, to make a Pye of 258
Shrimps in Jelly, to dress 274
Slic'd Pudding with Dates, to make 274
Sillabub, to make 27
Silmy of Woockcocks, to make 250
Soles, to stew 50
—— to boil 73
Soop de Sante, the French Way 75
——— au Bourgeois, to make 131

Soop

INDEX.

Soop in Balneo Moria, to dreſs	278
—— Puree of Artichokes, to make	157
—— Diſh, to garniſh	7
Spaniſh Olio, to make	239
Splace, to boil	73
Squob Pye, to make	127
Strong Broth, to make	5
Sturgeon, roaſted	304
———— broil'd	304
Suet, (or Hunter's) Pudding, to make	18
Swan for a Pye, to order	300
Sweet-breads, to roaſt	35
Sweet-breads, to marinade	118
Sweet-bread Patty, to make	134
Syrrup of Violets, Clove Pinks, or Gilliflowers, to make	100

T

Tanſey, to make	19
Tench, to dreſs	124
——— to bake	125
——— Carp, Trout, or Pike, to make a Pye of	129
Teal, to roaſt	296
Tongue, to boil	77
Tort de Moy, to make	41
Tripes, to fry	50
Trouts, to pickle, like Charr	139
——— to pot red	139
——— to ſtew the Dutch Way	140
Turbat Pye, to make	54
Turnips, to boil and order	171
Turkey, or Pullet, to braiſe	215
——— Pye, to make	256
——— Figs in Jelly	295
——— to boil, with Oyſter Sauce	13
——— to roaſt	28
——— to mince	29
——— Figs in Syrrup	110
——— Pullets, Chickens, or Partridges a la Smithergall, to dreſs	126

U

Udder, to boil	77
Umble Pye, to make	185

V

Veal Collops, to dreſs	32
—— Sweet Breads, to ragoo	59
—— Cutlets, to marinade	68
—— Pye, to make	102
—— Olives, to make	107
—— Cutlets, to make	162
—— a la Haſtereaux, to dreſs	272
—— forc'd and daub'd, to dreſs	135
—— Cutlets, to farce	262
Velvet Cream, to make	321
Veniſon, a la Royal, to make	166
———— a Shoulder of, to roaſt	167
———— to haſh	195
———— Paſty, to make	158
———— Haunch of, to boil	170
———— in Stakes, called a Civet to dreſs	194
———— a Ragoo of, to make	195
Vermicelly Soop, to make	46
Virginia Trouts, to dreſs	123

W

Wafer Paper, to make	309
Walnuts, to pickle	284
———— to pickle white	180
———— to preſerve	180
———— to make keep all the Year	181
Water Tart, to make	303
Weavers, a Fiſh ſo called, to dreſs	195
Weet Ears, to roaſt	231
Welſh Flummery, to make	80
White Plumbs, to preſerve	321
———— Puddings, to make	271
———— Quince Marmalade, to make	316

White

INDEX.

White Marmalade of Quinces, to make 317
——— Cullis of a roast Pullet, to make 224
——— Collops, to make 33
——— Cabbage, to stew 52
——— Fricasey of Pigeons, to make 185
——— Cullis Meagre, to make 189
——— Jelly, to make 174

Whitins Lord Exeter's Way, to dress 112
Wigs, to make 99
Wild Ducks, to roast 14
Woodcocks a la Smithergall, to dress 218
——— and Partridges, to pot 251
——— Pye, to make 272
——— to roast 15

See the Whole Bills of Fare at the End of the Book.

ERRATA.

PAge 48, instead of more Truffles, Morels, &c. *read*, butter over all before it is closed to bake, and when baked, put in the Lare.—Instead of dish'd Sweet-breads, Carrots, Turnips, &c. in some Places, *read*, diced Sweet-breads, &c.—Page 93, for Eggs in Butter, *read*, Eggs in Batter.—Page 102, for *Des Oeufs au verjus*, read, *Pate de Veau*.—Page 111, for put in some Shredding, *read*, put in some shred Mint.—Page 150, for minc'd Sauce, *read*, Mint Sauce.—Page 231, for Land Rodes, *read*, Land Rales.— Page 271, for boil them, *read*, broil them.—Page 321, *read*, White Plumbs when scalded, skin them.———— Rock Candy, instead of setting it over a very hot Stove, *read*, set it on a drying Stove, or in a Closet near the Fire.—In the Bill of Fare for the Prebendaries, instead of a roast Pigeon Pye, *read*, a rais'd Pigeon Pye.

THACKER's
ART
OF
COOKERY.

JANUARY.

Directions for Salting Beef.

Instruction pour conserver du Beuf.

LET your salting Vessels be scoured out clean, and scalded once a Week; see the Beef be cold before you salt it; cut out all the Kernels, and look it well over, to see if you can find any Flyblows; which, if you do, take them clean out, and salt your Meat with common Salt; then put it into a Vessel that has a Conveniency to let the bloody Brine run from it; the next Day take it out, and salt it over again very well, pricking the skinny Pieces with the Point of a sharp Knife, or an Iron Skewer, to let in the Salt; joint the Brisket-pieces well with a Cleaver, for they will not take the Salt so soon as the other Pieces, then put it into the Tub again, (or Leaden

Veſſel, which is beſt) ſtop the Hole at the Bottom, and keep the ſecond Brine to the Meat; boil the bloody Brine that you ſaved, and ſtrain it through a Hair Sieve, let it ſtand to cool and ſettle, then pour what's clear of it on your Beef; in a Day or two take it up again, and examine it once more, for ſometimes the Flies will ſtrike it where you can't find out at firſt, and in three or four Days they will grow to large Maggots, which, on finding, cut them out clean, and rub that Part well with Salt and Vinegar, and it will not be perceived to have been touched.

How to ſalt Hams the Weſtphalia Way.
Jambon maniere de Veſtphalie.

A Ham of 18 lb. is to be ſalted with common Salt, and lay 24 Hours, to let the bloody Brine run from it, as it did from the Beef; then take four Ounces of Saltpetre, two Ounces of Bay Salt, half a Pound of coarſe Sugar, as much Cocheneal (pounded) as will lie on a Shilling, dry theſe Ingredients before the Fire, and rub your Ham well over with them, throwing away the bloody Brine, put it into your ſalting Veſſel again, turn it every Day, and rub it well with the Pickle; keep this Order for three Weeks, then hang it up to ſmoak in a Chimney for a Fortnight where Wood is burnt, and afterwards hang it in a convenient Place to keep for Uſe; it will be good in two Months.

N. B. There are convenient Places in London to dry Hams and Tongues: I have cured as good ones in London as ever was made Uſe of.

The common Way of ſalting Hams.
Jambon a la maniere ordinaire.

LEAVE out the Sugar and Cocheneal, mix the reſt with common Salt, dry it well before the Fire,

ART of COOKERY.

Fire, salt your Hams well, then keep the same Order as above, except smoaking them. You may salt Bacon the same Way.

How to pickle Pork.
Porc a conservé.

CUT it into what Pieces you think proper; salt it well with common Salt; put it into an Earthen Jar 24 Hours; then take it up and let it drain; take the same Ingredients you used to the Westphalia Ham, except the Cochineal, in Proportion to your Weight; rub your Pork well with them; take the bloody Brine out of the Jar; pack in the Pork as close as you can; boil the Brine as you did for your Beef, and put the Clear to the Pork; lay a Weight on it to keep it tight down, and it will be fit to use in a Fortnight. You may cure Bacon any of these Ways; I have tried them all, and it proved good; let your Brine be cold before you put it to your Pork.

How to preserve Fish.
Poisson a preservé.

TAKE your Fish, when fresh, wash and clean them; put them into your Kettle with a Drainer in the Bottom; pour in as much hard Water as will cover them; put in a good Handful of Salt and a little Vinegar, let them boil till near enough; then take them up, and let them lie till cold; put your Liquor into an Earthen Pot to cool also; afterwards put in your Fish, and they will keep good two or three Days. When you would use them, put them into your Fish-kettle, with as much hard Water as will cover them; make them just boil over a brisk Fire, and they will eat near as well as when first taken. For further Particulars, look for dressing of Fish.

How

How to order and feed Fowls.

Volaille a nouriré.

DO not mix the Fowls together in Coops which you buy at different Times; but cut their Wings and Tails, and put them into a Yard three or four Days, (giving them different sorts of Meat) in which Time they will become acquainted, and take Meat better when you coop them. If you have not a convenient Yard, put them in a Room, (which is better) strew'd with gravelly Sand, and lay some Straw over that; set their different Meats in separate Things, as Barley-meal made into a pretty stiff Paste with warm Water, or Milk and Water, or the Liquor fresh Meat hath been boil'd in; sometimes mix Barley-meal and Chissel (or small Bran) together, other Times mix Oatmeal with any of these; save the Crumbs of Bread, Raspings, and Crusts, soak them in the Liquor aforesaid, and give them it for a Change; and sometimes give them Grain, as Barley, Oats or Wheat. Let the Room be washed once a Week, and give them fresh Gravel and Straw; feed them twice a Day; take the Meat from them if they don't eat it up, and mix it with fresh, and give it to them again in the Evening; at which Time be sure they have enough, for they like to feed as soon as it is light in the Morning; and what they leave, mix with fresh, and give to them about Noon. If you feed them in a Coop, keep the same Order, leaving out the Straw in Summer, and cleaning the Coops and Troughs every Day. Observe these Rules, and you'll never fail of having fat Poultry in a Fortnight's Time, if they are full of Flesh when you buy them; but if they are poor, it will take as much Time to make them fleshy, as to make the fleshy ones fat.

As the Ground-work of Cookery chiefly consists in

in making good strong Broth and Gravy; how to prepare these follows next of Course.

How to make Strong Broth.

Bouillon fort a fair.

TAKE a Leg of Beef, a Knockle of Veal, a Neck of Mutton, or what Quantity of these you please; cut them to Pieces; let them lie to soak in a good Quantity of Water, to take the Blood out of them; then wash your Meat very clean; put it into a Pot big enough, with a good Faggot of Sweet-Herbs, some Turnips, two or three Carrots, half a dozen Onions, some Salt, and Whole Pepper; put as much Water to it as will cover it, and let your Water be as clear as you can get. Some People object against Spring Water, but I do not, if it has no bad Taste, for some Reasons I shall give when it comes in Course: Let your Pot boil gently, and keep scumming it, and as it boils away put in some more boiling Water; keep this Order till your Meat be boil'd enough; then strain it first through a Cullender, then through a Hair-sieve; put it into a shallow Vessel; set it in an airy Place to cool, if you have Time: Before you use it, take the Fat off the Top, and the Settlement from the Bottom. This strong Broth is proper for several Uses. which I shall mention hereafter.

How to draw Gravey.

Jus a fair.

CUT some Slices of Bacon, and lay at the Bottom of your Gravy-Pan, with sliced Carrot; then cut some Slices of lean Beef, the Thickness of your Hand, and lay upon that; put in some Sweet-Herbs, with Salt and Pepper; set it over a slow Fire, covered close; let it stew till all the Gravy is

drawn

drawn out of the Meat, and fallen to the Bottom, and is very brown; then having some strong Broth ready, as before-mentioned, put it into your Gravy-Pan, and let it boil softly till you have got all the Goodness out of your Meat; scum it well; when enough, strain it off as you did the strong Broth. This Gravy is for Soop mixt with strong Broth and other Ingredients, which I shall mention in the Directions given for Soops. This Gravy serves likewise for all Sorts of wild and tame Fools; but for Ducks, and Fowls of that Kind, put in one Spoonful of Red Wine, but no more of it than can be just tasted. In its other Particulars relating to Fowls, I refer you to to its proper Place.

Note, Sometimes we use Veal ordered as above; sometimes we mix Veal, Mutton, and Beef together.

Gravy Soop.

Potage au jus.

TAKE six Heads of good Celeri, Endive, Beets, Spinage, &c. clean them very well, and shred them not too small; put these into a Stew-Pan, with a Piece of Butter, and a little Salt, and let them stew; then put in some Gravy; add to them till you get as much as will do for your Dish; put in some Vermicelli, and if you please, some forced Meat-balls; in the Middle, put a forced Lettice, a Fowl, or a Duck, a Knockle of Veal, or a French Roll, (as your Conveniency or Fancy suits) with some Roll sliced and dried before the Fire. Your Soop may be made higher or lower, as you think proper, by mixing the strong Broth and Gravy; adding a Faggot of Sweet-Herbs, consisting of about an Handful, composed of Thyme, Parsly, Sweet-Leeks, Lemon, Marjoram, &c.

N. B. You may slice four or five Onions and stew them with your Herbs.

ART of COOKERY.

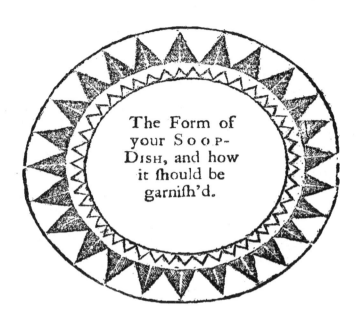

Explanation of the Garnishing of your Soop Dish.

THE first Rim next the Soop is to be Paste, in the same Form as in the Figure; the second or outer Rim is to be made of Turnips parboiled, cut in Pieces, and laid in Form as in the said Figure; and the Vacancies between each Square of the outer Rim are to be filled up with Carrots cut small in one Open; and Spinage, &c. in the other, and so alternately.

To dress a Cod's Head, with fry'd Fish around.

Tête de Morue accommodé.

TAKE out the Cod's Gills and clean it very well; then tie it up with Pack-thread, and put it into the Fish-kettle, with a large Handful of Salt; cover it with hard Water, (for that causes the Fish to boil hard and firm) let it boil softly on a slow Fire for half an Hour, then make the frying Fish ready, by skinning them, &c. which done, take out their Eyes, turn them round, and put their Tails through the Holes of their Eyes; wash them in Small Beer, and Flour them well; some wash them over with beaten Yolks of Eggs, and drudge them with Flour and fine Bread Crumbs. Let your frying Ingredients be good Beef or Mutton Suet well render'd and strained, or Beef-drippings, if clean from Dross; put your Fat in to the Frying-pan, and make it sufficiently hot, which is to be perceived by its beginning to turn of a brownish Colour; then put in your Fish; do not fill your Pan too full, and take great Care they do not burn; fry them of a Gold colour, then take them up and put them on your Fish-plate before the Fire to drain; if your Fish are large, fry them slow, if small, the quicker the better.

To make Fish Sauce.

Sauße au Poißon.

TAKE a Pint of Good strong Broth, half a Pint of White-Wine, four Anchovies, the Juice of a Lemon, some sliced Horse-radish, some whole Peppercorns, a little Mace, two middling Onions, and a small Faggot of sweet Herbs; let these boil till half be wasted, strain it, and draw your Butter with it, you may add Crab, Lobster, Oysters, Shrimps, or Cockles

kles as you please; if the Sauce is not thick enough, work a Piece of Butter in Flour, and thicken it with that.

How to boil Salmon.
Saumon á Accommodé.

SCALE it and cut it down the Middle, take what Part of it you think most proper, and put as much hard Water into your Kettle (with a Handful of Salt) as will cover the Fish. Make the Water boil first, then put in the Fish, which must only boil gently, (for if it boils fast it will break) half a large Salmon will take half an Hour boiling, and so in Proportion; make the same Sauce to it as you did for the Cod's Head, and add to it some Spawn of Lobster bruised, with a little Red-Wine; some prefer Herbs and Butter mixt with the Juice of Lemon, which you will find explained in the dressing of Mackarel.

How to boil a Ham.
Jambon á Accommodé.

CRACK the Shank Bone, pare the black off the Inside, and if your Ham be dry, lay it in Water all Night before you use it; tie it up in a coarse Cloth with a Cord, and lay a Stick over the Copper; tie the Cord to it so as to let the Ham swim in the middle of the Copper; it will take five Hours boiling, if a large one; skin it and rub it over with the Yolk of an Egg; drudge it with fine Bread Crumbs, and brown it in an Oven, or before the Fire.

How to roast a Surloin of Beef.
Longe de Beuf Accommodé.

CUT the Chine off the Inside; joint it a little with a Cleaver; crack the Bones at the thin End; spit it as straight as you can, but the thin Side must be

B hea-

heaviest; skewer the Skin next the Chine, and lay it down with the Chine next the Fire, but at a good Distance off; let it lie so for a Quarter of an Hour, then take it up and paper it, lay it down again, and set the Jack a-going; let it roast three Hours, or three Hours and a Half, as it is in bigness; then take off the Paper, dridge it and take it up. Garnish with Horse-Radish and Pickles.

How to hash a Calf's Head.

Tête de Veau Hachez.

CLEAN it well, and wash the Blood quite out of it; boil it tender; cut one Half in Slices, with the Tongue or without it; cut the other Half round, and wash it over with the Yolk of an Egg; then sprinkl it over with shred Thyme, Parsley, a little Salt, Mutmeg, and Bread Crumbs; lay it to the Fire to brown, and baste it with Butter.

Another Way.

D'un autre Maniere.

IS to take out the Bones, and cut the thick Part thereof into two square Pieces; brown them as above directed; then clean the Brains, and boil them with a little Sage, Parsley, and Salt; when enough, chop them together, putting in a little Butter, Pepper, and Vinegar; then cut the Top off a Roll; take out the Crum; wash it over with oyl'd Butter; brown it before the Fire, and split the Tongue in two; then make your Hash ready in this Manner; put almost a Quarter of a Pound of Butter into your Stew-pan; keep it stirring till dissolved; put in a large Onion with a small Faggot of sweet Herbs; dust Flour into it; then put in your sliced Calf's Head; toss it up, and put in a Pint of good brown Gravy, a little
Pep-

Pepper, Salt, forc'd Meat Balls, and a little White-Wine; tofs it all together, let it ftew till it is of the Thicknefs of Cream; then put it in your Difh, and the Roll with Brains in the Middle; the two fquare Pieces on each Side, and the fplit Tongue to anfwer that; garnifh your Difh with Rafhers of Bacon, Lemon, and Barberries. If you keep half the Head whole, and brown as before-mentioned, lay it in the Middle, then cut the Tongue in Slices and put it into the Hafh; cut the Brains in little Pieces; order them as you did the brown'd half of the Head, and add it to the above Garnifh of your Difh.

To drefs Mutton Cutlets.

Cotelettes de Mouton.

TAKE a Neck of Mutton, cut it Bone by Bone, flat them with a Cleaver, trim them round with a Knife, to make them all alike as nigh as you can; then order them as you did the brown'd Half of the Calf's Head (as above) brown them on both Sides; broil them before the Fire, and take Care they are not done too much; let your Sauce be Gravy and Butter, with a few Capers chopped fmall, and a little Onion; thicken it with a Piece of Butter wrapped up in Flour; put your Sauce into the Difh, and lay your Cutlets handfomely on. Garnifh them with Capers, Horfe-Radifh, and Barberries. I fhall have Occafion hereafter to mention fome different Ways of dreffing Cutlets.

To make a boil'd Bread Pudding, with baked ones round it.

Boudin au Pain.

TAKE a Three-penny fine Loaf, pare off the Cruft, cut it in Slices, rub it through a Cullender,

der, put the Crumbs into a stew Pan, boil as much Milk as will moisten them; mix all well, and cover it; then beat ten Eggs and put to it, with some grated Nutmeg, and as much Sugar well powder'd as will sweeten it to your Taste; boil as much of it in a fine Cloth, (which must be buttered, flour'd, and tied tight) as will lie handsomely in the middle of your Dish; then add to the remainder you left, some Suet cut small, or Marrow, with some Currans washed and picked, and well dry'd by the Fire; mix all together, put in a little more Salt and Butter; then take some earthen Cups, butter them and sprinkle them with a little Suet chop'd small, fill them, which done, turn your little Puddings out of the Pans, cut them in two, and lay them round the boiled one; then grate on some Sugar; stick the middle Pudding with Almonds sliced, or Sweatmeats, which you please. The Sauce may be made of Whitewine and Sugar, the Juice of an Orange and Melted Butter; or plain Butter only. The boiled Pudding will be ready in an Hour, or little more; and the little Puddings will bake in the same Time.

To make a Florentine of Calves Feet.

Florandine et la forme.

WASH them well and clean them from Hairs, boil them tender, let them be strained from their Liquor, and stand to cool; take out the Bones, and shred the Meat small; take the Weight of your Meat in Suet, and shred it also, with three or four Apples and some green Lemon Peel; mix all together with a pound of Currans, (pick'd, wash'd, and dry'd before the Fire) half a Pound of Raisins, stoned and chop'd; season it with Salt, Nutmeg, and beaten Cinnamon; put in half a Pound of Sugar, half a Pint of
White-

White-Wine, and fill your Dish; you may put in some candied Peel, as Orange, Lemon, or Citron, which you please; crofs bar it, and put a Border of Puff Paste round, as you see in the following Draught.

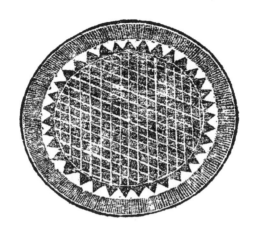

To boil a Turkey with Oyster Sauce.

Dindon accommodé avec des Huitres.

DRAW it, and beat down the Breast Bone, (if required) which must be done thus; lay a Cloth under the Turkey, and another on the Breast, then give it a hard Stroke with the flat Side of a Cleaver, then singe it, wash it well, truss it for boiling, butter and flour the Breast, tye it in a Cloth, boil it in hard Water, and it will look the whiter; so will all Fowls, Fish and Flesh; but good clear soft Water is better for any Thing that is old; a middling one will boil in an Hour and a Half, but a very large one will take two Hours. For Sauce take an hundred Oysters, or what Quantity you please, when opened wash them clean from the Pieces of Shells and Sand, take the

clear

clear of their Liquor, put it in your Stew-pan with the Oysters, and stew them, but not too much, take them up, and take off their Beards, clean your Stew-pan and put in your Oysters again, with the clear Part of the Liquor, and half a Pint of good strong Broth or Gravy, a large Onion, a small Faggot of sweet Herbs, Half a Lemon, a little grated Nutmeg, and a little White-Wine; draw it up thick, with a Pound of Butter, and pour this over your Turkey. Garnish it with Lemon, Barberries, &c.

To boil Fowls.

Volailles accommodé.

THEY must be boiled the same Way as you did the above Turkey; dish them with green Sprouts boiled nicely in hard Water, pour drawn Butter over them, and garnish them with diced Carrots, and Eggs boiled hard and chop'd.

How to roast Wild Ducks.

Canards sauvages Roti's.

TRUSS them, put a Bit of Butter dipped in Salt in their Bellies, spit them and lay them down to roast; then singe, baste and flour them; they must not be roasted too much. The Sauce for them you will find under the Directions for drawing of Gravy, (Page 5 and 6.) I shall give particular Directions concerning trussing all Sorts of Fowls hereafter.

How to roast a Hare.

Lievre Roti.

SKIN it, and take the Guts quite out, and clean it from the Blood with a wet Cloth, put a Pudding in the Belly

Belly of it; then truss, spit, and roast it in the following Manner; lay it a good Distance from the Fire, and baste it well with Butter, then salt and flour it; when it has been down about half an Hour, put it nigher the Fire, and baste it over again; if you keep a good Fire and it is a young Hare, one Hour will roast it. Froth it up just before you take it from the Fire; take some of the Pudding out, and mix it with Butter, and Gravy, put it into the Dish and lay the Hare thereon. Garnish it with Lemon and green Parsley, or Barberries; you may lard it with Bacon, or cover the Back with a Lard of Bacon.

How to make a Pudding for a Hare.

Boudin pour une Lievre.

TAKE two Ounces of Suet, shred it small, soak the Crum of a Penny Brick in Cream, put in some Thyme, Parsley, a Bit of Onion, an Anchovy, and a little Lemon Peel shred fine; season it with Pepper, Salt, and Nutmeg; break in an Egg, work it all together, and put it in the Hare; sew it up, and roast it as above.

To roast Woodcocks.

Becasses roti.

PICK and truss them with their Heads on, spit them across, with their Intrails in them; make some white Bread Toasts, and lay under them as they roast to catch what falls from them; do not roast them too much; pour some melted Butter on the Toasts when in the Dish, froth up the Woodcocks, draw them off the Spit and lay them on the Toasts, put in a little Gravy. Garnish with Lemon and Barberries.

How

How to stew Pears.

Poirs etuvée.

GET some of the largest baking Pears you can, pare them, but leave on the Stalks; put them into an earthen Vessel, with some Pieces of Pewter; and to one Dozen, put a Bottle of Red Wine, two Pounds of Sugar, about ten Cloves, some Lemon Peel, with as much hard Water as will cover them; put in as much Cotchineal pounded as will lie on a Shilling, tied in a Linen Cloth; then tye brown Paper over the Top of your Vessel, and bake it in a slow Oven till they be baked tender; when you use them, pour some of the Syrup upon them. The Pieces of Pewter adds much to their Colour, and the finer the Sugar, the clearer your Pears will be.

To make Raspberry Cream.

Creme aux Framboises.

TAKE half a Pint of Preserved Raspberries, or Jaum, boil a Pint and a half of Cream, and when it is cold, mix the Raspberries with a Pint of it; if it be not sweet enough, make it to your Taste; then take the other half Pint and wisk it to a Froth, put it into a Glass Bason, and lay the Froth on the Top of it; you may strew Caraway Comfits on it if you please.

To make Blawmange.

Blanch à Manger.

TAKE two Ounces of Hartshorn, and a Set of Calves Feet, well cleaned and washed, split them and take out the long Bones, and the Bit of black in

the

the Middle; put them into a very clean well tinn'd Pot, or a large Sauce-pan, with Spring-water; boil them till they come to a ſtrong Jelly, which you may find by taking a little in a Spoon; and ſet it to cool; when 'tis boil'd enough you will have a Quart of Liquor; ſtrain it through a Napkin; ſet it to cool; take the Top clean off, and the Jelly clean from the Bottom; mix it with a Quarter of a Pound of Almonds well beat, the Juice of a large Lemon, a little Orange Flower Water, a few Drops of Ratafia, or a Laurel Leaf or two bruis'd; ſweeten it with double-refin'd Sugar; put in a Pint of good Cream; let it ſimmer over a ſlow Charcoal Fire; keep it ſtirring; ſtrain it through a Napkin; and keep it ſtirring till 'tis pretty cold; then put it into your Glaſs-baſon; ſtick it with blanch'd Almonds, cut in four the long Way. You may colour them if you pleaſe, for a Change, ſome with Cochineal, and others with Saffron; boil them in Sugar and Water, with the Colours tied in Muſlin Rags.

How to make an Orange Pudding.

Boudin d'Orange.

TAKE four Naples Biſcuits, grate them fine; boil a Pint of Cream and a Pint of Milk together; put it to your Biſcuits, and ſweeten it to your Taſte; grate in the Rind of a Seville Orange, and ſqueeze in the Juice; colour it with a little Saffron, tied up in a fine Cloth, and ſoak'd in three or four Spoonfuls of Sack or Orange-flower Water, which put into your Pudding; then ſlice in half a candied Orange Peel; and beat eight Eggs fine; ſtrain them, and grate in Half a Nutmeg; put in a little Salt; mince the Marrow of Half a Marrow Bone, or a Quarter of a Pound of melted Butter, which put in, and mix all together; butter your Diſh; fill it and put a Border of

C   Puff-

Puff-paste round it; it will bake in Half an Hour. Note, Your Milk and Cream must be Wine-Measure.

How to make a Lemon Pudding.

Boudin aux Citrons.

Also a Carrot Pudding.

Boudin aux Carotes.

BOTH these Puddings are made as the above, only you must first boil your Carrots, and beat them fine in a Mortar; you may boil your Orange or Lemon Peel also, and beat it fine; but then you must take the Rind of two. The Sauce for Orange or Lemon Puddings is Sack, Sugar, Butter, and Half an Orange to an Orange Pudding, and Half a Lemon to a Lemon Pudding; but instead of either, in the Carrot Pudding, you must put Orange-flower Water.

To make a Suet (or Hunter's) Pudding.

Boudin aux Chasseurs.

TAKE a Pound of Flour; the Crumb of a Penny Roll soak'd in hot Milk; a Pound of Suet, cut fine; a little Salt; Half a Nutmeg; a little Sugar; Half a Pound of Currans; Half a Pound of Raisins, ston'd and chopp'd; and eight Eggs; mix it very stiff with cold Milk; boil it three Hours at least; you may put in Sweet-meats if you would have it richer.

N. B. You may make any Sort of Pudding, putting eight Eggs to a Quart of Milk; as, Almonds, Chesnuts, &c. beating them in a Mortar; a Quarter of a Pound is sufficient to a Quart of Milk and four Naples Biscuits, thicken'd over a Fire; stick some, cut in Quarters, on the Top of your Pudding.

A Tansey.

Tanaise.

TAKE four Biscuits, the Crumb of a French Roll; boil a Pint of Milk, and a Pint of Cream; and put to it Half a Pint of Spinage Juice ſtrain'd; grate in Half a Nutmeg; beat a little Mace and Cinnamon; put in a little Tanſey; beat it with your Spinage; ſweeten it to your Taſte; put to it a Quarter of a Pound of Butter; beat twelve Eggs; leave out the Whites of two; ſtrain them through a Sieve; put all together into a Stew-pan; keep it ſtirring, till thick, with a Whiſk; butter the Pan you bake it in; alſo butter a Paper, and put it at the Bottom; then put in your Tanſey; Half an Hour will bake it; which done, turn it in your Diſh; take off your Paper, and grate on ſome Sugar; divide a Seville Orange in eight; ſtick the top with Sweat-meats, that is, Citron, Orange, and Lemon Peel.

Directions *for making all Sorts of* Puff Paste, *&c.*

Pate feüilletée.

TAKE a Pound of Flour; rub in it a Quarter of a Pound of Butter; break two Eggs into it; make it into Paſte with cold Water; roll out your Paſte into a ſquare Sheet; lay Bits of Butter all over it; flour it, and fold it up at both Ends; lay one over the other in the Middle; beat it with a Rolling Pin, and roll it out again; keep doing thus, till you have uſed a Pound of Butter: If you dridge in fine Powder Sugar every Time, it makes it Paſte Royal. This Paſte is for all Sorts of Sweetmeats, Tarts, Puffs, or cut Covers for Puddings, &c.

Pasty-Paste.

Pate commune, ordinaire, brisée.

IS made with six Pounds of Butter to a Peck of Flour; rub into the Flour three Pounds of Butter; make it Paste with six Eggs and cold Water; roll it out as you did the above Puff-paste, and keep the same Order till all your Butter be spent.

Hot Butter Paste for Standing Pies.

Pate blanche pour les gros Pâtez.

PUT two Pounds of Butter to a Peck of Flour; boil the Butter in Water, and make your Paste very stiff: But if for Tarts not so stiff.

To make a Marrow Pudding.

Poudin de Mouëlle formée.

CUT four Naples Biscuits; rub them through a Cullender, with the Crumb of a French-roll; boil a Pint of Milk with a Pint of Cream; put it to the Biscuit and cover all down; then beat eight Eggs; strain them and put them to the Pudding, with as much fine Sugar as will sweeten it; grate in Half a Nutmeg, and put in a little Salt with a little Rosewater; then wash Half a Pound of Currans; rub and dry them, and mix all together. This done, put your Pudding into the Stew-pan, and set it over a Charcoal Fire; keep it stirring with a Whisk till it be thick; then put it into your Dish, and let stand to cool; then put in your Marrow, in Pieces, about

the

ART of COOKERY.

the same Quantity as is contain'd in one Marrow bone. Put a Rim of Puff paste round your Dish; and lay on the Cover, cut in the following Form:

Three Quarters of an Hour will bake it: You may ice the Cover, and the Rim also, if you please. Directions concerning Icing will be given in a more proper Place afterwards.

How to make a rais'd Pigeon Pye.

Paté de Pigeons elevée, et la forme.

PICK, draw, and singe the Pigeons; cut off the Wings at the second Joint; truss them; take Pepper, Salt, and minc'd Parsley, mix'd together; and work a Bit of of Butter, as big as a Walnut, among it, which put into the Belly of each Pigeon, and rub their Outsides with the same Seasoning. Your Pye being rais'd and set in Form, lay in your Pigeons, with forc'd Meat, and Yolks of hard Eggs; lay

lay thin Slices of Butter over all; then close your Pye, and garnish the Lid as in the following Figure, which is also the Form of your Pye.

When it is half bak'd, draw it, and put in some good strong Broth. One Hour and an Half will bake it. You may make the Pye in a Dish, with the same Ingredients, using Pasty paste instead of hot Paste.

F E B.

FEBRUARY.

To make Peas-Soup.

Potage aux Pois à l'Angloise.

TAKE a Quart of Split-peas; wash them; and put them into a Pot big enough, with a Scrag of Mutton, a Knuckle of Veal, a Piece of Bacon, some whole Pepper, five or six Onions, a Faggot of sweet Herbs. Put as much Water in as will cover them, and set the Pot on the Fire; let it boil softly till the Meat is in Rags, and the Peas in a Pulp (but take the Bacon up before it is too much); as the Liquor boils away put in boiling Water; strain your Soop through a Cullender, working the Peas through with a Laddle; then pass it through a Hair Sieve to make it the smoother; take six Heads of Sallery, and two Leeks; cut and wash them clean; and stew them tender, with a Piece of Butter in a Pan; add to it some strong Broth; put in your pulp'd Peas, and some dry'd Mint, sifted fine; cut the Bacon in Pieces like Dice; and put them in, with some French bread cut the same Way, and fried in Butter; scum the Fat clean off; dish it with a French-Roll in the Middle; and season it with Salt and Pepper to your Taste. You may put in some shred Spinage if you please.

To boil a Leg of Lamb.

Gigot d'Agneau bouilli.

SOAK it in warm Water for an Hour; make your Pot very clean; and see it be well tinn'd; set it on the Fire, with very clean Water; and when it boils scum it; then take your Lamb and dry it with a Cloth; rub the upper Side with Butter; flour it and tie it in a Cloth: One Hour will boil it. As for the Loin, cut it into Stakes, and order them as you did the Mutton Cutlets [which see Page 11.] otherwise broil them plain, just as you think best. Having some Spinage boil'd and well drain'd, put it in the Bottom of your Dish; lay the Leg of Lamb in the Middle; and put the Stakes round it; garnish the Dish with Carrots, cut in small Dice, slic'd Lemon, &c. You may dress a Leg of Veal the same Way; it will take two Hours, or two Hours and an Half boiling; dish it with Bacon and Greens; garnish with Carrots and scop'd Turnips. Send a Boat or Cup with melted Butter to the Table with it: and you may put a little over your Meat if you see Occasion.

To roast a Neat's Tongue.

Langue de Beuf roti.

BOIL it pretty tender; blanch it, that is, take off the Skin: If you have a small Udder to answer the Tongue it will be better; then a Marrow bone (as mention'd in the Bill of Fare) which Udder must also be boil'd tender: Spit the Tongue through the Root; then the thin End will lie upon the Spit towards the Point; pare off the Out-side of the Udder, and cut it in the Shape of a Tongue; spit it through the thick Part, with the thin End opposite the Tongue; fasten the thin Ends with a Skewer and Pack thread; wash them over with the Yolks of Eggs; drudge them with Bread Crumbs rubb'd through a Cullender; roast them of a Gold Colour; baste them with Butter, and draw them carefully; dish them with Gravy Sauce, and Venison Sauce, or Curran Jelly in a Cup. If you send the Tongue up with a Marrow bone, let it be cut at both Ends, that it may stand by itself; then

break

break it exactly in the Middle; cut all the Meat clean from the Bone; put some Flour on the Marrow, and squeeze it hard on; boil them an Hour. Dish them on each Side the Tongue, with Toasts of Bread, and Sauce, as before, or with Greens, Carrots, &c.

How to stew a Hare.
Lievre cuit à l'etuvée.

CUT the Hare off below the Shoulders; and cut the Fore Parts as for a Fricasey; put it into a Sauce-pan, with a Faggot of sweet Herbs, two large Onions, an Anchovy, Half a Lemon (the Peel being taken off) Half a Pint of Red Wine, a Pint of good Gravy, some whole Pepper-Corns, a little Mace, Half a Pound of good Bacon (the Skin taken off and par'd clean) stew these all together over a slow Fire till the Hare is tender, keeping it close cover'd all the Time; as the Liquor stews away, add more Gravy or strong Broth; take your Meat out; strain the Liquor through a Sieve; put a Piece of Butter into a Stew-pan; brown it with a little Flour; put in your Liquor and the Hare; let it stew till it is the Thickness of a thin Cream; season it with Salt and Nutmeg to your Taste; cut a Bit off each Leg of the other Part of the Hare, to make it look handsome; and stew it with the Fore Part; then put a small Iron Skewer into the Back-bone; drive it in fast; skewer the Legs with two Skewers; spit it; and tie that Skewer, which you drove in, to the Spit, to keep it tight, so roast it; baste it well with Butter, and sprinkle on it a little Salt: This done, heat the stew'd Part of the Hare, and put it in the Dish, with the roast Part in the Middle; cut the Bacon in Slices, and lay over it; garnish it with Lemon and Barberries.

To make Forc'd Meat.

Godiveau à faire.

TAKE Half a Pound of Veal, free from Skins, &c. chop it fine, with the same Quantity of Beef-Suet, a little Thyme, Parsley, Lemon Skin chop'd fine, a little Pepper, Nutmeg, and Salt; chop also a little Bacon, with two Anchovies, a little Shallot, and the Crumbs of a Penny Roll; work all together with two Eggs; beat it fine in a Mortar, and it is fit for Use. Take Care you don't season it too high: The best Way to try it is, by boiling or frying a Bit, and tasting it, by which you may have the better Guess. The stuffing of a Turkey's Crop is made the same Way, only leave out the Veal, and add the like Quantity of Suet, with but a little Thyme and Parsley. By adding more sweet Herbs, it is good Stuffing for a Fillet of Veal: Also by adding to this Half a Pint of Cream, it makes a good Pudding for a Hare, Leveret, or Rabbit.

The best Way to Dress and Roast a Pig.

Cochon roti.

AFTER your Pig is kill'd put it into warm Water, wash it clean, then put it into as much cold Water as will cover it, and set it on the Fire; keep it often turning till you find the Hair will come off, then take it out; if the Hair don't come off clean, put it in again (for the Hair will come as well off this Way as with Rosin): This done, open it, and take the Entrails out clean; wash and rub it dry both within and without; put some Bread Crumbs in the Belly, with a little Salt and shred Sage; sew it up, skewer it, and spit it, lay it a good Distance from the Fire till it be well dry'd; then rub it over with

Sweet

Sweet Oil, and it will roaſt well; if you have no Oil, oil ſome Butter, and take the Clear of it; when it is roaſted, cut off the Head, and cut the Pig off the Spit, exactly down the Middle; put it into the Diſh, and part the Under Jaw from the Upper; cut off the Ears, and take out the Brains. Garniſh the Pig with the Under Jaw cut in two, ſlic'd Lemon, and the Ears; mix the Brains with the Gravy, and what comes out of the Pig, with melted Butter; make it hot, and put it to the Pig.

To make an Apple Pye.

Paté de Pommes.

LET your Paſte be Paſte-Royal; pare, quarter, and core your Apples; ſheet a Diſh that will be ſuitable to the reſt of your Side Diſhes; put ſome Sugar at the Bottom; lay in a Row of Apples; put in a little Lemon Peel, cut fine, a little Cinnamon; lay on more Apples and Sugar upon them; then put on the Lid, cloſe it, and ice it. One Hour will bake it.——— The Iceing: Beat an Egg to Froth; waſh your Pye over with it; drudge on ſome fine powder'd Sugar, ſprinkle it with Roſe-water, and take Care the Iceing is not too much colour'd.

To make a Sillibub.

Boiſſon refraichiſſante.

TAKE a Quart of good Cream, whip it to a Froth with a Whiſk; take off the Froth as it riſes, and put it on a coarſe Sieve to drain; then take either Red or White Wine, or both, and ſweeten it to your Taſte, with double refin'd Sugar; if you meaſure the Wine, by putting as much in the Glaſs as you would have, you need ſweeten no more; ſome put in Whites of Eggs, a Piece of Lemon Peel, a Stick of Cinnamon, and some White Wine, and Sugar to the Cream, and whisk it to a Froth as before; but that Froth will not stand so long, nor keep so well, or look so white.

To make Jellies.

Gelée pour faire.

TAKE a Set of Calf's Feet, or what Quantity you think proper, (considering the Number of Jellies you design to make) a Set of large Feet will afford three Pints of Stock, if mix'd with a little Hart's Horn, two Quarts or more; when it is boil'd strain it; take off the Fat when cold, and the Sediment from the Bottom; to a Quart of Jelly take four Whites of Eggs beat to a Froth; a Pint of Rhenish Wine, the Juice of three or four Lemons, as much double-refin'd Sugar as will sweeten it to your Taste; stir all together, set it on a Charcoal Fire till it boils, then put it into your Jelly-bag (it being ready fix'd); put it two or three Times through till it is very fine, then put it into your Glasses. Some put in Brandy, and the outside Rine of a Lemon, with a Stick of Cinnamon; but it will colour them high, and the Brandy will cause them to turn of a bluish Colour if they stand. Jellies both eat and look the best when they are fresh made: If you use Lemon Juice instead of Wine, it is best in Summer.

To roast a Turkey.

Dindon pour Roti.

TRUSS it, put a Piece of Butter wrapt in Salt in the Belly, and some Stuffing in the Crop; (as in Page 26.) break down the Breast-bone before you truss it; then spit and roast it at a slow Fire; it will be enough in an Hour, or an Hour and an Half, just as it is in Bignefs. Difh it with Gravy-fauce and Saufages, and Bread Sauce in a Cup.—Partridges are roafted the fame Way, and have the fame Sauce; Half an Hour will roaft them. You may lard either Turkey or Partridge with Bacon.

The following are a few ufeful INSTRUCTIONS *how to manage Things that have been left, after Company have been at Dinner, and they unexpectedly ftay Supper; fo that by adding a few, you may make up a Table of five, feven, or nine Difhes in the following Manner:*

Fry'd Fifh, or Veal Cutlets.

Tarts.   Flummery.

Minc'd Turkey.   Jellies.   Hafh'd Duck.

Rafberry-Cream.   Cheefe-Cakes.

A Pigeroom of Mutton.

To mince a Turkey.
Dindon haché.

TAKE the White of the Turkey, and mince it fine; put it into a Stew-pan, with a little clean Water, a Bit of Lemon Peel cut fmall, a little Cream, the Yolk of an Egg beat, a Bit of Butter wrap'd in Flour, a Sprig of Thyme, and a little Parfley ty'd in a Bunch, with a large Onion, which put in whole, grate in fome Nutmeg, fqueeze in a little Lemon, put

put in Salt to your Taste, and make it hot over a Charcoal Fire. Dish it with Sippets of White Bread: If the Legs be left, cut them cross and cross; pepper salt, and broil them, and lay them in the Middle of the Mince. Mind to take out the Onion and Herbs.——Veal and Partridges are minced the same Way.

To hash a Duck.

Canards hashé.

CUT it into handsome Pieces; make some Water scalding hot, and put your Duck therein, which will take off the strong oily Taste; put a Piece of Butter into a Sew-pan, make it hot; take the Duck out of the Water, dry and flour it, and put it into the Stew-pan; toss it up; put in a little Onion shred small, with a small Faggot of Sweet Herbs; add to it some good Gravy; put in a small Matter of Pepper; let your Liquor be the Thickness of Cream; squeeze in a little Lemon. Garnish it with Barberries and Lemon: Some chuse Red Wine in it.

N. B. Your Mince or Hash must be no more than just thoroughly hot; for if they stew, they will be hard and tough.——I shall give further Instructions in the Bills of Fare, that you may always meet with something to make up a Supper quickly.

To coller Beef.

Beuf en ruelle.

TAKE the Middle Part of a Brisket; bone it, and take off the Skin; get a Quarter of a Pound of Salt-Petre, two Ounces of Bay-Salt mix'd with a Pound of common Salt; powder the Salt-Petre and Bay-Salt, and salt your Beef well with it, turning it every Day and rubbing it well with the Pickle for four or five Days; then wash it clean, dry it with a Cloth, and take Thyme, Parsley, Beets, Spinage, and Pot-Marjoram shred fine, Half an Ounce of Pepper, a large Nutmeg, a few Cloves and Mace beat also fine; then shred a Pound of Suet very fine, mix all together, and season your Beef with it; roll it up, and then roll it in a Cloth; tie it tight at both Ends, and bind it about well with coarse Incle; boil or bake it in hard Water till it is tender, then unbind it and roll it up again in the Cloth, tying it up tight at both Ends, and binding it again; tie it up to a Hook and hang a sufficient Weight at the Bottom to keep it tight and make it firm, or press it between two Boards (which you think best or most convenient); thus let it abide till next Day, then take it out of the Cloth, and keep it in a thick Sheet of Paper, butter'd and wrapt in a coarse Cloth. When you use any, cut the Coller in two, and set one Half upright in the Middle of your Dish, and cut some Slices off the other Part, and lay round it. Garnish with green Parsley or Laurel Leaves, or any other Thing else that looks pretty.

To marinade Fish.

Poisson marinée.

WHEN you have a Dish of Fish, and the Fish that are fry'd are chargeable, and you would have them preserv'd for another Dish, make Pickle in the following Manner: Take a Quart of hard Water, and boil it with Salt and Vinegar; put thereto a little White Wine, some whole Pepper, Mace, and two or three Onions slic'd, with some Horse-raddish; put it into an Earthen Pan, and when it is cold, put in your Fish; 'twill keep good three or four Days: The Sauce is commonly Oil and Vinegar. If this Pickle is good when you have us'd your Fish, you may boil it half away, and put to it five or six Ancho-vies;

vies; strain it, and keep it in a Bottle. It will be good to put into Fish Sauce; three or four Spoonfuls will be enough at a Time, mix'd with strong Broth or Gravy, and other Ingredients as directed in Page 5.

To dress Veal Collops.

Collops de Veau roux.

TAKE a Leg of a well-fed Calf; cut the best of it into Slices, the Breadth of three Fingers, and the Thickness of Half a Crown; spread them on a clean Board or Table; hack them with the Back of a Knife; drudge them with a little Flour; put a Bit of Butter into your Stew-pan, just as much as will moisten the Bottom, but no more; keep it stirring till the Butter be melted, and lay your Collops in one by one, till you have cover'd the Bottom of your Pan; set them over a quick Fire; let them be a little brown, then turn them, and brown the other Side; be sure not to do them too much; put them out into an Earthen Pan, and spread them; for if they lie thick, one on another, they will be hard and tough; clean your Pan, and fry the rest in the same Manner; when all are done, rub your Pan out with some good strong Broth; save it in a Pot; take a Piece of Butter, put it into your Pan, and set it on the Fire; drudge in some Flour, put in a Faggot of sweet Herbs, with a large Onion; keep it stirring till brown; strain in the Liquor that you rub'd out your Pan with, after frying the Collops; if that is not enough, add some good Gravy, put in some forc'd Meat Balls, made as in Page 26, some pickled Mushrooms, some Juice of Lemon, a little White Wine, grate in a little Nutmeg; you may put in some Lamb Stones and Sweet Breads cut and fry'd, or garnish the Collops with them; boil it to the Thickness of thin Cream; put in the Collops, toss them together, make them just
tho-

thoroughly hot; dish them with the Udder of the Veal stuff'd with Forc'd Meat, and wash'd over with the Yolk of an Egg drudg'd with Bread Crumbs, and roasted, baked, or brown'd in the Dripping Pan; lay it in the Middle: Garnish your Dish with Artichoke Bottoms, Cucumbers, or any Pickle you please; season it with Salt to your Taste.

How to make white Collops.
Collops de Veau blanc.

CUT them as thin as you can, hack them as you did the other, put a Quarter of a Pound of Butter into your Stew-Pan with a Fag of Sweet Herbs, a whole Onion, and a little Salt; keep them stirring with a wooden Ladle till they are turned White; put them into an earthen Pan as you did the other; take half a Pint of Cream, the Yolks of two or three Eggs, some good strong Broth, a Bit of Butter worked in Flour, some Nutmeg, White Wine, Anchovy shred fine, with a little Onion, using the same Ingredients as in the brown Collops; but the Forc'd-Meat-Balls must be boil'd. The Artichokes before-mentioned are the Bottoms preserv'd in the Season, which I shall treat of in the proper Time of the Year.

A Breast of Veal may be done White: Spit it on an Iron Skewer, parboil it in Spring-water, stew it in strong Broth till very tender, and use the same Ingredients as in the white Collops, and the same Spices in Sewing as in the brown Collops.

To pickle Oysters.
Huitres Confit.

TAKE an hundred Oysters, and open them without cutting; wash them in Salt and Water clean from the Shells; then take a Quart of Spring-water, put thereto an Handful of Salt, boil it in a Sauce Pan well tin'd, scum it, and put in your Oysters; let them boil two or three Minutes, according as they are in Bigness; take them out of the Liquor, and put them on the Bottom of a Sieve, spreading them single to cool; strain the Liquor that came from them when you open'd them, and put it to the Liquor you boil'd them in, with eight or ten Blades of Mace, half a Nutmeg, half a Pint of White Wine, a few whole Pepper Corns, a Quarter of a Pint of Vinegar; boil it twenty Minutes; put it into a Jar which will hold both it and the Oysters; let it stand to cool, then put in your Oysters; tie them down with a Bladder dipped in Vinegar and Leather over that; when you use any of them, moisten the Bladder with warm Water, and it will come easily off; otherwise you may bung them down as you do a Barrel, and tie Leather over it. This Pickle is good in several Sauces, and particularly in Fish Sauce.

To scollop Oysters.

Huitres escalope.

OPEN and clean them as before; butter your Scallop Shells; rub some White Bread Crumbs through a Cullender; put as much Butter into a Stew Pan as will moisten them; set them over the Fire; keep them stirring with a wooden Ladle till they begin to be crisp; put some of them into the Bottom of your Shells, and lay in your Oysters with some Bits of Butter; put a Spoonful or two of their Liquor into each Shell, and Bread Crumbs on the Top, to cover the Oysters well; set them in an Oven, or on a Grediron over a slow Fire till they are stew'd enough, and brown them with a Salamander or Fire Shovel. Some stew them in their Liquor first, and put in a little White Wine and Nutmeg, and Bread Crumbs,
with-

ART *of* COOKERY.   35

without doing any other Thing to them firſt, and lay on Bits of Butter on the Top of them, keeping the ſame Order as above-mentioned. Some chuſe to have the Oyſters bearded.

To roaſt Sweet-breads.
Ris de Veau roti.

PArboil them and ſpit them on a Lark-ſpit, tie it to another Spit, waſh them over with the Yolks of Eggs, drudge them over with Bread Crumbs, and a little Salt; when they have been ſome Time at the Fire baſte them: Three Quarters of an Hour will roaſt them, then draw and diſh them. You muſt draw your Butter with Gravy, ſqueezing in a little Lemon; garniſh your Diſh with Lemon and fry'd Parſley.

A Fiſh Pye in the Shape of a Fiſh, as in the Figure below.
Paté de Poiſſon en forme de Poiſſon.

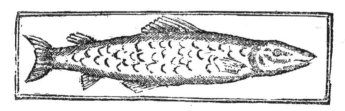

TAKE a Salmon Trout, ſcale and clean it, cut off the Head, and make Stuffing to put in the Belly in the following Manner: Take two Ounces of Beef Suet ſhred fine, the Crumb of a Penny Loaf ſoak'd in good Gravy or ſtrong Broth, ſome Sweet-herbs ſhred fine, with two Anchovies, and a little Lemon-peel; ſeaſon it with Pepper, Salt, and Nutmeg; make it into Paſte with an Egg; put it into the Belly of the Fiſh, taking off the Fins and Tail; then make a Paſte of two Pounds of Flour; rub into it one

Pound

Pound of Butter, as in the Directions for Pasty-paste; make it very stiff with two Eggs, &c. roll it into an oval Sheet; lay in your Fish, and make the Shape of the Head of the same Paste, and join it to the Fish: You may turn the Fish in the Shape of a Half Moon, or streight, as in the Figure; close it on the Back; cut off the Paste that over-covers the Fish, and make all tight about it. Then make another Paste of half a Hoop of Flour, and two Ounces of Butter boil'd in Salt Water; make it stiff; roll it out, and lay your Fish in that; wash it over with melted Butter, and close that Paste over the other, making the Shape of a Fin on the Back, and two Fins on each Side, just let into the outside Paste; then make Holes for the Eyes, and roll a Bit of the Paste you made for the outside Work in a little Lamp-black to colour it; then roll a Bit round like a Marble for the Eyes, and put a Bit of white Paste round that, and fix it in the Holes for the Eyes; then make the Shape of the Gills (as you may see by the natural Fish) and take Part of the Red and fix it in, to make it look as near Nature as you can; this done, fix in the natural Tail, or make one artificial of some of the colour'd Paste; then roll out some of the colour'd Paste thin, and some of the white Paste; cut it out with a Thimble to imitate the Scales, then wet the Pye, and lay on one black and one white, beginning at the Tail, and let one reach a little over the other, so continue doing till you come to the Gills; cut the Back-fin in Nicks on the Top with a Pair of Scissars to make it look more natural, then wash it over with the Yolk of an Egg, and drudge it with Bread Crumbs grated fine; bake it an Hour and a Half in a slow Oven, and when it is enough send it dish'd with two Cups of Sauce, one of plain Butter, the other Fish Sauce.

N. B. The outside Paste (which is thrown away) will come clean from the inside Paste, which is to be
eat

ART *of* COOKERY.   37

eat with the Fish. It eats very well cold with Oil and Vinegar.

To make a Plumb-Cake.

Gâteau des Raisins.

TAKE three Pounds of fine Flour well dried, half an Ounce of Cinnamon and Mace, with one large Nutmeg, three Quarters of a Pound of fine Sugar pounded and sifted, a little Salt, mix all together in a large Bowl; put to it one Pint of Ale Yeast, with two Pound and a Half of Butter melted, mix them together with half a Pint of Sack, make a Hole in the Middle of the Flour and put it in, and mix it with Part thereof to the Thickness of a thin Batter-Pudding; sprinkle some of the Flour over it, lay a Stick cross the Bowl, and a Cloth over all, and set it to the Fire to rise; when it is risen up beat it with your Hand till it be smooth; then take three Pounds of Currans, well wash'd and dry'd before the Fire, with one Pound of Raisins ston'd and chop'd; Lemon, Orange and Citron Peel two Ounces of each sliced thin, mix these well in your Cake; have your Hoop well paper'd without and within; butter it within and flour it, then put in your Cake; let it stand to rise, and set it in a good Oven; when it is colour'd paper it. Two Hours and a Half will bake it.

You may put in more Fruit if you would have it richer, and, if then it be too thick, add eight Eggs well beat and strain'd.

To make the Iceing.

Glace pour le Gâteau.

TAKE one Pound and a Half of fine Sugar, beat and sifted, put it into an earthen Pan, break in the White of an Egg, and beat it well; then break in another, and beat it again, so keep doing till you have
used

used six Whites; beat it till it be white and light, then spread it all over the Cake, and set it into the Oven again to harden; so draw it.

To make a Seed-Cake.

Gâteau confit.

TAKE half a Quartern of Flour dry'd, a little Nutmeg and Cinnamon well pounded, one Pint of Cream, three or four Spoonfuls of good Yeast, half a Pound of Butter beat to a Cream, four Eggs beat, two Ounces of Carraway Seeds a little bruis'd, and a Quarter of a Pound of fine Sugar sifted; mix your dry Things together, and the wet together, made warm, and order them as you did in the Plumb-Cake above; when it is risen beat it for half an Hour, and then put it into your Cake-Pan; an Hour and a Half will bake it, and if a good Oven an Hour will do; paper it when risen, and when enough wash it over with the White of an Egg well beat, with a little Rose or Orange-flower Water, sift on some fine Sugar, and strew on some candied Carraway Seeds; set it in the Oven till harden'd.

A Pigeroom of Mutton.

Pigeroome de Mouton.

ROAST a Shoulder, but not too much, cut the Meat off, leave the Blade Bone handsome, wash it over with the Yolk of an Egg, and order it as you do the broil'd Calf's Head in Page 10; add to it a little Pepper beaten, and leave out the Nutmeg; take the rest of the Mutton, and cut off the Skin and most of the Fat, mince it fine; get your Stew Pan, and put therein a Pint of good Gravy, an Onion shred fine, some Parsley, and a little Thyme; let these stew a little, then put in a Handful of Capors cut a little, also

also a little Vinegar, and your minced Mutton, with a Piece of Butter wrap'd in Flour to thicken it; season it with Pepper and Salt to your Taste, make it just hot, and dish it with the broil'd Blade Bone in the Middle. Garnish with poach'd Eggs and Spinage.

This is a good Side Dish for Dinner: You may mince any Part of Mutton, boil'd or roasted, and order it as before for a Supper Dish.——Poach your Eggs in the following Manner; break six new-laid Eggs into a Bason, take Care you don't break the Yolks; make some spring or hard Water boil, with a little Salt in it; scum it, put in your Eggs, stir them round with a small wooden Ladle; have some Toasts ready butter'd and cut oval, take up the Eggs with a Slice that is full of Holes to drain the Water clean from them; lay them on the Toasts, and put them round the Mince, with some Toasts cut like Sippets, and cover'd with stew'd Spinage and laid between the Eggs, with a round one in the Middle, with a poach'd Egg, or Spinage, as you like it: Let your Spinage be well butter'd before you put it on the Toasts; put to it a little Pepper, and as much Vinegar as you can just taste.

To make a Custard.
Flanc pour faire.

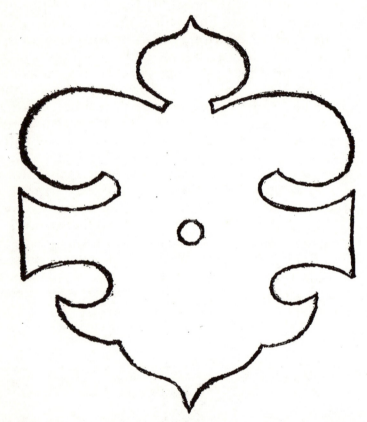

TAKE a Quart of Milk or Cream, and boil it with a Stick of Cinnamon, three or four Blades of Mace, a Laurel Leaf or two bruised, and a Piece of Lemon Peel; let it boil softly for ten Minutes; keep it stirring with a small Whisk to hinder it from setting to the Bottom; strain it thro' a Sieve; then beat eight Eggs and strain them; sweeten it to your Taste with fine Sugar; set it on the Fire again, and keep it stirring till it begins to thicken; then take it off, and

keep

keep it stirring five or six Minutes; put it into Cups or Glasses; or having a Crust rais'd, and set in the above Form, and dry'd in the Oven, fill it and bake it: Take great Care not to bake it too much; it is enough when it rises.

To make Almond Custards.

Flanc aux Amandes.

BLanch a Quarter of a Pound of Almonds, pound them in a marble Mortar very fine, put a little Milk to them to keep them from oiling, rub them thro' a Hair Sieve, order your Matters as before; stir in your Almonds and fill your Custards; stick the Tops with some blanch'd ones cut in Quarters the long Way.

To make a Tort de Moy.

Tourte de mouelle.

BLanch half a Pound of Almonds, and beat them as above; mince the white Part of a Fowl or Capon, or Part of a Turkey; mix the Almonds and these together, with a Quarter of a Pound of candied Citron, Orange, and Lemon-peel; pound your Meat and Almonds together with two Spoonfuls of boil'd Spinage; break in an Egg, beat it again, and so keep doing till you have used six Eggs; season it with Salt, Cinamon, Nutmeg, and Mace; sweeten it with fine Sugar; put to it three Quarters of a Pint of Cream, and two grated Biscuits, mix all together in a Stew Pan, set it over the Fire, and keep it stirring till it be thicken'd, and begins to be almost cold; then put in the Marrow of one Marrow-bone shred fine; put a Border of Puff Paste round your Dish, as done in the Marrow Pudding, p. 20; put in your Meat, and lay on it a cut Cover; ice it and bake it.

To make Cheese Cakes.

Caſſe Muſeau.

TAKE a Gallon of Milk and warm it, then take it off, and put to it ſome Rennet or Yearning; mix them together and ſet it to gather a Curd, which done, break it with your Hand, and put it into a thin Strainer; tie it, and hang it up to drain the Whey from it; then rub it thro' a Hair Sieve, with three Quarters of a Pound of Butter; beat four or five Eggs and put to it, grate in a large Nutmeg: You may put in Roſe or Orange Flower Water, and a little Cream; if it be too thick you may beat it with your Hand and it will make it lighter; you may add to it ſome grated Biſcuit if you pleaſe; put in half a Pound of Currans waſh'd and dry'd; ſweeten it to your Taſte; ſheet your Pans with Puff Paſte, and fill them; ſtrew ſome Currans on the Top, and bake them.

How to make a Biſcuit Cake.

Gateau Biſquit.

TAKE a Pound of freſh Butter, beat it with your Hand to a Cream; break as many Eggs as will fill a Pint, beat them well, put them to the Butter a little and a little at a Time, ſtill keeping beating till you have put all in; then take a Pound of fine Flour well dry'd, put a little at a Time of that in, keeping beating till that is all in, then put in a Pound of fine Sugar ſifted, doing in the ſame Manner, and a little Salt; keep beating it from the Beginning to the End: It will bake in an Hour; paper your Pan or Pans, put in the Cake, and bake it in a briſk Oven; take Care they are not ſcorch'd; you may put in an Ounce of Carraway Seeds if you pleaſe.

Another Biscuit Cake.

Autre Gateau.

TAKE the same Quantity of Eggs as above, leave out three Whites, and add to them one Pound of Flour, in the same Manner as before directed, then a Pound of Sugar; beat it for an Hour, put it in a Pan and bake it. This Cake is proper for Puddings or any Thing of that kind.

To preserve Oranges and Lemons.

Orangés confit.

CUT a round Hole at the Stalk, scoop out all the Meat, rasp off the outside Rind, put them to soak in cold Water for two Days, shifting them into fresh Water twice every Day; pick out the white Skin from the Pulp of your Oranges, make a strong Syrup of their Weight of double refin'd Sugar, boil it almost to a Candy Height, put in the Pulp, keep it stirring till clear, put it into a Gally Pot, paper it down till wanted; then take your Orange Outsides out of Water, and put them into a Pot big enough, with Plenty of Water, boil them till tender; put them into fresh cold Water, let them lie twenty-four Hours; to six Oranges take three Pounds of Sugar, boil it to a Syrup with a Pint and a half of Water, take off the Scum, and put in your Oranges; let them boil a little, put them into a Pot with the Syrup to them, let them lie three or four Days, then put them into your preserving Pan again, and boil them to a Candy, and fill them with the Pulp you boil'd before, first making it hot, put in the Bit you cut out, (it being candied also with the rest) set them in a drying Stove to dry, and they will be candied all over; if you would keep them in Syrup, don't boil them the last Time; then you may make use of your Marmalet for something else:

Lemons are done the same Way; you may preserve them in Halves or Quarters as you see proper. Some chuse to put in a little Paring of the Rind boil'd tender, and beat and boil'd clear in Syrup, and mixt with the Marmalet, also a little Orange Flower Water and Juice of Lemons. You may fill Halves or Quarters the same Way as you do the whole ones; but take out the Seeds of both Orange and Lemon Marmalet.

To dry Oranges and Lemons in Knots.

Limons en neuds.

TAKE out the Meat as in the above Receipt, let the Skins lie till next Day, then cut off the outside Rind with a Knife as whole as you can, let them lie till the next Day; then boil them tender, and put them into cold Water for twenty-four Hours; then take them out, and dry them before the Fire; make a Syrup of fine Sugar as much as will cover them, put them in when the Syrup is almost cold, let them lie three or four Days, then give them a boil, and keep them till you want them; then candy them out of the Syrup as you did the whole Orange and Lemon Skins: You may cut the white Part of the Peel into Rings, and do it in the same Manner as you did the other.

To make China Orange Chips.

Oranges de la China en Buchettes.

PARE them thin with a sharp Knife, and order them as you did the others above: You need not let them lie in Water after they are boil'd, but put them in Syrup directly, drying them before you put them in; let them lie a Week and you may candy them.

To

To make Orange Drops.

Oranges en goutieres.

TAKE as many Oranges as you think proper, pare them pretty thick, boil those Parings very tender, afterwards beat them very fine, and rub them thru' a Hair Sieve; to a Pound of this Pulp put a Pound and an half of fine Sugar sifted, mix all well, putting thereto as much of the Orange Juice as will make it pretty thin; put all into your Preserving-Pan, set it over a slow Fire, keep it stirring till it looks clear and is pretty thick, let it stand till almost cold, drop it on Glass Plates, and dry it; turn it the next Day, and it will be dry in two or three Days: You may make Lemon Drops the same Way, or Marmalet, adding the Meat pick'd clean from the Skins and Seeds, but then they must not be squeez'd.

To make Orange Paste.

Des Oranges en Pâte.

TAKE what Quantity of Seville Oranges you please, rasp off the red Rind, cut them in two, and take out the Meat, pick the Stones out of it, boil the white Rinds tender, drain the Water well from them, and beat them very fine; to one Pound of this Rind put a Pint and a half of your Meat; mix all together, put it into your Preserving-Pan and make it hot; then put in three Pounds of fine Sugar sifted, stir it till the Sugar be dissolv'd; put in the Juice of three Lemons, stir it well together, and put it into Glasses of what Form you please, and dry them in a Drying-stove; turn it next Day and dry the other Side.

MARCH

MARCH.

Vermicelly Soop.

Potage de Vermicelli.

TAKE a Knuckle and Neck of Veal, and a Scrag of Mutton; cut them to Pieces; lay them to soak in warm Water to soak the Blood out, and wash them clean; but them in a Pot that will hold them, and two Gallons of Water; set them on a Stove, put in some Salt, two large Onions, a Carrot, two or three Turnips, a Bit of lean Ham, a Faggot of Herbs, a little whole Pepper, three or four Blades of Mace; let it boil softly, keep it scumming; put in a Bundle of Cellary; let it boil till all the Goodness is out of the Meat; strain it, scum off the Fat, pour off the Clear, put to it the Crust of a French Roll; dridge as much Vermicelly boil'd in strong Broth as will do, let it simmer over the Fire. Dish it with a Knuckle of Veal; in the Middle, or the best Part of it, you may garnish your Dish as in Page 7; if any Broth be left draw your Gravy with it.

To stew a Breast of Veal white.

Pour etuver une Poitrine de Veau blanche.

PArboil your Veal, let it cool, lard it with Bacon, lay in the Bottom of an oval Stew-pan some Slices of Bacon and Veal, season it with Salt, Pepper, Mace, sweet Herbs, some sliced Onions; lay in your Veal, the fleshy Side down; lay over it the same as under, keep a slow Fire under, put some on the Cover, let it stew an Hour, put in some good Broth, stew it till tender; take it up, and take the Clear of
the

the Liquor, and make a white Lare for it and put on it. Garnish your Dish as for white Veal Collops; you'll find the Lare for it where Lares are treated of, and put in it some Forc'd-meat Balls, pickled Mushroons, and drest Sweet-breeds.

To force a Leg of Lamb.

Jigot d' Agneau farcies.

TAKE a large Leg of Lamb, bone it to the last Joint, take Care you don't cut through the Skin; make the Forcing as follows, of Veal, Beef-Marrow, a little Bacon, Parsly, Thyme, Bread-crumbs, Nutmeg, Salt, a few Capers; shred all fine, put in two Eggs, leave out one White, work all well together; rub the In-side of the Leg with the Yolk of an Egg, put in the Force, skewer it up, and tie it with Pack-thread; roast it or bake it as it suits best. Make a Ragoo of Morils, Forc'd-meat Balls, and Mushroons, which I shall mention afterwards.

To boil and stuff a Round of Beef.

Ruelle de Beuf farci.

LET it be cut pretty thick, salt it, and rub it with fresh Salt every Day for four Days, then wash it and stuff it with Beef Suet, shred Parsley, a few Bread Crumbs, and a little Salt; tie it in a Cloth and cord it tight, and boil it in a Copper that will hold it with a good deal of Water, keep scumming it, and it will look white and well; it will take four Hours boiling if it be large. Dish it, and garnish your Dish with Carrots and Turnips. Send Greens in a little Dish.

A bak'd Plumb-Pudding.

Boudin de Raisins au Four.

TAKE the Crumb of a Three-penny fine Loaf, rub it through a Cullinder, shread a Pound of good Beef Suet, a Ponnd of Raisins ston'd and chopt, Half a Pound of Currans, some Sugar, some Orange and Lemon Peel candied, sliced thin; mix all together, put in a little Salt, grate in some Nutmeg, beat ten Eggs, mix it with Milk not too thin; butter a Paper, and lay it in the Bottom of your Dish; pour it in and bake it; you may put in a Glass of Brandy, turn it in the Dish; when you design to send it in, take the Paper clean off and grate on some Sugar. Garnish with Seville Orange.

Patty Devo.

Paté de Veau.

BOIL a Calf's Head, prepared as for a Hash; put to the Hash a Pint of Oisters, with six Yolks of Eggs boil'd hard, some Rashers of Bacon, first boil'd in Vinegar. Make your Pye in a Dish, with Puff-paste, put in your Hash, lay on the Eggs and the Bacon, close your Pye, and bake it an Hour and a Half; take off the Lid from off the Fat, and make a white Lare for it as for white Collops, Page 33, the Hash prepar'd as in Page 10. N. B. Wash your Pye over with the Yolk of an Egg and a little Cream before you send it to the Oven, and likewise cut the Lid round that you may the easier take it off to put in the Lare, Sweet-breeds, more Truffels, Asparagus Tops, &c. season with Pepper, Salt, and Nutmeg; put Butter at the Top of all.

Her-

ART of COOKERY.

Herrico of Mutton.

Mouton en Aricot.

TAKE a Neck of Mutton, cut two Bones and two together, cut off the Chine, flour and fry them in Butter; then make a Brown; put in two Quarts of Gravey, with a Faggot of Herbs, a large Onion, some whole Pepper Corns, a Blade or two of Mace, some Anchovy, Half a Pint of White Wine; let these stew for two Hours, till the Meat is pretty tender; then having some Carrots and Turnips blanch'd and dish'd, put in Half a Pint of each, with some Capers, and the Juice of Half a Lemon; scum off the Fat; Dish it, and garnish your Dish with Pickles and Barberries, thicken it with a Brown.

To collar Pig.

Cochon de Lait en Ruelle en Rouleau.

STICK, scald, and clean your Pig; cut off the Head, cut it down the Back, take out the Bones and Entrails, put it into warm Water to soak out the Blood, shift it three or four Times till it looks very white; take it up, dry it with a Cloth; then shred some Sage, Parsley, and a little Thyme, a good Handful of Salt, some beaten Pepper, Nutmeg, and Mace; wash it over with Yolks of Eggs; season it with the above Ingredients, then roll it up in a Cloth, tie it tight at each End, bind it tight with Inckle; boil it in hard Water till tender; then untie and unroll it, and do it up again as it was at first; hang it to a Hook with a Weight at the Bottom till it be cold; then make a Pickle for it of Bran Water and Salt boil'd and strain'd; put in some Vinegar; take your Collar, put it into this Pickle when cold. When you want to use any of it, slice it, and garnish it with Parsley.

To stew Soles.

De Soles etuvée.

TAKE off the black Skin, scrape, gut, and clean them, wash them in Small Beer, rub them well with Flour, and fry them as you are directed in Page 18; then make a brown with Butter and Flour, put in Half a Pint of Fish-Sauce Stock, as in Page 18, with a little Shallot, shred fine, and Half a Pint of White Wine; let them stew two Minutes cover'd over a slow Fire; take them up with the Scummer, and dish them; add to the Sauce a little Lemon Juice and a Ladle full of drawn Butter. You may put in Lobster, Oisters, or Shrimps, as you like. Garnish with Lemon, Horse-raddish, and Barberries.

To fry Tripes.

Tripes frit.

TAKE some good double Tripe, cut it in square Pieces or in what Form you please, dry it well with a Cloth, make a Batter for it of Yolks of Eggs, Salt, and Flour, mix'd with Small Beer; let your Batter be thick enough or it will fly off the Tripe; take a Stew-Pan with a good Quantity of Fat prepared as for frying of Fish; dip the Tripe in the Batter and fry it of a fine brown Colour; don't fry too much at a Time, and take Care it does not burn; put it on a Drainer before the Fire to drain the Fat from it. Dish it. The Sauce is Butter, Mustard, and Vinegar, in a Boat or Cup. Cow Heels are fried the same Way; first split them, slice some Onions, salt and flour them, and fry them in clarified Butter. Garnish the Feet with them: The Sauce is as for the Tripe.

To roast Chickens.

Poulets roti.

LET them be pickt clean, and drawn; break down the Breast Bones; skewer them; put in their Bellies a Bit of Salt, with some Parsley and Butter; roast them brown, first singe them, baste them with Butter, and flour them; the Sauce is Parsley and Butter, with a little Salt, and the Juice of Lemon or Gravey. Garnish with Lemon, Parsley, and Barberries.——Young Rabbits are roasted the same Way, add the Livers, scalded and chopt, to the Sauce.—— Young Turkies are roasted the same Way; leave out the Parsley, and truss them with their Heads on.—— Partridges are truss'd the same as Turkies, with their Heads on or off: The Sauce is white Bread Crumbs boil'd in fine strong Broth, or Water, with whole Pepper Corns, Salt, and an Onion; when enough, put in a little Cream, and a Piece of Butter; send Gravey in the Dish, and the Sauce in a Cup or Boat. ——Pigeons are roasted the same as Chickens; the Sauce the same. Any of these may be larded if so liked.

How to boil Asparagus.

Des Asperges à cuire.

IT eats with any of the above Roasts, except Partridges; wash them and scrape them, that is the white Ends; take the brown Leaves off the Tops or green Ends; wash and tie them in small Bundles, and boil them in hard Water and a little Salt till tender, but not too much; toast some Bread slic'd thin and butter'd; lay them between your Fowls; lay the Asparagus on them, with their Heads to the Middle of the Dish, and the Fowls, with their Breasts to the Rim of the Dish; put melted Butter on the Aspargus,

and

and send it in hot. — There are several Ways of dressing Asparagus, whereof I shall give you some Particulars as follow.

Asparagus à la Cream.
Asperges à la Créême.

CUT the green Ends off your Grass, and blanche them in boiling Water, and toss them in a Stew-Pan, with a Piece of good Butter; dridge in a little Flour; moisten them with a little good strong Broth made of Veal or Fowl; make a white Lare for them as in Veal Collops white; toss them up, and dish them with a Chicken Loaf or Turkey Loaf in the Middle, or Partridge: The Mince prepared as in Page 42. The Loaf for the Mince must be a large French Roll; cut off the Top, take out the Crumb, rub it within and without with Butter, set it in an Oven or before the Fire till crisp, or fry it in clarified Butter; put in your Mince, lay on the Top, and set it in the Middle of the Dish. Garnish your Dish with potch'd Eggs, Spinage and Rashers of Bacon, or with Parsley and Lemon, or Seville Orange.

Asparagus with brown Sauce.
Asperges avec une Sauße roux.

CUT them as before, and toss them with Butter, and dridge in some Flour, put in some good Gravey, chop a little Onion with Half an Anchovy; stew them softly till tender, grate in a little Nutmeg; put in a little Pepper; and salt a Spoonful of White Wine, and squeeze in a little Lemon; toss all together. Dish it and garnish it as before.

Asparagus in Amblit.

Asperges en Omelet.

BLanch them and tofs them in Butter, dridge in a little Flour, moiften it with ftrong Broth, put in fome white Lare; then fhred a Bit of lean Ham fine, and put in; tofs all up together; beat fix Eggs; put in Half a Pint of Cream, a little Salt, two or three Spoonfuls of Flour; melt a Piece of Butter, and mix all together, and fry it like a Pancake; heat your Afparagus, put the Cake in the Difh, which fhould be a China one, and the Edges of the Cake to ftand up; then put in the Afparagus; cut a Seville Orange in eight Parts, and lay on the Edge of the Difh to keep up the Cake, and fend it in hot.

A Pig Pye.

Paté de Cochon de lait.

AFTER dreft and clean'd, fkin and bone it; cut it in four Pieces, prepare your Pye the French Way; lay the two hind Quarters in the Bottom, having a pickled Neat's Tongue boil'd, blanch'd, and flic'd; then firft feafon your Pig with Pepper and Salt, and a little Sage, and a good Handful of Parfley chopt fine, twelve Eggs boil'd hard, the Yolks chopt, and lay Half of them on the Pig; then fome Slices of Tongue, then the two Fore Quarters feafon'd as before, then fome more Tongue, then the reft of the Eggs, then lay Butter on all, clofe it and bake it; when bak'd, let it ftand till cold, and fend it to the Table for a Middle Difh.

To make a Turbat Pye.

Paté de Turbot.

TAKE a Turbat or Part of it, clean it and scrape it, and lay it in a Dish; scotch it under and over; season it with Pepper and Salt, Sweet-Herbs with Leaves, make some forc'd Meat of Fish, first blanch a Pint of Oisters and put in; lay the forc'd Meat on that, and Butter over all; lid it and bake it in a moderate Oven two Hours; cut up the Lid and make a Lare for it of Half a Pint of the Stock as directed for Fish Sauce, Page 8; draw it up with Butter to the Thickness of a Cream, pour it on the Pye, lay on the Lid, and dish it up.

Pigeons Compote.

Pigeons en compote.

PICK, draw, and truss them as for Boiling, singe them, lay some Rashers of Bacon in the Bottom of a Stew-Pan; force your Pigeons with a little forc'd Meat, and a good deal of Parsley in it; lay some Slices of Beef on your Bacon; season it with Pepper and Salt; lay in your Pigeons with their Breasts down, then put in a Faggot of Sweet Herbs, an Onion stuck with three or four Cloves, put in four Blades of Mace, lay Rashers of Bacon on the Pigeons, and Beef season'd as before on that, cover it close, set it on a slow Fire to stew till tender; take them up, and put them in a Dish cover'd down, strain the Liquor from the Meat, scum off the Fat, take a clean Pan, make a light Brown, put in Half a Pint of Gravey, with the Liquor you strain'd; put in some dish'd Sweet Breeds, pickled Mushroons, the Juice of a Lemon, a Spoonful of White Wine, grate in some Nutmeg, put in the Pigeons, let them stew a little. Dish them, and garnish with Parberries and Lemon. You may make a white Lare for them, for a Change, with the same Ingredients.

N. B. I shall mention some different Ways of dressing Lamb, the common Ways being so well known.

To roast Lamb the French Way.

TAKE a Fore Quarter, truss it, and lard the Neck Part of it; wash the other Part with the Yolk of an Egg and melted Butter; dridge it with Bread Crumbs and Salt; spit it first, then paper it, and roast it of a fine brown Colour; dridge it again with the same, adding a little shred Parsley and a little Flour; let it go Half a Score Turns, and draw it; let the Sauce be Lemon and Gravey. Garnish with Seville Orange.

To ragoo Lamb.

Ragoût d'Agneau.

TAKE a Breast and Neck, part the Breast from the Neck, cut each in three Pieces, lard them, take Half a Pound of Butter, and brown them in a Stew-Pan; then make a Brown, put in a Quart of good Gravey, a Faggot of Herbs, an Onion stuck with Cloves, some whole Pepper and Mace, a Gill of White Wine, add forc'd Meat Balls, Morels, Mushrooms, the Juice of a Lemon; let it stew till tender. Dish it; garnish with Barberries and Lemon.

Fricasy of Lamb.

Agneau en Fricaſſée.

CUT a Loin of Lamb in Pieces, order your Stew-Pan as for the Pigeons, instead of Beef use Veal, the Ingredients the same to make the white Lare; take Half a Pint of Cream, the Yolks of three Eggs, a little Anchovey and Onion shred small, a little White Wine, Nutmeg and Salt, a Bit of Butter work'd in Flour; stir it till it is thick, but don't let it boil if it prove too thick; add a little more Cream, take the brown Skin from your Lamb; toss it up in this, add a little Parsley boil'd and chopt; put in the rest of the Ingredients, make it thorough hot, but don't let it boil. Dish it; the Garnishing as for most Made-Dishes, which I have before-mention'd.

To fricasy Chickens.

Poulets en Fricassée.

SKIN your Chickens, cut them in Pieces as you carve them when roasted; order your Stew-Pan as you did for the Lamb; let the Chickens be soak'd well in warm Water to take out the Blood, dry them well, and lay them in your Stew-Pan; then cover and stew them as directed for the Lamb; make a white Lare, and toss them in it, with the same Ingredients, viz. Mushroons, Morels, forc'd Meat Balls, Aspargus Tops, Artichoke Bottoms, &c. leave out the Parsley.—Young Rabbits are done the same Way.——Another Way for Chickens or Rabbits: Prepare them as before, butter your Pan well, lay in your Chickens, put in some whole Pepper, three or four Blades of Mace, an Onion, a Faggot of Sweet Herbs; strinkle in some Salt, cover it close and stew it on a slow Fire till tender; take them out, and put them in your white Lare, throw in Liquor, toss all together, with the same Ingredients as above, and dish them.

To fricasy them brown.

Poulets en Fricassée roux.

CUT them as you did before; flour them, and fry them in clarified Butter; then make a Brown for them; put in some good Gravey, with Ingredients as for brown Collops. See Page 32. Stew them a little, and dish them: This is for Rabbits as well as Chickens.

N. B. As the common Way of dressing Salmon is so well known, I shall give you the different Ways of dressing it, as it is done several Ways abroad, as well as at the grand Tables in England.

To dress Salmon à la Braise.

Saumon à la Braise.

TAKE what Part of the Salmon you would do this Way, tie it with Pack-thread, lay it on a Drainer; then lay some Rashers of Bacon in the Bottom of an oval Stew-pan, with some Slices of Veal season'd with Sweet Herbs, Pepper, Salt, and Nutmeg; lay your Fish and Drainer on that; cover your Salmon with Veal season'd as before; put on the Cover, set it on a slow Fire, with some on the Lid, let it stew an Hour; if it be Half a Salmon, you must put in a Bottle of Champaign or White Wine if it do not cover your Fish, add some good strong Broth; the Pan you do it in should but hold the Fish in Length and Breadth; then let it stew a little to give it the Relish of the Liquor, take it up carefully; take off the Veal and Pack-thread; make your Sauce of some of the Liquor, some Oisters, or Lobster, a little Onion and Anchovy, shred fine, thicken'd with a light Brown; you may bruize some of your Spawn with the Juice of a Lemon; set it on the Fire, let it simmer a little, put in a Ladle-full or two of drawn Butter; lade it up altogether, slide off your Salmon from the Drainer into your oval Dish; put on some of the Sauce, and send the rest in a Boat. Garnish with Horse Raddish and Lemon.

N. B. You may dress any large Fish the same Way.

To broil Salmon.

Saumon Grilées.

CUT your Salmon in Slices, wash it over with oil'd Butter, sprinkle on some Salt, butter a Sheet of Writing-Paper, lay it on a Gridiron, lay on your Salmon; make a Charcoal Fire on a broiling Stove; set on your Gridiron at a pretty good Height that it may broil slowly and not burn, turn the Salmon, when it is enough, dish it with this Sauce; take an Anchovy, with a Shallot shred fine, a few shred Capers; put in a little Pepper, Salt, and Nutmeg, with a little Fish Stock, made as before directed; draw it up with Butter, put the Sauce in the Dish, lay on the broil'd Salmon. Garnish it with fry'd Parsley and Lemon.——You may dress a Chain of Salmon the same Way.

To dress Salmon au Court Boüillon.

Saumon au Court Boüillon.

TAKE the Head-part of a Salmon, scrape, draw, and clean it, score the Sides deep, that it may take the Relish of the Marinade the better; season it with Pepper, Salt, Onion, and Anchovies, shred fine, Parsley, and sliced Lemon; make a Forc'd-meat of Fish, and put in the Belly of the Salmon; tie it with Pack-thread, and lay it in an oval Stew-Pan; put to it hard Water, Wine, and Vinegar enough to cover it; set it on a Stove-Fire to boil, when enough put it in an oval Soop-Dish with some of the Liquor it was boil'd in; make the Sauce of boil'd Fennel, Parsley, and a little Mint, a few Capers and scalded Goosberries; let your Butter be drawn thick, the Herbs chopt fine, mix all together and put the Sauce in a Boat. Garnish your Fish with raw Parsley and scrap'd Horse-Raddish.

To dress Salmon meagre.

Saumon en Maigre.

TAKE a Tail, lard it with the Flesh of Eels, tie it with Pack-thread, and put it into an oval Stew-Pan, brown a Piece of Butter, dridge in some Flour, moisten it with Broth made of Fish; put to it a Bottle of Champaign, let the Liquor cover it, let it stew till enough, first season it with whole Pepper, Mace, Salt, Onion, Sweet Herbs and Vinegar; then make a Ragoo of Oisters, the Liver, and Mushrooms; take off the Pack-thread, dish it, and put some of the Ragoo over it, and send some up in a Boat. Garnish it as you do other Fish.—There are several more Ways to dress Salmon, some I shall mention hereafter.

I shall mention some Ragoos and Sauces for Fish.

To make a Ragoo of Truffles for Fish.

Ragout de Truffes.

BOIL your Truffles in Water till tender; take off the black Edges with a sharp Knife; then make a Brown; put in some Stock of Fish Sauce, as in Page 8, and stew them over a slow Fire; put in a Ladle-full of drawn Butter, and use it where proper, &c.

To ragoo Veal Sweet Breeds.

Ris de Veau en Ragoût.

WASH and blanch them in boiling Water; cut them in pretty thick Slices; flour them and toss them up in clarified Butter, moisten them with good Gravey; let them stew four Minutes, scum off the Fat, put in a Glass of White Wine, squeeze in some Lemon; put in some pickled Mushrooms, the

Yolks

Yolks of Eggs boil'd hard, some Forc'd meat Balls; thicken with a Brown made of the Cullis of Veal and Ham. This is for a Side Dish, or to add to made Dishes, as you will find hereafter.

To make a Ragoo of Morels.

Morilles en Ragoût.

CUT off the Stalks, cut them in two, and wash them very clean from the Sand; boil them in Salt and Water; put a Piece of Butter into a Stew-Pan, brown it, dredge in some Flour, moisten them with Fish Stock, squeeze in some Lemon, grate in some Nutmeg, add to it a little drawn Butter, and the Yolk of an Egg beaten with a Spoonful of Verjuice; and toss all together.

As there is Cullis often mention'd to thicken made Dishes, I shall insert one that serves for most in the brown Way.

To make a Cullis of Veal and Ham.

Coulis de Veau et de Jambon.

TAKE four Pound of Veal, a Pound of the Lean of a Ham; cut them into thin Slices, butter the Bottom of a Stew-Pan, lay in the Ham, the Veal on that, slice in some Onion, a Carrot, put in some Sweet Herbs, two Heads of Celery, whole Pepper, and Mace; cover it close, set it on a stove Fire, let it stew till it is brown at the Bottom; take Care it does not burn; then having some good strong Broth and Gravey, put to it a Quart of each, with the Crust of a French Roll; let it simmer Half away, strain it, and let it stand to cool; take the Fat from the Top, and the Sediment from the Bottom; take Half a Pound of good Butter, put it into a Stew-Pan with an Onion stuck with Cloves; put in a large Handful of Flour; stick the Onion on the Point of your

your Knife, ftir it with the Onion till it be of a light Brown; put in the Cullis, ftir all together, keep it ftirring till it is almoft cold, that it may the better incorporate together; put it in an earthen Pot, tie it clofe down, and keep it for Ufe. A Spoonful of this will thicken a made Difh or Fifh Sauce, or any Thing that requires thickening or binding together, and it gives a good Relifh.

You may make a common Brown, with a Piece of Butter and Flour; ftir it till brown, put in fome good Gravey, and all Things that are proper for the Difh you are making of; add Lemon and Seafoning to your Tafte.

Beef a la Braife.

Beuf à la braife.

TAKE the thin End of a Surloin of Beef, bone it, and take off the outfide Skin, then cut fome Bacon to lard it with, that will fit a large Dobin-Pin; take fome Parfley and Thime fhred fine, mixt with Pepper and Salt, rub the Lard in this, and lard your Beef at the thick End quite through, bind it with Pack-thread to keep it from cracking, cover the Bottom of your Brazen Pan with Rafhers of Bacon, and on that Slices of lean Beef, feafon'd with Pepper, Salt, Herbs, Onions, &c. put in your Beef with the flefhy Side down, feafon the upper Part as you did the lower, and lay on Bacon and Slices of Beef alfo; fet it on a flow Fire, firft put in a Bottle of Champaign Wine, cover it clofe, let it ftew for four or five Hours; make a Ragoo for it as follows:

Put in fome good Gravey into a Stew-Pan with difh'd Sweet-breeds, Turnips difh'd and blanch'd, Carrots, &c. Mufhrooms, Ox Palates, and pickled Cucumbers fliced, ftew all together till tender, thicken it with fome Cullis as above; take up your Beef, lay it in
the

the Dish, strain the Liquor from the Meat the Beef was brais'd in, scum off the Fat, put the Liquor to the Ragoo, make all hot, put it on the Beef, garnish with dish'd Turnips and Carrots, Greens, or Spinage, &c. this is the Way of braising: Fowls and Fish are done the same Way, making Use of Ingredients proper to each Sort.

I shall give you an Account of, and how several Ragoos are made of Vegetables, as well as of other Things, proper to use in this Way of Dressing, and for Sauces for several Sorts of Roasts, &c.

To make a Ragoo of Turnips.

Ragoût de navets.

PARE them, slice and dice them, and blanch them in boiling Water; toss them up in melted Butter; add to them some Gravey-Vinegar that has stood on beaten Pepper two or three Days; put in some Salt, thicken it with a Brown, or some Cullis as above. Carrots are done the same Way; as likewise is Celery cleaned and cut an Inch long.

To stew white Cabbage.

Choux cabus à l'etuvée.

TAKE a Cabbage that is light, cut it in 4 Pieces, take out the Stalk or Core, blanch it in Water, take it up and drain it well; then cut it crossways, begin at the upper End as thin as you can, stew it in strong Broth, add an Onion shred fine, let it stew till tender; put in some Salt and Vinegar, with a Ladleful of drawn Butter; thicken it with a Cullis or a Piece of Butter worked in Flour: If you would have it very white, put in a Gill of Cream, but don't let it boil up after, if you do it will cruddle: If you would have it brown, use Gravey instead of strong Broth.

To ragoo Colliflowers.

Choux fleurs en ragoût.

CUT off the Tops, blanch them in boiling Water, and drain them, tofs them in a Stew-Pan in melted Butter, dridge in a little Flour, put in a little Salt, and a little Vinegar that has been in Pepper, let them ftew till tender. This is proper to eat with roaft Lamb, &c.

To ragoo Onions.

Des Onions en ragoût.

TAKE half a dozen large Onions, cut them in two, flice them thin, blanch them in two or three Waters, drain them, dry, and fry them a little in clarified Butter, dridge in fome Flour; put to them half a Pint of Gravey, a little Pepper, Salt, and Vinegar; put to it a Spoonful of Muftard, and let all ftew till the Onions are tender. This Sauce is proper for Tripe, Ox Feet, or Hogs Feet and Ears, or for broil'd Herrings, &c.

To ftew Cucumbers.

Concombres etuvée.

TAKE fix or eight Cucumbers, pare and cut them down the Middle, and take out the Seeds; cut each half in four Pieces, falt them, and fet them to drain, flour them, and tofs them up in clarified Butter; put in a Pint of good Gravey, an Onion fhred fine, fome Pepper and Vinegar, let them ftew on a flow Fire till tender; if they be not thick enough put in fome Cullis as beforementioned.

To ragoo Lobsters.

Ragoût d'Ecrevices.

TAKE out the Meat of the Tails and Claws, cut it in small Pieces, boil eight or ten Morels; take off the Stalks, cut them open, wash them clean, shred them with some pickled Mushrooms, mince a small Onion with half an Anchovey, make a Brown with Butter and Flour; put in half a Pint of Gravey, put all together with a little Pepper and Vinegar, let them simmer on a slow Fire; dish them on Sippets.

To make a Ragoo of Ox Palates.

Ragoût de Palais de Beuf.

CLEAN them, boil and skin them, cut them in Pieces, make a Brown; put in a Pint of Gravey, some Onion, and Anchovey shred fine, a Faggot of Sweet-herbs, the Juice of a Lemon, some Mushrooms; put in the Palates, let them stew till tender: You may put in Forc'd-Meat-Balls, the Yolks of hard Eggs, and lard and roast a Sweet-Bread for the Middle.

I shall mention some Dishes in Meagre for Lent and Fish Days.

To make a Meagre Soop.

Potage Maigre.

TAKE a Quart of Peas, pick and wash them clean; put to them six Quarts of Water, with some whole Pepper, half a dozen Cloves, a little Mace, two Parsnips, two Carrots, six Turnips, six large Onions; clean and slice all these, boil all till tender and the Peas broke, strain this through a Cullinder; take six Heads of Celery, take off the Outside, wash and pare the Roots, shred them with a Knife; take

take two good Handfuls of Spinage, pick, wash, and shred it, also two Onions; put half a Pound of Butter in a Stew-Pan, put to it your Herbs with some Salt, cover it, and stew it tender; keep it stirring now and then or it will burn; moisten it with some of the Broth that you have already prepared, then dice two large Turnips, and blanch them; then take ten Morels, take off the Stalks, cut them through and wash them from the Sand, and shred them fine; make a Brown, put in your Turnips and Morels, add to it some more of your Broth, with two Anchovies, and an Onion shred fine; then put all together; put in as much Vermicelly as you think proper, stew all together till enough, salt it to your Taste, prepare some French Bread as you do for other Soops, or fry it; dish it with a French Rowl in the Middle; garnish as for other Soops.

N. B. Most Meagre Soops made of Herbs are prepared from the same Stock as above, as Onion, Turnips, Spinage, or Peas, the Peas rub'd thro' a Cullinder, adding dry'd Mint; you may leave out the Morels; Onions blanch'd in two or three Waters, boil'd tender, and rub'd thro' a Cullinder; Turnips the same, Spinage the same, take only the clear of your Stock, boil in it a French Rowl or two sliced, and rub them through the Cullinder to thicken your Soops. These Soops go by the Name that they chiefly consist of, as Turnip Soop, Onion Soop, &c.

Lobster Soop.

Potage d' Ecrevices.

TAKE three or four Lobsters, pound the Spawn, add to it some Fish Broth, made as follows; take what Sort of Fish you can get, that is to say, Scates, Thornback, Codlins, Haddocks, Eels, Roach or Dares, or what Part of these you can best get, cut them in Pieces firſt, ſcrape, draw, and gill them; ſave ſome of the Fleſh to make Forc'd-Meat of; put your Fiſh into a Kettle of Water, with ſome Onions, Pepper, Mace, Salt, Parſnips, Turnips, Celery, and a Faggot of Sweet herbs, with five or ſix Anchovies, ſome Cruſts of Bread; let it boil for two Hours, add to it boiling Water, ſtrain it; this ſerves for all Fiſh Soops: Some uſe it for White, by beating half a Pound of Almonds blanch'd and beat, with Yolks of hard Eggs, adding ſome Cream: To make brown Soop of the ſame, take ſome Butter, and butter the Bottom of a Stew-Pan, ſlice in ſome Carrot, Turnip, Parſnip, and Leaks, cover it cloſe, let it on a ſlow Fire till it begins to brown, dridge in ſome Flour, put in ſome of your Broth; then make your Soop with this, and with the beforementioned, as Celery, Turnip, &c. &c.

To make Forc'd-Meat of the Fleſh of Fiſh.

Godiveau de Poiſſon.

CHOP it fine, mix it with Bread Crumbs, Sweet-herbs and Spices, put in a good Piece of Butter, three or four Eggs, work all together with an Anchovey ſhred fine with a little Onion, make it in the Shape of a Roll, bake it and put it in the Middle of your Soop Diſh; make a Ragoo of ſome of your Lobſter, with ſome of the Fiſh Stock, thicken'd with a Brown; fill your Forc'd-Meat with that; mince the reſt of your Lobſter and put into your Soop, with ſome of the Forc'd-Meat made in ſmall Balls like a ſmall Nutmeg, firſt blanch'd in boiling Water; put likewiſe the Cruſt of a French Roll cut in Pieces the Bigneſs of a Shilling, and dry'd before the Fire; garniſh your Diſh with Lobſter Spawn, and Lemon laid on green Leaves.

Of Morels.

Morils à sechée.

MORELS are an Excrement of the Earth that grow near the Water and Foot of Trees; we find them generally in this Month and April; when you have gathered them, wash them from the Sand, string them and hang them up in a warm Place to dry. We use them in most Ragoos; the Particulars I shall mention in their proper Places.

To dress Haddocks the Dutch Way.

Haddocks à l'Hollandois.

SCALE and gut them, wash them and gash them on each Side, put them in cold Water half an Hour, wash them out of that and put them in your Kettle with a Drainer at the Bottom, and as much Water as will cover them, with a Handful of Salt, and some Vinegar, some Lemon-Peel, and a Faggot of Sweet-herbs; if they be not very large they will boil in a quarter of an Hour; whilst they are boiling, get some Turnips, pare, slice, and dice them. In Holland they boil them with the Fish, drain them well, and put them into drawn Butter and boil'd Parsley shred or chopt fine; put in a little Salt, and squeeze in some Lemon; lay toasted Bread in the Bottom of your Dish, pour some of the Sauce on them, lay in your Haddocks, and pour the rest of the Sauce over them: You may brown your Stew-Pan with a Piece of Butter and Flour, and toss up your Turnips in that, and moisten it with Fish Stock; add to it as much Butter (drawn up with it) as will do; put to it your Parsley and Lemon.

You may do Codlins, Soles, or Whitens the same Way, or large Splace, &c. The Fish Stock is what I mentioned before.

To dress several Sorts of Fish the French Way.

Poisson's accommodé à la maniere Francois.

SCALE, clean, and wash them, that is to say, Trout, Salmon, Soles, Codlin, Whitens, &c. take the Flesh from the Bones and Skin, mince it, put it into a Stew-Pan, cover it, and set it on a slow Fire till it turns white ; then lay it on your shredding Block or Board, shred some Parsley, Truffles, and Chives, or Shallot fine ; brown a Stew-Pan with some Butter and Flour, put in your Hash, season it with Pepper, Salt, and Lemon, moisten it with Fish Stock as above, take some of this, add to it some grated Bread, with two Yolks of Eggs ; take the Bone of your Fish with the Head on, and lay this upon it, shape it like the Fish, butter a Tin Plate, lay it on it, wash it over with the Yolk of an Egg and melted Butter, and bake it, put it in the Middle of the Dish, heat the rest of your Hash, and lay all round it ; garnish with Lemon and Barberries: You may force a large Fish with this, prepared as above ; add in some Anchovey and White Wine, turn your Fish round, and fasten it with a Skewer, or tie it ; make an Incision on each Side the Back-bone, fill it with the Forcing, and put some in the Belly, wash it with melted Butter and Yolks of Eggs, strew on it grated Bread, and bake it in a proper Thing, dish it, and make the Sauce as in Page 8 ; if on a Fish Day use the Stock mentioned for meagre Dishes, with the rest of the Ingredients, as you think most proper.

To marinade Veal Cutlets.

Cottelets de Veau Marinée.

TAKE a Neck of Veal, cut it Bone by Bone, take off the Bit of the Chine with your Clever, bare the Ends of the Bones an Inch, flat them with your

your Cleaver, make a Marinade for them as follows: Take a Pint of Water, half a Pint of Vinegar, some whole Pepper, Mace, sliced Onion, Parsley, Salt, Thyme, sliced Lemon, and a little White Wine; let them lie in this two Hours, then take them out; dry them with a Cloth; then make a Batter of Flour, the Yolks of six Eggs, the Juice of a Lemon, a little White Wine, some melted Butter, and a little Cream; make it as thick as for Tripe, dip the Cutlets in it, and fry them in clarified Butter, dish them, and garnish them with fried Parsley.

Chickens may be cut in Quarters, marinaded and dress'd the same Way, or Rabbits, or a Leveret; but you must send sweet Sauce to the Leveret, as Bread Crumbs boil'd in Red Wine, with a Stick of Cinnamon and Sugar, or Curran Jelly.

This Marinade serves for Fish as well as Flesh and Fowls. It heightens the Taste and makes it more agreeable to the Palate.

To fry Salt Fish.

De au Morue frit.

WATER a Tail of Salt Fish till it is very fresh, cut it in Slices, dry it well, dridge it with Flour, and fry it in clarified Butter; garnish it with Parsnips boil'd and dish'd, and fry'd Parsley: You may set a Bason with Egg Sauce in the Middle, or plain Butter, or a Poivrade Sauce, made as follows:

Take Water, Vinegar, and White Wine, of each a like Quantity, put in some Pepper, Salt, and Shallot, threadfine, with some Lemon, and a little Anchovey; boil all together and strain it.

Dry'd Salmon is dress'd the same Way, and most Sorts of dry'd Fish.

Salt

Salt Fish Pye.

Paté de la Moruë.

LET your Salt Fish be well watered and boiled, take the Fish from the Bones; then take a fresh Codlin, clean and wash it, take the Flesh from the Skin and Bones, shred it with Sweet-herbs and Spices, but no Salt, mix it with a sufficient Quantity of Butter, put some in the Bottom of your Pye, lay Salt Fish on that, then lay the rest of your other Fish on that, Salt Fish on that again, hard Eggs on that, with Butter on the Top: Some put Parsnips boil'd and dish'd, and some Potatoes, and leave out the Eggs; so close it and bake it; first wash it over with the Yolk of an Egg and a Spoonful of Cream; cut the Lid round with a sharp Knife that you may the easier take it off; when baked, take off the Fat or Oil with a Spoon, having some Parsley boil'd and chop'd, with a Spoonful of Capers, and a little shred Onion, draw your Butter with a little Fish Broth, put in the Onion and the rest, put it in the Pye, lay on the Lid, and send it up.

Oister Loaves.

Pain aux Huitres.

OPEN as many Oisters as you think will fill the Quantity of Loaves you would have; wash them out of their Liquor, put them in a Stew-pan with a Blade or two of Mace, some whole Pepper Corns; put in the Clear of their Liquor, with a little White Wine, and the Juice of a Lemon; grate in a little Nutmeg, add a little good Gravey; draw all up together with good Butter the Thickness of Cream, take out the Mace and Pepper, and fill your Loaves, prepared as follows:

Cut off the Tops, take out the Crumbs and fry them brown in Butter, or butter them within and without, and let them in an Oven till crisp.

ART *of* COOKERY. 71

To fry Oisters.

Des Huitres frit.

MAKE a Batter for them as for Tripe, (p. 50) and fry them in clarified Butter, or beat some Yolks of Eggs mix'd with melted Butter, dip them in that, and dridge them with fine Bread Crumbs, shred Parsley, and a little Flour, fry'd as before: You may send them in Plates, garnished with fry'd Parsley, with a Cup of melted Butter, and the Juice of an Orange in the Middle: You may garnish boil'd Fowls, Turkies, or Chickens with them, or Fish, or any Thing proper to eat with Oysters.

To make Petty Patties of Fish.

Petiits Pâtez de Poisson.

TAKE the Flesh of what Fish you can best get, with some Parsley, Capers, Chives, Salt, Pepper, Nutmeg, the Yolk of an Egg, and a little Anchovey; pound all in a Mortar with a good Piece of Butter; make them of Puff Paste, a little bigger than a Crown Piece; wash them with the Yolk of an Egg, and bake them: You may send them in on a little Dish or Plate, or garnish boil'd Fish with them when you cannot get Fish to fry: You may make Patties of Oisters; season them with the same Herbs and Spice, but don't chop them, but lay them in whole with Butter on them; make them bigger or less as you like.

To pot Lobsters.

Ecrevisses empotée.

SPIT them through the Bodies with a Lark Spit, and tie them to another Spit; lay them to the Fire, and roast them, when they are red they are enough, baste them with Butter, and salt them; take

them

them up, take out the Meat of the Tails and Claws, put it into a Pot, season it with Pepper, Salt, and Mace, put on as much Butter as will cover them handsomely, tie them down with a Paper, and bake them an Hour; take out the Lobster, let it drain well in a Cullinder, then put it in the Pot you design to keep it in, press it down tight, scum off the Clear of the Butter, fill up the Pot, and let it stand to cool: Some bruise the Spawn and put in to make it redder, but you must strain the Butter through a Sieve to take the Bits of Spawn out; let it stand to settle, then scum off the Clear: Let all your Lobsters be cover'd in the Pot; they will keep a Quarter of a Year done this Way.

To roast Lobsters.

Ecrevisses roti.

SPIT them as before, lay them to the Fire, baste them with Butter, and salt them well; when they are enough take them up and crack the Claws; split the Tails, dish them with a Cup or Boat of plain Butter, garnish with Seville Orange.

If you would broil them, baste them with Vinegar and Butter, salt them as before, cut them up as before, lay them on the Gridiron, and broil them on a clear Fire; serve them up with the same Garnishing, &c.

To cream Lobsters.

Ecrevisses à la crême.

WHEN boil'd take out the Meat of the Tails and Claws, cut it in square Pieces, make a white Lare for it, see for white Lare; you may put an Oyster Loaf in the Middle; garnish with Lemon, Barberries, &c. or Seville Orange and Parsley.

To boil Splace, Flounders, or Soles.

Pliés, Carrelets ou Soles a cuir.

CLEAN and scrape them, and take out their Bowels on the brown Side, boil them in hard Water, Salt and Vinegar ten Minutes, without they be very large; let the Sauce be Parsley and Butter, the Juice of Lemon, and a little Salt; or you may make Fish Sauce as directed in Page 8; garnish with Horse Raddish and Lemon.

To pickle Salmon.

Saumon confit au sel & au vinaigre.

CUT it in six Pieces first, chine it and take out the Entrails, rub it dry with a Cloth, take out the Gills, and stitch the Head where you took out the Gills to the Body with a Needle and Thread, to keep the Head from breaking off; then put your Fish on a Drainer that will hold them without laying one upon another; put as much hard Water to it as will cover it when in your Kettle, and a sufficient Quantity of Salt, with an Ounce of Salt-petre; let it boil half an Hour, take it up and let it stand on the Drainer till cold; put to your Pickle some Vinegar, just to taste it, with some whole Pepper and Mace; let it boil a quarter of an Hour, strain it and let it stand to cool; put your Pickle in the Vessel you intend to keep it in; put in your Salmon, put sweet Oil on it; and keep it close covered for Use. This Pickle will keep good for six Weeks.

N. B. You must leave the Bone in on one Side, and leave the Scales on.—You may leave out the Salt-petre if you please.

To pickle Salmon like Sturgeon.
Saumon confit à la maniere d'Esturgeon.

TAKE a fresh Salmon, cut it in three Pieces, take out the Entrails and the Gills, don't scale it, rub the Blood clean out with a Cloth, tie it with Bass as Sturgeon is tied, put as much hard Water as will cover it in your Kettle, with a good Handful or two of Salt, and an Ounce of Salt-petre, let it boil ten Minutes; put in your Salmon, let it boil forty Minutes, if a large one an Hour; take it out, let it stand to drain and cool; add to your Pickle a Pint of Vinegar, a Quart of White Wine, some Cloves, Mace, and whole Pepper, three or four Bay Leaves; boil all for a Quarter of an Hour, strain it, let it cool, put it in your Pot with the Salmon; cover it close, and keep it for Use.

APRIL.

APRIL.

Soop de Sante the French Way.
Potage de Santé.

TAKE ten or twelve Pounds of Beef, the Scrag End of a Neck of Mutton, prepared as in Page 49; the Gravey is done the same Way, only use Veal instead of Beef; the Herbs the same, only add three or four Onions; let there be a Fowl in the Middle, and garnish your Dish with Spinage, and Rashers of Bacon that are free from Rust, cut out of the Middle of the Flitch, &c.

Dress your Salmon as you think will be best liked: There are several different Ways which I have already mentioned.

To make a Pudding of Herbs.
Boudin d'Herbes.

TAKE a Penny Brick, cut off the Crust, rub the Crumbs through a Cullinder; put to it Sweet Marjoram, Thyme, a little Penny-royal, and Parsley; mince all very fine, beat half a Nutmeg, some Cinnamon and Mace, half a Pound of Currans, half a Pound of Raisins stew'd and chop'd, half a Pound of Beef Suet, a quarter of a Pound of Sugar beat, eight Eggs, leave out four Whites, put in a little Salt, beat your Eggs, mix all together with as much Cream as will make it stiff; butter a Cloth, and flour it, tie it up tight, and boil it two Hours and a half: The Sauce is White Wine, Butter, and Sugar.

To make a Pupton of Lobsters.
Poupeton d'Ecrevices.

TAKE a Couple of Lobsters, boil them, take the Meat out of the Tails and Claws, cut it in Dice; then take the Spawn and bruise it in a Marble Mortar very fine; then take the Flesh of what Fish you can get, make it into Forc'd-Meat as you would with Veal; let your Pupton-Pan be garnish'd, lay on a Sheet of Forc'd-Meat on that; then ragoo your Lobster with some Forc'd-Meat Balls, Oisters, and hard Eggs; look for ragoo'd Lobsters, fill your Pan, lay on a Cover of Forc'd-Meat, close and bake it an Hour; when baked, loosen it round the Edge with a Knife, lay the Dish on it; if you design to send it in, turn it in the Dish, take off the Pan, cut out a Hole in the Middle where the Slice of Lemon lies, put in some Gravey and Butter, and lay on the Piece again; garnish it with shred Fennel, Lemon, &c.

To dress a Pullet à la Braise.
Poulets à la braise.

TRuss it as for boiling, lard it with Bacon, season it with Pepper and Salt; garnish the Bottom of a Stew-Pan with Rashers of Bacon, lay on them Slices of Veal, season'd with Pepper, Salt, Onion, Sweet-herbs, and Slices of Lemon; cut off the outside Rind, put a Piece of Forc'd-Meat in the Belly, lay in the Fowl with the Breast down, lay on it as under; set it on a slow Fire, make a Fire above, and let it stew for an Hour; then look at it for Fear it should burn, then put in a Quart of good strong Broth, let it stew till tender, take it up and drain it; make a Ragoo for it as you'll find in ragoo'd Sweet-Breeds, Page 59: Garnish with Lemon and Forc'd-Meat Patties, or Patties of Oisters.

ART *of* COOKERY.   77

To daub a Neck of Veal.
Collet de veau à la daub.

LARD it with large Lardoners of Bacon, feafon'd with Salt, Nutmeg, fhred Parfley, Lemon-Peel, and a little Thyme, roll your Bacon in this, and lard your Veal pretty thick, that is, the beft End of the Neck; fpit it, and lay on it a Sheet of Forc'd-Meat tied on as you would on Venifon, with Paper on it; roaft it, and when enough, take off the Paper and Forc'd-Meat, bafte and dridge it, let it brown, and difh it with the Forc'd-Meat cut like Sippets, and laid round, with a Ragoo of Sweet-Breeds put under it.

To boil a Tongue and Udder.
La Langue et at Tettin de Beuf a cuire.

THE Udder will take five Hours boiling, if it be an old one; if a young one, it will boil in the fame Time the Tongue will, which is in three Hours or lefs; when boiled, take the Skin of the Tongue and pare it, and the Udder likewife; then wafh them over with a little melted Butter, and the Yolk of an Egg, dridge them with Bread Crumbs, and brown them before the Fire, or give them a few Turns on a Spit to make them crifp; difh them with Turnips, Carrots, and Greens between: You may fend a little Curran Jelly in a Cup, or Venifon. Some like to eat them without Greens when they are brown'd.

How to drefs young Ducks.
Jeune Canards appreté.

CUT their Throats, let them bleed well, then put them into Water; make fome Water fcalding hot, and fcald off their Down; then lay them on a Cloth with their Breafts down and their Feet turned under them; then take a Brick and cover it with a Cloth, lay one Duck next the Brick with a Cloth be-

tween

tween them, then the next Duck close to that, and so on; then lay a Brick next the Outside one to keep them streight, lay a Board on the Top with a small Weight on it to keep it down; let them be cover'd all over with a wet Cloth, let them lie till cold, then take care how you draw them; cut off their Wings to the last Joint next the Body, then truss them handsomely; put a Bit of Butter rub'd in Salt into their Bellies, roast them at a good Distance from the Fire; when they are dry, singe them, and baste with Butter before you take them up; rasp some Crust off a French Roll or Brick, shred it fine with Salt, mix it with Flour, baste them and dridge them with it; let them go two or three Turns, and take them up; dish them, and send Gravey in the Dish; garnish with Orange and scalded Goosberries; send green Sauce in a Boat or Cup, made as follows; take Sorril, and beat it in a Mortar, squeeze out the Juice through a Cloth, sweeten it with Sugar, put to it some scalded Goosberries, put in some Butter, dridge in some Flour, stir it on the Fire till it be as thick as Cream; if you can't get fresh Goosberries, take bottled ones. —Geese are done the same Way, only take off their Legs to put to the rest of the Giblets to stew, or for a Pye, as you like best.

To roast Rabbits.
Lapins à rotir.

Rabbits being now young and small it will not be amiss to force them, that is, to make Puddings for their Bellies; skin, clean, and truss them, two together, then make the Forcing; take the Crumb of a French Roll, rub it thro' a Cullinder, add as much Suet to it shred very fine, with a Handful of Parsley pick'd, wash'd, and chop'd, likewise half an Anchovey, a Shallot, and a little Lemon-Peel and Salt; mix all together with the Yolk of an Egg and a little Cream, fill them with this, sew them up, and roast them; let their Sauce be their Livers and Parsley,
miz'd

mix'd with drawn Butter; take the Galls off the Livers.

To make Rice Cream.
Crême au Ris.

TAKE a Pint and a half of Cream, three Spoonfuls of the Flour of Rice; put in a Stick of Cinnamon, set it on the Fire, keep it stirring with a Whisk till it be thick, take it off and let it cool a little; put in as much fine Sugar as will sweeten it, beat the Yolks of three Eggs with a little Salt, mix all together well, set it on the Fire again, add a little fresh Cream, stir it till all be well incorporated, put it in the Dish you design it to go in, let it stand till quite cold; then take a Thread and mark it cross and cross again, then you have it in four equal Parts; then divide each Part in two, that will make it in eight; then with a Tea-Spoon take out every other one very exactly, first separate them with a Knife; then take as much Rasberry Jame as you think will do, put to it half a Pint of Red Wine, set it on the Fire till the Jame is dissolved, strain it through a Sieve, and fill the Places up with it where you took the other Cream out; stick the Cream, two Parts, with blanch'd Almonds, and the other two with candied Lemon, or Orange-Peel, or Citron; or you may let the Cream abide whole, and divide it as directed; stick four Quarters as above, and lay Rasp-Cream between; if you take some out, you may mix it with a little fresh Cream; add to it some Sugar, and the Yolk of an Egg or two, stir it on the Fire till all is mix'd together, put it into Cups, and turn it out into another Dish: Garnish it as you like, &c.

To make Almond Snow.
Des Amandes en niege.

TAKE a Quarter of a Pound of Sweet Almonds, blanch and beat them very fine, add now and then a little Cream; then put to them the Remainder
of

of a Quart, put to it half a Pint of White Wine, some Nutmeg, the Rind of a Lemon, a Spoonful of Rose-Water; sweeten it to your Taste with double-refined Sugar, strain it into a Bason, and beat it up with a Whisk till it frothe very high; then put it into your Dish or Bason.

To make Welch Flummery.
Flomorée à la manière Galles.

TAKE half a Peck of Wheat Bran, put it into an earthen Vessel, put as much Water to it as will cover it three or four Inches; let it stand three or four Days, stir it two or three Times a Day, then strain it thro' a Sieve, and press the Water out of it as much as you can, or strain it through a Napkin, and squeeze it well with your Hands; then take the Liquor, put it into a Stew-pan, set it on the Fire, keep it stirring till it be thick, put it in Cups till cold, then turn it out: You may boil in it some Cinnamon and Lemon-Peel; sweeten it, and add to it some Cream to make it look White: It is eaten with Wine and Sugar. You may send it up in a Bason, and garnish it with Seville Orange.

To make a cold Cream Foul.
Crême avec Gelée de Corinth.

TAKE a Quart of Cream, sweeten it to your Taste with fine Sugar, put it into a Silver Stew-Pan or Sauce-Pan, or a Stew-Pan well tin'd, set it on a gentle Fire to boil; then take the Yolks of ten or twelve Eggs with a little cold Cream, and put them to the hot Cream; keep them stirring till it is thick, but not to boil after the Eggs are put in; then slice some Naples Biscuit and lay them in the Bottom of the Dish; pour it on the Sippets, and lay over it Curran Jelly.

ART of COOKERY.

How to make a Rosa-solis of Spinage.
Rosoli oux Epinards.

TAKE half a Pound of Spinage when boil'd and squeez'd from the Water, mince it fine; put to it a Quarter of a Pound of Sugar, a Quarter of a Pound of Butter melted in half a Pint of Cream; mince two Ounces of Citron very small, and the Yolks of six Eggs boil'd hard, a little Salt and Nutmeg, and a little Cinnamon; warm all over the Fire in a Stew-Pan, stir it, and set it to cool; then make it like the Florentine in Page 13.

How to order and roast a Hog's Haslet.
Fressure de Pourceau à rotir.

CUT some of the Liver and Heart into Pieces as near as you can of a Bigness, with some of the Skirt and Bits of the Fat; season all with Pepper, Salt, Sage, and Parsley; spit it on a small Spit, a Piece of one and a Piece of another, till you have spitted all; then wrap it round with the Caul, and tie it on with Packthread; baste it with Butter; when enough, draw it, and lay it handsomely in your Dish: Your Sauce may be Mustard, Butter, and Vinegar: Some like Apple Sauce, some Gravey, Butter, and a little minc'd Onion.

To make Bacon Froyce.
Fraize au lard.

MAKE a Batter of Eggs, Flour, and Cream, well beat; cut some Bacon into thin Slices and fry it in Butter; put half of your Batter on it, let it fry till you can turn it; then turn it, and put on the rest of the Batter; so turn it three or four Times, keep adding a little Butter; take care it don't burn: Your Quantity may be a Pint of Flour, eight Eggs, and as much Cream as will make it into a Batter.—This will do for a Side Dish.

To make a made Dish of Beef, like Beef A-la-mode.
Beuf à la Guinguet.

CUT two large Slices off a Buttock of Beef; hack them with the Back of a Knife, season them with Sweet-herbs, Pepper, and Salt; lay some Slices of Bacon in the Bottom of a Stew-pan, then one Slice of your Beef on them, then lay some Bacon on that; then put in some minc'd Onion, lay on the other Beef on that, and season the Top; lay on some Bits of Butter, cover it close, set it on a slow Fire to stew, then turn it and cover it again; let it stew a little longer; then make a Brown in another Stew-Pan; put in a Pint of good Gravey, with some pickled Mushrooms, Cucumbers, and some Morels; put in a Glass of Red Wine, let them boil a little; then put it to your Beef, let it stew till tender; put it in your Dish, first lay in some Sippets of White Bread: Garnish with Pickles.

To make Biscuit for Chocolate, or to eat as you like best.
Bisquit au Chocolat.

TAKE half a Peck of Flour, dry it well; beat sixteen Eggs, mix them with half a Pint of good Yest that is not bitter, and half a Pint of Cream; warm as much Water as you think will make it like White Bread; let it stand to rise, then work it well; butter a Tin Pan that you bake a Cake in, put it in and bake it; let it lie two Days, first rasp it, then cut it into Slices like Toasts, and strew them over with powder'd Sugar; dry it in a warm Stove or Oven, turn them and sugar them again; do so three or four Times; keep them in a dry Place.

To make Almond Butter.
Amandes au beurre.

TAKE sixteen Eggs, beat them well, and strain them into a Quart of Cream; set all on a clear slow Fire, and keep stirring it; when it is ready to boil,

ART *of* COOKERY.   83

boil, put to it a Quarter of a Pint of Sack, ſtir it till it comes to a Curd, ſtrain the Whey from it, blanch a Quarter of a Pound of Almonds, and beat them in a Marble Mortar with a little Roſe Water ; mix the Curd and Almonds together, and beat them again, adding Loaf Sugar powder'd to your Taſte ; beat it till it be as fine as Butter : You may put it in what Form you pleaſe, and garniſh it with Biſcuit. It will keep good three Weeks.

To make a Biſcuit to garniſh with.
Biſquits pour garniture.

TAKE three Whites of Eggs, take out the Treads, beat them well ; then add as much Sugar pounded and ſifted as will make it like a thick Cream ; add Flour to make it to a ſoft Paſte, work it well, and make it up in round or long ones ; ice, and bake them in a ſlow Oven.

To make Andoulians.
Andoulians.

TAKE the Guts of a Hog, turn and ſcour them ; lay them in Water 24 Hours, then wipe them dry, and turn the fat Side outwards; take ſome Sage, chop it fine ; then take ſome Pepper, Cloves, Mace, and Nutmeg ; pound them in a Mortar ; mix all together with ſome Salt, ſeaſon the fat Side of the Guts ; then turn that Side inward again, and draw one Gut over the other to what Bigneſs you pleaſe ; tie them faſt at both Ends, and boil them in Salt and Water ; then broil them, and eat them with Muſtard and Vinegar.

Andouillets.
Andouillets.

TAKE a Pound of Veal, Half a Pound of Bacon and Half a Pound of Beef Suet chopt fine with Sweet Herbs, and the Yolks of ſix Eggs boil'd hard, add Pepper and Nutmeg ; you may try a Bit of it to taſte

if

if the Bacon has made it falt enough; if not, put in some Salt, with a few Bread Crumbs; make these up the Bigness of an Egg, and wash them over with the Yolks of Eggs, and wrap them up in the Pieces of Veal; then egg them over again, and dridge them with Bread Crumbs; bake them in an Oven; let the Sauce be Gravey, Butter, Vinegar, and a little Mustard, drawn up together; or you may roll it in Veal Collops, hack'd with the Back of a Knife, and seasen'd with Sweet Herbs and Spices order'd as before, with the Caul over all; or you may put the Forc'd-meat in Guts prepar'd as above, and drest the same Way: The Sauce the same. You may garnish Fowls or Turkeys with them.

To fry Hog's Liver.
Foie de Cochon frit.

SLICE it, but not too thin, strinkle it with Salt, flour and fry it in Butter, but not too much; for if you do, it quite spoils it; then make a Brown for it, as mention'd in several Places before; add to it a little good Gravey, and a little Onion chopt fine, with a little Parsley; put in a little Vinegar; let it be the Thickness of a Cream; put it in your Dish, lay on the Liver. Garnish it with fry'd Parsley and Rashers of Bacon. You may fry some Sweet Breeds with it; or you may fry the Fat with it that is call'd, the Croe, &c.——A Lamb's Liver may be done the same Way.——Or a Calf's Liver, the Heart stuft and roasted, and set up in the Middle; or you may lard them, and likewise lard some of the Slices of the Liver before you fry it; but leave out the Rashers.

To dress a Fowl, Capon, or Turkey in Balneomariae.
Dindon ou Chapon en Balneo Maria.

WHEN clean'd and sing'd, lard it with Bacon, fill the Body with Rice wash'd and dry'd; then take two Pound of Beef Stakes, season them
with

with Pepper, Salt, and Sweet Herbs; then take a Pan big enough to hold them and the Fowl; lay some Stakes at the Bottom, and the Fowl on them, with two Pound of a Fillet of Veal season'd on the Fowl, and the rest of the Beef Stakes on that; take a Cover that will fit it tight, paste it down, and set it in a Pot of Water; take Care the Water do not boil over the Pan your Fowl is in; if it does not keep well down, lay a Weight on the Top of it; let it boil four Hours, as the Liquor boils away put more boiling Water into your Kettle; then take it off, and let it stand till you have prepar'd a Ragoo of Sweet Breeds, as in Page, 59, take the Meat off your Fowl, and lay the Fowl in the Dish; let the Dish be rim'd as you were directed before, and garnish'd with potcht Eggs, Spinage, and Rashers of Bacon; strain your Liquor from the Meat, lay some of the Veal under the Fowl, with some Sippets of Bread round; scum off the Fat, make the Liquor hot, and pour it on; if there be too little, add a Ladle-full of strong Broth; pour the Ragoo of Sweet Breeds on the Breast of the Fowl, and send it up.

To dress Barbels, Pike, or Salmon, in Court Boüillon.
Poisson apprêté au Court Bouillon.

TAKE a large Barbel, or any of these, draw and clean it, but do not scale it; lay it in a Dish, and throw on it Vinegar and Salt, made scalding hot; then set your Fish-Pan over the Fire, with as much Water as you think will cover your Fish; put in some whole Pepper, Mace, three or four slic'd Onions, some Horse Raddish, a Faggot of Sweet Herbs; let it boil, then put in your Fish, with the Salt and Vinegar; first turn your Fish round, fasten the Tail in the Mouth, and put it on a Fish Drainer; when it is boil'd enough, take it up, take off all the Scales clean, and put it in your Dish. Garnish it with Parsley and Garden Cresses; send the Sauce in a Boat. Let your Sauce be as directed in Page 8.

To dress Eels a la Doube.
Anquilles à la Daube.

TAKE some of the large Silver Eels, if you cannot get them so large as you would have them; take two when clean'd, skin'd, and bon'd; take the Bone and Entrails out at the Back, lay the thick End one Way, and the thin End the other; take one or two, with the Flesh of some other Fish, and make a Force of them, season'd with Pepper, Salt, Nutmeg, Mace, Parsley, and a little Sage; take another Eel and cut it into Pieces long-ways, long enough to reach over the other two a-cross; first season them, then lay on some of your Forcing, then the Pieces a-cross, then the rest on that; so you may make your Collar as big as you please; then roll it up, and put it into a Cloth, roll it in that, tie it tight at both Ends, and bind it with Tape; then boil it in half Wine and half Water, with Half a Pint of Vinegar; let it boil an Hour, then take it up, loosen it, and tie it up tighter, by binding it a-fresh; let it hang up till cold; put the Liquor into a Pot you design to keep it in; when it and the Collar is cold take it out of the Cloth, and put them together for Use; when you use it, slice it, and send with it a Rammolade, which is made as follows, to be eaten with Fish pickled, collar'd, or any cold Fish: It is composed of Parsley, Shallot, Anchovies and Capers, shred very small, with a little Pepper, Oil, and Vinegar, or Lemon, Nutmeg, and Salt: If you please you may shred in a little Fennel, and garnish it with the same.

To Collar Eels.
Des Aquilles accommodée.

ORDER them as you did before; you may put two together if you cannot get them big enough, and cut some to lie a-cross; first wash them over with the Yolks of Eggs, and season them with Thyme, Parsley, Sage, Pepper, Salt, Nutmeg, and Mace,

Mace, the Herbs finely chopt, the Spices well beat; lay on your Pieces a-cross, and season them; likewise roll them up in a Cloth; tie and bind them as before; boil them in Salt Water and Vinegar, when enough unbind them and untie the Ends; tie them up tight, and bind them with Tape as before; hang them up till cold, then put the Pickle in a Pot that will hold them; untie them and keep them in the Pickle.

How to roast a large Eel.
Anquille large Roti.

RUB your Eel well with Salt, wash it and rub it well with a Cloth to take off the Slime, skin it down to the Tail; take out the Entrails, rub it dry, then cut Notches on each Side, an Inch from each other; then make a Force as follows: Take the Crumb of a Penny Brick, rub it through a Cullender, take Parsley, Thyme, Sweet Marjoram, Chives, an Anchovey, a little Lemon Peel, Nutmeg, Pepper, Salt, Mace, shred and beat all fine; mix it with a Slice of good Butter, and the Yolks of two Eggs; mix all well together, and fill the Incisions and the Belly of the Eel with this; draw the Skin over all, and tie it at both Ends; prick it with a large Needle or a Fork in several Places; then tie it to a Spit, and roast it, or turn it round, or broil it on a Gridiron, over a slow Charcoal Fire; turn it several Times. Dish it and garnish it with fried Parsley and Lemon; let the Sauce be Butter, Lemon, a few Capers, shred fine, with some boil'd Parsley, and a little Anchovey; you may put in a little White Wine.

Spitch-cockt Eels.
Des Auquilles Grillée.

SPitch-cockt Eels are done the same Way; leave out the Force, only make Use of the Herbs and Spices; then cut the Eels on the Sides as before; rub them well with the Spices and Herbs, and draw on the

the Skins again; tie and broil them as before; let the Sauce be Butter, Vinegar, or Lemon, with a little Anchovey.

To boil Eels.
Anquilles boülli.

SKIN and clean them; if they be small or middle Size, turn them round; if large, cut them into what Pieces you like; set on a Pan with Salt, Water, and a little Vinegar; boil them till they be pretty tender, take them up to drain; let your Sauce be Butter, Vinegar, a little Pepper, and boil'd and shred Parsley. Garnish with raw Parsley.

If you would fry them, order them as before; make a Marinade for them of Salt, Vinegar, whole Pepper, and Water; let them lie in it an Hour, take them out, flour them well, and fry them in clarified Butter. Garnish with fried Parsley; send with them a Boat of plain Butter.

To make an Eel Pye:
Paté des Anguilles.

CLEAN them, cut them into Pieces, season them with Pepper, Salt, and a little Nutmeg; lay some Butter in the Bottom of your Pye; season them with Pepper, Salt, some shred Parsley, and a little Onion; lay them in with Butter on the Top; put in a little strong Broth, with a little White Wine; close your Pye, wash it over with an Egg and a little Cream, and bake it; when it comes from the Oven, take off the Lid, scum off the Fat; put in some Gravey, Lemon, and Butter.

To stew Eels.
Anquilles etuvée.

CUT them in Pieces as before, toss them up in some clarified Butter, dridge in some Flour, put in some strong Broth and Gravey, Pepper, Salt, Anchovey, White Wine, a Faggot of Sweet Herbs,
Nut-

Nutmeg, and the Juice of a Lemon; cut some Sippets, and lay in the Bottom of your Dish; dish your Eels on them first; let them be toss'd up with a little melted Butter. Garnish with raw Parsley, &c.

To dress Eels a la Braise.
Des Anguilles à la Braise.

TAKE the largest Eels you can get, skin, gut, and clean them; cut them in Pieces, three Inches long; season them with Spices and Sweet Herbs; then cut some Slices off a Fillet of Veal, hack them with the Back of a Knife, season them likewise, and roll the Eels in them; then take a Stew-Pan that will hold them; lay some Slices of interlarded Bacon in the Bottom, with some Slices of lean Beef on that, season'd also; then lay in your Eels with some Beef season'd on them; take Care you don't make it too salt; then cover it with a Cover that has a Rim on it, set it on a Stove, with a slow Fire under, and a Fire on the Top; let it stew gently for an Hour; then make a Ragoo for them, brown another Stew-Pan with a Piece of Butter and Flour; put in a Pint of Gravey, or what Quantity you think will do for your Fish; squeeze in a Lemon, put in some shred Parsley, Capers, Morels clean'd and shred, with some pickled Mushrooms; let this be the Thickness of a Cream; take up your Eels; let them drain from the Fat, take them out of the Veal; lay them in your Dish, strain the Liquor from the Meat, scum off the Fat, put the Gravey into the Sauce, make it hot, and put it over your Eels. Garnish with Barberries and Lemon; send it hot if you please; you may keep them cold, and eat them with a Rammolade, as you will find in the Index.

To dress a Lamb's Head with the Appurtenances.
Tête d'Agneau avec la Fressure.

TAKE a Lamb's Head, cleave and clean it well, lay it to soak in warm Water, chop off the Chop Bones, then boil it; take off a Piece of the Liver to fry,

fry, and the Heart, and boil the reſt; you muſt keep the Lights down with a Beef Fork, if you have not a Fork for the Purpoſe; when it is boil'd, mince the Lights and Liver with the reſt; take off the Thropple-Pipe, then cut the Head in two, and ſeaſon one Half as you do a Veal Cutlet, and broil it; keep the other Half warm in the Pot; ſtuff and broil the Heart; ſlice and fry the Liver that you cut off; then put ſome ſtrong Broth to your Mince, with ſome boil'd Parſley, chopt with a little Onion and a Piece of Butter work'd in Flour, to thicken it; grate in ſome Nutmeg, put in ſome Salt, and a little Vinegar, toſs all together; then have ſome Raſhers of Bacon ready, Half a Dozen potcht Eggs, and ſome boil'd Spinage; put your Mince in the Diſh, firſt made hot; lay in the two Half Heads, and the Heart in the Middle, with the fried Liver round and the Raſhers of Bacon; then lay on the Spinage on the Rim of the Diſh, and the Eggs on that; ſend all up hot, with a Boat of drawn Butter. You may fry the Brains; blanch the Tongue and ſlit it, and lay it on each Side of the Heart, and the fried Brains round.

To roaſt a Calf's Head.
Tête de Veau roti.

LET it be cut off with the Skin on, lay it to ſoak in warm Water, waſh it well, ſcald off the Hair, ſplit it, take out the ſnotty Bones; cut out the Tongue, blanch it and ſkin it; waſh the Head in ſeveral Waters; take the Brains and clean them; mince the Tongue with the Brains, ſome Parſley, Thyme, Sage, Salt, and Nutmeg; add ſome Suet ſhred fine, with a Score of Oiſters; mix all together with ſome grated Bread, a little Vinegar, and the Yolks of three or four Eggs; put all within the Head, firſt cut off the Chops with a Cleaver, and fill the Places where the Brains come out; let the Eyes be taken out, and an Iron Skewer be put through, and at the thin End of the Chops likewiſe to faſten it to the Spit; lard one Side;

raiſe

raife up the Skin of the other Side, and put in fome Forc'd-meat, fkewer it down tight again, fpit and roaft it, and bafte it well with Butter; then make a Ragoo with Oifters, and put it in the Bottom of your Difh; untie and pull out the Skewers, take out the Stuffing and mix it with Gravey and Butter for the Sauce; fry fome Oifters to garnifh it with, and Rafhers of Bacon, with Barberries and Lemon; fo you may take which Way you like beft, or you may bake it in an Oven; rub it over with a Yolk of an Egg, and dridge it with Bread Crumbs; obferve to lay it flat in your Difh, with the Flefh-fide upwards.

To drefs Chickens the Polifh Way.
Poulets à la Polonoife.

CLEAN, trufs, and finge them; lard them with fome Ham and fome fat Bacon; make a Stuffing of their Livers with fat Bacon, Sweet Herbs, Spices, and the Yolks of Eggs, fill their Bellies with it; fpit and roaft them, and bafte with Butter when they are near enough; take a clean Fire-fhovel, make it hot, lay on the Shovel fome fat Bacon, and bafte them with it; but take Care you do not black them when they are enough. Difh them with a hot Rammolade, as beforemention'd in Page 86. Garnifh them with Lemon and raw Parfley.

To make Italian Cream.
Crême à l'Italiene.

TAKE half Milk and half Cream, (to what Quantity you pleafe) according to the Bignefs of your Difh; boil it with a Stick of Cinnamon, fweeten it to your Tafte; if a Quart, take the Yolks of fix Eggs beat with with a little Salt, and ftrain it three or four Times through a Sieve; then mince fome Citron; put fome of your Cream into your Difh; fet it very even in a Baking-pan, over a Stove, with a flow Fire; cover it, let it ftand till it be hardened; then lay on fome of your candied Peel; then put in fome more of your

Cream,

Cream, let it harden likewife; then lay on fome more Peel, and put on the Remainder of the Cream; ftick the Top with fome more Peel, and fome Almonds blanch'd and cut in four; lay on the Cover and put on fome Fire on the Top; let it be colour'd of a brown Colour; take Care you do not burn it at the Bottom, a very fmall Fire will do: This will do for a Difh in a Defert, or for a fecond Courfe Difh. You may bake Tanzey Cuftards or Tarts, or any fine Pudding, this Way.

As there are feveral Ways to drefs Eggs, I fhall mention them here, they being very ferviceable to add to a Table when there is a Scarcity of other Things: They are proper to eat with feveral other Difhes as I fhall mention.

Eggs in Cramp-pine, for a Side Difh.
Des Oeufs en Cramp-pine.

TAKE two Sweet Breeds, blanch and cut them in fquare Bits; a Slice off a well-fed Ham, a Quarter of an Inch thick, cut in Dice; take Half a Score Morels, a few Mufhrooms, and an Anchovey; clean and mince them fine, with a little Shallot, tofs them up in a little clarified Butter, dridge in a little Flour, put in a Pint of good Gravey, grate in a little Nutmeg, fqueeze in Half a Lemon, fet it to ftew over a flow Fire Half an Hour; then fet it off, and take ten Eggs, leave out five Whites, add to them a little White Wine, with a little Salt, (but firft tafte your Ragoo if it won't make it falt enough) beat them and ftrain them through a Sieve into your Ragoo, it being cold; mix all together, then take a Stew-pan that will hold it, and butter it; then lay fome Rafhers of Bacon all round the Sides of your Pan, an Inch off one another; lay a Piece of Bacon in the Bottom of your Pan, cut like a Star; then lay it exactly for the Points to go againft each Rafher of Bacon; then fcald fome Parfley, and fhred it fine; boil four Eggs and mince them fine alfo, and lay the Parfley between the

Rafhers

ART of COOKERY.

Rashers of Bacon; then next to that lay some of your Eggs, then Parsley again, so alternately; then having some good Forc'd-meat, lay it over all in thin Pieces so that none of the Bottom can be seen; then wash it all within with the Yolks of Eggs; then put in your Ragoo and Eggs, cover it with the Caul of Veal, close it tight all round, and bake it; then loosen it with the Point of a Knife, lay your Dish on it, and turn it into it. Garnish it with raw Parsley, and Seville Orange cut in Quarters.

Poach'd Eggs in Gravey.
Des Oeufs au jus.

TAKE six or eight Eggs, (them that are new laid) break them carefully into a Vessel, set a Stew-pan over the Fire with hard Water, when it boils pour in your Eggs all together, then with your Egg-slice stir them round gently, and the Whites will the better wrap round the Yolks; when the Whites are hardened, take them up and lay them in your Dish. Garnish the Dish with boil'd Spinage and Rashers of Bacon; then having Half a Pint of good Gravey, made hot, with some Pepper, Vinegar, and a little Onion shred fine, and a little Salt; strain it through a Sieve upon them, send them up hot.

To dress Eggs with Verjuice.
Des Oeufs au Verjus.

BEAT twelve Eggs, or what Number you please; put a Piece of Butter into your Stew-Pan, with a little Verjuice, Salt, and Nutmeg; stir all together till it be thick; then having some thin Toasts laid in the Bottom of your Dish; dish the Eggs on them, and garnish them with Seville Orange and chopt Parsley.

To dress Eggs in Butter.
Des Oeufs frioient en Batter.

BOIL Spinage to the Bigness of two Eggs, shred it fine, take as much fat Bacon that is as big as one

one Egg, shred it fine, boil eight Eggs hard, mince them, that is, the Yolks; put all into a Mortar, with the Yolks of four raw Eggs, grate in a little Nutmeg, put in a little beaten Pepper, with a Spoonful of Vinegar; salt it to your Taste, beat it to a Paste, take an earthen Pan that is not too big, cut a Piece of fat Bacon thin and round, to fit the Bottom of the Pan; make up the Compound, and lay it in; leave Half an Inch betwixt it and the Sides of the Pan; butter the Sides, and lay in Rashers of Bacon all round; then make a Batter of Flour, two Yolks of Eggs, a little Beef Suet shred fine, with a little Salt; make it into a stiff Batter with Cream, and beat it well; put it in the Pot, and cover the Meat in the Middle, an Inch over the Top; bake it, when it is bak'd turn it into your Dish, and garnish it with your Whites of Eggs that were left off the Yolks, shred fine. Let the Sauce be Butter, Gravey, with some Vinegar, White Wine thicken'd with a Brown. You may mince a little Ham, and a Sweet-breed, if you have them.

To make Rhenish Wine Cream.

Crême au Vin de Rhin.

TAKE a Pint of Rhenish, a Stick of Cinnamon; put it into a Stew-Pan, with Half a Pound of Loaf Sugar; while this is boiling, beat six Eggs well with a Whisk, and strain them through a Sieve, add to them a Quarter of a Pound of Sugar, beat and sifted; take your Wine off the Fire, let it stand till almost cold, put in your Eggs by Degrees, keep stirring, when all is in set it on the Fire, keep stirring it very fast till it be the Thickness of a Cream; squeeze in a Lemon, put in a little Orange-flower Water. Put it into Glasses.

To preserve Asparagus.

Des Asperges Confit.

CUT off the hard Part of the Stalk, boil the rest in Butter and Salt a Minute; put them into
Water

Water till cold, then drain them dry; put them into a Vessel that will hold them without breaking, boil Half Water and Half Vinegar, and put to them enough to cover them; then render some Beef Suet, and put it to the Butter and Salt you fried them in; cut a Paper to fit the Vessel you put them in, and butter it; put on the Fat to cover all over, that no Air can get in; and keep them in a Place, not too hot nor too cold; when you would use them, first soak them in warm Water.

N. B. Put in a Handful of Salt to the Vinegar and Water, when boiling.

To make Dutch Beef.
Beuf à l' Hollandoise.

TAKE ten Pounds of Buttock Beef that is well fed, salt it with common Salt 24 Hours; put away the bloody Brine, then take four Ounces of Salt Petre pounded, and Half a Pint of Bay Salt, Half a Pound of coarse Sugar, and a little Cochineal; mix all together, being beat and dried by the Fire; rub the Beef well, and rub and turn it every Day for three Weeks; then tie it in a coarse Cloth, and bind it tight with Tape, and hang it in a Chimney to dry; turn it up-side down every Day till well dried; then boil it in Pump-Water till tender; slice or scrape it. It is commonly eaten with Bread and Butter.

To candy Angelica.
Angelique confit.

TAKE the tender Stalks, boil them in hard Water till tender; put them in cold Water, and let them lie to cool; then take off the Skin by raising it with a Needle, or carefully scrape it off with a Penknife; then put in some Vine, or Curranberry Leaves in the Bottom of a Brass Pan; lay in your Angelica, put in a Spoonful of Vitriol Water, with a little Allum; lay on more Leaves, cover them with hard Water, put on the Cover of the Pan, set them on a slow

slow Charcoal Fire, but don't let it boil but simmer till it be very green; then put them in cold Water again, and shift it three or four Times; then take double the Weight of Sugar, if a Pound, Half a Pint of Water; boil and scum it, dry your Angelica, and tie it in Knots, or put it in what Form you please; put it into the Syrup, and boil it till clear; put it into a Pot that will hold it, cover it down when cold, first cut a Piece of Writing Paper that will fit the Pot; dip it in Brandy, put Paper and Leather over that. I shall give Directions for candying it, and some others after.

To preserve green Apricots.

Apricots confit.

GAther them when you can easily run a Pin through them; let them be the greenest you can get; take a Flannel Cloth, wet it and dip it in Salt, and rub them till you have rub'd all the Ruffness off them; first put them into cold Water, then put them into fresh hard Water, with some Leaves, as you did the Angelica, order'd the same Way, set them on a slow Fire to simmer till tender and green; then take them out, and put them into cold hard Water, shift them five or six Times; take their Weight and Half their Weight of double-refin'd Sugar, pound and sift it; make a Syrup of their Weight of Sugar with Half a Pint of Water to a Pound of Sugar; boil it and scum it, let it stand to cool, then put in the Apricots, set them on the Fire, and let them boil up; keep stirring them and add the rest of the Sugar by Degrees; keep stirring them till they be clear; if they offer to crack, take them off and set them on again, keep adding the Sugar till all the Sugar is in, and they very clear; put them in Pots order'd as you did the Angelica. If you would candy the Angelica or Apricots, after they have lain some Time in the Syrup; take them out, and let them drain from the Syrup, dridge them with double-refin'd Sugar, pounded and sifted;
lay

lay them on wired Sieves, and dry them in a drying Stove or in the Sun, or in a flow Oven; turn and sift on more Sugar till they are candied and dry; paper a Box with Writing Paper, and lay Paper over them; keep them in a dry Place.

To make Sagoe Soop.

Potage de Sagoe.

TAKE a Quarter of a Pound of Sagoe, wash it clean, put to it two Quarts of Water, a Stick of Cinnamon, and a little Sugar; let it boil till tender, then put in a Bottle of red Port, grate in a little Nutmeg, keep it stirring or it will set to the Bottom, add more Sugar to your Taste; then take two Naples Biscuits, slice them thin, and let them dry by the Fire; put the Biscuit in the Dish you design to put your Soop in; let the Soop boil five Minutes after the Wine is in. Dish it up, pare the Rind off a Lemon, and put in five or six Slices; send it away quick, for if it stands there will rise a Scum.

To pickle Asparagus.

Des Asperges confit au Vinaigre.

TAKE off the Leaves to the Bud at the End, and cut them about two Inches long; put them in Salt and Water, strong enough to bear an Egg; shift them every other Day for nine Days; then boil some Salt and Water, and put to them; cover them close, and they will turn yellow; then drain them from that Pickle, and put as much Vinegar to them as will cover them; let them on a slow Fire cover'd close, that no Steam can come out, and they will turn green; be sure you do not let them boil; if they be not green enough the first Time, let them stand in the Pan till the next Day, and set them on again, and they will soon be green enough; let the Pan be a Brass one you green them in; you may green them in Salt and Water if you please, and put in a

little

little Vitriol Water, a Bit of Allum, and use Leaves as you did with the Apricots; then boil your Vinegar and Spices, and let it cool; dry your Asparagus, and put it into your Pickle in a Jar, and tie it down with a Bladder and Leather; when you take any out use a little wooden Ladle; the Spices are Pepper, Mace, Ginger, and Dill.

To make a Sagoe Pudding.
Boudin de Sagoe.

TAKE a Quarter of a Pound, wash and boil it tender in Milk, take Care it does not set to the Bottom; if it sticks to the Bottom, shift it into a clean Stew-Pan, first renge it in Water, and put in a Stick of Cinnamon, keep it stirring till it be thick, take out the Cinnamon, beat ten Eggs, leave out four Whites; put in a little Salt, and sweeten it with fine Sugar to your Taste, strain the Eggs through a Sieve, put in a little Salt, grate in a little Nutmeg, mix all together; butter a fine Cloth, tie it up tight, and boil it an Hour: The Sauce is a little White Wine, Sugar, Butter, and the Juice of a Seville Orange, drawn up thick; you may bake it if you please, put in a Border of Puff-Paste round the Dish; adding Half a Quarter of a Pound of melted Butter, mixt well with the Pudding; you may put in a few Currans, laying on some candied Orange, Lemon, or Citron Peel slic'd thin; Half an Hour will bake it.

To make Sagoe Cream.
Créme au Sagoe.

WASH it in three or four Waters, boil it tender as you did for the Pudding; lay it on a Sieve to drain, then boil as much Cream as you think will do; let it stand to cool, put in the Sagoe, sweeten it to your Taste; take out the Cinnamon, you may beat Half a Dozen bitter Almonds, tie them in a Muslin Rag, and boil them in the Cream; or you may

may put in a little Orange-flower Water or Rose Water, as you like; mix it well and fill your Glasses, or send it up in a Glass Bason.

To make Wigs.
Petites Gateaux.

TAKE a Pound and a Half of Flour, Half a Pint of Milk, a Quarter of a Pound of Butter, warm the Milk and Butter, let it be Blood warm; then put in a Quarter of a Pint of good Ale Yeast; mix two Ounces of Sugar with your Flour, and a Quarter of an Ounce of Caraway Seeds bruiz'd, a little Salt strew'd in your Liquid, and make it into Paste; make them up and lay them on Tins; let them stand to rise, wash them over with the Yolk of an Egg and a little Cream; you may strew on them some Caraway Comfits, or bake them plain; Half an Hour will bake them.

To make Almond Cakes.
Gateaux d' Amandes.

BLanch a Pound of Almonds in warm Water, beat them fine in a Marble Mortar, keep adding a little Rose Water, add Half a Pound of Sugar by Degrees finely sifted; add the Whites of two Eggs, and likewise two Spoonfuls of Flour, beat all well together; butter your Pans, put them in, dridge them with fine Sugar, and bake them of a light Brown; then draw them out, and turn them on Papers, then set them in a little again and they will be much whiter. Keep them in a dry Place.

To make Cowslip Wine.
Vin aux Bouillons.

TAKE three Gallons of Water and three Pounds of Sugar; boil all an Hour, scum it very well; then put it into a Cask, with the Rinds of three Lemons and six Quarts of Cowslips pickt from the Stalks; cut a Slice off a Penny Loaf, and toast it well on each

Side; let it cool, and spread on it some good Yeast as you would butter it, and put it into the Cask after you have stirr'd it; the Casks should have a square Bung Hole; or you may put in two Spoonfuls of Yeast, as it is in Goodness, but be sure you do not put in too much; but it will not keep so well nor fine so well without some Yeast; so I take a Toast order'd as above to be the best Way; you may work it in a Stand if you have not a convenient Cask; stir it with a Stick, let it work for three or four Days, then tap it with a Basket Cock, or put a thin Cloth over the End of the Cock; draw it into another Vessel, put to it a Quart of good Brandy, and the Juice of three Lemons; put in a Quarter of a Pound of Loaf Sugar, and a Quarter of a Pound of Raisins ston'd; let it stand for three Weeks, and bottle it; set it in a cold Place, it will keep a Year. Some use Mallaga or Mountain, instead of Brandy; and some make it without either, for present Use.

To make Syrup of Violets, Clove Pinks, or Gilliflowers.

CUT off the colour'd Part of the Flowers from the White, and sprinkle them with Water only, to wet them; put them into a Jar, cork it, and tie it tight down that no Air can get in; set it in a Pan of Water, and put a Weight on the Top that it may not fall on one Side; let it boil for two Hours, strain out the Juice to a Pint; put a Pound and a Half of fine Sugar to it; set it on the Fire in a Silver Saucepan; stir and scum it till it begins to boil; put it into Gally-Pots, wet a Bladder in Brandy and lay on it, with a Leather over it, and tie it when cold.

Another Way.

TAKE a Quarter of a Pound of Flowers clipt from the white Part, and put them into an Earthen Vessel; boil a Pint of Spring Water, put it to the Flowers, and let it stand close cover'd an Hour,

then

then strain the Liquor from the Flowers, and put to it two Pounds of double-refined Sugar, pounded and sifted; then set it on a clear Coal Fire to simmer, but not boil; let it stand to cool, and order it as you did the other.

For Marygold Syrup, boil the Flowers in Water, that is, two Ounces to a Pint, and use a Pound of Sugar the same as above, or boil the Water, and put it to them two Hours.

To make Birch Wine.
Vin de bouleau.

TO every Gallon of Birch Water take two Pounds of Loaf Sugar, the Juice and Rind of two Seville Oranges, and a Pint of good Brandy, boil it half an Hour, scum it, let it stand to cool and settle; pour it into a clean Tub or Earthen Vessel, put to it a little good Ale Yeast, let it work twelve Hours close cover'd, then tun it into a Vessel; let it stand six Weeks, and bottle it; keep it in a cool Place; it will be fit to drink in a Month or six Months.

To make Naples Biscuit.
Bisquit de Naples.

TAKE a Pound of the finest Flour, and a Pound of fine Sugar finely powder'd, mix them together, then beat ten Eggs, and strain them through a Sieve, stir and beat them with a wooden Beater for an Hour; then paper your Pans, fill them three Parts full, and bake them half an Hour; you may add an Ounce of double-refined Sugar pounded and sifted, and half an Ounce of Caraway Seeds bruis'd, and two Spoonfuls of Rose Water, make them into what Forms you please, and bake them as above; or you may leave out the Seeds, and strew them with Caraway Comfits.

N. B. The longer you beat Biscuit or fine Cakes, the better they are.

To make a Veal Pye.
Des Oeufs au verjus.

CUT some Slices of a Fillet of Veal, hack them with the Back of a Knife, wash them with the Yolks of Eggs, season them with Pepper, Salt, Nutmeg, Mace, Thyme, Parsley, Bread Crumbs, and a little Lemon-Peel mine'd fine, as also the Thyme and Parsley; let the Collops be all of a Size and an even Number, when season'd with the aforesaid Ingredients; mix all together, roll them up like little Collars, then cut the Kell in as many Pieces, egg them, and roll the Veal in them; your Paste being made, and the Dish sheeted, butter the Bottom, and lay them in; then cut off some Tops of Asparagus, and blanch them in Salt and Water, and some Cabbage Lettice cut in Dice; then boil some Eggs hard, and make some Forc'd-Meat Balls; lay them in between the Rolls of Veal, then one of Yolks of Eggs opposite, then more Yolks, next to that Asparagus, the same opposite again, then Forc'd-Meat Balls as before, then the Lettice, so they will lie in eight Parts, one to answer the other; lay Butter over all, lid it, and bake it; when baked have a Ragoo of Morels ready, with some pickled Mushrooms; cut off the Lid, pour it all over, lay it on again, and send it to the Table.

MAY.

MAY.

How to make a green Peas Soop.
Potage purée vert.

MAKE your Stock as directed for Peas Soop for February; take blue Peas instead of white, if you have not Plenty of green Peas, and take three or four Handfuls of the Tops of green Peas, with the same Quantity of Spinage, pound them in a Mortar, and squeeze out the Juice through a fine thin Cloth; then shred a Handful of green Mint, and take some Spray of Asparagus, cut it as far as it is tender the Bigness of Peas, and blanch it in Salt and Water; then cut some young Onions, likewise your Asparagus being strain'd off, take a Quarter of a Pound of Butter and put it into a Stew-Pan, big enough to hold the Quantity of Soop you would have; dust in some Flour, put in your Asparagus, Onions, and Mint, toss it up and moisten it with some of your Stock, season it with a little Pepper and Salt to your Taste, keep adding more of the Stock, and stir it from the Bottom; every Time you put any in let it simmer till it is smooth and as thick as you would have it; then put in your Greening and stir it, but don't let it boil; scum off the Fat; dish it with a boil'd Chicken in the Middle, and diced Bread fry'd in Butter: Garnish your Dish with boil'd Spinage and Rashers of Bacon; for this Soop, make your Stock of green Peas if you can get them. I mention this Way in case you should have a Desire to make a Soop of this Kind sooner than Peas are plentiful: It may be taken for the greater Rarity.

To dress a Brit, commonly called Turbat, with Lobster Sauce.
Turbot appreté.

SCRAPE and clean it; rub it with Salt to take off the Slime, and wash it well; put it into a convenient Thing that will hold it, with a Bottom under it, and cover it with hard Water; put in a Handful of Salt, put on the Cover, and let it boil gently for half an Hour; if it be a large one it will take more; take it up and let it drain; then take one or two Lobsters, chuse them Berry ones, and bruise the Berries in a Marble Mortar, with the Juice of a Lemon; take out the Meat from the Tails and Claws; cut it into small Dice, take a Pint of Fish Stock as in Page 8, put in the Lobster with the Spawn, if a large Fish and a Pound of Butter; dust in some Flour to make it of a proper Thickness; dish up your Fish, and garnish with Horse-raddish, Lemon, and Barberries.

To make a Rice-Pudding.
Boudin au Ris.

TAKE half a Pound, wash and pick it clean, put it to boil tender in three Pints of Milk, keep it stirring now and then with a wooden Ladle, or it will set to the Bottom; when thick enough, take it off; (you may put in a Stick of Cinnamon, and two or three Blades of Mace in the boiling) then beat seven Eggs, and strain them through a Sieve; grate in half a Nutmeg, melt a Quarter of a Pound of Butter, wash half a Pound of Currans, rub them dry, and mix all together; rim your Dish with Puff-Paste, strew in a little Salt, put it into the Dish; lay on the Top some candid Lemon-Peel, or Citron cut thin, bake it an Hour in a moderate Oven: You may put a cut Cover on it if you please, as directed before: You may make it plain, leaving out the Currans and the Sweet-Meats; the rest, the same as above-mentioned.

ART of COOKERY.

To order and roast a Chine of Mutton.
Echine de Mouton roti.

CUT it handsomely, and skin it; put in two Iron Skewers thro' the hollow Part next the Rump; then take a larger Iron Skewer and put it into the other End of the Mutton where the Back Marrow is, and drive it in pretty tight; take a large Wood Skewer, and cut a Slit in it at the thick End; take a double Packthread, and place it in the Slit, so as you may draw it through the Meat as with a Pack-needle; if you have a Pack-needle it will do better, begin at the under Side within six Inches of the thin End; as nigh the Back Bone as you can, draw the Packthread half through, then put it through again on the other Side of the Back Bone; leave both the Ends long enough to tie to the Spit; cut off the Needle, and take your Spit and spit it through the two Skewers at the Rump End; put it as far on the Spit as you would have it to suit your Fire, then tie it tight to the Spit, with the Skewer at the other End; then lay the Spit on the Table with the Back of the Mutton down, press the Spit tight down, and tie the Packthread that you drew through the Mutton to the Spit very tight; then turn your Meat and paper it; if you have a ballance Skewer put it on the Spit to make it turn even; lay it down to roast at a good Distance from the Fire; it will take two Hours to roast leisurely; if large, two Hours and a half: You may loosen the Fat from the Lean on one Side, begin close to the Chine, and with a sharp Knife skin it three Inches down towards the Side, but don't cut it off, nor through; then cut out the Lean and the Fillets out of the Inside, and prepare it as directed in the Receipt for a Pigeroone of Mutton; lay it on the Chine, and cover it with the Fat; set it before the Fire, and dridge it with Flour; dish it with Gravey in the Dish, and garnish with Horse-raddish and Pickles.

To force Chickens.
Poulets forcie.

TAKE the Galls off their Livers, and mince them with Sweet-herbs, compos'd as before, with Pepper, Nutmeg, and a little Salt, a Bit of lean and fat Bacon, a little Beef Suet, a few Bread Crumbs, shred all fine, and put in two or three Yolks of Eggs; mix all well together, and force the Bellies and Crops with this; skewer and spit them; tie them at the Vents and Necks, cover them with Bards of Bacon, and Paper over that; tie all on with Packthread, and roast them gently an Hour; let the Sauce be Lemon, Gravey, and Butter drawn up pretty thick.

To boil a Neat's Tongue.
Langue de Beuf bouilli.

BOIL it two Hours, if a large one two Hours and a half, skin it, and cut it to stand handsomely in the Dish; get some young Cabbage and Turnips boil'd and laid handsomely round it, with melted Butter in a small Boat, or you may roast it as directed before.

Rabbits boil'd with Asparagus A-la-cream.
Lapins bouilli aux Asperges.

TRUSS them proper for boiling, and boil them in hard Water, but wash them in three or four warm Waters to take the Blood out the better; whilst they are boiling, take a hundred Asparagus, cut off the green Ends, and take off the Leaves as directed for boiling; boil them pretty tender in Salt and Water, then make a Lare for them; take half a Pint of Cream, the Yolks of two Eggs, a little good strong Broth, a Piece of Butter work'd in Flour, a little grated Nutmeg, two Spoonfuls of White Wine, the Juice of half a Lemon, half an Anchovey shred fine, with a small Onion; put all into a Stew-Pan with the Asparagus Tops, keep stirring them till they be the Thick-

Thickness of Cream; take Care it don't boil for fear it may curdle; dish your Rabbits, and pour over them the Lare, and garnish with Barberries and Lemon.

To make Veal Olives.
Olives de Veau.

CUT eight Slices off a Leg of Veal as broad as four Fingers, as thick as a Crown Piece, and all of a Size; hack them with the Back of a large Knife, wash them over with the Yolks of Eggs, season them with Sweet-herbs, Salt, and Nutmeg; lay on some Forc'd-Meat, made as in Page 26; roll them up like little Collars, then cut some thin Slices of Bacon (which is call'd Bards of Bacon) the Size of the Slices of Veal, tie them round with Packthread, lay them in a convenient Thing to bake, wash them over with Eggs, and dridge them with Bread Crumbs; bake them an Hour in a moderate Oven; then make a Ragoo for them as for brown Veal Collops; lay them handsomely in the Dish: Garnish with Lemon and pickled Mushrooms.

To marinade and dress Lambs Trotters.
Pieds d'Agneau marinée.

TAKE what Quantity you please, wash them and scald them as you do Calves' Feet, then boil them tender; take out the long Bones, slit them in two down the Middle, put them into an earthen Pan, and put to them two Parts of Water and one of Vinegar, some Mace, whole Pepper, and a Faggot of Sweet-herbs, a large Onion slic'd, and a sufficient Quantity of Salt; let them lie in this four Hours, then take them out, flour them well, and fry them brown in clarified Beef or Mutton Suet; let your Sauce be Gravey and Butter drawn up pretty thick; grate in a little Nutmeg: Garnish with fry'd Parsley and Seville Oranges cut in Quarters.

To make Ramkins.
Ramquins a faire.

TAKE three French Rolls, cut them even in the Middle the Top from the Bottom; take out some of the Crumbs, rub them all over with Butter, and set them in an Oven two Minutes; take them out; then take a Quarter of a Pound of the Crumb of an old well tasted mellow Cheese, the Yolks of four raw Eggs and one White, half a Quarter of a Pound of good Butter; put all into a Marble Mortar, with a little grated Nutmeg, and two Spoonfuls of White Wine, beat all to a Paste; then fill the Loaves and set them in the Oven, and bake them of a gold Colour; send them up hot.

To make Goosberry Cream.
Crême aux Groseilles.

TAKE a Quart of Goosberries, scald them, and rub them thro' a coarse Sieve with a wooden Spoon; put as much fine Sugar to it as will make it very sweet; take a Quart of Cream and boil it with a Stick of Cinnamon, and a Piece of Lemon-Peel; then beat four Yolks of Eggs, strain them, and put the Cream strain'd to them; put in a little Sugar, clean your Pan, put it into it again, and keep stirring it with a Whisk till it boils; take it off, and let it stand to cool; your Goosberries being cool likewise, mix all together, and fill your Glasses.

To make a green Apricot Tart.
Tourte d'Abricots verd.

GAther as many as will fill the Tart-Pan you propose, but try them first if you can run a Pin easily thro' them, then they will do, and order them as you'll see for Preserving; fill your Tart-Pan, first sheet it, then put in a sufficient Quantity of fine Sugar, close it, cut the Lid all round within half an Inch of the

Rim,

ART *of* COOKERY.   109

Rim, then cut it acrofs and acrofs to make it in four Parts, then cut each Part in two again, and that will make it in eight Parts; then ice it, and bake it in a moderate Oven an Hour; take off the Lid Piece by Piece, firſt part them with a Knife, and lay them in the Diſh you deſign to ſend it up in; place them as you would Sippets, the Points to come to the Outſide of the Diſh; then take out the Fruit out of the Tart and the Syrup, and put in the Fruit again without the Syrup; take half a Pint of Cream and a little Milk, boil it, and ſet it to cool; then beat a good Handful of Spinage without waſhing, and pound it in a Mortar; ſtrain or ſqueeze it thro' a Cloth, and put it to your Cream; put in enough to make it very green; then beat four Yolks of Eggs, ſtrain them in, and ſweeten it to your Taſte; put in a little Orange Flower Water, ſtir all together, put it into a clean Stew-Pan, ſet it on the Fire, and ſtir it with a Whiſk till it is the Thickneſs of Cream, put it into your Tart, but don't quite cover your Fruit, then ſet it in the Diſh in the Middle of the Lid, when cold ſend it up: If your Apricots prove too hard, take preſerved ones. This Greening is properly call'd a Newil.

If you rim a Diſh with Puff-Paſte and take a Pint of Cream, a Pint of Milk, 12 Yolks of Eggs, and Spinage Juice, ſufficient to make it very green, and Eggs according to the Quantity of Juice, put in a good Piece of Butter, and prepare it as you are directed above; fill your Diſh, bake it, and ſtick it with candied Lemon-Peel cut in thin long its; it is call'd a Lemon Newil; inſtead of Orange Flower Water, ſqueeze in a little Lemon Juice, if ſtuck with Orange-Peel, and uſe Orange Juice, it is call'd Orange Newil; if ſtuck with blanch'd Almonds, it is call'd an Almond Newil.

To ice China-Oranges.
Oranges de la Chine Galcée.

TAKE a sharp Pen-knife and cut a little Bit out of the End, and take all the Peel off in Slips, but take Care you do i't cut thro' the white Peel to let out the Juice; if you do, you will spoil it for this Design; then beat up some Whites of Eggs to a Froth, and roll the Oranges in it; then having some double-refin'd Sugar beat and sifted, roll the Oranges in it, and set them in a slow Oven to dry: You may blow Eggs and roll them in the Eggs, then in small colour'd Comfits, dry'd; stop one Hole, and fill them with some Newil, with a small Funnel, and set them upright in fine Sugar; or you may fill them with Custard or Flummery; observe how the Newil is made in the last Receipt.

Turkey Figs in Syrups.
Figues de Turquei confit.

CHUSE the best you can get; set them on the Fire in warm Water; let them boil softly till they be plump; take them out to dry and cool; to a Dozen take half a Pint of Water, and half a Pound of fine Sugar, boil and scum it; put in your Figs, and let them boil in it till they be thoroughly penetrated with the Syrup; squeeze in a little Juice of Lemon, and put in a little Orange Flower Water; give them another boil, and they are fit for Use.

As to the Remainder of the Bill of Fare look for the Receipts in their proper Places.

To boil Peas.
Des Pois bouilli.

SHILL them, set on some hard Water on the Fire and make it boil, put in your Peas; tie up some Mint in a Bundle, and boil it with them; when they are tender enough strain them from the Water; put them into a Stew-Pan with a Piece of Butter, dust

in

in a little Flour, set them on the Fire, toss them up till the Butter be melted, strinkle in a little Salt, dish them up, chop the Mint, and garnish your Dish with them ; or you may send them (without tossing up) with a Cup of drawn Buttter in the Middle.

To stew Peas.
Des Pois etuvée.

TAKE what Quantity you please, put a Piece of Butter in your Stew-Pan ; put in your Peas with an Onion shred, and some Cabbage Lettice shred ; put in a few Pepper Corns and a Blade or two of Mace, with Sweet-herbs ; set it on a slow Fire, take care it don't burn, moisten them with a little Water boiling hot, keep repeating till tender ; then put in a little good Gravey, salt them to your Taste, work a Piece of Butter in Flour to thicken them, toss them up, let them be the Thickness of a Cream ; take out your Sweet-herbs, grate in a little Nutmeg ; dish them, and garnish them with Rashers of Bacon : The French put in Cream and Sugar ; but that I don't approve of.

Another Way : Prepare your Peas as before, and when they are tender put in strong Broth, with a little Shreding in it ; leave out the Gravey ; put in half a Pint of Cream : Dish and garnish them as before.

Fricandeaux of Pigeons.
De Pigeons en Fricandeaux.

PUT their Legs in their Bodies as for boiling ; cut them down the Back ; put a Skewer thro' them to keep them open ; singe and lard them with Bacon ; fry them brown in clarified Butter ; stew them tender in Gravey, and make a Ragoo for them as for ragoo'd Veal : Take out the Skewers.

To dress a Pike the Dutch Way.
Brochets à l'Hollandi.

SCALE, gut, and wash it, clean it, cut it in Slices as you do Cod-fish for Crimping, that is about an Inch thick, put it into hard Water an Hour, then set on a Pan with hard Water, and a pretty deal of Salt, some slic'd Horse-raddish, whole Pepper, three or four Blades of Mace, a slic'd Onion, a Faggot of Sweet-herbs, and some Vinegar ; let it boil fifteen Minutes, lay a Napkin handsomely in a Dish ; tie the Head with Packthread before you boil it ; dish the Head in the Middle, lay the Slices round, and green Parsley about it ; let the Sauce be Lemon and Butter, or you may send it in with Sauce as directed in Page 8 : They use oil'd Butter for Sauce in Holland : Send the Sauce up in Boats set in with the Fish. Cod-fish is drest the same Way.

To broil Whitens Lord Exeter's Way, (whom I had the Honour to serve.)
Des Merlans Grillé.

GUT, and rub them dry ; clean, and flour them ; rub on the Flour with your Hand ; light some Charcoal and lay it on the Hearth : If you have not a convenient Place for that Purpose, set on your Gridiron, and lay on your Whitens ; broil them leisurely, turn them two or three Times, take Care they don't scorch ; take one Anchovey, shred it fine with a little Onion, put it into a Stew-Pan, with half a Pint of good Red Port, squeeze in half a Lemon, grate in a little Nutmeg, let it simmer a little, slice half a Pound of Butter, dust in a little Flour, and draw it up to the Thickness of a Cream ; dish your Whitens, and set the Sauce in a Boat in the Middle : Garnish with fry'd Parsley, Lemon, &c.

Lobsters in Jelly.
Des Ecrevice de mer en gellé.

FIRST prepare a strong Stock of Calves Feet and Icing-glass; put to it some Mace, whole Pepper, Vinegar, Salt, with the Whites of three or four Eggs well beat, stir all together, set it on the Fire to boil till it breaks, run it thro' a Jelly Bag and it will be as clear as Rock Water; then put a little in the Bottom of the Pot you design for your Lobsters, let it stand to cool; then lay in some of your Lobster with slic'd Lemon pickt, Fennel cut, and lay it in a pretty Form, so continue till you have laid in all; then fill it up with Jelly, let it stand to be very cold, set it in warm Water to loosen, and turn it into the Dish you design to send it in; so you may order Shrimps, Prawns, Crawfish, or any small Fish: Clean your small Fish, and put them into Salt Water and Vinegar, set them on a slow Fire to simmer, but not boil, for fear they should break; take them up carefully and lay them on a Drainer to drain and cool; then order the Pot as you did for your Lobsters, then lay in your Fish with Fennil and Lemon as before, but place the Fish with their Backs downwards; fill your Pot with the same Sort of Jelly as you order'd for the Lobsters, turn it out as you did the other, then the Fish will look as if they were swimming.

To make a Ham Pye.
Paté de jambon.

BOIL your Ham pretty tender, skin it, and when it is cold take out the Bones and shape it handsomely; then raise a Coffin, (or make it the French Way) paper it, lay Butter on the Top, and close it; bake it for two Hours; if to be eat hot, take off the Lid, and take off as much Fat as you can, and put in a Ragoo of Sweet-breads as before directed.

A Pye may be made of Beef the same Way; first
brase

braſe your Beef, and faſhion it as you would have it for a Pye made as above, or in a Diſh as you like; ſeaſon it with Pepper and Salt, put in ſome good Gravey, cloſe it, and bake it three or four Hours as it is in Bigneſs: Garniſh it as you think proper; when your Pye is bak'd, cut a Hole in the Lid, and put in a Ragoo as you like; ſee Ragoos.

To make a Patty of Calves Brains.
Paté de Cervilles de tête de Veau.

WASH, clean, and boil the Brains, with ſome Parſley ſhred fine; chop the Brains a little, put to them a little Pepper, Salt, and Nutmeg, with a little Vinegar; then blanch ſome Aſparagus Tops in a Stew-Pan with ſome Butter, let them cool, lay in the Brains, then the Aſparagus, then ſome Forc'd-Meat Balls, with ſome Yolks of hard Eggs, cloſe and bake it; when baked cut off the Lid, and put in ſome Gravey and Butter; if it be not tart enough, ſqueeze in a little Lemon, and lay on the Lid; take it out of the Patty Pan, and diſh it up: You may make it a Side Diſh when you have a Calf's Head-Haſh, and lay the Tongue in the Middle; let your Paſte be Puff Paſte.

To roaſt a Calf's Liver.
Foie de Veau roti.

LARD it with Bacon dipt in Savory Herbs, Pepper, and Salt; ſpit it, and tie on it a Veal-Kell, roaſt it at a ſlow Fire, baſte it with Butter; when it is enough, diſh it: Let the Sauce be Butter Gravey and the Juice of a Lemon; garniſh with fry'd Parſley and Raſhers of Bacon.

Chickens dreſt A-la braiſe.
Poulets à-la-braiſe.

TAKE good Chickens, break down the Breaſt Bones, truſs them and interlard them with Ba-

Bacon; then lay some Bards of Bacon in the Bottom of a Stew-Pan, with some Slices of Veal flatted, with a Clever on the Bacon, season'd with Sweet-herbs, Spices, and Salt; then lay in your Chickens with their Breasts downwards, then some Veal, order'd and season'd as before, on them; set them on a slow Fire, make a Fire above and below, let them stew gently, and moisten them with strong Broth; let them stew till they be pretty tender: You may make a Ragoo for them of Veal, Sweet-breads, Pallets, Oysters, or of any other Thing as before-mentioned; strain the Liquor from the Meat, scum off the Fat, and put the Gravey into your Ragoo. Partridges, Ducks, or any large Fowl may be done the same Way, chusing proper Ragoos for the different Sorts of Fowls, as you'll find before.

To make green Sauce.
Sause vert.

TAKE some green Wheat and Sorril, pound it in a Mortar, and a Piece of stale Bread season'd with Pepper and Salt; put in a little Gravey, and strain it: This Sauce is proper for boil'd Veal and Lamb; add a little drawn Butter and Sugar.

To make a Salpicon for Roast Meats, as Beef, Mutton, Veal, or Lamb.
Salpicon.

TAKE what Quantity of Cucumbers you please, cut them in two, longways, take out the Seeds, then cut them in Dice, or as you like; lay them in an Earthen Dish, strinkle them over with Salt and Pepper, put to them some slic'd Onions and some Vinegar, shake them together, and let them lie an Hour; then drain and dry them, and toss them up in Butter; moisten them with good Gravey, let them stew till tender: You may add Sweet-breads, Morels, Trufles, Lamb stones and Pallets, Coxcombs, Mushrooms, or any

any of these that you can get; bind it with a Cullis made of Ham and Veal, or make a Brown, and put your Salpicon to it; let it be the Thickness of a Cream: You may send it up under your Meat, or cut a Piece out of the thickest Part and mince it; put it to your Salpicon, fill the Hole with it, and send the rest as a Side Dish: If you would make it for Veal, add to it some Ham minc'd fine, toss'd up in it; if for Mutton, put in some minc'd Capers, and leave out the Ham: You may add shred Thyme, Parsley, Chives, &c. as you like.

Beef Stakes collar'd.
Cottelets de Beuf en ruelle.

CUT some Stakes out of the Middle of a Rump, and flat them with a Cleaver; cut them even, and make a Fore'd-Meat for them as follows; take some Veal, Marrow, and Sweet Herbs, season'd with Pepper, Salt, some Lemon-Peel shred fine, some Onion, an Anchovey shred fine, some Morels or Mushrooms shred fine, some Bread Crumbs, let all be shred very fine, mixt with five or six Yolks of Eggs, and beat in a Mortar; wash your Stakes with Yolks of Eggs, and season with Sweet-Herbs and a little Salt; lay on your Fore'd Meat thin, roll them up and wrap them in Kells of Veal or thin Bards of Bacon, tie them round with Packthread, cut them even at each End, and stew them A-la-braise as directed before till tender, drain them from the Fat, take the Bacon off the Ends and cut them in two; set them up, and make a Ragoo for them, or send them up with a Salpicon.

Beets to fry.
Bête rave frit.

TAKE the largest you can get, bake them in a Pot as you do Pears, with Red Wine and Water, Spices, and a little Cotchineal pounded and tied in in a Rag; when they are bak'd tender, take them out to cool, cut them in thick Slices, and make a Batter for them of White Wine, Yolks of Eggs, Flour, and shred Parsley; grate in a little Nutmeg, add a little Cream, make your Batter thick, dip in the Slices of Beef, and fry them in Hog's Lard or clarified Butter; dish them with a Cup of drawn Butter in the Middle; garnish with fry'd Parsley: You may bake them with Sugar, Cloves, and Cinnamon, and the Ingredients as before; observe to tie the Pot down with brown Paper; make the Batter as before, leave out the Parsley, cut them in thinner Slices, and fry them in clarified Butter or good clean Fat, first dipt in the Batter, and send them up as you do Apple Fritters with powder'd Sugar over them: You may garnish them with Seville or China Orange, as you like.

To dress a Calf's Liver A-la-braise.
Foie de veau à-la-braise.

LARD it with large Lardowns of Bacon rub'd in Sweet-herbs minc'd fine, and fine Pepper and Salt; lay Bards of Bacon at the Bottom of a Stew-Pan, Beef Stakes on that, season with Pepper, Salt, Onions, and Sweet-Herbs; lay in your Liver season'd as before, then Bacon on that, then Beef Stakes on that, season'd likewise; stew it as you do other Things a-la braise, moisten it with good Gravey, let it stew till tender, take it up, strain the Liquor, scum off the Fat, thicken it with a Cullis, or make a Brown for it; put in some minc'd Chives and Parsley, let it stew a little, put in a little Vinegar, put in the Liver, make it thoroughly hot, dish it, put in a Ladleful of drawn Butter, draw it and the Sauce up together; let your Dish be rim'd, garnish it with Spinage, poach'd Eggs, and Rashers of Bacon; pour the Sauce hot over the Liver and send it up.

To marinade Sweet-Breads.
Ris de veau marinée.

BLANCH them, and cut them into what Pieces you like; make your Marinade of White Wine, Water, and Vinegar, put in it Salt, whole Pepper, Mace, two or three slic'd Onions, Sweet-herbs, and two or three Cloves; grate in some Nutmeg, let your Sweet-Breads lie in it two or three Hours, then having ready some clarified Butter, make it pretty hot in in a Stew-Pan; take out your Sweet-Breads, put them in a Dish, take a good Handful of Flour and strew over them; stir them up with your Hands and the Flour will stick to them like Batter; put them in one by one, fry them of a brown Colour, put them on a Drainer to drain before the Fire; dish them on fry'd Parsley, with a Cup of drawn Butter in the Middle.

To make Salamagundy.
Salmagondin.

TAKE the Breasts of Turkies, Fowls, or Chickens, and mince them fine, or some white Veal, or both; boil four Eggs hard, chop the Whites by themselves, and the Yolks by themselves; shred some Capers and an Apple or two, and some lean Ham or Neat's Tongue; then take a middle-siz'd Funnel, and put a little of one Sort of your minc'd Things into it, first stop the Pipe of the Funnel with a Cork, then put in a little of another Sort, and so continue till you have fill'd your Funnel; press it tight down, lay your Dish on it you design to send it up in, turn it up and place the Funnel in the Middle of the Dish, put your Thumbs to each Side of the Funnel to keep it in the Middle of the Dish, give it a good Thump on the Dresser, and take off the Funnel; garnish it with Lettice, slic'd Lemon, and Anchovies wash'd and stript off the Bones; lay round it three or four small Onions: This is commonly eat with Oil and Vinegar.

ART of COOKERY.

To dress a Dutch White Herring.
Horangues Hollandoise apprétée.

SCALE and wash it; take the Flesh off the Bones, and mince it fine with Apple, Onion, and a few Capers; mix some Oil and Vinegar with the Yolks of two or three hard Eggs, put in a little Mustard, mix all together, send it on a Plate or little Dish; garnish it with raw Parsley and Lemon.

Lettice to farce.
Laitue farcie.

TAKE as many Cabbage Lettice as you like, and blanch them in scalding Water; take the Flesh of a roast Turkey, Fowl, or Chickens, and mince it fine with some Ham, Mushrooms, or Morels, first blanch'd and shred fine with some Parsley, Onion, and Marrow, with the Crumb of some stale Bread rub'd thro' a Cullender; take the Yolks of three or four Eggs, season them with Pepper, a little Salt, (if the Ham don't make it salt enough) and Nutmeg, work it all together into a Paste, pound it in a Mortar; then open your Lettice, Leaf by Leaf, till you come to the Heart, cut that out, wash it over with Yolks of Eggs, fill the Middle with the farcing, and bring the Leaves up all round, wash them over with the Yolks of Eggs and melted Butter, dridge them over with Bread Crumbs and a little Salt, put them into a convenient Thing to bake in a slow Oven: You may send them up with stew'd Peas under, or with a Ragoo of Sweet-Breads; or garnish made Dishes with them.

To preserve Cherries.
Cerises confit.

THE Cherries that come in this Month are not so proper to preserve as they are that come in next, so I think proper to treat on them in full there.

Strawberries come in this Month, they are commonly

ly eat with Cream and Sugar, or with Wine and Sugar; some like them made into Tarts: You may preserve them or make a Jame of them. I shall treat larger of them when Raspberries come in.

An Ammulet of Ham to make.
Omelet de Jambon..

TAKE twelve Eggs, beat them well, put in a little Salt, and half a Pint of Cream; strain them thro' a Sieve, put them into a Stew-pan with a good Piece of Butter, and some boil'd Ham shred fine; mix all together, and keep them stirring with a Spoon Ladle till thicken'd; put it in your Dish, brown it with a Salamander; let the Sauce be melted Butter, put in a little Parsley boil'd and chop'd, squeeze in some Lemon, or put in a little Vinegar and Pepper.

You may make it without Ham, and put in shred Thyme and Parsley. You may make it of Asparagus Tops, first boil'd tender in Salt and Water: You may fry one Half of your Eggs of one Side, and put them in your Dish with the Sides up that are not fry'd; then lay on your Asparagus, then fry the other Part and turn it on that; then serve it up with the Juice of an Orange and Butter.

You may make many Sorts of Ammulets after this Manner; as for Example, take a Kidney of Veal roasted the Fat and all, mince it fine; then beat fourteen Eggs, squeeze in some Lemon, put in half a Quarter of a Pound of fine Sugar, grate in a little Nutmeg, put in a little White Wine, with a little candied Citron minc'd fine, add a little Salt, mix all together, fry it in clarified Butter, ice it with Sugar, set it in an Oven for two Minutes, or set it before the Fire to glaze, or glaze it with a Salamander: The Sauce is Butter, White Wine and Sugar.

You may make one of Apples, pair'd, cored, cut in Dice, and fry'd in Butter till tender, order'd as before

fore, the Apples are commonly made use of, instead of the Kidney prepared as aforesaid.

To make Hotch-Pot.

Hoche Pot.

TAKE four square Pieces of Brisket Beef, soak it in Water; then take a Pot that will hold two Gallons of Water, put in the Beef, and let it boil some Time, or till it be half boil'd; then take a Loin of Mutton, and cut it into square Pieces, skin and wash it, and put it in; then take a Breast of Veal, and cut it into Pieces, wash and put it in; put in some Salt, whole Pepper, and a little Mace, with five or six Onions; then cut three or four handsome Bits of Bacon, and boil it in a Pot by itself till it be tender, skin and pare it, and keep it hot in the Liquor till you dish it up; then take some Carrots and Turnips par'd, cut in Dice, and fried in Butter, with some Cellery, and two or three slic'd Onions; dridge in some Flour, put in some of the strong Broth, let them to simmer till tender, then having some good Gravey, put it to it; strain in the rest of the Liquor that the Meat was boil'd in, scum off the Fat, then rim a large Soop Dish as you are directed in the first Number. Garnish it with Spinage, Cabbage, and Carrots, first lay in your Meat, the Bacon next the Veal, to intermix one with the other, with toasted Bread cut like Sippits, then put in your Soop on it. You may have a boil'd Fowl in the Middle, if you please. I have often drest this Dish for a Gentleman that I served, to be ready when he came from Hunting.— You may shred some Cabbage and put in, in the stewing of the Turnips and Carrots.

To make a Rabbit Pye.

Paté des Lapins.

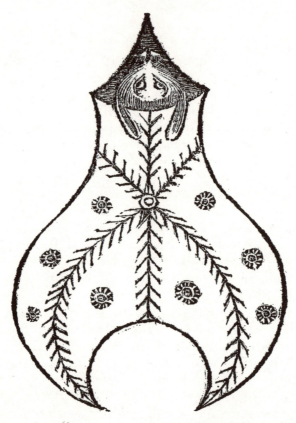

TAKE a Cupple, or two, of Rabbits, skin and clean them, cut them into Pieces as you do for a Fricasy, season them with Pepper and Salt, with a good Handful of Parsley shred fine; then raise a Coffin in the Form as above: Make some Forc'd-meat, and make it into Balls; boil some Eggs hard, and take the Yolks, lay some Rabbit in the Bottom, then Butter on that, then some Forc'd-meat, then more Rabbit on that; then the Yolks of Eggs, and more Forc'd-meat and Butter. Close and garnish it as in the Figure; wash it over with the Yolk of an Egg and a little Cream; paper it, and bake it two Hours in a good foaking Oven; when bak'd, put in fome good Gravey; take off the Paper from the Bottom and Sides. Difh it, and fend it up.

A Hare Pye is made the fame Way, only put in Half a Pint of Red Wine before you lid it, and bake it Half an Hour longer. You may make them in a Difh, with Puff or Pafty-Pafte; and, when bak'd, you may put in a Ragoo of Sweet-breads, Morels, and Truffles, as you will find before-mention'd.

To make Chocolate Cream.
Crême Chocolate.

BOIL a Quart of Milk and Cream, mix'd and fweeten'd to your Tafte; then fcrape as much Chocolate as will give it the Colour, then boil it, keeping ftirring it with a Whifk, but firft put in three or four Yolks of Eggs beaten; ftrain it, and put it into Glaffes or a Glafs Bowl.

Chickens Bullio blance with Endive, &c.
Poulets bouilli blanc.

DRAW, finge, and trufs your Chickens, lay them to foak in warm Water for two Hours; take them out of that Water, and wafh them in cold Water, put them in a Pot in a good deal of Water that is very clear, put in a little Salt, let them boil Half an Hour; blanch two or three Heads of Endive in boiling Water, drain and cut them like Cellery; take a Piece of Butter and brown it in a Stew-pan, with a little Flour; put in the Endive, ftir it and fome minc'd Onion, put in fome good Gravey, with a little Anchovey, fhred Capers, and a little boil'd Ham or Tongue minc'd, fqueeze in a little Lemon, mix all together, with a Ladle-ful of drawn Butter; pour it over them when difh'd. Garnifh them as you like.

Rabbit Surprize.
Lapins en Surprise.

ROAST off two, three, or four Rabbits, according to the Size of your Dish; cut off their Heads, take the Meat off their Backs to the Bone, fill up the Places with Forc'd-meat; wash them over with the Yolks of Eggs and melted Butter, dridge them with Bread Crumbs, Salt, and minc'd Parsley; lay on them some Bards of Bacon, and brown them off in the Oven; then mince the Meat you took out of their Backs, put a Piece of Butter into a Stew-pan, put in your minc'd Meat, with an Onion, and a Faggot of Sweet Herbs, stir it till it is thoroughly hot, dridge in a little Flour, put in some Gravey, squeeze in a little Lemon, grate in a little Nutmeg, put in some melted Butter, stir all together, put it into your Dish, and lay on the Rabbits. Garnish them with fried Parsley and Lemon.

To dress Tench.
Tanches apprêté.

SCALE, gut, and clean them, dry them and flour them, fry them in clarified Butter; take them out, dridge in a little Flour, put in a Bottle of White Wine, or what Quantity will do for your Fish, with some strong Broth, a little Mace, some whole Pepper Corns, a Faggot of Sweet Herbs, some Anchovey, and Onion shred fine, grate in a little Nutmeg, squeeze in a Lemon, let them stew for Half an Hour: You may put in Oisters, Shrimps, and Lobsters, as directed in Page 8. Dish them, with a Scummer, lay on some of the Sauce, and put some in a Boat. Garnish with Horse Raddish and Lemon; salt them to your Taste.

Chickens à la Chiringrate.
Poulets Chiringrate.

SINGE and truss them as for boiling; lard and brown them with Butter; take them out, dridge in

ART of COOKERY.

in a little Flour, put in some good Gravey, stew them in it, with a Faggot of Herbs and Onion, squeeze in some Lemon, put in some Sweet Breads slic'd, with some Morels; cut some Slices of Ham that are boil'd, or Tongue, warm them in the Ragoo. Dish up the Chickens, lay the Ham round, scum off the Fat, and pour the Ragoo over them: You may put in some Forc'd-meat Balls if you please, or force your Chickens with some.

To bake Tench.
Tanches apprêté au Four.

SCALE and clean them, dry them, take a Stew-pan, butter the Bottom, lay in some thin Slices of Veal season'd with Pepper, Salt, some shred Thyme and Parsley, a slic'd Onion; lay the Tench on that, then mix the Yolk of an Egg, and some oil'd Butter, and wash them over with that; shred some Parsley Leaves mix'd with Bread Crumbs, Pepper, and Salt, and strew over them; bake them in a moderate Oven, then make a Ragoo of Lobsters or Crab-Fish, or make a Sauce for them as directed in Page 8; put the Sauce in the Dish, take them up carefully with a Slice, and lay them on the Sauce. Garnish with Lemon and fried Parsley.

You may bake Trouts the same Way, Carpe, Haddocks, or a Pike: You may force them as directed for a Roast Pike.

To dress a Duck with Claret.
Canards apprêté avec du vin rouge.

CLEAN, truss, and singe it; put a Piece of Butter rubb'd in Salt in the Belly of it, spit and three Parts roast it; craw it and cut it up, but leave it hanging together, put a little Salt in the Incisions, warm three or four Spoonfuls of Wine, squeeze in a little Lemon or Orange, lay a Bit of Onion in every Incision, lay a warm Plate on the Breast, and press it hard; put the

warm

warm Wine over it, and send it up hot. A young Duck drest this Way eats very fine.

To dress Turkeys, Pullets, Chickens, or Partridges à la Smithergall.
Dindons, Poulards, Poulets, ou Perdrix la Smithergall.

MAKE Forc'd-meat as directed in Page 26, and work it hollow, in the Shape of a French Roll; make four, five, or six, according to the Size of your Dish; then chop some coarse Meat, as a Neck of Beef, or any Thing you can spare; season it and fill the Forc'd-meat with it; lay a Bit of Forc'd-meat on the Top, then paper them round with Writing Paper; wash the Tops over with Yolks of Eggs and melted Butter; dridge them with Bread Crumbs, bake them of a gold Colour, and not too much, but first cut some Bards of Bacon thin and round to set them on before you bake them, bake them on a Massireen, take a sharp Knife, and cut a round Piece out of the Tops; take out the Meat you put in, and take the Meat off the Bones of your Turkey, Pullet, Chicken, or Partridge, after they are three Parts roasted, and slice it very thin, and toss it up in a white Lare, as for white Veal Collops, see Page 32, or you may order it as you mince a Turkey, in Page 29, and fill the Forc'd-meat with either of these; set them a little in the Oven to heat, put on the Tops of your Forc'd-meat again. Send them up with fried Parsley round them; you may take Rolls, cut a Bit off the Tops, take out the Crumbs, butter them well within and without, set them in the Oven to crisp or set them before the Fire, but keep them turning for Fear they should burn; then you may call them by the Name of the Fowl they are fill'd with; if Turkey, Turkey Loaves; if Partridge, Partridge Loaves; so for the rest. You may provide some little Earthen Pans to make the aforesaid Dish in, and order them as you do a Pulpotoon, as you will find before-mention'd.

Ducks

Ducks a la Braise with Onions.
Canards à la Braise.

TRUSS your Ducks as for boiling; garnish the Bottom of a Stew-pan with some Bards of Bacon and some Slices of lean Beef, flat the Beef with a Cleaver, season it with Thyme, Parsley, sliced Onion, Pepper, Salt, some Cellery, brown the Breasts of your Ducks in a Stew-pan with a Piece of Butter, keep them moving or they will burn; when brown'd, take them out, and lay them in the Stew-pan that you have prepar'd, with their Breasts down; then lay Slices of Beef on them, season'd as before; put on the Cover, set them on a slow Fire, put some Fire on the Cover, let them stew till pretty tender. In most Noblemens Kitchens they have oval Pans to suit most or all Things that are to be done in this Way, which make them do much better. Then get forty or fifty Onions about the Bigness of a Nutmeg, blanch them in Salt and Water, then make a Brown, put in some good Gravey, with a little White Wine, Lemon, and a little Anchovey min'd fine; let it stew till the Onions be tender; take out your Ducks and put them in this, strain the Liquor they were stew'd in, scum off the Fat, add it to the rest; dish them, and garnish with Lemon and Barberries. You may dress a Goose the same Way, or send it up wth stew'd Peas as before directed. There are several Ways to send up a Goose or Duck, as with stew'd Cellery, ragoo'd Turnips, Carrots, stew'd Cabbage, or with Olives, Capers, &c. You will find these mention'd in their proper Places.

To make a Squob Pye as they make it in Devonshire.
Paté de Pigeoneaux à la Paisan.

TAKE a Neck of Mutton, cut it in Pieces, Bone by Bone, flat them with a Cleaver, cut them handsomely, take off most Part of the Fat, season them with Pepper and Salt, raise a Pye or make it in a Dish, lay some Chops in the Bottom; then having some Apples pair'd, cor'd, and slic'd, some Onions peel'd and sl c'd; likewise lay a Lare of Apples and Onions over the Mutton, then some Stakes on that again, then Apples and Onions on that; season the Top as before, lid your Pye, and bake it two Hours.

To dress Virginia Trouts.
Truites à la Virginie.

TAKE as many pickled Herrings as you please, scale them, and lay them to soak in warm Water twenty-four Hours, wash them out, and dry them with a Cloth; season the Bottom of your Pot with Mace, Pepper, slic'd Onion, and shred Parsley; lay in a Lare of Herrings, then some more Seasoning on them, with some Lemon Peel, and a little red Saunders tied up in a Cloth, then more Herrings on that, so continue till you have put them all in; put to them some Red Wine and Vinegar, Half one and Half the other, almost to cover them; tie them down with a double brown Paper, bake them in a moderate Oven four Hours, let them stand to cool, eat them with the Liquor.

To farce Sheep Trotters.
Pieds de Mouton farcie.

SCALD them well, and wash them clean, stew them in strong Broth; take out the long Bones, open the Feet with a sharp Knife, and take out the little Bones; leave one Side of the Foot as whole as you can, then wash them over with the Yolks of Eggs, and lay on some good Forc'd-meat; roll them up handsomely, butter a convenient Thing, lay them in it, egg them, and strew over them some fine Bread Crumbs, and bake them of a fine Colour. Dish them, and pour over them a Ragoo made of Sweet Breads shred fine, or a Cullis of Mushrooms, which you can get best, or with boil'd Parsley, minc'd Capers, Butter, and Gravey. Garnish with fried Parsley.

ART of COOKERY.

To make a Pye of Tench, Carpe, Trout, or Pike.

YOU may make them as directed in Page 35, or in a Dish or rais'd Pye, as you like, seafon'd as there directed; put into the Pye a good deal of Butter, some shred Parsley, and a few Capers shred fine; close it, and wash it over with melted Butter and the Yolk of an Egg; bake it two Hours, when bak'd, cut off the Lid, take off the Fat as clean as you can, and make a Lare for it as directed before; lay on the Lid again, and send it up hot.

To make Rice Fritters.
Bignets de Ris.

TAKE some ground Rice, if you can get it; if not, take some whole Rice, and wash it in three or four Waters, dry it, and pound it in a Mortar, and sift it through a fine Sieve; put it into a Stew-pan with some Milk, set it on the Fire and keep it stirring till it is thicken'd; then add more Milk, and stir it till it is thicken'd again; then take it off, and beat as many Eggs as will do, according to the Quantity, if a Pint of it take six Eggs; sweeten it to your Taste, mince some Lemon or Orange Peel that is candied, and put in with a little melted Butter; put in a little Salt, stir all together, squeeze in a little Lemon or Orange Juice, and fry them in clarified Butter, clean Fat, or Hog's Lard; put in a Spoonful at a Time, turn them and fry them of a light brown Colour; put them in a Cullinder to drain before the Fire; dish them, and dridge them with fine Sugar, and send them up. You may garnish with Seville Orange.

To make natural Gravey of Beef or Mutton.
Jus de Beuf ou du Mouton naturelle.

TAKE a fleshy Piece of Beef without Bones, spit, and three Parts roast it; salt it as it roasts, take it up and prick it full of Holes, with a sharp-pointed Skewer;

Skewer; ftrew on fome more Salt, put it in a Tin Dripping-pan, lay a Board on it, and fet it in a Prefs; prefs it hard to force out the Gravey, then pour it into a Pan, and having fome good ftrong Broth, put fome on it, and prefs it again; do fo for three or four Times, then take out your Beef, cut it in Pieces, and put it into your Broth Pot. You may do the fame by a Leg of Mutton or any Sort of Fowl that you would have natural Gravey from. This Gravey very much heightens your Soops and made Difhes.

JUNE

JUNE.

Soop au Bourgeois.
Potage au Bourgeois.

TAKE four or five Cabbage Lettices, cut them in four, wafh and cut them thin a-crofs, put them in a Cullinder and ftrinkle a little Salt over them; then take fix middling Cucumbers, pare and flice them, and ftrinkle fome Salt on them; then take two large Onions, peel and cut them in two, and flice them; then take a Quarter of a Pound of Butter; put it into a Stew-pan with your Herbs, ftir them till your Butter be melted; then cover them clofe, let them ftew foftly till they are pretty tender; then put in a Pint of young Peas, tofs all together, put in as much ftrong Broth as you think will do for your Soop; let it all boil up, then fet it on one Side of your Stove-fire to keep hot and fimmer; fcum off all the Fat, then having a young Fowl roafted very pale, which may be done by papering it and roafting it at a good Diftance from the Fire; rim your Difh, put in the Soop, with fome French Roll flic'd, and dried before the Fire, and the Fowl in the Middle. Garnifh the Difh with Spinage and Rafhers of Bacon.

To roaft a Pike.
Brochets roti.

SCALE, clean, and rub it dry with a Cloth within and without; then make a Farce of Fifh of what Sort you can get, take it clean from the Bones, fhred it fine, mix it with Sweet Herbs, two Anchovies, a little Onion, grate in a little Nutmeg, fhred a little Lemon Peel, mix all together with a Quarter of a Pound of Butter, and the Yolks of two Eggs; put it into the Belly of the Pike, few it up, fpit it as even as you can, and tie it to the Spit with Laths, but they muft not be made of Fir, for it will give the Fifh a Tafte; be fure to faften the Laths tight to the Spit, bafte it with Butter; if it be a large Pike it will take an Hour roafting; falt it as it roafts, then having an oval Difh, take up the Pike and lay it in the Difh, untie the Laths, draw out the Spit and make a Sauce for it, as directed in Page 8. Garnifh with Horfe Raddifh and Lemon; mind to draw the Thread out of the Belly.

As to boiling the Ham, you will find the Direction in Page 9. Take a Difh that will hold it handfomely, and rim it; then fheet Half a Dozen Petty-pans with Cuftard Pafte, prick them with a Fork to keep them from bliftering, and bake them on the Rim of your Difh, your Pafte being bak'd, take them out of the Pans, fet them on the Rim of your Difh, firft fpread on fome Spinage or other Greens, that they may ftand firm; place your Ham in the Difh, and garnifh it with any Thing you pleafe to hide the Bottom of the Difh; then blanch your Beans and fill your Pafte-patties, put a little Butter to them: You may likewife fend four Plates round the Ham, one of Colliflowers, one of Carrots, one of white Cabbage, one of Savoys or Spinage, or what you like.

To roaft a Haunch of Venifon.

Gigot de Venaifon roti.

BREAK the Shank, cut a Piece off the hinder Side like a Beef-Stake to make it lie flat in the Difh, fpit it even, and as little through the Fat as poffible; butter a Paper, and lay on the Outfide of your Venifon; then make a Piece of coarfe Pafte, roll it out thin, and lay it on the Paper; then lay another Sheet of Paper over that, tie all on with Packthread, roaft it two Hours and a Half at a good foaking Fire, make the Sauce of fine Bread Crumbs, Red Wine,

Wine, a Stick of Cinnamon, with as much Sugar as will sweeten it to your Taste. Some make it all of Wine and Sugar, boil'd to the Thickness of a Cream; some use Currant Jelly.

N. B. Take off the Paste and Paper, dridge it with Flour, salt it, and let it brown before you send it up.

Hare in Collops.
Lievre en Fillets.

SKIN and clean your Hare, take the Flesh clean from the Back-bone, and off the Legs, take off the Shoulders, cut off the Head, make a Pudding, and fill the Carcass with it; cut it from the Back bone, rub it over with Yolks of Eggs, dridge it with Bread Crumbs and bake it, split the Head, and order it the same Way; baste it with Butter; whilst it is baking, cut the Flesh off your Hare in thin Slices, hack it with the Back of a Knife, as you do Veal Collops, and fry them the same Way, but not too much, if a young Hare; if an old one, you must stew it in Gravey till tender, make a Brown, put in some Gravey, with a Faggot of Sweet Herbs, some Onion shred fine with Anchovey; put in Half a Pint of Red Wine, some Pepper and Salt, squeeze in some Lemon, grate in a little Nutmeg; when the Hare is tender, and the Sauce the Thickness of a thin Cream, dish it, take the Carcass, split it in two, lay it in the Middle with the Pudding upwards, the Head laid in with the Brains up. Garnish with Barberries and Lemon.

Chickens and Rice.
Poulets au Ris.

CLEAN, truss, and singe them; lay them to soak in warm Water, stew them in strong Broth till they be enough; wash three Ounces of Rice in three or four Waters, and stew it in strong Broth till tender then make a Brown, or use some Cullis drawn from Ham and Veal; if you have no Cullis, nor cannot have conveniently, proceed with your Brown, putting some of your strong Broth and some Gravey to it; strain your Rice and put it in, salt it to your Taste, squeeze in a little Lemon, put in a Ladleful of drawn Butter, grate in a little Nutmeg, stir all together, lay your Chickens in the Dish, pour over them the Sauce. Garnish them with creed Rice, coloured with Saffron.

To make Sweet-bread Patty.
Paté de Ris de Veau.

TAKE Half a Dozen, blanch them, and cut them into Pieces; toss them up in a Ragoo with Forc'd meat Balls, Yolks of hard Eggs, Mushrooms. [See Ragoo'd Sweet-breads] Sheet your Patty-pan with hot Butter Paste; put in your Sweet-breads, season them higher than for a Ragoo; lid it with Puff-paste, wash it over with the Yolk of an Egg, and a little Cream; cut the Lid round with a sharp Knife, that you may the easier take it off when bak'd; an Hour will bake it; when bak'd put in some Gravey and Butter, and lay on the Lid again.

To make a Potato Pudding.

BOIL and peel as many as you think will do, pound them in a Mortar with some Cream, till it be very fine; if you think it be not fine enough, rub it through a Cullinder; put it into a Stew-pan, with a good Piece of Butter, some Salt, and as much Sugar as will sweeten it to your Taste; grate in Half a Nutmeg, shred some Citron and Orange Peel, or Lemon, very fine; then beat the Yolks of ten Eggs, mix all together; rim your Dish with Puff paste, put in your Pudding, bake it an Hour: You may put in a few Currans if you like it, and a Glass of Sack, with a little Orange Flower Water, White Wine, Sugar, and Butter; with the Juice of an Orange, mixt together for the Sauce.

Duck.

Ducks and Onions.
Canards aux Onions.

CLEAN, truss, and singe them; put a Piece of Butter, rubb'd in Salt, in their Bellies; spit and roast them, but not too much; take four large Onions, peel and cut them in two, slice them thin, toss them up in a Stew pan, with a Piece of Butter, till they begin to turn brown, dridge in a little Flour, put in some good Gravey, with a Glass of Red Wine, and a few Capers, shred fine, a little Pepper and Salt. Dish your Duck, carbinate them, and pour the Sauce over them.

Veal forc'd and dob'd.
Veau farcie à la Daube.

TAKE a Leg of Veal, cut a large Slice off the hinder Side, take off the Skin, lard the upper Side of that Piece very well; then, with a sharp Knife, open it in the Middle, rub it within with the Yolk of an Egg, put in some good Forc'd-meat, squeeze it flat with your Hand; take a good Piece of Butter, and put it into a Stew-pan, fry it brown on both Sides; take it out, make a Brown for it, and stew it till it be tender; send it up with a Ragoo of Sorrel, made in this Manner: Get a good Handful of Sorrel, wash and pick it, blanch it in boiling Water, take a Piece of Butter, put it into a Stew-pan, shred the Sorrel, and put it in, with the Juice of an Orange; dust in a little Flour, put in a little strong Broth, stir all together, salt it to your Taste, grate in a little Nutmeg, make the Veal hot, lay it in the Dish, pour this Sauce over it. You may cut off the Shank or Knuckle of the Veal and stuff and roast the other Part, or use it as you please.

To roast Moor-game by some call'd Heath Pouts.
Moorgame roti Coc de Bruyere.

PICK, crop, and clean them well within from the Heath; put a Piece of Butter, rubb'd in Salt in their Bellies ; trufs them with their Heads and Feet on, fpit, finge, and bafte them : You muft roaft them like a wild Duck, full in their Gravey. Make Bread Sauce for them, as for a Turkey ; fend it in a Cup or Boat, and Gravey in the Difh. Turkies are done the fame Way ; but force their Crops with good Forc'd-meat. See more, where Turkies are treated of.

To make Clouted Cream, as it is made in Devonshire.
Crême brouillé.

TAKE the Milk that is milk'd at Night, and ftrain it into an Earthen Veffel ; let it ftand till the next Morning, then fet it on a fmall Charcoal-Fire in the fame Pan, difturb it as little as poffible ; let it ftand till it juft pimples up, but be fure you do not let it boil ; take it carefully off, and fet it in a cool Place till the next Morning ; then take off the Cream with a Slice, and lay it on your Difh, to eat with your Strawberries. Six Quarts of Milk will do for two little Difhes order'd as above.

To preferve Codlins green.
Codelins à rendre verd et confire.

GATHER them when they are the Bignefs of a Golden Pippin, lay fome Vine Leaves in the Bottom of a Stew-pan ; if you cannot get Vine Leaves, take Curran-berry Tree Leaves ; lay your Codlins on them, then more Leaves on the Top ; cover them, and fet them on a flow Fire, take Care they do not crack ; when they will peel, put them into cold Water, take off their Peels ; then put fome frefh Leaves in your Pan again, a Brafs Pan is beft, if you have one, lay in your Codlins, put as much hard Water to them as will cover chem ; then a Bit of Verdigreafe, the Bignefs of a large Hafel Nut, finely powder'd, and put into Half a Pint of diftilled Vinegar, and about the fame Quantity of Allum powder'd ;
like-

likewife with a little Bay Salt; put all into a Bottle, shake it, and let it ftand till clear; put to your Codlins a fmall Spoonful, lay more Leaves on the Top, cover them down clofe, fet them on a flow Fire for an Hour, and they will be as green as Grafs; take them out, and put them into cold Water till they be quite cold, then take them out, take out their Nofes, and with a Bodkin, make a Hole in them to the Heart; then weigh the Codlins, and take double their Weight of Sugar, the fineft you can get, pound it in a Mortar, and fift it through a Sieve; then make a Sirrup of Half of it, put in your Codlins firft, fkim it, keep them moving, with a Silver Ladle; if they crack take them off, and let them ftand a little, and ftrinkle in fome of the Sugar you kept out; fet them on again, let them boil up again, ftill keep them moving that they may do all Sides alike; take them off again, and ftrinkle in more Sugar, keep this Order till they be clear.

N B. If you fet them by before they be thorougly done they will fhrivel, and then you cannot get that out again; you may put in fome Lemon Peel in the doing of them, that is rafpt off the Lemons; you may lay fome of it on the Apples, when you fend them to Table; if you would keep them long, you muft make a frefh Sirrup for them, or they will turn brown when you fend them to Table, fend them in Codlin Jelly, or Jelly made from fome other Sort of Apples; put them in a Pot when cold, cut a fheet of Writing-Paper to fit the Pot, dip it in Brandy, and lay it on, tie it down with Leather if to keep long, you may put on a wet Bladder firft.

To preferve Cucumbers.
Coucombres à comfire.

GATHER the ftrighteft and greeneft you can; get them that are but half grown, rub them with Salt, let them lie in Salt and Water twenty four Hours; then boil them in hard Water till they be
pretty

pretty tender, cut a Bit off the pale End, and skoop out the Seed with a small Skoop, but don't take any out of the Cucumber, only the Seeds; but first green them as you did the Codlins; they are preserved the same Way; when they are almost done, put in a little Orange Flower Water, and the Juice of a Lemon, the rest is all the same; boil them till they be clear, and they will look like Citron.

To pot a Hare.
Lievre conservé.

SKIN and rub it clean, salt it with common Salt, and Salt-Petre, twenty-four Hours; first cut it to Pieces, put it into a Pot with two Pounds of Butter, and a little Pepper; tie it over with a double Paper, bake it four Hours, take out the Meat, and pick it clean from the Bones; put it into a Mortar, with a little Nutmeg and Mace beat fine, and two Anchovies wash'd, chopt and min'd fine, with some of the clear Butter; pound it fine, and put it into the Pot you would have it in; put the rest of the clarified Butter on the Top, let it stand to cool.

To pot Beef.
Beuf à conservé.

TAKE what Quantity you please off a Buttock of Beef, salt it as you did the Hare, but it must lie longer in Salt, according to the Bigness and Thickness of your Meat; then put it into a convenient Pot, with as much Butter as you think will do; tie the Pot as before, and bake it till it is quite tender; then take two, three, or four Anchovies minc'd fine, put them into a Mortar, put in a small Quantity of beaten Mace and Nutmeg, pound it very fine with some of the Clear of the Butter that it was bak'd with; put it into your Pot or Pots, and fill them with clarified Butter.

To pickle Trouts like Charr.
Truites confit au Vinaigre.

TAKE your Trouts, and clean them, put them into a Pot with half Water and half Vinegar; take some Powder of red Sanders, tied up in a thin Cloth, dip it in the Liquor, and squeeze it, and leave it in the Pot; put in some whole Pepper and Mace, put in a little Salt, that is, according to the Quantity; lay in your Trouts with their Heads, one, one Way, and another, another; strinkle some Salt on the Top, let the Liquor just cover them, tie them down with double Paper, and bake them four or five Hours in a slow Oven; let them stand to cool; then dish them with green Fennel over them.

To pot them red.
Les confire rouge.

TAKE some Salt and Water, and boil it with some red Sanders and a little Saffron, let the Brine be pretty strong; when it is cold, put in your Trouts, let them lie twenty-four Hours, then take them out, and put them into a Cloth, and dry them very well; put them into a Pot, season them with Pepper, Nutmeg, and Mace, lay Butter on the Top, tie them down, aud bake them two Hours; take them carefully out of the Pot, and lay them in the Pot you design to keep them in; scum off the clear Butter, and fill up the Pot, if you have not enough, clarify some more. They will be near as fine as Charr. You may do any small Fish the same Way, after they have lain in the pickle as before. You may dry, flour, and broil them; and send them up with plain Butter.

To make Lemonade.
Lemonade.

TAKE a Gallon of Spring Water, and two Pounds of Loaf Sugar, boil them softly an Hour; when the Liquor is almost cold, put to them the Juice of

twelve

twelve Lemons; then make a brown Toast and spread it with Yest, and put it to the Liquor; let it stand twenty-four Hours, then take the clear Liquor, and put it into a Vessel, with two Quarts of White Wine; let it stand two Days, then bottle it; if it be not sweet enough, put a little more Sugar in each Bottle.

To stew Trouts the Dutch Way.
Trouts etuvé.

SCALE, wash, and gut them, put them into a Stew-pan, first make a Brown, as directed in several Places before-mention'd; toss them up in that, then put in Half a Pint of White Wine, and Half a Pint of good strong Broth or Gravey, with some whole Pepper and Mace, a Faggot of sweet Herbs, some Parsley, Anchovey, and Onion shred fine; salt it to your Taste, grate in a little Nutmeg, put in four Yolks of Eggs boil'd hard, and shred fine; take out the sweet Herbs, put in a little Lemon. Dish them on Sippets of white Bread; send up some Fish-Sauce in a Boat.

To pickle Currants.
Corinth a confire.

TAKE red or white Currants before they are ripe; take as much distilled Vinegar as will cover them, to a Quart put Half a Pound of Loaf Sugar, boil and skim it; take it off the Fire, and put in your Currants, let them a good Distance from the Fire, let them simmer a little; take them out, let the Liquor cool, put them in a Jar, and keep them under with an earthen Plate or Saucer; tie them down with a Bladder.—Grapes may be done the same Way.

To perch Almonds.
Des Amanes à la Praline.

TAKE a Pound of fine Loaf Sugar pounded and sifted, take Half a Pint of Water, and a little Orange-Flower Water; put it into your preserving Pan,

Pan, boil it to a Candy Height; take three Quarters of a Pound of Jorden Almonds blanch'd and dried, put them into the Syrrup, keep them stirring over the Fire till they are dry and crisp; then put them into a paper'd Box, and keep them dry.

To make Catchup of Mushrooms.
Catchop pour faire.

GATHER the freshest Flabs you can get, cut off the Root-Ends, take off the rough Skin, which will peel off with a Knife, break them to Pieces with your Hands, put them into an earthen Pan, salt them pretty well, let them stand for twenty-four Hours; then tie a Paper over them, and bake them in a moderate Oven; press all the Liquor out of them, let it stand to settle; to a Quart of Catchup take Half a Pint of Red Wine, and Half a Pint of Vinegar, some Pepper, Mace, and six Anchovies chopt fine, with a large Onion; boil it altogether and strain it through a Sieve; let it settle, then bottle and cork it tight, and set it in a cool Place. You may keep the plain Catchup, and add some Spice to it, and boil it; let it stand to settle; it is proper to be used in all made Dishes that are brown, and in all Hashes of Flesh and Fowls, and in Fish Sauce; a small Matter will do. I shall treat now of Mushrooms this Time of the Year being the first of their coming, but Michaelmas is the best Time of the Year for pickling of them; they are then firmer.

To preserve Mushrooms for any Use.
Champignons à confire.

TAKE small Buttons, cut their Stalk Ends off, and wash them very clean with a Flannel Cloth, put them into fresh Water, and shift them every Hour till you can't perceive the Water discolour'd; then make a Brine of Salt and Water, and boil them in it; let them stand in their Liquor till they be cold; then

then make a Brine for them of common and Bay Salt, boil it well, let it stand to cool, and filter it through a filtering Paper; bottle your Mushrooms, and fill the Bottles with this Brine; put a little Oil on the Top of them, and cork them tight, and keep them in a cold Place; when you would make use of them, shift them in several warm Waters till they be fresh.

To pickle Mushrooms.
Champignons conservée.

PRepare them as above, and boil them in Salt and Water; let them stand to cool in their Liquor, then drain them well, and put them into distill'd Vinegar; put on a little Oil, cork them, and tie them down with a Bladder.

To fricasy them.
En fricassée.

CLEAN and soak them in two or three Waters; put in a good Piece of Butter, with a Faggot of Sweet Herbs, an Onion, some whole Pepper, and a little Mace; cover them close, and let them stew; strinkle in a little Salt; when they are enough take them off; if there be too much Liquor, put some out; to a little Dish take Half a Pint of Cream, the Yolks of two Eggs, a Bit of Butter work'd in Flour, a little White Wine, Anchovey, and Onion chopt fine, grate in a little Nutmeg, toss all up together, and dish them: If you have any large ones, skin them, and take out the Inside; season them with Pepper and Salt, then grate or rub some stale Bread through a Cullinder, and lay Bread Crumbs on them; then baste it with Butter, broil them before the Fire, or brown them in an Oven, and garnish your Fricasy with them; they are proper to eat with Beef, Mutton, Veal, or Lamb roasted, or with Beef Stakes, Mutton Chops, or Veal Cutlets, or to garnish them that are made in the made Way of any of the Meats above-mention'd.

To fricasy them brown.
Champignons accommodé.

PUT a Piece of Butter into a Stew-pan, with the Mushrooms, clean'd as above directed, with a Faggot of Sweet Herbs, some Salt, Pepper, Mace, and an Onion; let them stew till they are enough, then put some out, and clean your Pan; put in a Piece of Butter, dridge in some Flour, make it brown, put in some Gravey, squeeze in some Lemon, grate in a little Nutmeg; let all stew till it is the Thickness of a Cream. You may send them under any Roast-meat as above-mention'd, or make a Dish of them by themselves.—N. B. Observe to take out the Faggot of Sweet Herbs and the Onion.

To dry Mushrooms.
Champignons en Fricasíée roux.

CLEAN, and dry them in a flow Oven, or put them on a String, and dry them as you do Morels.

To make Mushroom Loaves.

PRepare your Loaves as you do for Oisters, and fill them with the white Fricasy, or the Brown, which you like best; the smallest are best for this Use.

Mushrooms are to be made use of in several other Things, which I shall mention hereafter.

To bottle Goosberries.
Groseilles en Bouteilles.

GET them that are three Parts grown, take off their Stalks and Noses, set on a Pan of hard Water, make it boil, take it off the Fire; put in your Goosberries, and let them lie till they turn white, but take Care they don't crack; strain them into a Cullinder, lay them on a coarse Cloth, and cover them with another; let them lie till they be cold,

cold, bottle them, and stamp the Bottle on a Cloth to settle them, cork them tight; cut off the Top of the Corks, rosin them over, and set them in a cold Place.

To preserve Gooseberries.
Geoseilles confit..

TAKE the largest you can get, when they are green and hard, pick them, and put some Curran-tree Leaves into the Bottom of the Brass-Pan; lay in the Gooseberries, put in a Spoonful of Greening, as prepared for green Codlins; put in as much hard Water as will cover them, lay Leaves on the Top, cover them close, set them on a very slow Fire three or four Hours, take Care they don't crack; when they are green take them out, and put them in cold Water, let them lie till cold, then make a Syrrup for them pretty strong, of fine Sugar; let it stand to cool, put in the Gooseberries, let them be dried with a Cloth, set them on a slow Fire, keep them stirring, and now and then sprinkle in some Sugar that is pounded and sifted; let them simmer til clear; put them in Pots and tie them down with Leather.

To pickle Gooseberries.
Groseilles au Vinaigre.

PICK them, and put them into a strong Brine of Salt and Water twenty-four Hours; then green them as for preserving, and put them into distill'd Vinegar, order'd as you did the pickled Mushrooms.

To make an Acid of Gooseberries fit for Punch.

TAKE them that are full grown, pound them in a Mortar, and press all the Juice out of them; let it stand to settle, put it into Bottles, that is, the Clear, for it will be as fine as Water in twenty-four Hours; put a little Oil in each Bottle, cork it tight, and set it in a cold Place; if you put some Elder Flowers to it, and let it stand two or three Days; then

then ſtrain it, let it ſtand to ſettle, and bottle it as before. This will give a very agreeable Flavour to ſeveral Things in the made Way and Sauces.

To make Gooſberry Cream.
Crême aux Groſeilles.

CODDEL and rub them through a coarſe Sieve; put it into a Stew-pan, with as much fine Sugar as will ſweeten it to your Taſte, ſet it on the Fire, ſtir it till it looks pretty clear; take it off, then take half Milk and half Cream, according to the Quantity you would have; ſet it on the Fire to boil, with a Stick of Cinnamon, and a Piece of Lemon Peel; beat the Yolks of three Eggs, that is, to a Quart, mix the Eggs and Milk together, ſtrain it through a Sieve, and thicken it as below, ſtir it till it be pretty cold, put in a little Nip of Salt to take off the Rawneſs of the Gooſberries, mix all together, ſtir it, and fill a Glaſs Baſon with it, or put it into Jelly Glaſſes, as you like beſt. If you would have it white, take Whites of Eggs inſtead of Yolks; whiſk them well, and mix them with the Milk, and ſtrain it as before; ſet it on the Fire, keep it ſtirring till it be a little thicken'd; ſtir it till it be cold, then mix it with your Gooſberries.

To make Tarts of Gooſberries.
Des Tartes aux Groſeilles.

WHEN they are green, ſcald them as for bottleing, fill your Tarts, and ſweeten them with fine Sugar, cut your Lids and ice them with fine Sugar, bake them in a quick Oven, and they will look clear and well. You may make Tarts of the preſerved ones; ſheet your Pans with Sugar-Paſte, and bake the Paſte by itſelf; then having ſome Covers made like a little Scale (you may have them made of Tin) you may cut their Lids on them, in the ſame Manner you do a Crocaunt Cover; ice them and take them off, fill your Tarts, and lay on your Covers. You may order any preserved Fruit the same Way. You must butter the Tins before you lay on the Paste to cut it.

To make Goosberry Wine.
Vin aux Groseilles.

TAKE the ripe white Berries, put them into a Vessel, and pour on them a sufficient Quantity of boiling Water; cover the Vessel very close, let them stand till the Liquor is impregnated with the Juice a Month; draw it out and put it into another Vessel, and put as much fine Sugar to it as will sweeten it; stir it well together till it is all in a Ferment, let it stand to settle and fine; cover it close, then bottle it. You may put in it some Orange Peel, if you like the Flavour. If you would drink it soon, put into each Bottle a Bit of Sugar, and two or three Raisins.

To make Goosberry Jelly.
Du Gellée aux Groseilles.

TAKE what Quantity of Juice you please, order'd as you did that for bottling; put to it a sufficient Quantity of Sugar, boil, and skim it when it is cold; put in your preserv'd Fruit with it, into what Glasses you please. This Jelly is much better than Apple Jelly: If you make a good Quantity of this, it will serve you all the Year to make into Jelly, or for other Things, as above-mention'd.—— To make Clear-Cakes of them. See Apricots.

To make a Marmalade of Roses and Almonds.
Des Roses en Marmalade.

TAKE Half a Pound, blanch and beat them very fine, with Rose-Water; take two Ounces of the Leaves of Damask Roses, beat fine likewise; take three Quarters of a Pound of double-refin'd Sugar, break it into Pieces, moisten it with Water; let it boil

ART of COOKERY.

boil to a Candy-height, skim it, and put in your Almonds and Roses, let it boil up, and keep it stiring for a Minute; put it into a Flue-Pot, that you may the easier cut it out when cold; tie it down with a double Paper, keep it in a dry Place.

To dry Roses.
Des Roses à Seché.

PICK off the Leaves, and put them into large Pewter Dishes, and set them in the Sun to dry, turn them till they be quite dry; don't put too many together, put them into large Mouth Bottles, cork'd close, and keep them in a dry Place.

To make Rose Water.
Eau de Roses.

TAKE Roses when just blown, gather them when the Sun has dried off the Dew; pick the Leaves from the Stalks and Seeds, spread the Leaves on a Cloth till they are dry from any Moisture; then put as many as you can conveniently into a Pewter Still; put on the Top, and paste it round; then having your Bottle clean and dry, place your Bottle to the Nose of the Still, and tie a Cloth round it to keep in the Scent; then make a slow Fire under your Still, when it begins to drop you may increase it a little, but take Care you don't make your Fire too fierce; when it begins to slack, draw out your Fire by Degrees; when it has done dropping take off the Top of the Still, and turn the Cake, and let it lie till quite dry. Some put these Cakes amongst their Cloaths.

To make Artichokes keep all the Year.
Artichaux à garder tout l' Année.

ARtichokes being of great Use in Cookery, I shall begin with the Method of keeping them all the Year. Take a Quantity of Water, suitable to the Artichokes, that is, what will cover them, make it

into

into a strong Brine, boil it very well, let your Salt be Bay and Common Salt, strain it and let it stand to settle, then pare off the Leaves with a sharp Knife, and boil them till you can take out the Chokes; put them into Water as you do them, then scrape them clean, and cut a Lemon in two and rub them with it, to make them white; then boil them a little more in Salt-Water and Vinegar; put your first Brine into the Vessel you design to keep them in, then put in your Artichoaks, let the last Liquor that you boil'd, stand to cool and settle, and poor the clear of that in likewise; then put Oil on the Top, first lay on a Slate to keep them under the Pickle, tie them down with Leather to keep for your Use; when you would Use any of them, steep them in warm Water, to take out the Salt; when you have prepared them, as for putting them into the Pickle, you may string them on a Packthread with a packing Needle, and hang them up in the Kitchen to dry, or dry them in a slack Oven. You may keep them another Way, pare them as you did at first, take out the Chokes, and put them into Water, or they will turn black, then rub them with Lemon as before, and put them into Flour, then lay them on splinted Sives, or wired ives, and dry them in an Oven, as you are directed above, keep them in a Box, in a dry Place; when you would use them, soke them twenty four Hours in warm Water, and boil them tender, and they will eat very well.

To dress Artichokes.
Artichaux opreté.

I Shall mention some different Ways of dressing them. I shall first mention the plain Way, though known by most People; let your Artichokes be cut with their Stalks on them, two Hands long, then break the Stalk off from the Artichokes, and it will draw out the Strings from the Bottoms, especially if they are kept a Day or two; cut a Bit of the Tops off, and put them into Water, wash them well and boil
them

them in hard Water, till you can draw out a Leaf easily, then dish them with a Cup of melted Butter in the Middle. When your Artichokes are prepared and orded as for Pickling, then boil them quite tender, in the same Sort of Liquor as in the last Direction for pickling; then dish and send them up with plain Butter, or Butter and Gravey, and a little Juice of Lemon; you may garnish them with fried Artichokes, as here directed. Take the small ones and cut them in four, take out the Chokes; blanch them in boiling Water, dry and flour them, and fry them in clarified Butter; you may make a Dish of them, with a Cup of plain Butter in the Middle,

To fry Artichokes.
Des Artichaux frit.

TO fry Artichokes in Batter, when they are boiled, take off the Leaves and Chokes, cut the Bottoms in Pieces, lay them to marinate in Vinegar, Water, Salt, Pepper, and a sliced Onion, an Hour; take them out and make a stiff Batter for them of Eggs, Flour, a little Milk, Salt, and oil'd Butter; dip them in it and fry them in clarified Butter; send Butter up in a Cup, and garnish them with fryed Parsley; you may put in a little White Wine, that is, into the Batter, you may send them in with a white Lear; as for a white Fricasey, adding some fresh Mushrooms prepared as directed for a white Fricasey of Mushrooms. You may cut Artichokes in Pieces, and put them into any Thing done in the brown Way, and likewise in several Pyes, as I shall mention in their proper Places.

To preserve Currants.
Des Corinth à preservé.

TO preserve Currants, take the largest red ones you can get, lay the Bunches on the Bottom of a splinted Sieve, till the next Day, then pick as many from the Stalks as you think will be enough to make

into

into a Syrrup, for thofe you defign to preferve. Take to a Pound of Currants, a Pound and a Half of Sugar, make a Syrrup of a Pound of it, and a Pint of Currant Juice, let it boil very well, and fkim it, then put in your Currants, and ftir them now and then, having the other Half Pound of Sugar beat and fifted, put it in by Degrees, let them boil till they be clear, put them in Pots or Glaffes; if you would candy them, make a ftrong Syrrup, let it boil to a Candy-height, which you may know by dropping it on a Plate, put in your Currants, give them two or three Turns, and tie as many in a Bunch as you pleafe; lay them on a Sieve firft, drudge with Sugar, and dry them in a drying Stove, or in a flow Oven. You may fave the Syrrup to ufe with Cherries, Rafberries, Damfins, or Red Plumbs.

To make Currant Jelly.

TAKE a Pint of Water and a Pound of double-refin'd Sugar, make it into a Syrrup, boil it well and fkim it, let it boil till it comes almoft to a Candy height, then having fome Currants picked into a Jar or Pitcher, and let into a Pot of Water, ftopped clofe and boiled till the Currants burft, ftrain them through a Jelly Bag, and put a Pint of this Juice to the Syrrup before prepared; boil it for two Minutes and fkim it, and put it into Pots or Glaffes. Clear Cakes, fee Rafberries and Currant Jame, fee Rafberry Jame.

To drefs a Pig á la Smithergill.
Cochonde lait á la Smithergall.

AFTER your Pig is haired, cleaned, and wafhed very well, cut off the Head and cleave it down the Middle, as you would a Lamb; cut it into four Quarters, trufs it like Lamb, fpit it on a fmall Spit and roaft it till the Skin begins to ftiffen; fo that you can carve it like Roaft Pork, but firft take it from the Fire; you may cut the Skin into what flourifhes you
pleafe,

pleafe, then take a deep Stew-pan, and take a Drainer that will fit it, lay in your Pig with the Skin upwards; then having provided moft Sorts of Sweet Herbs, as Thyme, Parfley, Winter Savery, Sweet Margeram, Shallot, Onion, a Handful of Parfley Roots, fome Salt, a Bay Leaf or two, fome White Pepper and Mace, fome Coriander Seeds, a large Lemon cut in Slices; put in as much Salt as you think will do, then clean the Head, by cutting it on the under Side, and taking out the Throttle and the Guts; wafh it very clean, and bind it with Tape, to keep it whole, lay it in the Middle of the Pig, then faften or tie a Cloth round your Drainer and Pig, to keep it tight, and put in as much Water as will cover it, with a Pint of Vinegar, and a Quarter of a Pound of Rice, fome Veal, that is a Knockle, with a Scrag of Mutton chopped fmall Bones and all, foke it well in warm Water and put it to the Pig, cover it clofe and let it boil foftly, fkim it well, let it boil two Hours, then take it off, let it ftand to cool, take it up and lay it into a convenient Thing that will hold it, warm the Liquor and ftrain it, let it ftand to cool, take the Fat from the Top, and the Sediment from the Bottom, wipe the Pig clean from the Herbs and Spices, or wafh them off with fome of the Liquor ; if the Liquor be not tart enough, put in a little more Vinegar ; put the Pig into it when you would ufe it ; difh it on a China Difh, with the Head in the Middle, the two hind Quarters oppofite one to the other, and fore Quarters the fame; garnifh it with a good deal of raw Parfley and Siville Orange. If you would eat it hot, take the Skin and lard the leaneft Part, half roaft it, and ftew it as before; make a Ragoo for it. See ragoo'd Sweatbreads, or you may fend it up with ftew'd Cellery, or with Caper Sauce. If your Pig be large and fat, you may cut it as before, fkin, and lard it with Parfley ; having a Pot of Water boiling hot, put in your Pig for a Minute, take it up and fpit it ; dridge it with Flour, bafte it with Butter,

falt

salt it and roaſt it as you do Lamb, and you can ſcarce tell the Difference, if you eat it with Minced-Sauce.

To roaſt à Pig à-la-Grand-vell.
Cochon de lait à la Grandvell.

TAKE a nice fat Pig, and not above twelve Days old, let it be cleaned, take out the Liver, take off the Gall, mince it fine, with a little Beef Suit, ſome Parſley, a very little Thyme, ſome Bread Crumbs, a little Sage, Nutmeg, and Salt; put it into the Pig's Belly, ſow it up, ſkewer it, ſpit it, lay it at a Diſtance from the Fire, till it hardens, then rub it over with Olive Oil; when it is roaſted, cut it up, take out the Pudding, mix it with Butter and Gravey, and put it to the Pig; ſqueeze in alittle Lemon, ſend it up hot Pig the German Way; when it is ſcalded, drawn, and cleaned, cut it into Quarters and ſkin it, truſs it like Lamb, dridge it with Flour, and brown it in good Beef Droppings; take it out to drain, then make it brown with a good Piece of Butter, dridge in ſome Flour, put in ſome Gravey drawn from Ham and Veal; put in your Pig, ſeaſon it with an Onion ſtuck with Cloves, a Fagot of Sweet Herbs, Pepper, Salt, and Nutmeg; let it ſtew till almoſt enough, then put in Half a Pint of White Wine, then take Half a Hundred of Oiſters blanch and beard them, ſave the Liquor, make another brown, and put in your Oiſters and the Liquor, put in a few Capers, a little Anchovy and Onion ſhred fine, ſqueeze in ſome Lemon, ſtrain in ſome of the Liquor, then you may put in the Pig, ſkim off the Fat, and ſtrain in the reſt; you may put in ſome Olives ſtew'd, let the Sauce be the Thickneſs of a thin Cream, ſalt it to your Taſte, diſh the Pig, and pour the Sauce over it; garniſh it with fried Parſley and Lemon.

To make a white Fricaſey of a Pig.
Cochon de la en Fricaſée blanche.

WHEN cleaned, cut it into Pieces and ſkin it, let it lie to ſoke in warm Water, then take a
good

good Piece of Butter, put it into a Stew-pan, wash out your Pig and drain it well, put it to the Butter, with a large Onion, a Faggot of sweet Herbs, some whole Pepper, Mace, and a little Salt; cover it close, and set it on a slow Fire to stew till pretty tender, then wash it out from the Liquor, and put it into a clean Stew-pan, with a sufficient Quantity of Cream, the Yolks of three or four raw Eggs, an Anchovy shred fine, with a little Onion, some Parsley, a little Sage boiled and chopt, a Piece of Butter wrought in Flour; squeeze in some Lemon, put in a little White Wine, grate in a little Nutmeg; strain the Liquor in which the Pig was stew'd in; set it on the Fire, keep it stirring till it be the Thickness of a Cream; dish it, and garnish with raw Parsley and Lemon. You may fricasey it brown, the same Way you do a brown Fricasey of Chickens or Rabbits.

To dress a Pig the French Way.
Cochou de lait á la Francoise.

WHEN it is cleaned, spit it, lay it at a good Distance from the Fire, till it is hardened, then cut it up, and cut it into pretty handsome Pieces; stew it in half strong Broth and half Gravey, a Pint of White Wine; season it with Pepper, Mace, Nutmeg, some Onion shred fine, with two Anchovies; chop some Parsley, squeeze in some Lemon, put in a little Mint, and Thyme; when it is enough, dish it on Sippets, with the Liquor it was stew'd in, and skim off the Fat.

To dress Crabs.
Ecrevice Morpion accommodée.

BOIL them, take the Meat out of their Shells and Claws, cut the last, but not very small, put all into a Stew-pan with a little Butter, some Vinegar wherein Pepper has been steeped; grate in a little Nutmeg, salt it to your Taste; but if you put in Plenty of Salt in the boiling of them, they will be salt enough;

nough; clean the Shells very well; ſtir the Meat to mix all well together; put it into the Shells; garniſh with the ſmall Claws, and a little Fennel.

To butter Crabs.
Ecrevices au beurre.

ORDER them as you did before, but put in a little Gravey, and thicken them with a Piece of Butter wrought in Flour; ſend it in a Diſh with Sippets, of white Bread cut thin; you may ſend it in French Rolls, prepared as they are for Oiſters, and call them Crab Loaves.

To fry Cream.

TAKE half Cream and half Milk, ſet it on the Fire to boil, then ſtrinkle in ſome Flour, till it be pretty ſtiff, put in a little Salt, keep it ſtirring all the Time; then butter a Diſh that will conveniently hold it; put in the Cream; let it ſtand to cool; make a Batter of Eggs, Cream, and a little Flour; cut out your Cream in Pieces; roll them in this Batter, and fry them of a Gold Colour; lay them handſomely in a Chinea Diſh, with a Cup of Butter, Sugar, and White Wine in the Middle; garniſh with Seville Orange. Or you may put it into the Diſh you deſign to ſend it in, and rub it over with the White of an Egg, whipt to a Froth, mixed with a little melted Butter, and rubbed over it; drudge it with Sugar, and brown it with a Sallamander, then it is call'd Scotch'd Cream, garniſh it as before.

To make Cream Tarts.
Tartes á la Creme.

SHEET your Petty Pans as for Sweet-meat Tarts, then having ſome Cream prepared as follows; take half Milk and half Cream, and boil it; take half a Pint of Flows, put a little Cream to it, and ſtir it till it be ſmooth, beat the Yolks of eight Eggs; put as much

much Sugar as will fweaten them to your Tafte ; mix all together; put in a little Salt and a Piece of Butter; fet it on the Fire, ftir it till it be thickened ; your Milk and Cream when mixed, muft be a Quart ; then lay fome of the Cream in the Bottom of your Tarts ; then lay a Lare of Sweetmeat, either Citron, Orange, Lemon, or any dried Sweat-meat, or white-dried from the Syrrup ; then lay Cream on the Top ; fmooth them with a Knife, dridge on fine Sugar, and bake them.

To make a Pupton of Rabbits.
Poupetoà des Lapin.

CUT them as for a Fricafey, tofs them up in melted Butter, dridge in fome Flour, put in fome good Gravey, a whole Onion, a Faggot of fweet Herbs, fome Pepper and Salt, fhred a little Parfley, let all ftew till it is the thicknefs of a Cream ; let it ftand to cool, then make fome good Forc'd-meat and beat it well, then cut fome thin Slices of Bacon, and butter a Petty-pan with a clofe Bottom, or take an Earthen Pan that will conveniently hold it; lay a round Piece of Bacon in the Bottom, and long Slices round the Sides, leaving a Space between each Piece ; fill one Space with fcalded Parfley minced fine, and fill another with Rings of Vermicelly, fo as all round roll out a Sheet of Forc'd-meat, and lay over all, prefs it down with your Hand, put in your Rabbits, with fome Yolks of hard Eggs ; roll out another Sheet of Forc'd-meat and lid it, clofe it tight, and bake it two Hours ; when baked, loofen it round the Edges with a Knife ; turn it upfide down into the Difh you defign to fend it in ; cut a round Hole in the Top, put in fome Gravey, Butter, and the Juice of Lemon ; garnifh it with fried Parfley and Lemon.

To make a Neat's Foot Pudding.
Boudin des Pieds de Beuf.

TAKE all the Flefh clean off the Bones, fhred it very fine ; take the fame Quantity of Beef Suet,

fhred

shred fine likewise; take the Quantity of both of Bread Crumbs, rubbed through a Cullender, as many Currants as you think will do; you may put in candied Lemon, Orange, or Cittron Peal, as you like, shred or sliced fine. To one Foot take seven Eggs, put in some Salt, grated Nutmeg, and a little beaten Cinnamon; mix all together, with a little Milk, make it pretty stiff, butter and flour a Cloth, tie it up tight, and boil it two Hours; let the Sauce be Butter, White Wine, Sugar, and the Juice of an Orange. A Calf's Foot Pudding is made the same Way.

To make a Liver Pudding.
Boudins de foie de Veau.

A LIVER Pudding is made the same Way, but first boil it, and grate or shred it very fine; you may put a Glass of White Wine, Sack, or Brandy, in any of these Puddings as you like.

To make a Pudding Cake.
Boudin en Gateau.

TAKE a Pound of Flour, or what Quantity you please, take the same of Suet, shred very fine; warm a Pint of Milk, put in a Spoonful of good Yest, and six Eggs; make a Hole in the Middle of the Flour, strain in your Milk, Yest, and Eggs; put in a little Salt, stir it till it is the Thickness of a thin Batter, strew some Flour over it, set it before the Fire to rise, covered with a Cloth; then having a sufficient Quantity of Currants washed and picked, put them in with the Suet, grate in some Nutmeg, put in a little Cinnamon, and Rose Water, work it to a Paste with Cream; put in some candied Peal; butter a Baking Pan, put it in, and bake it two Hours, send it up with sweet Sauce as before.

To make Almond Milk.
Amandes au lait.

TAKE one Pound of sweet Almonds and six of bitter, blanch and pound them in a Mortar, put in a little Milk to keep them from oiling, beat them very fine, then boil a Quart of New-milk, let it stand till almost cold, mix the Almonds with it, and strain it through a Napkin; wring it tight to get all you can out of it, put it into a Stew-pan with a Stalk of Cinnamon; set it on a Stove, stirring it with a Whisk till it begins to thicken; put in as much Sugar as will sweeten it; put in a little Salt, cut some Naples Biscuit thin, and brown it before the Fire, put it into your Dish or Bason, pour the Milk on it and send it up.

Another Way. Take Milk and Cream as before, boil them with a Stick of Cinnamon, some Lemon Peal, a little Salt, and as much Sugar as will sweeten it; beat six Eggs, mix it with your Milk, strain all through a Sieve, and mix it with the same Quantity as before, ordered the same Way, put it into a Stew-pan, set it on the Fire, stir it till it begins to thicken; put it into a Glass Bason, and strew it over with Caraway Comforts, or stick it with Almonds.

To farce Sheeps Tongues.
Langues de Mouton farcie.

TAKE the largest you can get, rub them with Salt and wash them clean, then farce them as follows; take the Breasts of Fowls or Veal, a little Lean of a Ham, some Mushrooms, Parsley, two or three young Onions, Pepper, Salt, and a Piece of Beef Suet, with some Crumbs of Bread; mince all very fine, work it up with the Yolks of Eggs, pound it fine in a Mortar; then cut a Hole nigh the Roots of the Tongues and thrust your Finger the whole Length of them; break the Skin as little as possible; then stuff your Tongues with

with the Farce, and stew them a la-braise, as you are directed in several Places; moisten them with strong Broth, let them stew till they be almost enough; then take off their Skins, and egg and bread them, put them into an Oven to brown, or before the Fire, baste them with Butter, then make a Ragoo of two or three Veal Sweetbreads cut in Dice. See Sweetbreads how to make it. You may braise Sheep Rumps the same Way, and send some done with the Tongues. You may do Calf Tongues the same Way, or a Neat's Tongue, and send it up in the Middle of boiled Fowls, or with the Ragoo as before.

To make a Ragoo to use with a Neat's Tongue, &c.

Ragoût a une Langue.

TAKE a Stew-pan, put into it a Quarter of a Pound of Butter, stir it till melted, dridge in some Flour, stir it till it turns brown, put in some good Gravey; if you make use of it in Winter, you may use Carrots and Turnips cut in Dice and fried in clarified Butter, or small Onions pealed and scalded in Water, dried, and fried, put them into your Gravey prepared as above, seasoned with Pepper and Salt; stew in it a Faggot of sweet Herbs, put in a little Vinegar, or the Juice of a Lemon; let it stew till it tenders your Roots, and it is the Thickness of a Cream. This is good for Beef stew'd a-la-braise, or a Breast of Mutton; add to it some Capers; if for Beef, you may put in some Mustard; this a good Sauce for a thin Flank of Beef boiled tender.

JULY.

JULY.

Soop Puree of Artichokes.
Potage purée d'Artichaux.

BOIL a Dozen of the largeſt you can get, till tender, take off the Leaves, and rub the Bottoms through a Cullinder; be ſure to take out the Chokes; then leaving ſome good ſtrong Broth, made as directed before; add as much to the pulp'd Artichokes as will be enough for your Diſh; then take the Cruſts of two French Rolls, ſoak them in ſtrong Broth, and rub it through a Sieve or Cullinder; take ſome Cellery, waſh it, cut it ſmall, with two or three Onions ſhred fine, and two or three Cabbage Lettices; waſh all well, put a Piece of Butter into a Stew-pan, with your Herbs, and a little Salt; cover it cloſe, and ſtew it tender over a ſlow Fire; then put it to the reſt of your Soop, then pare in two or three Artichokes; take out the Chokes, and cut the Bottoms in ſmall Dice, and fry them in clarified Butter, and put them to your Soop; then fry ſome dic'd Bread, and drain it well; put the Bread into your Soop Diſh, ſkim all the Fat off the Soop; force a large Artichoke Bottom, and put it into the Middle of your Diſh. Diſh up your Soop, ſeaſon it to your Taſte, and garniſh it with blanch'd Lettice; ſend it up hot.

To boil Ling.
De la Moruë à Appreter.

TAKE a middling Ling, turn it round, boil it in hard Water, Vinegar, Pepper, and Salt, with two or three Onions, and a Drainer under it; when it is well boil'd take off the Skin, and ſet it to drain; ſlide it into your Diſh; ſend round it fried

Smelts or Soles, or what you can get. Garnish with fried Parsley and Lemon; send a Boat of Sauce, made as directed before for Fish.

To dress Scate or Thornback.
Raye accommodée

TAKE the out Guts, and the Head off, and skin it on both Sides as you do Soles; cut it into what Pieces you please; throw it into hard Water, and it will turn round; take it out and dry it, and rub it over with Eggs; dridge it with Salt and Bread Crumbs, bake it of a fine brown Colour, baste it with Butter, and lay it round your Ling, or send it by itself; it is commonly eat with Mustard and Butter, or boil'd, and sent up with Sauce as before.

To make a Venison Pasty.
Paté de Venaison à faire.

TAKE a Side of Venison, bone and skin it, and cut it into round Pieces; season it with Pepper and Salt, prick it with the Point of a Knife. Make some Paste as before directed, roll it into a Sheet, and cut it round; lay a Piece all round the Venison, then wet the Paste, and lay a Sheet over all, and garnish it handsomely; then butter a Paper and lay over it, and bake it in a moderate Oven four Hours; bake the Bones in a Pot, season'd with Pepper and Salt; put as much Water to them as will cover them, and tie them down with a double Paper; strain it through a Sieve, cut a Hole in the Top of the Pasty, and put in a sufficient Quantity of this Liquor; lay on the Piece again and send it up. Some bake the Venison first in coarse Paste; but I shall leave that to the Discretion of the Maker.

To make a Pupton of Apples.
Poupeton de Pommes.

PARE and cut your Apples, and make a Marmalade of them, with their Weight of Sugar; put in a Stick of Cinnamon; boil it till it be clear and pretty stiff; let it be cold, then rim a Dish that you design to put it in; you may lay in Cherries, Currants, or stew'd Pears in Quarters; cut a Cover in Puff-paste, and lay over it; ice it and bake it. Some mix the Marmalade with grated Naples Bisket and Yolks of raw Eggs.

To stew Golden Pippins or green Jennitons.

Des Pommes d'Or etuvée.

PARE and core them with a fine Scope; put them into cold Water, as much as will cover them, with a little Loaf-Sugar, a Stick of Cinnamon, some Lemon Rind cut like Thread; so cover them down with a Sheet of Writing-Paper, and set them on a gentle Fire; let them stew till they be very tender and clear; take them out, and boil up the Liquor with a little more Sugar; put them in Pots or Glasses.

To bake Apples red.

Des Pommes cuit au four.

PARE and core them; put them into a Pot with Sugar, and a little Cochineal, beat fine and tied in a fine Rag; cover them with coarse Paste, and bake them in a slow Oven till they be very tender; then mix them well and use them as you like, as for Puffs or Tarts, Apple Pyes, &c.

To make Apple Fritters.

Bignets des Pommes.

CORE and pare them; cut them in round Slices; scald them a little in Water; lay them on a Sieve to dry; then make a Batter of a Pint of Flour, Half a Pint of Cream, and six Eggs; leave out four Whites, beat them very well and strain them, put in a little potted Sugar, a little beaten Cinnamon, a little Salt, mix all well together; if that does not make it thin enough, add a little more Cream, but

X take

take Care you don't make it too thin; then dip in your Apples, Slice by Slice, and fry them in hot Lard or Suet render'd, or clarified Butter, which is the best; set them before the Fire, on a Drainer till you have fried all. Dish them and dridge on fine Sugar.

To make Pancakes of the same.
Des Gateaux mince frit an Poel.

PUT a little Fat in the Bottom of your Pan; then put in some Butter, but your butter must be made thinner; then lay on some Apples, then some Batter on them; fry them of a light Brown on both Sides; strew on Sugar betwixt each Pancake, and some on the Top. You may garnish your Dish with Seville Orange.

To make an Apple Tanzey.
Des Pommes au Tanaise.

PRepare your Apples as before; take two Naples Bisket, and rub them through a Cullinder, then boil a Quart of Cream and Milk, and put to it; cover it and let it stand, then beat twelve Eggs, leave out five Whites, and strain them in; put in Half a Pint of Spinage Juice, with a little Tanzey Juice, a Quarter of a Pound of Butter melted, and as much Sugar as will sweeten it to your Taste, grate in a little Nutmeg, mix all together, and stir it over the Fire till it be thick; butter a Paper and lay it in the Bottom of your Dish; put in some of the Tanzey, lay on some Apples, then Tanzey till your Dish is fill'd; then bake it, turn it into a Dish, take off the Paper, garnish it with Seville Orange, and grate in Sugar.

To make Mutton à la Royal.
Mouton à la Royal.

TAKE a Giggot of Mutton, that is, a Leg and Part of the Loin, cut like a Haunch of Venison; lard the thick Part of the Leg, paper it with double

double Paper, and half roaſt it; then lay in ſome Bards of Bacon, and Slices of lean Beef in the Bottom of a Stew-pan, ſeaſon'd with ſweet Herbs, Pepper, and Salt; then lay in your Mutton with the larded Side downwards, cover it as under, ſeaſon'd as before; ſet it on a ſlow Fire, lay ſome lighted Charcoal on the Lid; let it ſtew for an Hour, then put in a Pint of Claret; let it ſtew for another Hour, take Care it does not burn, if you find it in Danger, put in ſome good Gravey; make a Ragoo of Sweetbreads for it as directed. See Sweetbreads. Strain the Liquor from the Mutton, lay the Mutton in the Diſh, ſkim off the Fat, put the Gravey to your Ragoo, heat all together, and pour it over your Meat. Garniſh with fried Oiſters and Pickles.

To dreſs Chickens the Barbary Way.
Poulets à la Barbarie.

TRUSS them as for boiling, and break down their Breaſt-bones; ſinge them; let them lie in warm Water to ſoak out their Blood; then make a well-ſeaſon'd Forc'd-meat for them, with a good deal of Parſley, ſtuff their Bellies with it, and boil them in ſkim'd Milk, with a good Quantity of ſweet Herbs; let the Milk boil before you put them in, Half an Hour will boil them; then take them up, and dry them with a Cloth, egg and bread them; put them into an Oven to brown, then make the Sauce as follows: Take an Anchovey, ſhred it fine with an Onion, then ſhred a few Capers, and a pretty deal of Parſley; put a Piece of Butter into a Stew-pan, duſt in ſome Flour, ſtir it, and put in a Ladle-full of good Gravey; put in the Herbs and Capers with the Juice of Lemon, their Livers ſcalded and ſhred; mix all together with a Ladle-full of drawn Butter, and put it over your Chickens. Garniſh with Lemon and Barberries.

Rabbits

Rabbits à la Saingaraz.
Lapins à la Saingaraz.

TRUSS your Rabbits as you do a young Hare; make a Pudding for their Bellies of Beef Suet shred fine, with the Crumb of a French Roll soak'd in Cream, their Livers shred fine with Shallot and some Parsley; season it with Pepper, Salt, and Nutmeg, a little Lemon Peel minc'd fine; work it all together with an Egg, put it into their Bellies, sew them up and spit them; lay on their Backs Bards of Bacon, tie them on with Packthread, roast them, and baste them well with Butter; when they are enough take off the Bacon, and take out the Pudding that is in their Bellies, mix it with Gravey and Butter, and squeeze in some Lemon. Dish the Rabbits, and put the Sauce over them, lay on the Bards of Bacon, and garnish with Parsley and Lemon.

To make Veal Cutlets.
Cottelets de Veau.

CUT them off a Leg of Veal a Quarter of an Inch thick, let them be all of a Size as nigh as you can, hack them with the Back of a Knife, wash them over with the Yolks of Eggs and melted Butter, strinkle them over on both sides with Bread Crumbs, Parsley, and a little Thyme; broil them on a Charcoal Fire. The Sauce is Butter, Gravey, and Mushrooms. Garnish with Rashers of Bacon and Lemon.

To make Black Caps.
Des Pommes qu'on appelle Bounets noir.

TAKE what Quantity of Apples you please, cut them in two, take out the Cores, lay them in a flat bottom'd Dripping pan, and put to them some Red Wine sweeten'd with Sugar; lay in some Bits of Lemon Peel, wet the Apples with Water, dridge in some fine Sugar, and bake them in a hot Oven that

will

will make them black on the Tops; let them stand till they be tender, let them stand to cool; then take them up with a thin Knife, and fill the Skins with the Pulp that will stew out. Dish them and grate on Sugar. You may send up a Cup of Cream in the Middle.

To stew Barbel.
Barbeau etuvée.

SCALE and draw them, then fry them a little in Butter; take them out, and brown your Pan with Butter and Flour; put in a Quart of Red Wine, with two Anchovies shred fine, with a little Onion; put in a little whole Pepper and Mace, a Faggot of sweet Herbs, and the Juice of a Lemon; put in your Fish, and let them stew in this till they be enough; let your Pan be close covered. Dish them with the Sauce that is at them, add some melted Butter, take out the sweet Herbs. Garnish with Horse Raddish and Lemon.

To broil Barbel.

SCALE and draw them, wash and rub them dry with a Cloth, rub them well with Flour, rub your Gridiron with a Bit of fat Bacon, lay on the Fish, and broil them on a very slow Fire, turn them; then take a Gill of White Wine, with a little good strong Broth or Gravey, the Juice of Half a Lemon, a little Anchovey and Onion shred fine; put in your Butter, dust in a little Flour; draw up your Sauce pretty thick, put it in your Dish, and lay your Fish on it. Garnish with Barberries and Lemon.

To pickle Barbel.
Barbeau en conserve.

SEE TROUT.

To farce Beef.

TAKE a Rump or Part of the Ribs, or Surloin, spit and roast it; when it is almost enough,
draw

draw it, raise up the Skin, and cut as much off the Beef out as you like, shred it fine with some Pickles, Thyme, Parsley, and Onion, mix it with the Gravey, a little Pepper and Salt, and make it hot in a Stew-pan over the Fire, with a Piece of good Butter; then fill up the Place where you cut it out, lay it smooth, draw on the Skin again, and put it into an Oven for Half an Hour, first skewer down the Skin; then dish it up, and garnish with Horse-raddish, Pickles, and Toasts of White-Bread; you may put in a little Red Wine, if you please into your minc'd Beef. You may do a small Piece of Beef the same Way for a Side Dish; if you can't conveniently roast it, you may bake it or braise it, as you like. See Beef a la Braise.

To make a light Flour Pudding.
Boudiu commune au farine.

TAKE a Pint of Milk and a Pint of Cream and boil it, let it stand to cool, take the Yolks of twelve Eggs, beat them and run them through a Sieve; take four Spoonfuls of fine Flour, and put to it a little of your Milk and Cream, beat it well with a Wooden Spoon, mix the rest with your Eggs, put in a little Salt, mix it all together by Degrees, and beat it well; then butter and flour a fine Cloth, and tie it up and boil it an Hour and a Quarter; send it in with plain Butter, or with sweet Sauce. You may boil it in a Bason, and tie the Cloth over it.

To farce Cucumbers.
Concombres farcie.

TAKE out the Seeds with a Scoope, pare them and fill them with good Forc'd-meat; stew them a-la-brase, then make a Ragoo of sliced Cucumbers, as directed. See stewed Cucumbers.

To

ART of COOKERY.

To stew Cabbage.
Choux etuvée.

TAKE a small one, cut it through the Middle, take out the Heart, wash it well, fill the Middle with Forc'd-meat; put in some Mushrooms into your Forc'd-meat, first minced fine; then blanch your Cabbage in boiling Water, then squeeze it dry, and rub it with the Yolk of an Egg within, and then lay in your Forc'd-meat, bind it round with Packthread, and stew it a-la-brase; then take another Cabbage, and cut it in four, take out the Heart, cut it fine, with two or three Onions, wash it well and put a Piece of Butter into a Stew-pan; put in your sliced Cabbage and Onions, stir it, let it stew, put in a Ladle full of good Gravey; stew all together till tender; take up your whole Cabbage, lay it in your Dish, put over it the Ragoo and send it up.

To roast Quales.
Cailles roti.

TRUSS them with their Heads on, as you do Moore-game; roast them, let the Sauce be Gravey and Butter; garnish them with Bread Crumbs, borwn'd with butter.

Pigeons to farce and roast.

TAKE their Livers and mince them fine, with some Beef, sweet Parsley, a Bit of the Lean of a Ham, some Bread Crumbs, Nutmegs, and a little Thyme, and Pepper; stuff their Bellies with it; skewer them, spit and roast them; let the Sauce be Butter Gravey, Parsley, and Lemon.

To preserve Cherries.
Cerises preservé.

TAKE a Pound of the ripest Cherries, take off their Stalks, put to them a Pint of the Juice of Goosberries (see as before mentioned) boil them till you

you have the Colour taken out of them, strain them, and take half a Pint of that Liquor to a Pound of Cherries stewed, and a Pound of double refined Sugar pounded and sifted; put half of the Sugar to the Liquor, boil it and skim it, put in your Cherries, add the rest of the Sugar by Degrees, boil them till they be clear; put them into Pots or Glasses first, stir them till they be cold, or they will turn of a purple Colour; cut a Paper to fit the Vessel you put them in, dip it in Brandy, lay it on, tie them down, and keep them in a Place not too hot nor too cold.

To make Cherry Brandy Ratifie.
Cerises d'eou de vie.

TAKE the Stones of the Cherries you preserved, crack them in a Mortar, and put them to a Quart of the best Brandy, let it stand till you can get some good Black Cherries; then put in what Quantity you please, and sweeten it to your Taste.

To make a Semey of Venison.
Venasou Semey.

TAKE what Piece you like, soak it in warm Water, boil it a little in Salt and Water, then make a Paste, or Bread Crumbs, rubbed through a Cullinder, with White Wine and Butter boiled together, and sweetened with Sugar; mix some Flour with your Bread Crumbs, to make it hold together; make your Paste pretty stiff, then take an Earthen Dish the Bigness of the Dish you design to send it up in, that will conveniently hold it, butter the Bottom, and a Sheet of Writing Paper, then lay the Paper all over the Dish; roll out a Peace of your Paste, and lay on the Paper, then lay in your Venison, with the fat Side down; lay Bits of Butter on that, then roll out the rest of your Paste and lay over it and close it down; bake it till it be tender, then loosen the Edges of it, with a sharp pointed Knife, and lay it on the Dish you design to send

it

it in, and turn it upſide down, into the Diſh; take off the Writing-Paper, and lay a Border of Puff Paſte round the Rim of the Diſh, waſh it all over with an Egg beaten, and bake it till the Paſte is enough, and the other coloured fine; then take ſome Red-Wine, the Juice of a Lemon, Butter, Sugar, with ſome beaten Cinnamon; draw it up in a Stew pan, cut a round Hole in the Top, pour it in, lay on the Piece again, and ſend it up.

I ſhall mention ſome particular Ways of dreſſing Veniſon; but as I have obſerved, plain roaſted, bak'd or boil'd, is beſt liked by us Engliſh People.

Veniſon a la Royal.
Venaiſon a-la Royale.

TAKE a Haunch of Veniſon, and three Parts roaſt it; draw it and ſtew it a-la-braiſe, as you do a Piece of Beef; then make a Ragoo of Sweatbreads, Cucumbers, Aſparagus Tops; diſh it and pour over it the Ragoo; garniſh it with Seville Orange, and fried Parſley.

To roaſt a Shoulder of Veniſon.
Epaule de Veniſon.

LARD the lean Part with Bacon; roaſt it at a ſlow Fire, put into your Dripping-pan ſome White Wine, Salt, whole Pepper, an Onion ſliced; baſte it with that, take Care you do not roaſt it too much, then baſte it with Butter, and dridge it with Flour and Bread Crumbs, let it brown, and draw it; take the Liquor out of the Dripping-pan, and ſtrain it through a Sieve; ſkim off the Fat, make it hot, and put it under your Veniſon; you may ſend ſome Currant Jelly in a Cup or Boat, made warm with Red Wine; garniſh as you like beſt. You may dreſs any other Piece of Veniſon the ſame Way.

To make Cherry Wine.
Vin de Cerises.

TAKE what Quantity you please, stone them, and put them into a Hair Bag; put it into a Press to squeeze out the Juice to a Gallon; put two Pounds of Sugar, the finer the better; put it into a Vessel to work, when it has done stop it up; let it stand for two Months, then bottle it, it will be fit to drink in two Months more; if you would have it ripe sooner, put a little Sugar in when you bottle it. You may make Currant or Rasberry Wine the same Way: Some make them as they do Goosberry Wine, some put in Wine, some Brandy; but, in my Opinion, good Sugar, and Plenty of it, is the chief Ingredient in Made Wines; be sure you let it stand Half a Year before you bottle it, that is, if you allow Plenty of Sugar; if you do not, you must bottle it sooner, as above; for the longer you would have it keep, the sweeter you must make it; natural Juice is the best sweeten'd well, and Time enough given it. It will drink as well as most foreign Wines.

To preserve Rasberries whole, or Strawberries.
Fraises conservé.

GAther them before they be too ripe, put them into an Earthen Dish, strew on them some Loaf-Sugar, pounded and sifted; let them lie two Hours; make a strong Syrrup, according to the Quantity you would do, boil and skim it; put in your Straw or Rasberries, keep them stirring, strinkle in some Sugar now and then, boil them till they be clear, put them into Pots or Glasses; always observe to stir them till they are almost cold, before you put them up, it makes them keep their Colour the better.

To preserve Apricots.
De Apricots preservé.

TAKE them before they be too ripe, pare and stone them, and lay them in an Earthen Dish; pound and sift a Pound of double-refined Sugar, and put over them; let them lie till the Sugar is dissolv'd, put them into your preserving Pan, that is a Pound of Apricots to a Pound of Sugar; let them boil quick over a Charcoal Fire, strinkle in Half a Pound of Sugar more in the boiling, a little at a Time; let them boil till they be clear; put them in Pots or Glasses.

To dry Apricots.
Apricots seche.

LET them boil to a Candy Height, and put them on Glass-Plates to dry, dry them in a moderate Stove, and turn them with a thin Knife: To dry them another Way; take the largest you can get, pare and stone them, and fill them with double-refin'd Sugar; sift some Sugar on a Massareen, lay on the Apricots, and sift Sugar all over them; then set them in a moderate Oven for an Hour, drain the Liquor from them, sift on more Sugar, set them in again; if they run out, make them up round, and keep this Order till they be dry; then put them into Boxes, paper'd with Writing-Paper.

To make Apricot Clear-cakes.
Des Apricots transparent.

PARE them, and scald them in Water; strain the Water from them; take the Apricots from the Stones, and rub them through a coarse Sieve; to every Pound of Pulp take a Pound of double-refin'd Sugar, pounded and sifted; put Half of it to the Pulp, and boil it till it be clear; take the other Half, put a Quarter of a Pint of Water to it, and boil it to a Candy Height; skim it, put in your Apricots, and stir it well; put it into Glasses and dry it; let your
Glasses

Glaſſes be of what Form you pleaſe, when they are dry looſen them round the Edges, and you may turn them out.

White Plumbs are done the ſame Way, only ſcalded to take off their Skins.

To boil a Haunch of Veniſon.
Gigot de Venaiſon boulli.

SALT it well with common Salt, let it lie four Days, turn and rub it every Day, waſh it in Water, tie it up in a Cloth, and boil it in a good deal of Water; if it be a large one it will take three Hours; then diſh it and ſend it up with Colliflowers, Carrots, Turnips, Savoy, Cabbages, as you like beſt, or Kidney Beans, or mix ſome of theſe, as you pleaſe. Send drawn Butter in a Boat. I ſhall lay down ſome Methods of boiling your Roots and Greens, though they may be known by a great many, but I preſume not by all.

To boil green Sprouts.
De jeun Choux bouili.

TAKE off the Outſide Leaves and lay them by themſelves, cut the Hearts a-croſs and a croſs, put them into Water, and boil them in hard Water; but put in no Salt, for that hardens them, and makes them longer a boiling; when they are tender, ſtrain them and preſs out the Water, put them into an Earthen Pot, ſtrinkle a little Salt on them, and cover them down; ſet them by the Fire to keep hot till you want them; then ſtrip the other Leaves off the Stalks, and waſh and broil them as you did the other, in freſh hard Water, then order them as before. You may boil Savoys, Broclie, or any green Herb, the ſame Way; in ordering your Greens in this Manner you will ſave Half of them, which a great many throw away.

To boil and order Carrots.
Des Carrotes bouilli.

CUT off the out-fide Skin with a fharp Knife, boil them tender, flit them in Quarters, cut them in fmall Bits, and keep them in warm Water till wanted.

To order and boil Turnips.
Navets bouilli.

PARE them as far as the Skin goes; if you leave any of the Skin on, it makes them eat bitter; cut the large ones in two, boil them in hard Water, and they will look white and well; dice them, or fqueeze and mafh them with a Piece of Butter, as beft lik'd; put them into an Earthen Pot, keep them hot, and falt them to your Tafte.

To boil young Cabbage.
Des Choux bouilli.

ORDER them as you did the green Sprouts: A large Cabbage, cut into four Parts, cut out the large Stalks, part all the Leaves, and boil it in hard Water till tender. Order it as you do Sprouts.

To make a Sauce called a Poiverade.
Saufe poivreade.

TAKE fome Vinegar, White Wine Water, the White of a Leek, fliced thin, three or four Slices of Lemon, fome whole Pepper and Salt; ftew it over the Fire, mince a Shallot or two very fine, put the Shallot into a Boat or Bafon; boil the reft in a Sauce-pan, ftrain it, and put the Liquor to the Shallot. You will find it mention'd in many Receipts of the Book where it is to be ufed.

To make a Sauce Robert.
Saufe Robert.

TAKE fome Onions, peel and flice them, cut them like Dice, ftrinkle them with Salt, dridge

over

over them a little Flour, fry them brown in clarified Butter, keep them constantly moving for fear they should burn, put in some good Gravey with some Vinegar, Mustard, and beaten Pepper. This is proper Sauce for Hog's Feet and Ears, thicken'd with a Cullis of Veal and Ham, or a Piece of Butter mix'd with Flour, It is proper for fried Tripe or Neat's Feet fried with Batter mix'd with some melted Butter, your Dish being garnished with fried Onions.

To make Jelly of Lemons, or Oranges.
Gellé de Limmons.

TAKE the clearest, and them that have the thickest Rinds; rasp the Out sides off with a fine Grater, cut a Bit off from the Stalk, and skoop out all the Inside, but leave the outside Rind as thick as you can; put them into Water, and shift them every Day for nine Days; boil them in a good deal of Water, then take some well tasted Apples, pare and slice them, and stew them in Water till they are tender; also, you must observe to have Water and Apples enough, so that the Water may taste pretty strong of the Apples, and to have sufficient to make your Syrrup of; when it is strain'd from the Apples, let it stand to settle; take off the Clear; to a Pint of this Liquid, take a Pound of double-refin'd Sugar, boil it to a Sirrup; your Oranges being boil'd tender, but not to break, let them lie to soak a little in cold Water; take them out and put them to your Sirrup; you must have as much more Sirrup as will do for the Oranges, because I have prepar'd it in this Manner, to send it to the Table in small Glasses, as you do Currants, or any other Jelly; then when your Oranges are boil'd in this Sirrup a Quarter of an Hour, take them up, and put them into a Pot that will conveniently hold them without lying one upon another; then take the Pulp that you skoop'd out of your Oranges, put to it some of the Jelly of the Apples,

ples, bruize it well with a wooden Ladle or Spoon, strain it into an Earthen Pot through a fine Sieve or Cloth; the Liquid being first made warm, put it to your Sirrup that the Oranges were boil'd in; let it all boil together for ten Minutes, skim it well, and put it to your Oranges; let them stand till the next Day, lay Writing-Paper over them close to the Oranges; then put all together into your Preserving-Pan again, and boil them till they are very clear; put them into your Pot again, order'd as before, the Pot tied over with Paper and Leather; when you make Use of any of the Jelly, as before mention'd, put it into Glasses, with some of the Orange sliced thin. You may make Marmalade of Oranges, they being prepared in this Manner, pounded in a Mortar, and boil'd in some of the aforesaid Liquor till it is clear and thick; put it into what Sort of Moulds or Glasses you please; when you would use any of them, open the Edges with a large Needle, and turn them out into little Glass Plates. You may candy any of the whole Oranges at Pleasure, by making of a strong Sirrup and boiling it to a Candy-Height; keep them moving in your Preserving-Pan, till the Sirrup begins to candy; take them out, and put them into your drying Stove, some in Halves and some in Quarters. You may do as before directed in the preparing of the whole ones, to make into Marmalade, or to cut to put into your Jelly.

To make Jelly of Pippins:

Gellé des Pommes.

TAKE a Dozen of Golden Pippins, pare and core them, slice them into three Pints of clear Water, put to them a Pound of double refin'd Sugar, boil them till they are all of an Amber Colour and smooth, put them into what Shape of Glasses you like, and keep it for your Use. You may boil them into a Marmalade, and put them into Glasses, as you were directed

for

for Marmalade of Orange; turn them out the same, and stick them with candied Lemon Peel.

To make a white Jelly.
Gellé blanc à faire.

TAKE Half a Pound of Almons, put them into hot Water till you can take off the Skins, beat them in a Mortar, with a little Orange Flower Water, and a little Cream, till they are very fine ; then take some Jelly of Calves Feet, boil in it some Icing-glass till it is a very strong Jelly; strain it, put to it Half a Pint of White Wine, squeeze in the Juice of two Lemons, sweeten it to your Taste with fine Sugar, mix it with your Almonds, wring it through a Cloth, put it into a well-tinn'd Stew-pan, with a Piece of Cinnamon, and Lemon Peel ; set it on the Fire, and keep it stirring, with a Whisk, till it begins to thicken, which will be in two or three Minutes; take it off, keep it stirring till it is almost cold ; then take some Eggs, and make a Hole at each End of them, and blow them dry ; then stop one End with a Bit of Paste, and fill them at the other End with some of this Jelly. You may colour some of the Jelly, Red, Yellow, or Blue, just as you like ; when they are cold, rub them over with beaten Whites of Eggs, and roll them in small-coloured Comfits ; put some fine Sugar in your Dish, set them up on one End, and garnish them with dried Sweet-meats. You may keep some of them plain, by breaking the Shells of them ; and taking off the Jelly ; put some fine Jelly in the Bottom of your Dish ; lay in your Eggs on their Sides, lay betwixt and about them some fine Lemon Peel about six Inches long, cut like Straws, and boil'd in Sirrup till clear ; then take some Chocolate, put it into Water, sweeten it with a little Loaf Sugar ; put into it some Ringlets of Vermicelly, let it lie to soak in that till it is a little colour'd ; take them out with a little Slice ; lay them on the Back of a Sieve to drain,

when

when they are drain'd well, lay them all round the Edge of your Dish; this is call'd a Hen's Nest.

How to make a Lumber Pye.

Lumber Pye.

RAISE a Pye to the Height of a Custard in the Dish you design to make it in; cut out the Bottom, then take some Pork, Veal, and Beef Suet, season it with Nutmeg, Pepper, Salt, and sweet Herbs; make it into Rolls the Thickness of a large Eel, three Inches long, being first minced like Forc'd-meat; then take the Caul of Veal, cut it in two Pieces the Breadth and Length of your Rolls; rub it over with Yolks of Eggs, rub them all over with that, and roll them in it; lay them into your Pye, put one in the Middle made round, fill up the Vacancies with Sweet-breads, blanch'd and cut in Dice; season it as you did the rest, put in some Yolks of Eggs boil'd hard; lay on them a Rasher of interlarded Bacon, put in some Bits of Butter upon the Sweet-breads; put in Half a Pint of good strong Broth or Gravey; close your Pye with the same Paste you raised it of, then lay a Border of Puff-Paste, all round the Dish Edge, and join it close to your Pye; mark it all round with a marking Stick or a Skewer; pare it off from the Edge of your Dish, brush it all over with the Yolk of an Egg, and a little Cream; bake it an Hour and a Half, when baked, cut off the Lid, and make a Ragoo of Mushrooms and Morels, as you have directed in several other Places; put in a few Capers shred, a Glass of White Wine; skim the Fat off your Pye as much as you can, put in the Ragoo, cut your Lid in eight Pieces, like Sippets; stick them in the Pye, and send it up.

N. B. As I could not get some Things into their proper Months when they were in Season, I shall mention them here, and mention the Months they are to be done in.

To make Claer Fritters.

Bignets de clarie.

TAKE the Leaves all of a Size as near as you can, cut off the Stalks, wash them in Water, blanch them in boiling Water, then beat twelve Yolks of Eggs, mix'd with a little White Wine and Salt; then clarify some Butter, make it hot in your Frying-pan or Stew-pan, then dip your Leaves, one by one, into your Yolks of Eggs, and put them in your Pan smooth; fry them brown like Fritters, and set them before the Fire; then melt some Butter, with a little Juice of Lemon and Gravey, put it in a Cup, and set it in the Middle of your Dish; dish your Fritters round it, and garnish with fried Parsley and Seville Orange.—To be done in June.

How to make a Marmalade of Warden Pears.

Des Poirs en Marmalade.

PARE, and cut them in Slices from the Cores, put them into as much Water as will cover them, set them over a Fire, covered down close; put in a Stick of Cinnamon, a little Sugar, and two or three Cloves; when they are tender, pass them through a Cullinder, with a small wooden Ladle; then take a Pint of Water, and a Pound of double-refin'd Sugar, boil it to a Candy Height, and put in a Pint of the Pears, that you rub'd through the Cullinder; add to it Half a Pound of double-refin'd Sugar, beat to Powder; stir it till it be clear; put it into Pots or Glasses. This may be done in this Month.

To preserve Mulberries.

Meurs preservé.

GATHER them before they are too ripe, pick them from the Stalks, lay them in an earthen Pot, strew over them some double-refin'd powder'd Sugar; then take some of them that are thoroughly ripe,

ripe, squeeze out their Juice through a fine Cloth or Sieve; to a Pound of Mulberries take a Pound and a Half of double-refin'd Sugar; make it into a Sirrup, with a Pint and a Half of Mulberry Juice; squeeze in the Juice of two Seville Oranges or Lemons; skim it very well, put in the Mulberries, keep them moving in the Sirrup, and boil them till they are clear. Put them in Pots or Glasses for your Use.

How to make Marrow Loaves.
Pain de Mouelle.

TAKE Half a Dozen of French Rolls, cut a Piece off from the Tops, take out the Crumb, lay it to soak in Cream; take the Marrow of two Marrow-bones, shred it fine, take Half a Pint of Spinage Juice, take the Bread out of the Cream, put it into a Mortar, with a Piece of Butter, and the Spinage Juice; season it with Nutmeg and Salt; put in a Glass of White Wine, pound it all well together; put in your Marrow, squeeze in the Juice of a Lemon, mix all together; then fry the Rolls in clarified Butter, or rub them well with Butter within and without; set them in an Oven, or crisp them before a Fire, with the Pieces that you cut off the Tops; likewise put four Yolks of Eggs into the Mixture before-mention'd; mix all together, and fill the Rolls, bake them in an Oven an Hour. Dish them up, and garnish them with fried Parsley. These are properly called, *Marrow Loaves à la Smithergell.*

To dress Mutton the Turkish Way.
Mouton à la Turqeie.

TAKE a Leg of Mutton, cut it in Slices, flat it with a Cleaver; put it into a Stew-pan, wash a Quarter of a Pound of Rice, with some whole Pepper, and a little Mace; slice in three or four Onions, put as much Water to it as will cover it, put in a Faggot of Sweet Herbs, stew it over a slow Fire;

chop

chop the Bones of the Leg to Pieces, put it into a Pot, put to it three or four Turnips pared and sliced, a Carrot likewise, with four Heads of Celery, cut and wash'd clean; boil it well, and skim it; keep supplying your Mutton with this Broth; take Care your Mutton and Rice do not burn to the Bottom; when the Rice and Meat is tender, toast some Pieces of White Bread; dish it up in a Soop Dish; stick the Toasts all round, and send it for a Top-Dish of the first Course.

To make a Neat's Feet Pye.
Paté Pieds de Beuf.

TAKE two Neat's Feet, when boil'd and clean'd take out the Bones, mince them fine, put to them Half a Pound of Beef Suet chopt fine, Half a Dozen Apples, pared, cored and cut, Half a Pound of Currants and Raisins wash'd and pick'd clean, a Quarter of a Pound of fine Sugar, Half a Pint of White Wine, a little beaten Cinnamon, Nutmeg, and Mace; put in some Salt; sheet your Dish with Puff-paste; mix all your Ingredients well together, put them into the Pye, lid it, and bake it.

To bake Neat's Feet.
Pieds de Beuf au four.

CLEAN them as before, take out the long Bones, lard them with Bacon, brush them over with the Yolks of raw Eggs, season them with Pepper, Salt, and Sweet Herbs shred fine; put them into a convenient Thing, with a little Gravey at the Bottom; set them in an Oven for a Quarter of an Hour, draw them, and baste them well with melted Butter; let the larded Sides of them be uppermost, cover them with a Sheet of Paper; set them in the Oven again till they are baked tender, then draw them; dish them up handsomely. Garnish the Dish with fried Onions, make a Sauce Robert, and put under them, made as you will see before directed.

ART of COOKERY.

To make a Sweet Pye of a Neat's Tongue.
Paté de Langues de Beuf.

BOIL a fresh Tongue very tender, blanch it; when it is cold, cut it into thin Slices, and sheet your Dish with Puff-paste; season it lightly with Pepper, Nutmeg, Cinnamon, and Sugar, all finely beaten; then put into the Pye a Lare of Tongue, then strew over that some Currants and Raisins clean'd, wash'd, and pick'd; put in some Dates, ston'd and cut in Halves; lay on that some Marrow, cut in Dice, then lay on some more Tongue, then some Currants, Raisins, and Marrow, with some Grapes that are not too ripe, plain Butter over all; strew over it some fine Sugar, put in a Gill of Red Wine, close it, ice it, and bake it; when it is baked cut off the Lid, draw up some Butter, with a Gill of Red Wine, grate in some Nutmeg, put in some Sugar, with the Juice of a Seville Orange, dust in a little Flour, draw it all up thick, pour it over the Pye; cut the Lid in two, and lay it upon the Pye again, so that it may be seen what Sort of a Pye it is, and send it up.

To make Rasberry Jelly.
Gellé de Fraises.

PICK them, put them into a Pitcher, set it in a Pot that will conveniently hold it; put as much Water into the Pot as will reach three Parts or more, but not so high as it will boil away; let your Pitcher be stopp'd very close, let it boil till the Rasberries are become to a Mash, then strain them through a Flannel Bag, as you do Jelly; then take a Pint of Water, put into it a Pound of double-refin'd Sugar, skim it and boil it till it comes to a Candy Height; then put in a Pint of Rasberry Liquor, with a Quarter of a Pound of Loaf Sugar more, let it simmer over the Fire till the Sugar is all melted; skim it very well, and put it into Glasses. This is the best Way of making

king Jellies of Currants, Cherries, and Goosberries; observe that all the Fruit must be thoroughly ripe, and pick'd clean, that are done this Way. The Cherries must be ston'd and stalk'd, and to two Pounds of Cherries you must put in Half a Pint of Water. Goosberries the same, that is, any Fruit that has Stones in them must be taken out, as you did the Cherries.

To pickle Walnuts white.
Noix confit au Vinaigre blanc.

GATHER them at the same Time you did the other, stick a Fork in the Stalk End, pare off the green Peel with a very sharp Knife, and wipe the Knife often to keep it from colouring them, put them into Water as you pare them, then cut a Lemon in two, and rub them with it to make them keep white; put them into Salt Water and Vinegar; cover them, then set them on a Charcoal Fire to simmer, but not to boil; put them into wide-mouth'd Bottles, with distill'd Vinegar; put on a little sweet Oil, and tie them down, but first cork them.

To preserve Walnuts.
Noix à preservé.

GATHER them as before, and put them into Salt and Water, shift them every Day for a Week, then boil a Brine and put to them; let them stand till the next Day, strain them, and put some Vine Leaves into the Bottom of a Brass-pan; if you cannot get Vine Leaves conveniently, take Currant-Tree Leaves; lay on them your Walnuts, and more Leaves on them again; put to them as much hard Water as will cover them, and two or three Spoonfuls of greening, as directed in greening of Codlings; set them over a slow Fire for two or three Hours to tender them, but not to boil; you must do them carefully, then take them out, and put them into cold Water; then make a Syrrup of Powder Sugar; take double

their

ART of COOKERY.

their Weight, and to each Pound put also a Pint of Water; boil and skim it; then beat the White of an Egg very well; it will do for four Pound of Sugar, let the Sugar boil up, drop it in, stir it, and it will rise up; take it off the Fire, and let it stand a little, then skim off the Top, and the Bottom will be very clear; put in your Walnuts, set it on the Fire again, and let it simmer some Time; take it off and set it out again, so keep this Order till they look clear; put in the Juice of a Lemon, and some Orange Flower Water, let it simmer a little longer; take them off, and put them into Pots; tie them down when cold.

How to make Walnuts keep all the Year.
Noix à garder tout l'Année.

AS I am now treating of Walnuts I shall give you a Direction how to keep them all the Year, to eat as fresh as new gather'd, likewise Filberts, &c. When ripe and fit for gathering, take some Crabs, and stamp them, and lay a Lare of them and a Lare of Walnuts into an Earthen Pot, till you have fill'd it; let the Crabs be the last Lare, then cut a Paper to fit the Top of the Pot to go down within, then render some Mutton Suet, and shred it all over; when it is almost cold, let it be thick enough to keep out the Air. You may order Filberts the same Way, or Hazel Nuts; let their Husks be on; if they be quite ripe, and will shell, you may put them into Bottles and cork them tight, cut off the Tops of the Corks and rosin them down. You may bottle Walnuts the same Way, putting them into wide-mouth'd Bottles, or into Jars, if you cork them run Rosin over them, and tie them down with Leather.

AUGUST.

AUGUST.

To make a Craw-fish Soop.
Potage d'Ecrevices.

BOIL them, pull off the Tails, and pick off the Shells, then take off their Legs, and at the Ends next their Bodies you will find a little Bag, which you must take away, for it is bitter, then take out the woolly Part that is in their Bodies, and throw it away; put their Shells into a Marble Mortar, and pound them to a Paste; you may make your Stock of what Sort of Fish you can conveniently get, that is of Codfish, Scate, Whitings, Place, or Part of all; clean and wash them well, and boil them with Sweet Herbs and Onions, whole Pepper, and a little Mace; season it with Salt to your Taste; when boil'd enough, put in your pounded Craw-fish, stir all together and strain it through a Sieve; let it stand to settle, skim off the Top, and pour the Clear from the Bottom; take Care none of the Bottom goes in, for it will make your Soop taste sandy; take some of the Broth, and put in it the Crust of a Penny Brick; let it soak and simmer over the Fire till it is tender, then rub it through a Sieve, and put it to the rest of your Stock; then make some Forc'd-meat of some of your raw Fish, a middling-siz'd Whiting or small Codling, but a Carp is the best; leave the Head and the Back-bone whole, mince the Flesh with Marrow or good Beef Suet, sweet Herbs, season'd with Pepper, Salt, and Nutmeg; put in some Bread Crumbs, work it up with the Yolks of Eggs, and beat it fine in a Mortar; butter a Massereen, or a little Dish; lay on the Bone or Head of your Fish, turn it round, and fasten the Head to the Tail with a Pack-thread, then rub the
Bone

Bone over with Yolks of Eggs; lay on the Forc'd-meat, fashion it like the Fish, and rub it over with melted Butter; strinkle it all over with Bread-Crumbs, and bake it, your Soop being set on the Fire to boil softly, put in the Tails of your Craw fish, with some French Rolls slic'd and dried before the Fire, or fried in Butter; skim off the Fat, and dish it with bak'd Fish in the Middle; take Care how you take it off the Dish for Fear of breaking, first loosen it with a thin Knife. For further Particulars, see Lobster Soop.

To a-la-mode Beef.
Beuf à la Mode.

TAKE a little Round of a well-fed Heifer or Kiley, bind it round with a Cord; then take a a Piece of fat Bacon, and cut it into large Lard-downs; then shred a Handful of Parsley, with a little Thyme; mix it with Pepper and Salt, and roll your Lard-downs in it; then with a large Larding-pin, lard your Beef through; then put a Drainer into a Soop-pot, and put in the Beef; season it with whole Pepper, Mace, Salt, three or four Onions, two or three Carrots and Turnips, a Bottle of Rhenish Wine, with as much Water as will cover it; put on the Cover, and bake it with Houshold Bread; when bak'd make a Ragoo of Sweet-breads, dish'd Carrots and Turnips, make it pretty thin; dish it, take off the Curd, strain the Liquor, skim off the Fat, and put some of the Liquor to your Ragoo; take Care it does not make it too stalt, pour it over your Beef, then having some Sippets of White Bread dried before the Fire, or in an Oven; stick them all round, and send it up. You may garnish with Greens, &c.

To collar Pig like Brawn to be eat in Summer.
Cochon en ruelle à la maniere de Chair de Verrat.

YOU may make it a middle Dish: Take a fat, large, sucking Pig; let it be made very clean

A 2   from

from the Hairs, and cut off the Head close to the Ears, cut it even down the Back; take out the Bones and Entrails, wash it very clean, and put it into warm Water to soak out the Blood; shift it, and let it lie for twenty four Hours, dry it well with a Cloth; cut some of the thick Part of the Legs and Shoulders, and put them into the Middle; season it very well with Salt, then beat some Pepper and Mace very fine, and season it with it; then cut some large square Pieces of Bacon that will go quite a cross the Pig, three Inches a-part; then begin at the Tail-end and roll it up, and then in a Cloth tie it tight at both Ends, and rope it with Inckle; put it into a Pot, with Water enough, some Salt, and three or four Bay Leaves; let it boil till it is pretty tender, then having a Set of Neat's Feet, prepared as follows: Put them into a Pot, with Salt and Water, and boil them till you can easily take out the Bones, then cut them even, and spread them on a Tin Dripping-pan even, all of a Thickness, and the Length of your collar'd Pig, so that when it is cool it will stick all together; when the Pig is boil'd as above mention'd, tie it afresh at the Ends, and fresh wrap it with the Inckle, and hang it up to cool; then untie it, and with a thin Knife take the Neat's Feet off the Dripping-pan, roll them round the Pig; then roll all in the Cloth again, tie it, rope it as before, and boil it again for an Hour; then having a Tin Mould made the Thickness of your Collar, and the Length; set the Tin on a Board, untie one End of the Collar, and draw up the Cloth, or cut a Piece off the End that goes downwards, and put it into the Mould; then have a round Board that will go within it, and set a Weight on it that will press it very tight; let it stand till the next Day, then take it out, and make a Pickle for it in the following Manner: To a Gallon of Water, put in a good Handful of Salt, Half an Ounce of Salt-Petre, a Handful of Oatmeal, a Quart of Bran, a Pint of Vinegar, Half a Pint of Spirits of Wine; boil it and strain it through a Sieve, let it stand to cool, then take the Pig out of the Cloth, and rope it with clean Inckle, like Brawn; let it be covered with the Pickle, cover it as close from the Air as you can, and it will keep a Quarter of a Year: The Spirits of Wine will not make the Collar taste at all amiss, but make it keep a great while longer. This is a Secret worth knowing, to be made use of in any Thing of this Kind, in particular for Brawn.

To make an Umble Pye.
Omble Paté.

IT is made of the Heart, Liver, &c. of the Deer, either Buck or Doe; wash them, three Parts boil them, then mince them fine, and to a Pound of this take two Pounds of Beef Suet, shred very fine; then take two Pounds of Currants, well wash'd, rub'd dry, and pick'd clean, a Pound of Raisins ston'd and chopt; then take four large Apples, pare, core, and chop them; then slice thin two Ounces of candied Orange, Citron, and Lemon Peel, mix all together with Half a Pint of White Wine; mince the Rind of Half a Lemon, and squeeze in the Juice of a whole one; season it with Salt, Nutmeg, Cinnamon, and Mace; let all be well mixt, and fill your Pye, either rais'd or in a Dish; bake it two Hours in a moderate Oven.

To make a White Fricasy of Pigeons.
Pigeons en Fricassée Blanc.

CLEAN them; cut them in Quarters, wash them very well in warm Water; put a good Piece of Butter into a Stew-pan, with a Faggot of sweet Herbs, lay in your Pigeons with their Flesh Sides down, strew in some Salt, with some whole Pepper, and Mace; cover them down tight, and set them on a slow Fire to simmer till they be a little tender, then make a white Lare for them, as you will see for a White Fricasy of Chickens; put in the Liquor that came from them in the stewing, then having some Parsly boil'd, put in some shred fine, tols all up together; dish them, and send them up hot, garnish'd with Lemon and Barberries.

To dress Pullets a la Smithergell with Oysters.
Poulets au Smithrrgall.

TAKE two small Pullets that are fat, draw and truss them as for boiling, singe and let them lie in warm Water to soak out their Blood; then dry them with a Cloth, and take a score of pretty large Oisters, and shred them, with some Parsley and Beef Suet, a small Onion, some Bread Crumbs, Pepper, and a little Salt and Nutmeg; work it up with the Yolks of Eggs, put it into their Bellies, and spit them, then rub them over with Butter, lay on it a Handful of Parsly on their Breasts, and on it a large thin Slice of fat Bacon; tie it on with a Paper over all; and roast them; then having some Oisters blanc'd in their own Liquor, wash them out of it, and take off their Beards; put them into a Stew pan with their own Liquor, the Juice of Half a Lemon, two poonfuls of White Wine, Half a Pound of Butter, grate in a Nutmeg, mince Half an Anchovey, with a little Onion; put in Half a Pint of Cream, dust in a little Flour, set it on the Fire, draw it up thick, draw off the Fowls, and take all off their breasts; dish them, and pour the Sauce over them. Garnish with fried Oisters and Lemon.

Beef a la-Mode to eat cold.
Beuf à la Mode froid.

TAKE a Round of Beef, or Part of one, lard it with large Lardowns of Bacon, dipt in sweet Herbs and Spices; put it into an Earthen Pot that will conveniently hold it; first tie it round with Inckle; put to it a Bottle of Red Wine, an Ounce of Salt petre, some whole Pepper and Mace, with a Faggot of sweet Herbs,

Herbs, and as much hard Water as will cover it; put in some common Salt, do this in a Morning; let it stand till Night, then turn the other End downwards, tie over the Pot two Sheets of brown Paper, and bake it with Houshold Bread; let it stand to cool in the Pot, take the Fat off, let it to drain, and use it as collar'd Beef. If you would use it hot, make a Ragoo for it, as for a Herrico: See Herrico of Mutton; or send it up with ragoo'd Sweetbreads.

Neat's Tongue a la Braise.
Langue de Beuf à la Braise.

YOU must blanch and skin the Tongue, and cut off the Root; lard it as you did the Beef, then take a Stew-pan, and lay at the Bottom Rashers of Bacon, then Stakes of Beef season'd with sweet Herbs and Spices; lay in the Tongue, and lay Bacon and Beef above and below; cover it with a Cover that will fit, make a Fire above and below, let it stew four or five Hours, moisten it with strong Broth; when it is enough, send it up with a Ragoo of what you like. See Ragoos.

To pickle Neat's Tongues.
Langue de Beuf confit au Sel.

ORDER them as you do Hams the common Way for pickling to dry; and let them be done in the Westphalia Way.

To dress Cardoons.
Des Chardons appreté.

CLEAN, scrape, and cut them like Celery, an Inch long, blanch them in a Pot of hard Water, an Onion or two, a Faggot of sweet Herbs, some fat Bacon, and a Piece of Butter work'd in Flour; let them stew till tender, then make a Brown in a Stew pan, with Butter and Flour; put in some good Gravey, squeeze in some Lemon; put in some Pepper, Salt, and

and Nutmeg; let it stew till it is the Thickness of a Cream; dish it with Sippets of Bread under. Garnish with fried Parsley and Seville Orange or Lemon. You must strain them from the Liquor they were boil'd in, before you put them in the brown.

Cardoons Parmasan.
Des Chardons au Parmesan.

THEY are done some Times Parmasan, that is some Cheese scrap'd in, and put in Bread Crumbs, brown'd with a Salamander, or a hot Fireshovel. Parmasan is a Cheese, in Italy, so call'd. There are several Things done the same Way, which I shall mention in their proper Places.

To dress a Carp au Court Bouillon.
Des Carpes au Court Bouillon.

HAVING scaled and drawn your Carp, cut out the Fins and Gills; lay it in an Earthen Pan, and throw upon it some Vinegar and Salt, scalding hot; boil it in White Wine Vinegar and Water, with Onion, Pepper, and Butter; when it is boil'd, serve it up in a clean Napkin. Garnish with Parsley for the first Course, or send it in a Dish without a Napkin, with Sauce as directed in the first Number of this Book. Court Bouillon has been mentioned several Times, so I chuse to give you it in a particular Manner, that it may serve upon any Occasion, when you have a Mind to dress any Sort of Fish that Way: It is composed of Water, Vinegar, White Wine, Salt, Onion sliced, Horse Raddish, whole Pepper, a Bundle of sweet Herbs, boil'd all together; let it stand to cool, then put it into your Fish-Kettle; put in your Fish, boil it leisurely; observe the Sauce in dressing a Carp this Way.

To broil a Carp.
Des Carpes grillée.

SCALE it, take out the Entrails, and rub it clean with a wet Cloth; score it on the Sides, season it it with sweet Herbs shred fine, Bread Crumbs, Pepper, Salt, and Nutmeg; broil it in a double Gridiron, with butter'd Writing Paper under, and over it; shut down your Gridiron, set it on a Charcoal Fire to broil, turn your Gridiron often, then make Sauce for it as follows: Take Half a Pint of Red Wine, put it into a Stew-pan, with an Anchovey shred fine, with a little Onion, grate in a little Nutmeg, squeeze in the Juice of a Lemon, put to it six Ounces of Butter, dust in a little Flour, draw it up thick, unfasten your Gridiron, take off the upper Paper, and lay the Dish upon it that you defign to send it up in; turn it upside down into the Dish, take off the other Paper, pour your Sauce over it, garnish it with Horse Raddish and Lemon. You may dress Tench, Trout, or Salmon Trout, or Haddocks the same Way; send up plain Butter in a Bason.

A white Cullis Meagre.
Coulis blanc en Maigre.

TAKE what Sort of Fish you can conveniently get, clean them, and scale them, if required; wash and dry them with a Cloth, rub them over with Salt, let them lie two Hours, butter a convenient Thing, lay in your Fish, brush them over with melted Butter; set them in an Oven to bake; when bak'd, take the Flesh clean from the Bones; blanch a Handful of sweet Almonds, and pound them with the Flesh only of your Fish, and four or five Yolks of hard Eggs; take five or six Onions, two Carrots and two Parsnips, cut them in Slices, put them into a Stew-pan with Butter, and stew them, turning them from Time to Time over the Stove; and when they begin to brown, wet them with a thin Peas Broth; when this has boil'd for a Quarter of an Hour, strain it through a Sieve into another Stew-pan; season it with some Truffles, Mushrooms, a Leek, a little Parsley, a Couple of Cloves, and put in some Bread Crumbs as big as two Eggs; set it a simmering over a gentle Fire for a

Quarter

Quarter of an Hour, then mix amongst it your pounded Fish, Almonds, and Eggs; let it a simmering, but keep it from boiling, left you should change its Colour; strain it through a sieve, and use it for your Soups, and Ragoos, &c in eagre.

Mutton Cutlets in Batter.
Cottelets de Mouton en Pate.

CUT them handsomely off a Neck of Mutton, cut the Flesh off the Ends of the Bones, an Inch long, flat them with a Cleaver, lay them to marinate in Vinegar, Water, White Wine, a sliced Onion, a Faggot of Herbs, whole Pepper and Mace, and a little Salt for an Hour; then take the same out, make your Marinate boil in a Stew-pan over a Charcoal Fire, put in your Cutlets, let them simmer in it for two Minutes; take them out, let them lie to cool, rub them over with Yolks of Eggs, season them with Bread Crumbs and sweet Herbs, shred fine, a little Pepper and Salt; make a Batter for them as for Tripe, dip them in this Batter, and fry them in Hog's Lair; put some of the Marinate in, made hot and strain'd into a Boat, then dish your Cutlets round it. Garnish with Capers and fried Parsley.

To roast a Carp.
Carpe Roti.

TAKE a large fat He Carp, scale and clean it very well, take out the Entrails, make a Pudding for the Belly of it as follows; take the Melt, with the Flesh of a large Eel, two Anchovies, some Mushrooms, Sorrel, Parsley, Pepper, Salt, with a Piece of good Butter, some Crumbs of Bread, grated Nutmeg, the Yolks of two Eggs, and some Lemon Peel shred fine; chop and mix all together, pound it in a Mortar very fine; fill the Carp's Belly with it, and stew it up, then spit it on a convenient Spit; put the Spit in at the Mouth and out at the Tail, then provide

some

some Laths, made of Hazel, or any sweet Wood, fasten first one, let it be longer than the Carp, four Inches at each End, then place another Lath an Inch from that, rather longer than the other, and so all round the Carp, one short one and one long one, for the better Conveniency of its being fastened to the Spit; lay it down to roast, baste it with Butter and Red Wine, it will take an Hour roasting, if a large one; then lay it in your Dish, take off the Laths carefully, without breaking the Fish, draw out the Spit, take the Liquor it was basted with, skim off the Fat, strain it into a Stew-pan, add some more Wine to it, with Half a Pint of Gravey, a large Onion stuck with three or four Cloves, an Anchovy minc'd very fine; squeeze in the Juice of a Lemon or Seville Orange, shred a Spoonful of Capers, with a little blanch'd Parsley; put in a Score of Oisters, blanch'd and wash'd clean with the Clear of their Liquor; let all simmer a little over the Fire, put in three Quarters of a Pound of Butter; leave a Piece to work Flour in, enough to thicken the Sauce, draw it up all together to the Thickness of a Cream, pour some of the Thin of the Sauce over the Fish, and put the rest of the Sauce into a Boat. Garnish with Horse Raddish and Lemon, and Pattie Peters, made of the Forcing of the Carp; so you may roast Pike, or any other Sort of Fish that you chuse.

To butter Crabs.

Des Ecrevices à beurre.

BOIL them, take the Meat out of their Bodies, mix it with the Yolks of three or four hard Eggs, some White Wine Vinegar, Pepper, and Salt, strain it through a Sieve, and work it through with a Spoon; take the Meat out of their Claws, and mince it, mince an Anchovy, put all into a Stew pan together, put to it a Piece of Butter, dust in a little Flour, and stir it till it is the Thickness of a Cream; clean the Shell very well, and send it in it, or in a Plate with

B 2   Sippets

Sippets cut off a French Roll, and dried before the Fire.

To ragoo Crow-Fish.
Des Ecrevices en Ragoût.

WASH them well, and boil them in Water, then pick them; take off the Tails, and the rest of the Shells, having first taken out the Body, to make your Cullis; cut off the Ends of the Tails next the Body, and mix the rest with some Mushrooms and Truffles; toss up all together with a Morsel of Butter, then moisten it with a little strong Broth, and set it a simmering over a slow Fire, having season'd it with Salt, Pepper, and Onion; when it is enough, thicken it with a Cullis of Crow-Fish first, and serve it in warm Plates or little Dishes. See for Crow-fish Cullis.

To make new College Puddings.
Boudins à la Maniere des Colleges.

TAKE some Bread Crumbs rub'd through a Cullinder, with the equal Quantity of Beef Suet shred very fine, mix it together, season it with Cinnamon, Nutmeg, and Salt, put in a little Sack, Sugar, a Glass of Brandy, some Currants well wash'd and dried, some Raisins ston'd and chop'd; make it into Paste with Eggs, leave out Half the Whites, add to it a Spoonful of Ale Yest that is not bitter, mince some Lemon and candied Citron Peel, work all together, and set before the Fire to rise, make them up in the Shape of a Hen's Egg, fry them in clarified Butter over a slow Fire. There is a Receipt of this Sort before, try which you like best.

To make Rasp Jame.
Jam de Fraises.

PICK out the best of them, and take out their Stalks, put them into an Earthen Pot, and bruize all to Pieces; take the less Half and put them into a Stew pan, set them on a Charcoal Fire, and stir them

them till they be all to Pieces; then ſtrain and rub them through a coarſe Sieve to take out their Seeds; to a Pint of that take a Pound of fine Sugar, let it boil, and ſkim it; then take the Weight of the other Part of your Raſberries of fine Sugar, mix them together, ſtir them, and put them to the other; let all boil up quick till they be clear, take them off the Fire, ſtir them till they be almoſt cold, and put them into your Pots; inſtead of taking out their Seeds ſome put in Currant Jelly.

To make Raſberry Clear-Cakes.

Gateaux des Fraiſes tranſparante.

ORDER them as you did at firſt, that is, to take out their Seeds; take double their Weight of Sugar, put Half of your Sugar into your Preſerving-Pan; to a Pound of Sugar, put Half a Pint of Water, boil it to a Candy Height, take the reſt of the Sugar and put it into another reſerving Pan, with the Clear of your Raſberries, and boil it pretty high likewiſe; then put it to your Syrrup; ſet it on the Fire, and keep it ſtirring till all be well mixt and look clear, but don't let it boil; put it into what Form you pleaſe, dry them leiſurely, and put them into paper'd Boxes: This is the Way of making Clear-cakes of moſt Kinds of Fruit.

To boil Kidney Beans.

Des Aricots la Maniere de les accommodée.

STRING them, and cut them ſlant Ways about an Inch long; put them into Salt and Water for an Hour, ſet on ſome hard Water, make it boil, ſtrain your Beans, and put them into your boiling Water; let them boil till they be tender; ſtrain and diſh them as you do Green Peas.

To pickle Kidney Beans.
Des Aricots confit.

TAKE off the End that the Blossom is on, and put them into a strong Brine of Salt and Water, shift them every other Day for nine Days, then boil a fresh Brine and put to them, stop them down and let them stand till the next Day, and they will turn yellow; strain them from the Brine, dry them well, put them into a Brass-Pan, set them on a slow Fire, with as much White Wine Vinegar as will cover them close, and they will turn as green as Leeks; put them into a Jar; put to them what Spices you like, and tie them down; if they should mutter, strain them from the Pickle, and boil it with some fresh Vinegar; wipe your Beans, if they require it, and put them into the Pot again; let the Pickle stand to settle, and put the Clear to them again. Girkins are done the same Way; you may put to them a little Dill, if you please.

N. B. Potatoe Apples, Reddish Podes, Esturgeon Seeds, are also done the same Way.

To preserve Kidney Beans.
Des Aricots à garder tous l'Année.

PICK the young ones, put them into Salt and Water, shift them into fresh Salt and Water every Day for four Days; put them into fresh Salt and Water, set them on a slow Fire covered close to green, but don't let them boil; then strain them out, and put them into Pewter Dishes to dry; put them into a paper'd Box and keep them dry; when you would use any, soak them in warm Water to take out the Salt; make use of them as you do fresh ones.

To dress Venison in Stakes, call'd a Civet.
Venaison en Trenches.

TAKE a Neck of Venison, cut it in Stakes as you would Mutton, and flat them with a Cleaver; salt them a little, and let them lie a Quarter of an Hour.

ART of COOKERY. 195

Hour, then flour and fry them in Butter; brown your Stew pan with a little Butter and Flour, put in a Pint of Red Wine, squeeze in a Lemon, let the Stakes ſtew in it, but do not let them be too much done; ſweeten it with Sugar to your Taſte. Garniſh with Seville Orange, or Lemon and Barberries.

To make a Ragoo of Veniſon.
Venaiſon en Ragoût.

LARD what Piece you chuſe, flour and brown it in a Stew-Pan with Butter; take it out and dridge in ſome Flour, put in ſome good Gravey, an Onion ſhred fine, with an Anchovy, the Juice of a Lemon, ſome Red Wine, Pepper, and Salt, a little Nutmeg, a Faggot of ſweet Herbs; let it ſtew, cloſe covered, till it be very tender; diſh it with Toaſts of White Bread under it. Garniſh with Pickles and Lemon.

To haſh Veniſon.
Venaiſon hachée.

CUT it in thin Slices, from a Haunch that has been roaſted; put a good Piece of Butter into a Stew-pan, and put in your ſlic'd Veniſon, keep it ſtiring with a Spoon Ladle till it be thoroughly hot; put it into a Diſh, then make a rown with a Piece of Butter and Flour; put in ſome good Gravey, Pepper, Salt, pickled Girkins, and a few Capers ſhred a little; put in a little Pickle from the Girkins, a Spoonful of Catchup, a few Muſhrooms if you chuſe, a little Red Wine; let all ſtew together, put in your Haſh, let it juſt boil up, and diſh it on Sippets of White Bread. You may haſh Mutton the ſame Way, or roaſt Beef, &c.

To dreſs Weavers, a Fiſh ſo call'd.
Vives appreté.

THIS Fiſh I have not ſeen in the North, it is a Salt Water Fiſh. I ſhall mention ſome particular

cular Ways the French dress them; but they may be dress'd the same Ways we do Trouts boil'd, fried, stewed, potted, boil'd or bak'd; with the same Sort of Sauces, as Anchovy, Oisters, Lobsters, Shrimps, Crabs, Cockles, or Sauce as directed in the first Month of this Book. When you broil them, having clean'd and dried them, score them on the Sides with a sharp Knife, salt them, and dip them in clarified Butter; dridge them with Flour and Bread Crumbs, broil them on Writing Paper on a Gridiron, on a slow Fire; first butter the Paper, then take some Cabbage Lettice, take the Hearts of them, cut them in two, boil them a little in Salt and Water, and stew them in a Stew-pan with a good Piece of Butter, and a slic'd Onion; put in some Gravey, the Juice of a Lemon, season them with Pepper, Salt, and Nutmeg. If you would dress them meagre, put in Fish Broth instead of Gravey; add a little White Wine and a minc'd Anchovy; put the stew'd Lettice in the Dish, and lay on the Fish. Garnish with fried Parsley and Lemon.

To make Cabbage Soop.
Potage aux Choux.

TAKE a Knuckle of Veal, cut it to Pieces, with a Neck of Mutton; lay it in Water; take a young Cock, pick, singe, draw it, cut it in two, and lay them all to soak in warm Water; wash them out, and put them into a Pot with three or four Onions cut in two, three or four Turnips, likewise a Carrot, a Faggot of sweet Herbs, some whole Pepper, Mace, and some Salt; fill it with Water, boil it till all the Goodness is boil'd out of the Meat, and keep it skiming, strain it off, skim off the Fat, pour the Clear from the Bottom, then take a small, light, fine Cabbage, cut it in four, cut out the Stalks, shave it very thin, put a Piece of Butter into a Stew-pan, put in your Cabbage, with two or three sliced Onions, strinkle in a little Salt; set it to stew over a slow Stove Fire,

take

take Care it does not burn, put in some of your strong Broth; let your Stew-pan be big enough to hold the Soop, or put it into a Soop Kettle; set it over a Fire to stew softly, then force a small Cabbage, you will see how in the Receipt before given, boil it in the same Manner, lay it in the Middle of your Dish, lay in some Chippings of a French Brick dried before the Fire, put in a Ladleful of Soop or two, to moisten the Bread; lay round it three or four small Chickens boil'd white and well; salt your Soop to your Taste; your Dish being rim'd, garnish it with potch'd Eggs, Spinnage, and Rashers of Bacon broil'd before the Fire, but not too much; fill your Dish up with the Soop, and send it up.

To make Cream Toasts.
Rotis à la Cream.

TAKE a Quart of Cream, boil it with a Stick of Cinnamon, and the Half of a Lemon Peel; let it stand to cool, beat twelve Yolks of Eggs, mix them with your Cream, sweeten it with fine Sugar, strain it into a large Dish, then cut some Toasts off a Two-penny French Brick, about a Quarter of an Inch thick; lay them to soak in your Cream and Eggs, fry them in clarified Butter, be sure to let them be well soak'd and turn'd in the Cream; you must fry but one or two Slices at a Time; set them to drain before the Fire, then melt some Butter, with some White Wine and Sugar, with a little Dust of Flour; squeeze in the Juice of Half a Lemon, put the Sauce into a China Cup, set it in the Middle of the Dish; garnish it with a Seville Orange, cut in Quarters, dridge the Rim of the Dish with fine Sugar; dish the Toasts round the Cup, send it up hot.

Oysters in Jelly.
Huitres en Gellée.

TAKE some Jelly of Calves Feet, boil it with some Icing-glass till it is very strong, strain it through

through a Sieve, put to it Half a Pint of Red Wine, Cochineal beat, some whole Pepper and Mace, the Juice of two Lemons, the Whites of four Eggs beaten, a little Salt; mix all these together in a Stew pan, set it on the Fire to boil; when it breaks, run it through a Flannel Bag till it is very clear, then open your Oysters, take Care you do not cut them in the opening, set them on the Fire in their own Liquor, with some Mace and whole Pepper; let them stew till they are enough; wash them clean from the Shells and Sand; put some Jelly in the Bottom of the Pot you design to send them in; let it stand to cool, then lay in a Lare of Oysters, with some Slices of Seville Orange cut thin; cover them with some more Jelly, and lay Oysters on that again, then run on some more Jelly; so keep this Order till your Pot be quite full, then let it stand till the next Day, and turn it into your Dish as you are directed in the Receipts before of Fish in Jelly. Garnish with Seville Orange, cut in Quarters, and Sprigs of Fennel.

As to the rest of the Dishes, in the Bill of Fare, you will find the Receipts in their proper Places.

A Florentine of Apples and other Fruit.

Pommes en Florentine.

TAKE a Score of Golden Pippins, pare and core them, chop them grosly, mix them with Half a Pound of Currants, wash'd, dried, and pick'd clean, with a Pound of Raisins ston'd and chop'd, with Half a candied Orange and Lemon Peel shred fine, with the Marrow of one Marrow-bone shred also, the Juice of a Lemon, a Gill of Sack, some grated Nutmeg, some fine Sugar and Cinnamon; mix all together, put it into your Dish, with a Border of Puff-paste round it, and a cut Cover on the Top; ice it, and bake it.

To make a sweet Calf's Head Pye.
Paté d'une tête de Veau.

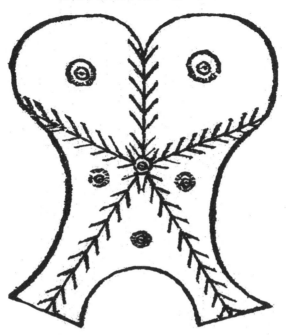

SPLIT, and wash the Head very clean, let it lie to soak in Water all Night; boil it pretty tender, let it lie to cool, cut it in Slices, season it with Salt, Nutmeg, Cinnamon, Mace, and a little Pepper, all beat very fine; sheet your Dish with cold Paste, lay in a Lare of Calf's Head, some Raisons ston'd, Currants dried and clean'd well; then lay in some more of the Head over that, with some Fruit over that as before; the Tongue being sliced and put in with the rest; keep this Order till it is all laid in; put in a little strong Broth, lay Butter on the Top, lid it, and bake it; when it is baked, melt half a pound of Butter, with half a Pint of White Wine, the Juice of a Seville Orange, and some Sugar; cut a Hole in the Lid of the Pye, and put it in; shake it all together, and send it up.

To make a Neat's Tongue Pye.
Paté des Langues de Beuf.

TAKE a fresh Tongue, boil it and skin it; cut it into Slices, season it with Pepper and Salt, sheet your Dish with Puff Paste, lay in some Slices of interlarded Bacon, throw over it some Thyme and Parsley shred very fine, then lay some Tongue all over that, so lay in all the Tongue, with some Bacon at the Top asunder, season'd as before; lay on some hard Eggs, that is, the Yolks, with some Pieces of Butter, put in a little good Gravey, squeeze in the Juice of a Lemon, lid it, and bake it.

Take off the Fat and put in a Ragoo of Sweetbreads.

To make a Lamb Pye.
Paté d'Agueau.

TAKE a Loin of Lamb, cut it in Stakes, flat it with a Cleaver, season it with Pepper, Salt, and Nutmeg, sheet your Dish as before, lay in the Stakes with Forc'd-Meat-Balls, and the Yolks of Eggs boil'd hard; strinkle over it some Parsley shred fine, with some Lemon Peel; lay on some Butter, put in a little good Gravey or strong Broth, lid it, bake it, and send it up.

Here I shall mention several Sorts of Sauces made the French Way for all Sorts of Fowls, Fish, and several Sorts of roast Meats.

To make Anchovey Sauce.
Sause d'Anchoies aux Pedrix.

WHSH your Anchovies, take out the Bones, mince them small, put them into a Stew-Pan, with some Cullis of Veal and Ham; put in a little Pepper and Vinegar, and make it hot. This is proper for Partridge, Moor Game, or garrinaded Rabbits; add thereto some minc'd Shallot.

To make Sauce with Westphalia Ham, for roasted Chickens, Turkey, or Lamb.

Sauce au Jambon aux Poulets.

CUT some Slices off it, beat them with a Rowling Pin, rub the Bottom of a Stew-Pan with a Bit of Butter, lay in the Slices of Ham, cover the Stew-Pan close, set it on a slow Fire till it begins to stick to the Pan; then having a Chicken boil'd into Broth, season'd with Pepper, Salt, and Sweet-herbs; put it all to your Ham, let it simmer gently over a Fire, strain it, and skim off the Fat, bind it with a Cullis of Veal and Ham, squeeze in a little Lemon, and it is fit for Use.

To make a Sauce for Capers.

Sause aux Canards & des Cercelles.

TAKE some of the same Gravey as in the last, put in some Capers shred fine, with a little Pepper, make it hot with a little Red Wine. This is proper for Ducks, Teel, or any Thing of that Kind; or for Mutton Cutlets, with a little Shallot shred fine.

Another Sauce for Ducks and Teel.

TAKE some Gravey drawn from Veal and Ham, squeeze in the Juice of a Seville Orange, put in a little Pepper, and make it hot.

To make a green Sauce.

Sauce vert à la maniere Francoise.

TAKE some green Wheat, pound it in a Mortar with the Crumb of a French Roll soak'd in strong Broth, squeeze and strain it through a Sieve; put to it the Juice of a Lemon, with a little Gravey. This Sauce is for Lamb: You may put to it a little Mint shred fine, and a little Sugar if you like it.

To make a Sauce for Woodcocks.

WHEN they are roasted take out their Thropples, throw away the Liver and Gizard, mince the rest very fine, season them with Pepper and Salt; put in a little Red Wine, thicken them with a Cullis of Veal and Ham; squeeze in a little Lemon, dish up your Woodcocks, and throw the Sauce over them.

To make a Sauce with Truffles.
Sause aux Trufles pour les rotis.

BLANCH them in boiling Water, cut the Black off the Edges, mince them with a little Anchovey and a few Chives, put in some Cullis of Veal and Ham, simmer it over a gentle Fire; send it up with any Joint of Butcher's Meat roasted: You may make Sauce of Morels and Mushrooms the same Way; put in some Juice of a Lemon, or a little Vinegar.

To make a Sauce for roast Mutton.
Sause au Mutton rotis.

PEEL some Shallots, mince them small, put them in the Dish you design to send your Meat in, put in some natural Gravey from Mutton with a little Pepper and Salt; put in a little Vinegar, garnish your Dish with Horse-raddish and Pickles; or this: Take some Veal Gravey, slice into it a Couple of Onions, season it with Pepper and Salt, put in a little Vinegar; let them simmer over the Fire for two Minutes, strain it over your Meat.

To make a Carbonade of Mutton.
Mutton en Carbonade.

CUT some Slices off a Leg, take off the Skin and Fat, flat them a little with a Cleaver, lard them with fat and lean Bacon, season'd with Sweet-Herbs, Pepper, and Salt; stew them a-la-braise, as you may see in several Receipts before; then make a Ragoo of Chesnuts, roast them in Embers, or in a Frying-pan, first cut off the little End or they will crack and fly out, let them be tender; then make a Brown with a Piece of Butter and a little Flour, put in some good Gravey with an Onion shred fine, put in a few Capers and your Chesnuts, let all stew till the Sauce is the Thickness of a thin Cream, lay your Mutton in the Dish, and pour the Sauce over them; peel the Husks off your Chesnuts before you put them into your Sauce: Garnish with Pickles.

To boil Rabbits the French Way.
Lapins a Cuire à Fraucoise.

TRUSS them as for boiling, lard them with Bacon, and let them lie to soak out their Blood in warm Water, then dry them, and wash them over with melted Butter; flour them, tie them in a Cloth, and boil them in a good deal of Water to make them look the whiter; then make the Sauce of their Livers scalded and minc'd, with some boil'd Parsley, a little White Wine, the Juice of a Lemon, and some pickled Barberries stript off their Stalks; grate in a little Nutmeg, put in a little Salt, dust in a little Flour, break in half a Pound of Butter, and draw it up all together; dish your Rabbits; and pour the Sauce over them: Garnish with Barberries and Lemon.

How to roast a Pheasant.
Phaisans roti.

PICK, draw, crop, and truss him, with his Head on; put a Piece of Butter dipt in Salt into his Belly; spit, singe, and baste it with Butter, take Care you don't roast it too much, draw it, and dish it; garnish the Dish with Bread Crumbs brown'd with Butter; send it with Gravey Sauce; save one of the long Feathers, and stick it upright in the Rump to shew what Bird it is.

To roast Plovers.
Pluviers roti.

PICK, draw, clean, and truss them with their Heads on; put Butter and Salt in their Bellies, spit them on a small Spit, singe and baste them with Butter: Some lay a Bard of Bacon on their Breasts, and fastens it with Packthread; when roasted, lay some butter'd Toasts in the Dish as you do for Woodcocks, sauce them with Butter and Gravey; garnish with Lemon.

To preserve Peaches in Brandy.
Pêches conservé en eau de vie.

SCALD them in Water, and let them simmer a little; then make a Syrrup of half Brandy and half Water, (a Pint to a Pound of double-refin'd Sugar) let it boil, and skim it well; then put in your Peaches, let them simmer a little, take them off, and let them stand a while, but keep them turning; set them on again and give them another turn, keep this Order for five or six Times; then put them into Pots, and tie them down as you do other Sweet-meats. Don't let them be too ripe when you get them.

To make Cakes for Breakfast.
Gâteaux pour dejeuné.

TARE a Pound of Flour, dry it well, rub in it three Quarters of a Pound of Butter, put in half a Pound of Currants wash'd and dry'd before the Fire; you may put in some fine Powder Sugar if you chuse it; make it into Paste with Water and three Eggs, work it well, roll it out, and make your Cakes of what Form you please: Remember to put in a little Salt, and two or three Spoonfuls of Sack if you like it; bake them in a quick Oven.

To make Portugal Cakes.
Gâteaux de Portugal.

TAKE a Pound of the finest Flour you can get, well dry'd, and a Pound of double-refin'd Sugar beat and sifted, mix them together; then take sixteen Ounces of Butter and work it to a Cream with your Hand, put in a little Rose-water, put in your Flour and Sugar by a little at a Time till half of it is in, keep beating all the Time; then break in six new-laid Eggs one at a Time, till you have got them all in, and the rest of your Flour and Sugar, beat it for half an Hour; after all is in, then put in a Pound of Currants wash'd, dry'd, and pick'd; having your Pans ready butter'd, half fill them, and bake them; but sift on some double-refin'd Sugar.

To make Clear Cakes of any Sort of Fruit, order'd as follows. I shall begin with Apples.
Gâteaux transparent aux Fruits.

TAKE what Quantity you please, core and pare them, put them into Water, boil them till they will jelly; take Care you don't put too much Water to your Apples; put in a little double-refin'd Sugar to make them keep their Colour; then strain them through a clean Sieve, let them stand till the next Day close cover'd; then take a Pound and Quarter of Sugar beat and sifted, put to it half a Pint of hard Water, boil and skim it till it is of a Candy-height, which you may know by lading it up, and if it fades it will do, or put a Drop upon a Plate and it is barr'd; then put in a Pint of your Jelly, stir it all well together, but don't let it boil, put it into flat Glasses to dry it in a drying Stove, turn them every Day till they be dry: You may order Currants, Goosberries, or any Sort of Fruit after the same Manner: Pick your Fruit off the Stalks. As to Goosberries, cut off the Stalks and the Noses, and let them be just ripe when you gather them:

The

The Currants muſt be quite ripe. As to Cherries, Plumbs, or Apricots, take out their Stones and their Skins off, make any of theſe into Pulp, as you are directed, and uſe the ſame Quantity of Sugar. The Reaſon for the Jelly ſtanding till the next Day, is to let it ſettle, if there is any Sediment in it, which you muſt take Care not to put in.

Some ſtrain the Jelly through a Muſlin Cloth, or through a fine Sieve, to make them ſmoother after it is mixt with Sugar.

To preſerve Peaches green. See green Apricots.

To dry Cherries.

GAther them when they are full ripe; take out their Stones with a ſharp Knife, put them into an Earthen Diſh, as you do them, and ſtrinkle on them ſome double-refin'd Sugar pounded and ſifted; to a Pound of Cherries take half a Pound of Sugar; then put them into your preſerving Pan, keep them moving, ſtrinkle in a little Sugar, let them boil up; then take them off the Fire and put them on wired or ſplinted Sieves to dry in a drying Stove, or in a very ſlow Oven; then put them into paper'd Boxes.

To dry Pears or Apples.
Poers & Pommes à Seché.

TAKE them when they are fit to eat. and put them into Tin Driping-Pans; ſet them into a moderate Oven to dry: They will take three Weeks drying moderately, turn them ev'ry Day, and flat them a little with your Hand. Keep them in paper'd Boxes.

To

ART of COOKERY.

To make Syrrup of Gilliflowers.
Oilets en Sirop.

CUT off the red Part, and put them into an Earthen Pan; when you have got the Quantity you would have, sprinkle them with Water, put them into a Pitcher stopt close, and set into a Pan of Water; let it boil two or three Hours, then strain out the Juice, and to a Pint take a Pound of double-refin'd Sugar, put all into a Silver Sauce pan, and make it just boil; keep it stirring till it be cold; bottle it up for Use. You may do Violets the same Way. Some soak the Flowers in Water and make it into Syrrup as above, and boil in it a few Cloves.

To broil Pigeons whole.
Pigeons grillé entier.

CLEAN them, and truss them as for boiling; make a Stuffing for them of a good deal of Parsley, some Beef Suet shred fine and mixt with a few Bread Crumbs, Pepper and Salt, work'd up with an Egg; put a Piece into all their Bellies, fasten up their Vents, and broil them before the Fire in a Tin Apple Roaster; turn them several Times till they be enough, baste them with Butter. The Sauce is Butter, Gravey, and the Juice of a Lemon. Dish and garnish them with raw Parsley and Lemon.

To make a Patty of Spinage a-la-Smithbergall.
Tourte aux Epinards.

PICK, wash, and scald your Spinage, sheet a sizable Patty-Pan with Puff Paste, chop the Spinage a little, and lay half of it into your Patty-Pan; then boil as many Eggs hard as will cover the Spinage, with Rashers of interlean Bacon between each Yolk of an Egg; season them with a little Pepper and Salt, that is, the Spinage and Eggs, but put none on the Bacon; then chop the Whites fine and strinkle all over them

them in the Patty; then lay on the rest of your Spinage season'd as before, lay on Bits of Butter, and lid your Pye; wash it over with a little Cream and the Yolk of an Egg; cut the Lid round an Inch within the Pye-Lid, that you may the easier take it off when it is bak'd: An Hour and a Half will bake it: Take it out of the Patty-Pan and dish it; take off the Lid and put in some Gravey and Butter, with the Juice of a Lemon; lay the Lid on, and send it up.

To cram Capon, Fowl and Turkey.
Pour fair nourrir des volailles.

MAKE Paste with Barley Meal sifted and Milk; make it stiff, and make it into Crams, thick in the Middle and narrow at both Ends; dip them in Milk, and cram your Fowls three Times a Day, that is, Morning, Noon, and Night, and they will be very fat in three Weeks.

I shall give you an Account of the Distempers that are frequent in Poultry, and how to cure them, as it was given to me by one that was well skill'd in that Way.

Pour faire guerir les Volailles.

THE Pip is a white thin Scale growing on the Tip of the Tongue, which makes them that they cannot feed: It proceeds for want of clean Water, and drinking bad Puddle-water, and eating filthy Meat: The Cure is to pull the Scale off with your Thumb Nail, and rub the Tongue with Salt. The Roup is a filthy Boil or Swelling that grows on the Rump; it will corrupt the whole Body, and is commonly known by the staring of the Feathers, or turning Backwards. To cure this you must pull off the Feathers, open the Sore, thrust out the Core, wash the Place with Salt and Water, or with Brine, put to it Rue and Butter, and it will cure it. The Flux is another Disorder which is got by eating too much moist Meat: The Cure is, you must scald Peas or Bran with
Li-

ART *of* COOKERY.

Liquor that fresh Meat have been boil'd in, and give them sometimes one and sometimes the other till they be well. The stopping of the Belly is contrary to the Flux, so that they cannot move: You must give them some Bites of Bread or Corn soak'd in Man's Urine, and anoint their Vents with Butter or Lard, and give them some Rue and Butter. To kill Lice that breed on them by eating corrupt Food, or for want of bathing in Sand, or Ashes, or such like: Take Pepper beat very small, mix it with warm Water, wash your Poultry therein, and it will kill all sorts of Vermin. If stung with a venomous Worm, &c. anoint the Place with Rue and Butter well pounded in a Mortar. If their Heads are swell'd, rub them with the same Ointment; and if their Eyes be sore, chew two or three Leaves of Groundivy, suck out the Juice, spit it into their Eyes, and it will certainly heal them.

To make Lemon Cream.
Crême aux Limons.

TAKE two large Lemons, pare off the outside Rind very thin, lay it to steep all Night in a Pint of hard Water cover'd by the Fire, the next Day squeeze into it the Juice of two Lemons, beat the Whites of four and the Yolk of one Egg, mix it with the Water and Lemon, sweeten it with double-refin'd Sugar to your Taste, strain it through a Sieve, put it into a Silver Sauce-Pan, keep it stirring till it begins to be thick, put it into Glasses. Orange Cream is made the same Way: Use Oranges instead of Lemon, and Yolks of Eggs instead of Whites: If it be not high enough coloured, colour it with Saffron.

Ti dress Pigeons en compote.
Pigeons en compote

SCALD them as you do Chickens cropt, draw them, singe and truss them as for boiling, wash them well in warm Water, blanch them in boiling Water,

ter, take them up and drain them; put a Piece of Butter into a Stew-Pan, with a Faggot of Sweet-Herbs, an Onion stuck with four Cloves; keep them moving, dust in some Flour, put in some strong Broth, let them stew till tender, take them up, strain the Liquor into a Pan, let it stand to settle, skim off the Fat, and pour off the clear; then put all into a clean Stew-Pan, with some Cream, the Juice of a Lemon, some Parsley boil'd and chop'd, grate in a little Nutmeg, put in a Spoonful or two of White Wine, with two Sweet-Breads boil'd and dish'd, some pickled Mushrooms, first soak'd in warm Water, a Piece of Butter work'd in Flour, with the Yolks of three or four raw Eggs, salt it to your Taste, set it on the Fire, and keep it stirring till it is the Thickness of a Cream; dish it, and garnish it with potch'd Eggs, boil'd Spinage, and Rashers of Bacon; send all up hot.

Pigeons a-la-Sante Menehout.
Pigeons à la-Saint Menhout.

TAKE the largest you can get, lard them with Bacon, garnish the Bottom of a Stew-Pan with Bacon, lay on that some thin Beef Stakes season'd with Pepper, Salt, Mace, Sweet-Herbs, sliced Onion, and Carrot; season your Pigeons with Pepper and Salt, stuff their Bellies with a good deal of Parsley, lay your Pigeons in with their Breasts down, lay on them Bards of Bacon and Beef Stakes season'd as before, cover them close, and stew them with a Fire above as below; when they have stew'd Half an Hour, put in some good strong Broth, half a Pint of Rhenish Wine, some Juice of Lemon, let them stew till tender, set them to drain, and make a Pickle for them of Bran and Water boil'd; put in the Liquor they were stew'd in, with some Vinegar; first strain off the Liquor from your Bran, boil them together, and let them stand to cool in the Pot you design to keep them in; put in your Pigeons: When you would use any, dish them
with

ART of COOKERY.

with green Parsley; if you would send them hot rub them over with Butter, dridge them with Bread Crumbs, and broil them before the Fire; make the Sauce of minc'd Capers, Chives, a little Vinegar, shred Parsley, Gravey, Butter made hot and poured over them, or rather put into the Dish, and the Pigeons laid on it: Garnish with green Parsley.

To broil Pigeons a la-Smethergall.
Pigeons grillé à-la-smithergal.

SLIT them down the Backs, season them with Pepper and salt, skewer them to keep them flat, put them into a Tin Pan to broil before the Fire, baste them with Butter, turn them, then baste them with Red Wine, turn them three or four Times, but don't broil them too much; dish them, let the Sauce be Butter, Lemon, a little Shallot shred fine and mixt with what is in the Pan they were broil'd in : Garnish with fry'd Parsley and Lemon.

To dress a Ham a-la-Braise.
Jambon à-la-Braise.

SOAK it in Water and pare it clean, boil it till it be half done, then take it up and skin it; take a convenient Kettle that will hold it, and lay Bards of Bacon at the Bottom, then Slices of Beef on that, season them with Sweet-Herbs and Spices, lay in your Ham, and cover it on the Top as under; peel three or four Onions, and slice them with two Carrots, four Turnips, six Heads of Cellery, and one Parsnip; mind to lay the Skin Side downwards that it may take the Realish the better; then put in a Bottle of Rhenish Wine, set it on a slow Fire to stew for five Hours, with a Fire above as below, moisten it sometimes with good strong Broth, let it stand to cool; then take it up and rub it over with the Yolks of two Eggs, dridge it with Bread Crumbs, brown it in an Oven or before the Fire; send it up garnish'd with raw Parsley. If you would

would send it up hot, you may send a Ragoo of Sweetbreads over it; garnish it with dish'd Carrots, Turnips, and stew'd Spinage.

To roast a Ham.
Jambon roti.

TAKE a Ham that has been cured about six Weeks or two Months, pare it, skin and spit it, roast it leisurely for three or four Hours according to the Bigness of it, and baste it with Rhenish Wine; strain the Wine it was basted with, put to it some good Gravey, skim off the Fat, and send it under the Ham; send Roots and Greens in a Dish by themselves: This Ham may be eat with Chickens, or Pigeons, &c.

To dress Gudgeons.
Goujons accommodé.

GUdgeons is a small Fresh-water Fish, and are commonly fry'd like Smelts; beat some Yolks of Eggs with a Spoonful or two of White Wine, dip your Fish in it, (after they are scalded and clean'd) and dridge with fine Bread Crumbs and Flour; fry them in good Lard, or fine Fat: Garnish them with fry'd Parsley and Lemon.

You may stew them and send them in Jelly as follows: Take two Calves' Feet, with some Icing Glass, put them when clean'd into a Sauce-Pan, with their long Bones taken out and split in two, with Salt, Pepper, Mace, and a little Vinegar; let them boil till the Jelly be strong with two Quarts of Water, then strain them through a Sieve; skim off the Fat or let it stand till cold, and then take off the Fat or Sediment from the Bottom; put it into a Stew-Pan with half a Pint of White Wine, four Whites of Eggs well beat, mix it all together, let it boil, and put it through a Jelly Bag; when it comes off fine, put a little into the Bottom of the Pot you design to put your Fish into, and lay in

some

some slic'd Lemon when the Jelly is cold in the Bottom of the Pot, then some Fennel pick'd in small Sprigs; then lay in some of your Fish, and lay more Lemon and Fennel on them, so continue till your Pot be full; fill it quite full with Jelly, let it stand till the next Day, dip it in warm Water, and turn it upside down into the Dish; garnish it with pick'd Fennel; take Care you don't stew your Fish too much.

How to boil a Goose.
Oye à culre.

LET it be well pick'd and sing'd, salt it as you do Bacon, for four Days; truss it for boiling, and boil it an Hour and a Half; then dish it and send it with stew'd Cabbage, or with ragoo'd Carrots and Turnips, or ragoo'd Cellery or Colliflowers, as you like.

If you would salt and dry it, let it lie in Salt nine Days, rub it with the Pickle every Day; then hang it up to dry, as you do Bacon, for three Weeks, and boil it and send it up as before.

To coller a Goose.
Oye en ruele.

BONE and cut it square, lay it to marinate in Half Wine and Half Water, and some Vinegar, Pepper, Salt, and some slic'd Onions; let it lie in this twenty-four Hours, then take it out, and shred Half a Pound of Ham, with six Anchovies; wash the Goose all over the In-side with Yolks of Eggs, then blanch some Spinage and Parsley, shred it fine, and lay all over it; then shred the Yolks of six or eight Eggs, and lay all over that; season it with Pepper and Salt, roll it up tight in a Cloth, bind it with Tape, tie it very tight at both Ends, boil it in the Liquor it was marinated in, adding as much Water as will cover it; let it boil till tender, untie and unbind it, and roll it up afresh; tie it tight at the Ends, and

and bind it with the Tape again; hang it up by one End, and tie a Weight at the other; let it hang till cold, let the Liquor be cold also; take the Fat off, and the Settling from the Bottom, and put it into an oval Pot that will hold it, and the Coller; take it out of the Cloth, and put it into the Pickle; when you would use any, slice some of it and lay it round your Dish; set the other Part upright in the Middle, and garnish with green Parsley.

To roast a Goose.
Oye roti.

TAKE three or four Onions, as they are for Bigness; slice them, and blanch them in boiling Water with some Sage; when it has boil'd a little, strain it and chop it fine, mix it with as much Salt as will season your Goose within, if it be fresh; then work it up with a Piece of Butter, and put it into the Belly of the Goose; skewer and spit it, singe, baste, dridge it, and salt it as it roasts; if it be a large Goose it will take an Hour and a Half roasting at a good Fire; let the Sauce be good Gravey; or Mustard, Gravey, Butter, and a little Vinegar, with Apple Sauce in a Plate.

Goose a-la-Braise.
Oye à la Braise.

SINGE and flat it with a Cleaver, lard it with with Bacon, take an oval Stew-pan, lay all over the Bottom Slices of Bacon, over that Slices of Beef, and on that Onions, Carrots slic'd with sweet Herbs, Pepper, Salt, and Mace; then lay in your Goose, and lay over it as under and season the same; set it on a slow Fire, let it have its own Cover, put some Fire on the Top; stew it so for three Quarters of an Hour till all the Gravey is drained down to the Bottom; take Care it does not burn, then put in some strong Broth, stew it till it be tender, then send it up with a Ragoo of Sweatbreads, or with any Ragoo of Roots, as you like.

like. See in several Places where there are Ragoos. Ducks are done the same Way.

To braise a Turkey or Pullet.
Dindon à la Braise.

YOU may do these as above, but send them up with Oysters or Sweetbreads, Mushrooms, and Forc'd-meat Balls ragoo'd.

Haddocs the Dutch Way.
Haddoc sorte de Merlans à l' Hollandoise.

SCALE, gut, and clean them, and throw them into Water for an Hour; then set on a Kettle that will hold them, put in hard Water, a Handful of Salt and some Vinegar; put in your Haddocs on a Fish Drainer, that you may take them up without breaking; when they are enough, drain them well, then having some Turnips pared, cut in Dice, and boil'd in Salt and Water, drain them very well, and toss them up in melted Butter; toast some thin Slices of White Bread, and lay in the Bottom of the Dish, lay on some of the Turnips and Butter, lay on your Fish, then having some Parsley boil'd and chopt, mix it with the rest of your Butter and Turnips, and pour it all over your Fish.

Haddocs are Fish that are much used in this Part of the Country, and the Ways of dressing them are so well know, I shall only mention how they are done Abroad.

To dress the Haddocs the Swiss Way.
Haddoc à la Suisse

CLEAN them, wash and lay them into a Marinate made of Half Water and Half Vinegar, some slic'd Onion, slic'd Lemon, whole Pepper, Mace, and some Salt; let them lie four Hours, then take them up and dry them well, fry them in clarified Butter, first rub them well with Flour, make the Sauce of some of the Marinate, an Anchovey chopt with a few

few Capers; draw your Butter with thefe, lay your Fifh in the Difh, and pour the Sauce over them.

To ſtew Haddocs.
Haddoc etuvé.

YOU may ſtew them as you do Tench, and fry them as you do Trouts; or ſalt, ſkin, and broil them, and eat them with Egg Sauce.

To dreſs a Hare the Swiſs Way.
Lievre à la Swiſſe.

SKIN and clean it, cut it into Pieces, and lard it with Bacon; flour it, and fry it in clarified Butter; then make a Brown with Butter, put in ſome good Gravey, Half a Pint of Red Wine, ſtew it till tender, put in ſome whole Pepper and Mace in the ſtewing, with a large Onion ſtuck with four Cloves, a Faggot of ſweet Herbs, an Anchovey chopt with Capers; ſqueeze in Half a Lemon, toſs all up together, let it be the Thickneſs of a Cream, take out the ſweet Herbs, and the Onion; diſh it up, and garniſh with Barberries and Lemon.

To boil Rabbits the Engliſh Way.
Lapins cuit à l'Angloiſe.

SKIN, clean, and truſs them, as you generally do for boiling; lay them to ſoak in warm Water, then take ſome clear Spring or Pump Water; put in a Piece of fat Bacon, cut to Pieces, with a Piece of Butter work'd in Flour, three or four Onions, ſliced thin, let them boil for about Half an Hour or better, according as they are to Age or Bigneſs; take a Score of Onions, peel off all the Out-ſide tough Skin, cut them in two, and throw them into Water; then boil them in a good deal of Water, when they are half boil'd, take out that Water, put in ſome freſh, and boil them till they are tender; ſtrain them through a Cullinder, and rub through into a Stew-pan with a wooden Ladle, to take out the tough Skins if there be

ART of COOKERY. 217

be any, or chop them upon a clean Board; dridge them over with a little Flour, falt them to your Tafte; fet them on the Fire in your Stew-pan, put to them Half a Pint of Cream, and Half a Pound of Butter cut into Pieces; ftir all together till it is as thick as a thick Cream; difh up your Rabbits, pour this all over them; garnifh them with pick'd Parfley foak'd in Water.

To drefs Beef tromblance.
Beuf tremblant.

TAKE the middle Piece of the Brifket, crack the the Bone fhort, wafh it very well, and put it into a Pot that will conveniently hold it; put into it a Patfnip pared and fliced, a Carrot ditto, with Half a Dozen Onions fliced, fix Heads of Cellery, Thyme, Winter Savory, two fweet Leeks, and a Handful of Parfley, three or four Turnips par'd and cut to Pieces, fome whole Pepper, Mace, Half a Pint of Vinegar, fome Salt, and a little Rhenifh Wine; let it ftew gently till it is very tender; you muft have a Bottom under it to take it up by; it muft ftew five or fix Hours, then prepare a Ragoo for it as follows: Take a Carrot, pare and cut it in Dice, three or four Turnips, likewife a Score of fmall Onions about as big as a Nutmeg, peel and blanch all in boiling Water; take four Sweet-breads blanch'd and cut in Dice; take a large Stew pan, put in Half a Pound of Butter, duft in fome Flour, ftir it with a Ladle till it begins to brown, throw in your Sweat-breads with the Carrots, Turnips, and Onions; keep fhaking the Pan for a Minute, put in a Pint of Gravey, add to it fome of the ftrong Broth your Beef is ftew'd in, let them ftew till they are tender, fkim off the Fat, difh up your Beef in a Soop Difh; garnifh the Difh with Greens and Spinage, ftick the Top of the Beef with Toafts, cut like Sippets, the Skin being taken off.

To boil a Leg of Veal the English Way.
Gigot de Veau cuit à l'Angloise.

SET on a Pot that will hold it, with a good deal of Water; cut off the Shank-end, lay it to soak in Water for two Hours, flour and tie it in a Cloth, boil it for two Hours and a Half or three, according to the Bigness of it; then take a handsome square Piece of interlarded Bacon, pare off the Rust if there be any, and boil it in a Pot by itself for two Hours; take off the Skin, rub it over with the Yolk of an Egg, dridge it with Bread Crumbs, brown it in an Oven, or before a Fire; then prepare some Roots or Greens as you like, order'd as before-directed; take it up, and take it out of the Cloth, let it drain from the Water, put it into the Dish, cut your Bacon in two, and lay to each Side the Shank-end of the Leg; dish your Roots and Greens handsomely round it; send it up with some Butter in a Boat.

To dress Woodcocks a la Smithergall.
Becasses à la Smithergall.

PICK, singe, and truss them; spit them on a small Spit, lay them down to a brisk Fire, baste them with Butter, roast them twenty-five Minutes, draw them and split them exactly in two down the Backs, cut off their Heads, take out their Entrails, throw away their Livers and Gizards, mince them with a small Onion and an Anchovey; put Half a Pint of Gravey into a Stew-pan, with a Quarter of a Pint of White Wine; lay in your Woodcocks, cover them close, let them stew for two Minutes, squeeze in some Lemon, put in some Butter melted very thick, salt it to your Taste; dish your Woodcocks upon Toasts, with their cut Sides down; throw the Sauce all over them; garnish them with Lemon and Barberries, and the Heads of the Woodcocks split.

ART of COOKERY.

To make Minc'd Pyes of Calves Hearts.
Paté haché au Corinth et Raisins.

TAKE three or four, as you like, open and wash them clean from the Blood; blanch them in boiling Water and Salt for two Minutes, take them out and drain them, cut them in Pieces, and let them lie to cool; shred them fine, take double their Weight of Beef Suet, cut, pick'd and shred; mix them together, then take the Weight of the Suet and the Hearts of Currants and Raisins ston'd and chopt; put the Fruit to the Meat, then take three or four Apples, par'd, cor'd, and shred also; then beat some Cinnamon, Nutmeg, and Mace; shred some Lemon Peel very fine, squeeze in the Juice of a Lemon, put in Half a Pint of Red Wine, a little Salt, with as much Sugar as will sweeten it to your Taste, candied Lemon, Orange, or Citron sliced thin; stir all well together, and fill your Pyes.

To dress Quails a-la-Braise.—See Chickens a-la-Braise.

To fricasy Quails.
Cailles à la Braise.

HALF-roast them, and make a Brown in a Stewpan with a Piece of Butter and Flour; put in some good Gravey, with some Mushrooms, a Bunch of sweet Herbs; season with Pepper, Salt, and Nutmeg, a Glass of Champaign Wine; squeeze in a little Lemon, put in your Quails, let them simmer for two or three Minutes; take out the sweet Herbs, and dish them; garnish with Lemon and Barberries.

To farce and roast Quails.
Cailles farcie et roti.

MAKE your Farce of Beef Suet and sweet Herbs, mixt with a few fine Bread Crumbs; season with Pepper, Salt, and Nutmeg; work it with an Egg, and farce their Bellies; spit them on a small Spit, singe and baste them with Butter, dridge them

with

with some fine Bread Crumbs, mixt with Flour and a little Salt; roast them of a fine brown Colour; let the Sauce be two or three Spoonfuls of White Wine, Gravey, the Juice of a Couple of Seville Oranges, a Shallot shred with a little Anchovey; mix all together, let it simmer for a Minute, and put it under your Quails; garnish with Seville Orange and dry Bread Crumbs.

To pickle and dry Sheeps' Tongues.
Langues de Mouton seché.

WASH them clean, pare the Roots handsomely, salt them, as you do your Hams, the Westphalia Way; turn and rub them with the Pickle every Day for a Fortnight; hang them up to dry, they will be fit to use in a Month's Time: when you will use them, boil them in Water, pretty tender; send them up cold; garnish with green Parsley.

Minc'd Pyes of Eggs.
Paté haché aux Oeufs.

TAKE their Weight of Beef Suet cut fine, chop the Eggs fine, and mix all together; take ten Golden Pippins, pare and core them, chop them fine, also season and order them; see how directed in Minc'd Pyes made of Calves Hearts; instead of Red Wine put in White; observe that the Eggs are to be boil'd hard as for a Sallet; you may make them of Mutton, either roasted or boil'd, or of Tripes, Veal, a Calf's Chaldron, or of a fresh Neat's Tongue, boil'd and peel'd, with the Roots off and shred fine; the same Ingredients as directed in Minced Pyes made of Calves' Hearts; a Neat's Tongue makes the best Pyes of all.

To stuff and roast a Fillet of Veal of a Quey Calf
Ruele de Veau farcie et roti.

CUT it what Size you please, make the Stuffing of Beef Suet, sweet Herbs, Bread Crumbs, Lemon Peel shred fine, season'd with Pepper, Salt, and
Nut-

Nutmeg; beat it fine in a Mortar, with the Yolks of three or four Eggs; make some Incisions with a sharp-pointed Knife, fill them with the Stuffing, skewer the Remainder under the Udder; spit and roast it, and baste with Butter; send it up with plain Butter; garnish with Seville Orange.

A Rump of Beef to roll.

Croupion de Beuf en rouleau.

BONE it, take out the Sinews, cut the thick Part of the Beef to make it lie all alike; lard it with large Lard-downs of Bacon, season'd with Pepper, Salt, and sweet Herbs; then make a Forc'd-meat of Veal, Beef Suet, the Yolks of Eggs boil'd hard, Bread Crumbs, Pepper, Salt, and Nutmeg, some Chives, and Lemon Peel, shred all very fine; beat it in a Mortar with the Yolks of Half a Dozen raw Eggs, rub the Inside of the Beef over with the Yolks of raw Eggs; blanch and shred Half a Score of Morels, mixt with the same Sort of Seasoning that you season'd the Lard-downs with; season the Beef all over with that, then lay your Forc'd-meat all over the Beef; begin at the small End, and roll it up, then roll it in a Cloth; tie it tight at each End with Packthread, then bind all over with Inckle very tight; order and boil it the same as you did the Beef-tromblance, it will take five or six Hours boiling; make a Ragoo of Cellery, Colliflowers, and Veal Sweet-breads; see the particular Places how made, mix all together; take your Beef up and drain it, lay it in the Dish; garnish it round with White Bread Toasts cut in Sippets; throw the Ragoo over the Beef; garnish the Dish with diced Carrots and Spinage.

To dress Beef Stakes the Italian Way.

Beuf en tranch à l'Italiene.

CUT them off the Ribs of Beef, hack them with the Back of your Kitchen Knife or Cleaver, sprinkle them all over with Elder Vinegar, season them with

with Pepper, Salt, and Coriander Seeds beat fine; lay them one upon another in a Dish, let them lie for an Hour; set your Gridiron over a clear Fire, rub it clean, then rub it with a Piece of fat Bacon, broil your Stakes quick, and turn them two or three Times; take Care they are not done too much; melt a Piece of Butter, with the Juice of a Seville Orange, the Gravey that comes from your Stakes, with a few Capers shred very fine; make your Dish very hot, lay in your Stakes, pour the Sauce over them; garnish with Horse Raddish and Pickles.

To dress a Neat's Tongue with Claret Sauce.
Langue de Beuf au Sause Vin rouge.

TAKE a large fresh Neat's Tongue, cut off the Pipe, leave the Roots whole, rub it well with Salt, and boil it tender; skin it, spit and roast it, stick it with Cloves, baste it with Butter, dridge it with Flour and Bread Crumbs; make the Sauce with Claret and Sugar, boil'd to the Thickness of a Cream; draw it, and dish it with Gravey under it; send up the Claret Sauce in a Boat; garnish with Seville Orange.

To roast a Neat's Tongue a-la-Smithergall.
Langne de Béuf à-la Smithergall.

ORDER it as in the last Receipt, spit it, take off the Skin of a Loin of Mutton, then take off all the Fat; rub the Tongue all over with the Yolks of Eggs, stick the thick Part with Cloves, lay on the Fat of the Mutton, skewer it and bind it on very tight with Packthread, wash that over with Yolks of Eggs as before, dridge it with fine Bread Crumbs, mixt with a little Cinnamon and Salt, roast it at a slow Fire for an Hour, draw it and take off the Packthread; send it up with Claret Sauce and Gravey as beforementioned; garnish with Seville Orange and Barberries. A Tongue ordered in this Manner eats not inferior to Venison.

ART of COOKERY.

To stew Beef-stakes.
Beuf en treuches etuvé.

TAKE some good Rump-stakes and hack them with the Back of a Knife, season them with Pepper and Salt, dridge them with a little Flour, fry them in Butter one by one just to give them a little brown Colour; then dridge in some Flour, stir it with a little wooden Ladle till it turns brown; then put in as much Gravey and strong Broth as you think will be sufficient to stew your Stakes in, put in an Onion or two sliced, some Pickles cut as you like; season with Pepper, Salt, and Nutmeg; salt it to your Taste, put in some Vinegar, with a Faggot of Sweetherbs, put in your Beef-stakes, cover them down close, stew them softly till they are very tender; then make some White Bread Toasts cut like Sippets, lay some in the Bottom of your Soop-Dish, dish up your Stakes, stick in the rest of your Sippets all round the Edge of your Dish; garnish with Horse-raddish and Pickles.

To fricasy Collyflowers brown.
Chouxfleurs en fricassée.

CUT the Flower off from the Stalk, blanch them in scalding Water for half a Minute, strain them into a Cullinder, drain them well from the Water, dridge on them a little Flour, tofs them up, fry them a little brown in clarified Butter, put in a Pint of Gravey, season with Pepper, Salt, a little Onion and Anchovey shred fine, squeeze in some Lemon, and dish them up.

To farce a Cabbage a-la-Smithergall.
Chox farcie.

TAKE a light Cabbage, tye it in a Cloth, boil it in a Pot a Quarter of an Hour, take it up and drain it from the Water, cut the Stalk End off very close, set it upon the Stalk End upon a Dish, draw down the Leaves one by one about four Leaves thick; then having some good Force-Meat prepared, wash the Leaves that you have laid down with the Yolk of an Egg, lay on some Force-Meat upon those Leaves very thin, with here and there a thin Rasher of interlard Bacon free from Rust; then wash that over with Yolks of Eggs, and let down some more Leaves over that again, so keep this Order till you have filled your Cabbage; then make it up all round in the Shape of your Cabbage as it was at first, wrap it in a Cloth, and tie it tight like the Collar of any Thing; tie it tight also at each End, boil it for two Hours, take it out of the Cloth, lay it in your Dish, and throw over it a Ragoo of Sweet-breads, either white or brown; garnish with Lemon and fry'd Parsley.

To make a white Cullis of a roast Pullet.
Coulis d'une blanc de Poulets.

TAKE off the Skin, and bone it; take a Handful of Sweet Almonds, blanch them and pound them in a Mortar, with the Breast or white Flesh of your Pullet, and the Yolks of four hard Eggs; when all this is well pounded together, take about two Pounds of Veal, some Ham of Bacon, cut it in Slices, and garnish the Bottom of your Stew-pan; put to it some Carrot and Parsnip sliced, and set it a sweating; when it begins to stick (before it has taken Colour) pour on it some good Broth, according to the Quantity of Cullis you intend to make; season it with Truffles, Mushrooms, a Leek, and Parsley; add to it the Bigness of a Couple of Eggs of Bread Crumbs, and let it simmer till the Veal be done enough; then take out your Slices of Veal, put in your Pullet, with the hard Eggs and Almonds that you pounded, and stir it about till it be very well mixt together; then set it over the Fire, but take Care that it does not boil for fear it turns brown; then strain it to use with your white Soop, Ragoos, &c.

To pickle green Figgs.
Figues confit au Vinagre.

GAther them in this Month, put them into a Brine of Salt and Water strong enough to bear an Egg, shift them every Day for eight Days; then green them as you do Cucumbers; make the Pickle of White Wine, Vinegar, and what Spices you like. Potatoe Apples are done the same Way.

To make elder Vinegar.
Sureau au Vinaigre.

ELder Flowers put into Vinegar give it a fine Flavour: The Buds put into Salt and Water, shifted every Day for four Days, green'd as you do other Pickles, and order'd as you do Kidney-beans, make a very pretty Pickle: As likewise Raddish, Pods, and Esturgeon Buds or Seeds.

To preserve Eringo Roots. (Some call it Sea Holley.)
Eringo espece Charden confit.

TAKE a Pound of these Roots, wash them clean, and boil them in hard Water till you can easily scrape off the outside Skin, put them into warm Water as you scrape them; then take two Pound of fine Loaf Sugar, put to it half a Pint of hard Water, let it stand in your Preserving-Pan till it be all melted; then set it on the Stove to boil; skim it and take out the Roots and put them in, let them boil till they be clear, stir them sometimes whilst they are doing, put them into an Earthen Pot that will conveniently hold them, and order them as you do other Preserves.

If you would candy them, boil them till the Sugar will candy, which you may know by dropping a Drop on a Plate; then take them out and put them on a wired Sieve, and dry them in a drying Stove.

To make Boulogne Sausages.
Sauscisse de Boulogne.

IT is a common Thing to make a Quantity of this Sort of Sausages together, because they will keep a long Time: Take three Pounds of a Buttock of Beef, three Pounds of a Leg of Pork, two Pounds of the fat of Pork, and a Pound of Beef Suet; season the Beef and Pork with four Ounces of Bay Salt, and an Ounce of Salt-petre well beat, with as much Cochineal as will lie on a Shilling, and a Quarter of a Pound of common Salt; rub your Meat well with them, and put them into an Earthen Vessel; rub and turn it every Day for four Days; then put it into a Pot, season it with Pepper, Mace, Thime, Sweet-marjoram, a little Winter Savory, a little Sage, a whole Nutmeg grated; shred your Suet very fine, and put it on the Top; then shred your Pork and put it in; then put in a Pint of Red Wine, tie it over with four Doubles of brown Paper, and bake it four Hours; then take out the Meat and strain it, pick it from the Skins and Sinews, put it into a large Mortar, pound it with the Fat skim'd off, and the Crumbs of a Penny Brick rub'd through a Cullinder, with six Anchovies wash'd, bon'd, and shred fine; when all is beat like a Paste, fill your Skins of what Size you please, tie them tight at the Ends, and hang them up in a Chimney to dry where Wood is burnt.

SEPTEMBER.

To make Jacobine Soop the Italian Way.
Potage au Jacobin à la manniere Italienne.

TAKE a large Knuckle of Veal, a Neck of Mutton, some Sweet-herbs, two or three Onions and Turnips, Salt, Pepper, and Mace; put it into a Pot that will hold it, fill it with clear Water, boil it softly, skim it very well as the Liquor boils away, fill it up with boiling Water, still keep it skimming; when the Meat is boil'd tender, strain it through a Sieve, let it stand to settle, take the Fat off the Top, then take the clear Broth from the Settling at the Bottom; then blanch and pound half a Pound of Almonds, mix them with some of the Broth and six Yolks of hard Eggs, rub them through a Strainer with the Crumbs of two French Rolls soak'd in some of the Broth; then take six Heads of Cellery cut and wash'd, three Turnips par'd and slic'd, two large Onions peel'd and slic'd, with a Faggot of Sweet-herbs, boil these in some more of the Broth till all be tender, then strain them and mix all together; then boil two Ounces of Rice in some of the Broth till it be tender, mix it with Bread Crumbs, Butter and Salt, with the Yolks of two Eggs; then take a large Fowl and truss it as for boiling, put the Rice into the Belly of it, spit and roast it; put it into your Soop, make all hot; put some dry'd Crusts of rasp'd Bread into the Bottom of the dish; dish your Soop with the Fowl in the Middle; garnish the Rim of the Dish with creed Rice colour'd with Saffron, and salt it to your Taste.

To dress Mackarel.
Maquereaux à sechée.

GUT and wash them, put them into Salt and cold water, set them on to boil; when they are enough, take them up to drain; then boil some Parsley, with a little Mint and Fennel, chop it fine, mix it with scalded Goosberries and drawn Butter, with a little Salt.

To broil Mackarel.

CLEAN and dry them very well, scotch them on the Sides, salt them, and let them lie an Hour; then rub them over with oil'd Butter, and broil them on a Gridiron over a slow Fire; turn them, then dish them. The Sauce as before.

To souse Mackarel.
Maquereaux au court bouillon.

BOIL them as before, take them up carefully and don't break the Skins; then add more Salt, put in some Vinegar, let it boil, let it stand to cool; then put in your Mackarel. When you send any to the Table, lay them in your Dish, and garnish them with Fennel.

To bake Mackarel.
Maqueraux cuit au four.

ORDER them as you did Herrings, beforementioned.

To make a Mackarel Pye.
Maquereaux en Paté.

CLEAN them, cut off their Heads, cut them into Pieces, season them with Pepper, Salt, and minc'd Fennel; sheet your Dish, lay in your Fish with Goosberries, lay Butter over all, lid it and bake it; melt your Butter with Gravey, dust in a little Flour, squeeze in some Lemon; cut up the Lid and put it into the Pye.

To salt and dry Mackarel.
Maquereaux salié et sechée.

RUB them with a Cloth, split them down their Backs, take out their Entrails and wipe them clean with a wet Cloth, salt them with bay and common Salt for two Days, skewer them open, tie them by the Tails to dry, broil and eat them with melted Butter and the Juice of a Lemon. Some like the Yolks of hard Eggs shred and mixt with the Sauce; some like the Sauce as before-mentioned.

To dress a Hare with Peas.
Lievre à-la-braise aux Pois.

TRUSS it short and put a Pudding in the Belly of it, lard it and stew it a-la-braise; then stew some Peas, and pulp them through a Cullinder; mix them with Butter, and pour all over the Hare when dish'd. How to stew the Peas, see stew'd Peas. How to braise the Hare, see Fowls a-la-brase.

To make a Pye of Mutton Olives.
Paté de Mouton aux Olives.

MAKE them as you do Veal Olives, but use no Bacon; sheet your Dish with Puff Paste and lay in the Olives, put the Yolk of an Egg boil'd hard betwixt each Olive, lay on some Bits of Butter, lid the Pye; put in a little Gravey, and bake it two Hours; when baked, chop some Capers, mix them with Gravey and Butter, cut up the Lid and pour it in, then lay on the Lid again.

To make a Damsin Pudding.
Boudin des Damsins.

TAKE off the Stalks; take out the Stones; make a Piece of Paste as you do Pasty Paste, butter a Cloth and lay it into a Bason or Dish, roll out the Paste and lay it on the Cloth; then put in the Damsins, put in as much Sugar as you think will sweeten it;

then

then wet the Edges, clofe it up, te it tight in the Cloth, boil it an Hour, turn it out of the Cloth into the Difh, melt fome Butter with White Wine and Sugar, and pour it over the Pudding; grate on fome Sugar and fend it up.

To order Damfins to preferve, and keep all the Year, for Tarts.

Damfins à garder tous l' Année.

PICK off their Stalks; nick them in the Seam with a fharp Knife; then take an Earthen Pot as broad at Bottom as at Top, lay fome Powder Sugar in the Bottom; then lay in a Lare of Damfins with their nickt Sides down, fpread Sugar all over them, lay in another Lare of Damfins and Sugar over them again; fo continue till you have fill'd the Pot; let Sugar be at Top; then tie them down with double Paper, bake them in a flow Oven two Hours, take them out, and let them ftand to cool; then put them into what Pots you like, lay a Piece of Writing-Paper clofe to them, put over it fome render'd Mutton Suet, and they will keep all the Year: Fill each Pot equally with Syrrup.

You may order Damfins the fame Way for a Sweet-Meat: Ufe double-refin'd Sugar beat and fifted, and make ufe of the fame Method; when they are bak'd and cold, make a Syrrup pretty ftrong with the Syrrup that comes from them, adding more Sugar; boil it, fkim it, and put in the Damfins, let them lie for three or four Days; then boil them till they be clear, put them into Pots and Glaffes, paper and tie them down as you do other Sweet-Meats.

Another Way.

Damfins confit.

TAKE off their Stalks, and nick them in the Seam; put them into your Preferving-Pan, ftrew over them fome double-refin'd Sugar, and let them

them stand till the next Day; then make a Syrrup for them of double their Weight of Sugar, skim it, put in your Damsins, let them boil till they be clear, set them sometimes off when they boil fast, for fear they should break; when they are done, put them up as before.

To roast Weet Ears.
Wheat-ears appretée.

WEET Ear is a Bird that is to be catched in Kent; they are to be roasted wrapt in Vine Leaves; first draw, singe, and truss them as you do Larks, put a thin Bit of Bacon betwixt every other Bird, baste them with Butter, dridge them with Bread Crumbs, Flour, and a little Salt; when they are enough, put Gravey and Butter into the Dish; garnish with crisp'd Bread Crumbs and Seville Orange.

To feed and dress Roofs and Reeves.
Ruffs and Rees nourrit & appretée.

THEY are a Lincolnshire Bird, bred in the fenny Part of the Country; they are a fine Nest Bird, and must be fed with creed Wheat and White Bread and Milk sweetned; they must have every one a Dish, for they won't eat one with another; they make a Contrivance for them to hide themselves, for as soon as you go into the Room they all fall a fighting: They must have clean Straw to lie on: Sometimes they give them creed Rice sweetened. I have known some feed their Chickens in this Manner. These Birds are chiefly roasted: Draw them and truss them as you do a wild Duck, but with their Heads on; singe them, put Butter and Salt in their Bellies. The Sauce is Butter and Gravey. Some like Bread Sauce to them, made as for Partridges: Garnish with butter'd Crumbs and Seville Orange, Land Rodes are drest in the same Manner. Teels as wild Ducks. As to feeding of Chickens, the Method above-mentioned is the best Way that is, if you go to the Expence of it.

it. When I ſerved Secretary Treby, they had a Coup made which kept each Bird by itſelf, the largeſt Sort at the Bottom, that held ſix Turkies or Geeſe; the next Row eight large Fowls; the next ten; the next twelve; and ſo on till you come to a Hole that would but hold a Quail; they were made with ſliding Doors, and they feil back according to the Depth of the Bird from the Breaſt to the Rump, when the Tail Feathers are cut or pull'd off; the Height that the Fowl can juſt ſtand upright, and it was left open at the further End at the Bottom for the Excrements to fall down; we never fail'd of having Fowls as fat as you would chuſe in three Weeks Time: Firſt take the Method as directed in the Beginning of this Book. This Coup was ſet in a Room built in the Yard for that Purpoſe; it had four Feet to it, that all the Dung was waſh'd away every Day, and a Run of Water went conſtantly through the Houſe. It had a Fire Place in it to warm it in the Winter Time. The Fowls were conſtantly fed three Times a Day, and their Troughs ſcalded every Day.

N. B. Some roaſt Roofs and Reeves cover'd with Vine Leaves and Bards of Bacon.

To make Damſin Wine.
Land Rails accommodée.

TAKE what Quantity of ripe Damſins you pleaſe, put them into a Tub, then put as much warm Water to them as will cover them; cover them cloſe, let them lie twenty-four Hours, or till they are fit to burſt, then add more warm Water to them; then put them into a Pan and boil them two Hours, then ſtrain and ſqueeze them hard in a Hair Cloth or Sieve, let it be luke-warm and work it with the Lees of good Wine; if you can't get Lees, ſpread ſome good Yeſt on a large Toaſt of Bread and put it in; when it hath wrought a while, tun it into a Wine Caſk; when it hath wrought two or three Days, put in ſome freſh Damſins and ſtop it up, let it ſtand in a cool Cellar
for

for two or three Months; then bottle it as you see Occasion. This Wine will drink much like Claret.

To make Damsin Wine another Way.
Vin de Damsins appretée.

TAKE four Gallons of Water, and put to it sixteen Pounds of Malaga Raisins, half a Peck of ripe Damsins; put all into a Cask that will hold it, stop it up, let it stand for six Days, stirring them every Day twice; then let them stand as long without stirring; then draw the Wine out of the Cask; then having half a Peck of Damsins put into an Earthen Vessel, put to them two Pounds of fine Sugar, tie them down, and bake them three Hours in a moderate Oven; then strain them through a Sieve, put it into a Wine Cask with the rest, stir it with a Stick, cork it lightly for a Week, then cork it tight, keep it in a cold Cellar, and bottle it at Discretion.

To make Cullis, or Damsin Cheese, as some call it, but 'tis properly a Conserve of them.
Confection de Prunes.

TAKE a Quart of ripe Fruit of either of them put to them a Pint of Red Wine, set them on a Stove, and stew them, close cover'd, till you can pulp them; then take out their Stones, and work them through a fine Cullinder or coarse Sieve, put to a Pint of this a Pound of double-refin'd Sugar, pounded and sifted; put them into your Preserving-pan, set it it on a Charcoal Fire, stir it with a Silver Spoon till it it clear and pretty thick; put it into your Pots to turn out, and dry it in your Drying-stove, slice it out, and cut it into any Form you like, or put it into small Glasses of different Forms as you like, or into Flummery Moulds, &c.

To make Marmalade of Quinces red.

Coigns en Marmalade rouge.

PARE and quarter them, take out the Cores; take the Cores and some of the worst of your Quinces, pare and slice them, and boil them in as much Water as will cover them; when boil'd tender, strain the the Liquor from them, put the other Quinces to it, and boil them as tender as you can; rub them through a Sieve, if the Liquor from the Quinces do not afford Liquor enough to boil them, add some Water to it; to every Pint of this Pulp put a Pound of double-refin'd Sugar finely powder'd, set it on a slow Fire, and put to it Half a Pint of Currant Jelly; let it simmer till it is of a fine Colour and clear, then put it into Pots or Glasses, as you like, or into any pretty Molds to turn out. You may do some with coarser Sugar for putting into Apple-Pyes, &c.—Some put in Jelly of Barberries instead of Currants; observe to slice your Quinces before you stew them; when your Marmalade is pretty stiff, you may make it into the Shape of Pears, cut them into Halves or Quarters, and dry them in your drying Stove.

To make Marmalade of Quinces white.

Coigns en Marmalade blanc.

TAKE the clearest Quinces you can get, pare, core, and slice them thin into Water, then boil them tender; take a Pound of double-refin'd Sugar, break it into Lumps, dip'd into Water, Bit by Bit, and put it into your Preserving pan; let it lie till it is all dissolved, then set it on a Charcoal Fire, let it boil till it comes to a Candy-height; then take your Quinces out of the Water you boil'd them in; put them to the Sugar, and keep them stirring till they be clear; put it into Pots, or order them as you did the red one.

ART of COOKERY.

To make Jelly of Quinces red.
Coigns en Gellée

PARE and core them, and put them into a Saucepan that will conveniently hold them, and has a Cover to it; set it on a slow Fire, fill it full of fine Water, let the Quinces be boil'd to Pieces, then run it through a Jelly Bag, to a Pint of this Liquor, take a Pound of double-refin'd Sugar; make the Sugar boil to a Candy-height, with Half a Pint of Water; then put in your Quince Liquor, set it on a slow Fire till it is incorporated together, but don't let it boil; put to it Half a Pint of the Syrrup of Barberries; see how made, where Barberries are treated of, then put it into Glasses. Another Way: Take a Pound of Quinces, par'd, cor'd, and slic'd; put them into an Earthen Jar, with Half a Pound of pick'd Barberries, and three Pints of clear Water, tie them down with a double strong Paper, bake them four Hours; then strain them through a Jelly Bag, take a Pound of double-refin'd Sugar to a Pint of this Liquor, but first boil the Sugar into a Candy-height, with Half a Pint of Water; then put in your Liquor, and order it as you did the other.

To pickle Barberries.
Barberries au Vinaigre.

PICK out the large Branches, make a strong Brine of Salt and Water, and put them in it; then stamp the rest of them, after they have lain in the Brine two Hours, strain it from the Berries, and put them that you stamp'd into the Brine; put in a Piece of Allum, and boil it; when it has boil'd Half an Hour, strain it again, then put your Barberries into a Jar, press them down tight, and put the Brine to them; lay on them a Slate, to keep them down under the Brine; tie them down with Leather, and set them in a cold Place.

To preserve Barberries.
Barberries en Conservé et Confit.

TAKE the finest Barberries you can get, and the largest and ripest; if any be bad, pick them off, lay the Bunches, one by one, and set them in the Sun for three or four Hours in a large Dish or Sieve; let them lie till the next Day, then make a Sirrup for them with Half a Pint of Water to a Pound of double-refin'd Sugar; let there be Syrrup enough for them to swim in without their lying one upon another; then take a Quantity of the other Barberries, and pick them off their Stalks, bruize them and boil them in as much Water as will a little more than cover them, then strain them through a Lawn Sieve, or through a fine Cloth; to Half a Pint put Half a Pound of Loaf Sugar, boil it to a Syrrup; put your Barberries, and the rest, into your Preserving-pan all together, and boil them quick till they be clear; then when they have lain some Time, and you have a Mind to candy them in Bunches, just dip them, Bunch by Bunch, in warm Water, and tie them to small Sticks with green Thread, and dridge them with double-refin'd Sugar, pounded and sifted; dry them in a Stove, turn them and sift them again; you should dry them on Glass-Plates, first sifted with Sugar, and then lay on your Bunches or Sprigs of Barberries; then, when dried, keep them in paper'd Boxes, in a dry Place; some take the Stones out of them before they do them: White and Red Currants may be done the same Way, but you need not have any White Jelly to put into the White Currant; the red ones require some Red Jelly to be put to them to heighten the Colour, and make the Fruit look better; the Syrrup that is left from your Barberries you should take great Care of, for it is the best and liveliest of all red Syrrups, to put to Cherries, Currants, or any Thing that is preserved red.

To dry Damsins or any Sort of Plumbs.

Damsins sechés

RUB them with a clean Cloth, lay them single in a flat bottom'd Tin Dripping-pan, and set them into a slow Oven; then turn them, put them on wir'd or splinted Sieves, and put them in again; keep this Order till they be quite dry, put them into strong Paper-bags prickt full of Holes, and hung up in a Kitchen, or where there is a constant Fire kept.

To pickle Red Cabbage.

Choux rouge en Confection.

TAKE one that is very red, cut it into four; take out all the large white Stalks, then cut it into thin shreds, put it into an Earthen Pot; to a Pound of Cabbage take a Quarter of a Pound of Salt, and an Ounce of Salt-petre; pound the Salt-petre, mix it with other Salt, and strinkle it over the Cabbage; press it down hard with a Board, and set a Weight on it; let it lie for six Hours, then take a Pint of Vinegar, the best you can get, and boil it with whole Mace, Pepper, and slic'd Ginger; then put the Cabbage into a Jar, pour on the Vinegar and Spices, lay something on it to keep the Cabbage under the Pickle; cover it down close, when it is cold tie it over with Leather, and keep it in a cold Place.— There is another Receipt of this, but both are good.

To pickle Potato-Apples.

Taupinenboure en Confection.

WHEN you gather them, rub them with a dry Cloth, and put them into Salt and Water as you do other Pickles; shift them every other Day for nine Days, then drain them from the Salt and Water, make a fresh Brine, boil it, and put it boiling hot on them; then let them stand till the next Day, and strain that Brine from them; then take as much White Wine Vinegar as will cover them, and put in it it Mace, Pepper, and raw Ginger, with a little Dill; put all together into a Brass-Pan, set it on a slow Fire, cover it close, and let it simmer till they be green; then put them into a Jar, cover them till they be cold, then tie them over as before directed, and set them in a cold Place.—Raddish Pods are done the same Way.

To pickle Onions.
Onions au Vinaigre.

TAKE the smallest white Onions you can get, peel them, and boil them in Salt and Water; they must boil but very little, then strain them and put them into distill'd Vinegar, in small Bottles, with Oil on the Tops of them; tie them over with Bladders first wet, and they will stick close to the Bottles.

To pickle Colliflowers the same Way, or Cabbage Stalks.
Choux Fleurs confit au Vinaigre.

CUT the Out-side hard Skin off; or large Cucumbers, par'd and slic'd, then put them into Salt and Water for twenty-four Hours, then strain'd from that, dried with a Cloth, and put into Vinegar, order'd as above.

To preserve green Figs.
Figues confit verd.

RUB them very well with Salt, and a Flannel Cloth first dipt in Water and squeez'd; put them into Water as you do them, then boil them very slow till they be tender, then green them as you do green Plumbs or Peaches; then put them into Water for two Hours, and cut them half Way down the Middle, and make a strong Syrrup of double their Weight of fine Sugar, let it boil almost to a Candy-height before you put them in, keep them stirring till they be clear, put them into Pots, let them stand till they be cold, then cut a Piece of Writing-Paper that will fit the Pot, dip it into Brandy, lay it close to the Fruit, and tie the Pot over with Leather; keep them in a Place pretty dry.

To preserve Pears.
Poirs confit.

PARE them very thin, and tender them in Water over a flow Fire; then take them out, make a Syrrup for them, as you did for the Figs, and order them them the same in the doing; you may dry them and the Figs, by laying them on Tin-Plates, dridging them with fine Sugar, and laying them a little open, that is, slip in one Half half-way off from the other, and let them remain fast at the Bottom; when you pare them, let their Stalks be kept on, and likewise on the Figs: If you design to dry them, you may put in some Juice of Lemon to them, and some Rust of Lemon Peel; put it in some Time before you take them up, that the Rine may boil clear.

To make a Spanish Olio.
Olio d'Espagne.

I Shall give you an Account of an Olio, but, in my Opinion a good English Hotch-potch is better: Take some strong Broth, made of a Leg of Beef, put it into a Pot big enough to hold the following Things; take Half a Dozen Pounds of Brisket Beef, cut it into square Pieces; let it boil some Time, and put in some Salt, skim it often; when it is three Parts boil'd, cut a Neck of Mutton into square Pieces, and put it in, still keep skimming it; you must have a Pot of boiling Water by to keep it filling up; then cut a Neck of Pork, and put it in, in the same Manner; then a Neck of Veal, cut the same Way; first wash and blanch your small Meat before you put it to your Beef; you may skin your Pork, if you chuse it, and roast it and the Mutton and Veal before you put them in; when your Meat is all stew'd near enough, then prepare the Roots and Herbs as follows: Take two or three Savoys, cut each in four Pieces; take four Carrots, cut a Hand's Breath, and in four long-ways; two Parsnips the same, first cut off the Out-side of both; six Heads of Celle-ry,

ry, cut the same; six Heads of Leeks, some Parsley Roots, some Cabbage Lettice; tie each Sort by itself, and stew them in some of the strong Broth, with a Dozen of small Turnips, twenty small Onions, some Carrots par'd round; likewise make a Brown, and toss them all up in it; take some fresh Broth and put to them, let them stew till tender, then taste the Broth they were stew'd in, and if it does not taste amiss put it to your Beef; then take three Chickens, four Pigeons, four Snipes, four Teals, a Dozen of Larks; let them be drawn, singed, and truss'd for boiling; you may lard some if you please, and half-roast them all; then make a Brown for them, and moisten it with some of the strong Broth; let them stew in it, put the largest in first; then stew a Quart of green Peas in some of the Broth, and pulp them through a Cullinder; then prepare a good many large Sippets of White Bread, dried in an Oven; then take a large Soop-Dish, raise a large Rim round it, and dry it in the Oven; then mix all your Meat and Fowls together, and let them stew a little to incorporate the Relish of all, one with another; then put all your Meat into a large broad Stew-pan, with the Fowls and Roots; skim the Fat off the Broth, and strain some of it into your Stew-pan or Gravey-pan; untie your Roots, Lettice, &c. and lay them in betwixt your Meats and Fowls; shake all together, and skim off what Fat you can; then have two Tereins ready, and put some dried Crusts of Bread in each; then take a large Silver Soop-Ladle, and begin to dish up; lay your Sippets of Bread in the Bottom of your Soop-Dish, then the Beef, skin'd and cut handsomely, then Mutton, then Veal, prick in some Sippets between; then with your Silver Ladle, lay in some Roots, &c. then your Pork, with your Chickens and Pigeons between, with some Rashers of Bacon, then your Savoys, Teals and Snipes; then pile the Larks in the Middle, having your Broth very hot fill the two Tereins.

reins, put some hot Broth to your Olio, and lay in the Turnips and Carrots, and all the rest of the Herbs and Roots, to fill up all the vacant Places; fill up the Dish with the Broth; garnish your Dish with Rashers of Bacon, Spinage, and potcht Eggs; send it in the Middle of the Table, with the Soops at Top and Bottom, and the rest of the Dishes you have provided to fill your Table, that is four added to these three; the Top Soop to be mov'd, with a Dish of Fish; the Bottom with roast Beef or Venison; the second Course, what you please.

To ragoo Oysters.
Huitres en Ragoût.

OPEN your Oisters, and put them into a Stew-pan with their Liquor, let them just boil up; take them off, wash them out of their Liquor, lay them on a Plate, and let the Liquor stand to settle; pour off the Clear of the Liquor, and put in your Oisters; then make a Brown, and put in some good Gravey, two or three Spoonfuls of White Wine, some Parsley, and a few Chives shred fine; grate in a little Nutmeg, shred a few pickled Mushrooms, and toss all up together; put in your Oisters and the Liquor; toss all up together; put some Sippets in your Dish, put in some melted Butter; don't let the Oisters boil after you have put them into the Ragoo; dish them, and garnish with Barberries and Lemon.

To broil Oysters in their Shells.
Des Huitres Grillée.

OPEN them, and put them into the deep Shells; clean them from the Shells and Sand, place them on a Gridiron; put to them a little Chives, Parsley shred fine, a little Pepper, Vinegar, and a little Bit of Butter; cover them with their upper Shells, set them into the Oven for a Quarter of an Hour; dish and send them up; you may broil them on a Stove, or put them into the Oven on a Dish; some like a few Bread Crumbs in them.

To farce Oysters.
Des Huitres farcie.

OPEN them, and blanch them in a little Water and their own Liquor; then shred them, with a little Shallot, Parsley, Pepper, and Anchovies; put in the Crumb of a Roll soak'd in Cream; season them with Nutmeg and a little Mace, put in three or four Yolks of Eggs, a Quarter of a Pound of Butter; mix all together, and beat it in a Marble Mortar, with two or three Spoonfuls of White Wine, and some Juice of Lemon; put it into Scallop-shells, put on them Bread Crumbs, set them into an Oven to brown; if they do not brown soon, brown them with a Salamander, and send them hot: You may make these into Patte Petets, made with Puff-Paste; make them small and round as you do Rasberry-Puffs, and garnish any Dish of Fowls, Turkey, or Veal, in a made Way or plain, as you like; or make a Dish of them, and if you add some Bread Crumbs to this Farce, there is nothing better for your Turkey or Fowls' Crops, either roasted or boiled.

To make Oyster Pancakes.
Gâteanx au Poel aux Huitres.

MAKE a Batter of Flour, Eggs, a little Salt, and Cream; make it to that Stiffness that it will run easily, then take some Butter; and clarify it, put some of it into your Pan, make it hot; put in as much Butter as will cover the Bottom of your Pan, then having your Oysters blanch'd and dried, lay some all over the Pancake, then put more Batter on them to cover them; when fried brown on one Side, turn it, and fry it brown on the other also; then dish it. Garnish with fried Parsley and Seville Orange.

ART of COOKERY. 243

To make Fritters of a Turkey Breast, Fowl, Partridge, Chicken, or Capon.

Bignets avec la Chair d'une Dindon.

TAKE two Ounces of the Flour of Rice, put to it a Pint of Milk and a Pint of Cream, mix it well together; put to it a Piece of Butter and a little Salt, set it on a Stove Fire, keep stirring till it is thick; take it off the Fire, and let it stand to cool, then beat ten Eggs, leave out six Whites, strain them through a Sieve into the Rice, stir all together, and mix it very well; then mince your Meat very fine, put to it as much minc'd Apple, some Suet shred fine; put in some Currants, wash'd, rub'd dry, and pickt, some candied Lemon, Orange, or Citron; some Cinnamon, Nutmeg, and Sugar, with a little Salt, and White Wine; mix all together; then set the Rice on the Fire again, and stir it till it is the Thickness of a thin Paste; let it cool again, then roll it out, and cut it into round Pieces; put in a Spoonful of your Mixture into as many as you chuse to fry; wet the Eggs, and cover them with another Piece of the same Size; close them down tight, that they may not burst in the frying; fry them in clarified Butter, or wash them over with an Egg, and bake them in an Oven.

To bake or fry Gurnets.

Rougets au Four ou frit.

CLEAN and gut them, wash and dry them well; then take Parsley, Thyme, Pepper, Salt, and Bread Crumbs, mix all together; then beat some Yolks of Eggs, with a little melted Butter; roll your Fish in it, and dridge them with the above Mixture; lay them into a convenient Thing, and bake them in an Oven, of a brown Colour; then make a Sauce for them as follows: Take some Mushrooms, an Anchovey, some Chives, mince all fine, then make a Brown; put in your Herbs, &c. with some good Gravey, squeeze in some Lemon, a Spoonful of White Wine, grate in a little Nutmeg, put in some melted Butter; put your Sauce into the Dish, and lay the Fish on it; garnish with fried Parsley and Lemon. You may fry them as you do any other Fish.

To dress Mullets.
Mullets accommodée.

YOU may dress them as you do Salmon Trouts that are bak'd or boil'd, with Sauce as directed for several other Sorts of Fish; or fried, if they be small.

To make Hartshorn Jelly.

TAKE a Pound of Hartshorn, put to it six Quarts of Water, boil it till two Quarts be wasted, then strain it through a Sieve, and let it stand till next Day; then take the Clear off the Top, and put to it eight Whites of Eggs, the Juice of six Lemons, as much Sugar as will sweeten it to your Taste; put in what you like as to Spices, stir all well together, set it on a slow Fire to boil, with a Bottle of Rhenish or White Wine; let it boil till it breaks, then run it through your Jelly Bag till it be as clear as Rock Water, and fill your Glasses: This is reckoned the finest Jelly that is made.

To pot Lampreys.
Lamproies empotée.

SKIN them, and take out the blue String that is in their Backs; cut them into Pieces, and season them with Pepper, Mace, Nutmeg, and Salt; to a Pound of Fish take a Pound and a Half of Butter; put your Fish into a Pot, put your Butter over them, tie them down with double Paper, bake them in a moderate Oven for four Hours; take them out, and let them drain in a Cullinder, then lay them round and round in your Pot, till you have fill'd it within an Inch of the Top; then skim off the clear Butter, and fill up the Pot to the Top; set the Pot even till cold.

ART *of* COOKERY

To stew Lampreys.
Lamproies en étuve.

SKIN them, and take out their Strings, clean and blanch them, dry them well, flour and fry them in clarified Butter; then make a Brown, put in some good Gravey, with a Handful of Parsley scalded and shred fine; put in some whole Pepper, Mace, and grate in a little Nutmeg, put in some Vinegar, let them stew till they be enough, put in a Glass of White Wine, squeeze in a little Lemon, put in some melted Butter, toss all up together; dish them up, and garnish with fried Parsley and Lemon; you may put in a few Capers shred fine.

To make Mould Fritters.
Bignets dressée dans une Forme.

YOU must provide some Moulds made of Tin of different Forms, like a Dolphin, a Coat of Arms, or any Fashion you like; then butter your Mould, and fill it Half full of Batter, made the same as for other Fritters; let your Fat be render'd Beef or Mutton Suet, or clarified Butter; let it be hot, then put in your Mould, with the Batter in it, fry it brown, and turn it out.

N. B. Your Moulds must be finely rivetted as well as soldered, or the hot Fat will unsolder them; be sure you have Fat to cover the Moulds.

To preserve Grapes.
Raisins confit.

TAKE them when they are large, but green, before they begin to turn; take out their Seeds, and let them lie on the Back of a Sieve twenty-four Hours, and set them in the Sun or before the Fire; then put them into a Pot, and strew some double-refin'd Sugar over them, pounded and sifted; then take as much Sugar as will make a Syrrup for them, enough for them to swim in, that is Half a Pint of

Water

Water to a Pound of Sugar; let your Syrrup be pretty strong; then put in your Grapes, with the Sugar to them, let them do softly till they be clear; keep putting them down with a Silver Spoon or Ladle, and skimming them; put them into a Pot large enough. You may dry them after they have lain some Time in the Syrrup.

Another Way.
Raisins confit d'une autre maniere.

PICK out their Stones, put them into hard Water; then put some of their Leaves into the Bottom of a Brass-Pan; lay in your Bunches of Grapes, with Vine Leaves between, then Leaves on them again; then take a Bit of Verdigrease, the Bigness of a large Nutmeg, pound it fine, and put it into a Viol Bottle, with as much Allum pounded; likewise put to it a Gill of White Wine Vinegar; shake the Bottle, and let it stand to settle, then put into your Grapes two or three Spoonfuls of this, with as much hard Water as will cover them; set them on a very slow Fire to green, do not let them boil, then take them out, and put them into cold Water; let them lie an Hour, then make a Syrrup for them as before, put them in Bunch by Bunch; let them just boil up, then set them off the Fire, cover'd down close for an Hour, then set them on again; keep this Order till they be clear, put them up as before-directed; let them lie in the Syrrup for a Month, then take them out, and drain their Syrrup from them, dridge them with double-refin'd Sugar sifted, lay them on Glass-Plates to dry in a Drying-stove, turn them every Day till they be quite dry; keep them in a paper'd Box, with Paper betwixt each Bunch; set them in a dry Place.

To make Italian Bisket.
Biscuit à l' Italienne.

TAKE a Pound of double-refin'd Sugar beat and sifted, put to it a Pound of the finest Flour you can

can get, mix them together; then take fix Eggs, beat them very well, and ftrain them through a Sieve; put them into Marble Mortar, put fome of your Flour and Sugar in, and beat it very well; fo keep putting the reft in, by little at a Time, till it be all in; you muft beat it an Hour without ceafing, then put a Sheet of Wafer Paper on a Sheet of Tin, drop on the Bifcuit, ftrew on them fome Carraway Comfits, and bake them off as quick as you can.

To make Macaroons.
Macaroni à faire.

TAKE two Ounces of fweet Almonds, blanch and peel them, beat them in a Marble Mortar, adding a little Cream and Orange Flower Water; then add by Degrees a Quarter of a Pound of double-refin'd Sugar fifted, and the Whites of three Eggs; beat it very well till it be of a convenient Thicknefs; if it fhould be too thin, add more Sugar; put it on Wafer Paper, dridge on Sugar, and bake them as you are directed above.

To drefs Mufcles different Ways.
Moules accommodé en plufieurs Manieres.

MUSCLES are Shell-Fifh not much valued, but order'd as below, I think they may be agreeable to fome: Wafh them, and pull off their Strings; put them into a Pot, ftrinkle on them a Handful of Salt, cover them down clofe, and fet them on a flow Fire till they will open: then take them out of their Shells, take off their Beards, take the Liquor and ftrain it; then take fome White Wine and Vinegar, and the Clear of their Liquor; put in it fome whole Pepper and Mace, give it a boil or two; put in your Mufcles, ftop them clofe, and keep them for your Ufe. You may fend them up on Plates, garnifh'd with raw Parfley, to be eat with Bread and Butter.

To fricasy them.
Moules en Fricassée.

YOU may fricasy them white, with a white Lare, as for Chickens. See fricasy'd Chickens.

You may dress them brown: Brown a Piece of Butter in a Stew-pan, put in a little Flour, shred in a little Onion, with some good Gravey; let it stew, grate in a little Nutmeg, shred and put in a little Parsley; then take out as many of your Muscles as you think will do, make them thoroughly hot, and dish them on Sippets; garnish them with fried Parsley.

To put them in Loaves scallop them like Oysters.
Moules au Pain aussi en Escalopes.

WHEN they are order'd as before, you may put them into Rolls, as you do Oysters, or as they are done White, which Way you like best: You may put the pickled Muscles into Fish-sauce, with some of their Liquor. You may use Cockles any of these Ways, or put them into Scallop-shells as you do Oysters.

To dress Perch.
Perches accommodé.

THEY are a fine Fish, if large, not inferior to Carp or Tench, and eat well stew'd; if small, they are good fried. You may bake, broil, or boil them as you do several Sorts of other Fish.

Pigeons a-la-Tartare.
Pigeons à la Tartar.

SINGE and truss them as for boiling, flat them with a Cleaver, season them with Pepper and Salt as for a Pye, dip them in melted Butter, dridge them with minc'd Parsley and Bread Crumbs, butter a Sheet of Writing-Paper, and lay it on a Gridiron, with the butter'd Side up, lay on your Pigeons, and broil them over a broiling Harth as there is in most large Kitchens;
but

but if you fhould not have fuch a convenient Place, you may broil them in the Chimney Corner, or upon the Hearth; firft light your Charcoal in a Stove, then lay Bricks the Square of your Gridiron, put the Charcoal into it, fet on your Pigeons, broil them leifurely, turn them often, and they will be of a fine Colour; then having fome Parfley minc'd fine, with a few Chives, Shallot, o Onion; mix them with minc'd Anchovey, a little Gravey, and a Piece of Butter work'd in Flour, the Juice of Half a Lemon; put all into a Stew-pan, grate in a little Nutmeg, put in a little Salt, fhred eight or ten pickl'd Mufhrooms, draw all up together as you do Butter; put the Sauce into the Difh, and lay one your Pigeons, that their Rumps may meet in the Middle; garnifh with Barberries and Lemon.

You may do Mutton Cutlets the fame Way, adding fome fhred Capers.

To drefs Pork Chops.
Cottelets de Porc.

YOU may broil Pork Chops as above; make Ufe of Sage inftead of Parfley; leave out the Capers, and put in a little Muftard.

This Way of broiling is the beft Way for moft fmall Things, as Sweet-breads fkewer'd on Silver-fkewers, Brotch-lights, Oyfters, Larks, or any fmall Birds, &c.

And all Sorts of Fifh; the large Fifh cut in Slices, about an Inch thick and flour'd, and the Gridiron fet a good Height from the Fire, that it may broil leifurely; you muft obferve, that none but your frefh Fifh will broil well; you need no Paper to the broiling of Fifh, all fmall Fifh broil whole; the particular Ways of ordering them, and their Sauce, look where each Sort is treated of. I have been particular in this Way of broiling, becaufe it is the very beft and fweeteft, and gives every Thing, fo broil'd, a much better Colour than any other Way.

To preserve Bonum Magnum Plumbs.
Bonum Magnum confit.

THROW them into boiling Water to raise the out-side Skin, peel it all off, cut them in the Nick to the Stone, put them into a Pot, strew on them some double-refin'd Sugar, let them lie three or four Hours; make a Sirrup for them, enough for them to swim in, let it boil till it be near of a Candy-Height, put in your Plumbs, with what is at them, let them do softly, keep them skimming and turning till they be clear, then put them into Pots.

To dress Larks.
Aloüettes accommodé.

PICK them clean, Heads and all; draw them, and turn down their Legs, as you do a Duck; spit them a-cross, on a Lark-spit, put a Bit of Butter, with a little Salt, into the Belly of each; singe and tie them to a small Spit; wash them over with the Yolks of Eggs and melted Butter, dridge them with fine Bread Crumbs mixt with Flour, and a little Salt; lay them down to the Fire, at a good Distance, to let the Coat fix on them; then drop on some more Butter, and dridge them again, till you have made them as plump as you can; garnish your Dish with Bread Crumbs, fried brown in Butter; send Gravey and Butter in a Boat, with a little Juice of Lemon.

To make a Silmy of Woodcocks.
Salmey des Becasses.

HALF-roast them, cut them in Quarters, put a Piece of Butter into a Stew-pan, make a Brown with Flour, toss the Woodcocks up in it; put in some good Gravey, a little White Wine, some Morels, Mushrooms, a little Onion and Anchovey shred fine, grate in a little Nutmeg, squeeze in some Lemon, salt it to your Taste; take their Ropes, take out the Liver and Gizard, chop the rest, and put it to your Woodcocks;

cocks; tofs all up together, put fome Truffles in the Bottom of your Difh, lay in your Woodcocks, pour on the Sauce; garnifh with Barberries and Lemon; take Care you do not let your Woodcocks be too much, and fkim off the Fat before you difh them; if the Anchovies do not make it Salt enough, put in Salt to your Tafte.

To pot Woodcocks and Partridges.
Becaſſes & Perdrix empoté.

PICK, finge, and draw them; take the bloody Part out of their Backs, rub out the Blood with a wet Cloth, feafon them with Pepper and Salt, and any other Spice you like; trufs them as for boiling, put them into a Pot big enough; you muft put Half a Pound of Butter to each Bird, if you pot them in fmall Pots; if you pot a large Pot, lefs will do; take out the Brains of the Woodcocks; if you pot them with their Bills on, pack them in the Pot you defign to bake them in; put the Butter on the Top, tie the Pot over with brown Paper; let them bake two Hours, take them out, and put them into a Cullinder, with their Vents down, to drain the Gravey out of them; then put them into the Pots you defign them to be potted in, and fill the Pots up with the Clear of the Butter; fet them very even till they be cold; take Care you don't put in any of the Settling of the Butter, for it will taint them: if your clear Butter does not hold out, put fome more Butter into the fame Pot, and fet it into the Oven to clarify.

OCTOBER.

To make Cockle Soop.
Potage aux Petoncles.

TAKE four Quarts of Cockles, put them into a convenient Pot, cover them close till they all open; pick them out of their Shells, and wash them in Water to clean them from the Sand; then take what Sort of Fish you can best get, cut it to Pieces, wash it, and put into a Pot of Water, with four large Onions, two or three Turnips, some Cellery, Thyme, Parsley, whole Pepper, Mace, some Salt, two Carrots, the Crust of a French Roll; let all boil softly for two Hours; let it stand to settle, after you have strained it through a Sieve; skim it, and pour off the Clear, then take some of the Clear, and put in it a Quart of green Peas, if you can get them; if not, take a Quart of blue Peas, boil them, and pulp them through a Cullinder; then take a good Handful of Sorrel, pick and shred it; take two Cabbage Lettices, cut them in four, and shred them fine Cross-ways; then shred two Onions, put a Piece of Butter into a Stew-pan, put in your Herbs, put to them a little Salt, cover them close, take Care they don't burn, moisten them with some of your Broth; then take the Kettle that you design to stew your Soop in, and put in your Herbs, the Peas, and the rest of the Broth; let them stew over a slow Fire till all is incorporated together; taste it, and if the Sorrel has not given it an agreeable Tartness, squeeze in a little Lemon; take a French Roll, cut a Piece off the Top, take out the Crumb, rub it with Butter within and without, put it into an Oven to harden, or set it before the Fire, and turn it, that it may not burn, put it into your Soop Dish;

let

let your Soop Dish be rim'd; tofs up your Cockles with a Piece of Butter, dridge in a little Flour, duft in a little Pepper, put in a little of your Broth, put in the Liquor that came from the Cockles; tofs all together when you are ready to difh, put fome Crufts of French Bread, dried before the Fire, and laid round your Roll in the Difh, put a Ladleful or two of your Soop to the Bread, fill the Roll with fome of your Cockles; garnifh the Rim of your Difh with fome of them, with fome Carrots, cut an Inch long, and fplit like Straws, that is a Heap of one, and a Heap of the other; put the reft of the Cockles into your Soop, ftir all together, and fill your Difh; firft fkim off the Fat that comes from the Butter, and fend it up hot.

I have been particular about this Soop, becaufe moft Soops, in Meagre, are made in this Manner; as, Mufcles, Oyfters, Shrimps, likewife any Sort of Roots that you would have the Soop go by the Name of, that is, the Rim of the Difh muft be garnifh'd with that particular Root or Herb, and the Roll in the Middle muft be fill'd with the fame, ordered in a proper Manner, as you will find, where directed for ragooing and ftewing of Vegetables. You muft broil three Pieces of Cod to put round the Roll of your Cockle Shop.

To make a Partridge Pye.

Paté aux Perdrix.

PICK, finge, and draw them; trufs them as for boiling; feafon them with Pepper and Salt, with a Piece of Butter put into the Bellies of them; then having your Pye rais'd and fet in a proper Form, lay in your Partridges, with fome Forc'd-meat and Yolks of hard Eggs between; lay on Butter over all, clofe and garnifh it in a proper Manner; wafh it over with the Yolk of an Egg, and bake it two Hours; when it is bak'd, put in fome Gravey; when you
defign

design to have it eaten cold, fill it up with clarified Butter.

To roast and order a Chine of Veal à la Smithergall.

LET it be cut out like a Chine of Mutton, spit it. See Chine of Mutton. Roast it leisurely; let the Veal be the smallest and whitest you can get; then make a Ragoo of Colliflowers, and put in your Dish; lay in your Veal, but first cut out the Kidnies, and lay them on each Side of the Veal; garnish with Seville Orange and Kidney-beans.

How to make a Patty of Oysters.
Paté aux Huitres.

MAKE some cold Paste, and sheet a Petty-Pan that will hold your Oysters; blanch them and wash them clean, put them into your Petty-Pan, with Yolks of hard Eggs, some Forc'd-meat Balls made of Fish; put in the Liquor, with two or three Spoonfuls of White Wine; season with Pepper, Nutmeg, shred Parsley, and a few Chives; if the Oysters do not make it salt enough, salt it to your Taste; put Butter all over, close and bake it an Hour; cut off the Lid, and make a White Lare for it, thicken your Lare over the Fire, keep it stirring; skim the Fat off your Pye, put in your Lare, lay on the Lid, and serve it up.

To make a Compot of Mushrooms.
Compote aux Champignons.

ORDER your Mushrooms as for a brown Fricasy, then take six Yolks of hard Eggs, with some Forc'd-meat Balls; let your Forc'd-meat be fried, put them to your Mushrooms, then blanch Half a Score Morels, all of a Size, as near as you can; take off their Stalks, stuff them with Forc'd-meat, and stew them in Gravey, with an Onion, and a Faggot of sweet Herbs; cover them close, and stew them over a slow Fire; rim the Edge of your Dish,
lay

lay in the Middle a French Roll, order'd as you did for the Cockle Soop, and fill it with some of your Mushrooms; lay round it the Morels and hard Eggs, squeeze a little Lemon into your Mushrooms, grate in a little Nutmeg, salt it to your Taste, tofs all up together, make it hot; if it be too thick, put in some of the Liquor your Morels were stewed in, pour it all over the rest, and garnish the Rim of your Dish with butter'd Bread Crumbs, crisp'd or dried.

To make Sausages,
Saucisses à faire.

TAKE some of the tenderest Part of Pork, and mince it fine; take the equal Weight of fat Pork, and mince it; season it with Pepper and Salt, a little Sage, Parsley, and Thyme, with a few Chives; shred your Herbs very fine, mix all together, with a few fine Bread Crumbs; pound it in a Mortar very fine; then having your Hog's Guts clean'd, fill them and tie them in proper Lengths, and boil, fry, or broil them, as you like. You may use them to Turkies, Fowls, or any Thing that Sausages are proper to be used with. There is a Receipt of this Kind, see which you like best.

To make a Sauce Robert.
Sauffe Robert.

TAKE an Onion, and slice it; put a Piece of Butter into a Stew-pan, put in your Onion, and keep it stirring with a wooden Ladle; put in some Cullis, drawn from Ham and Veal: then mince some Parsley, and put it in, with a small Matter of Thyme, put in a little Vinegar, let it boil up, put in a little Pepper, strain it through a Sieve; it for roasted Fowls, send it as it is; if for Mutton, put some Butter and minc'd Capers; if for Pork, leave out the Capers, and add a little Mustard.

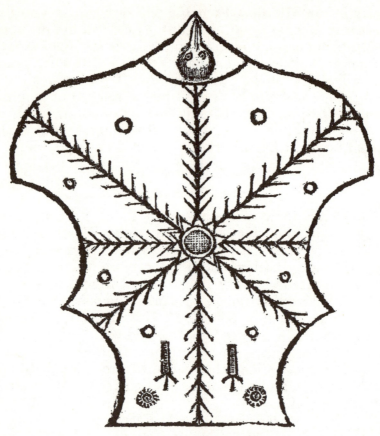

To make a Turkey Pye.
Paté de Dindon.

WHEN it is pick'd, drawn, and fing'd, bone it; you may bring the Bones out at the Breaſt whole, or cut it down the Back, and take out the Bones that Way; take Care you do not cut it through the Skin, then ſew it up, and tie up the Vents; make a Pan of Water boil, put in your Turkey, let it boil till it is plump; take out the Strings, and ſeaſon it with Pepper and Salt; having a Coffin rais'd to fit it, lay it in, with a Neat's Tongue boil'd, ſkin'd, and ſlic'd; lay in ſome Yolks of Eggs boil'd hard, with
two

ART of COOKERY. 257

two or three Pounds of Sausages; lay Butter over all, close it, and bake it; if to eat cold, fill it up with clarified Butter.

To make French Biscuits.
Bisquit à la Francoise.

TAKE six new-laid Eggs, leave out the Whites all but one, beat them very well, and strain them through a Sieve, but first weigh your Eggs with fine Flour; let their Weight be equal; put out the Flour, and weigh some fine Loaf Sugar as you did the Flour; mix the Flour and Sugar together; put in some candied Lemon Peel minc'd very fine, mix it with Sugar and Flour, put it to your Eggs in an Earthen Dish or Bowl, beat it with a Wooden Ladle till it comes to a Paste, drop it on Wafer Paper laid on a Tin Plate, and bake it, but not too much.

To make a Rabbit Pye.
Paté des Lapins.

TAKE three Rabbits, cut two into Pieces, truss one like a Liveret, and blanch it in boiling Water, season them with Pepper and Salt; take a small Loin of Pork, take off the Skin, cut it into Stakes, take out the Bones, season it as before; your Pye being made in the Form, as you may see in Page 122, lay in the Bottom of the Pye some of the Pork-stakes, then some of the Rabbit, then the rest of your Stakes, then some more Rabbit, then lay the whole one in the Middle, and if you have any more Bits of Rabbit, lay it round the whole one, lay Bits of Butter over all, close it, and press the Lid close to the whole Rabbit, that it may appear in its full Shape; you will see how it is garnished, by the Form; it will eat well cold, fill'd with clarified Butter; if to eat hot, boil some Parsley, shred it fine, mix it with drawn Butter and Gravey, squeeze in a little Lemon; it will take three Hours baking.

baking, if it be to be eat cold; if hot, two and a Half.

To make a Pye of Sheep's Tongues.
Paté des Langues de Mouton.

GET the largest you can, wash them, and salt them with Salt-Petre and common Salt; lay them into an Earthen Pot, and rub them with the Brine that comes from them every Day, and turn them; keep this Order for six Days; boil and skin them, cut off the Roots, raise a round Pye the Height of a Custard, lay in your Tongues, with the thick Ends to meet in the Middle; season them with Pepper, a little beaten Mace, and Cinnamon; lay a Yolk of an hard Egg betwixt each Tongue, with some Cutlets of Veal larded, laid over all, season'd as before; lay Butter over all, close it, and bake it; when bak'd, fill it with clarified Butter; keep it to eat cold.

To farce Chickens with Sweet Herbs and Bards of Bacon.
Poulets farcie.

LET your Chickens be clean pick'd and drawn, singe them, and put a Piece of Butter work'd in Salt, a few Chives and Parsley shred fine, into the Bellies of them; then raise up their Skins with your Finger all over their Breasts; cut some Pieces of fat Bacon to fit each Breast, season the Bacon with Parsley, Shallot, and Thyme minc'd fine; put in the Bacon betwixt the Skin and the Flesh, pull down the Skin over the Neck, and truss them for roasting; spit them, and cover them all over with fat Bacon, cut very thin; put Paper over all, tie the Paper Bacon on with Packthread, and roast them; take off the Paper and the outside Bacon; baste them with Butter, dridge them with the Raspings of French Bread made fine, mix'd with Flour and a little Salt; give them Half a Dozen Turns; dish them with a Cullis of Ham and Veal under them; garnish with Lemon and Barberries.

ART of COOKERY. 259

To farce Cocks' Combs to Ragoo.
Crêtes de Coqs farcie.

WASH them and par-boil them, strain them and let them cool; make a Forcing for them of Marrow, Veal, sweet Herbs, Pepper, Salt, Nutmeg, Bread Crumbs, a little Lemon Peel; mince all fine, mix it with the Yolk of an Egg, pound it fine in a Mortar; open the thick Ends with a sharp-pointed Knife, rub them within with some Yolks of Egg, fill them with your Forcing; take a Piece of Butter, put it into a Stew-pan, make a Brown with a little Flour, put in some good Gravey drawn from the Ham and Veal, put in your Combs, let them stew till tender; make a small Pulpotoon of Veal Sweet-breads, and put in the Middle of the Dish; dish your Cocks' Combs round it, squeeze in a little Lemon; garnish with Petit-Patties, made of some of your Forcing.

To preserve Cocks' Combs.
Crêtes de Coqes preservé.

COCKS' Combs are hard to come at in the Country, so I here give you a Receipt how to keep them a long Time, that when you are in London you may prepare some in the following Manner, to take into the Country with you; you may do a few at a Time, as you can get them: Clean them and put them into a Pot, season them with Pepper and Salt, put to them some Beef Suet shred fine, with some Butter; put these to the Combs, tie them over with Paper, and bake them, but not to much; take them out, and strain the Fat through a Sieve; clean out the Pot, lay in the Combs, skim off the Clear, and cover them over; set them to cool; so you may keep Sweet-breads, Lamb-stones, and several other Things, as Mushrooms clean'd, and put into a Stew-pan, with a good Piece of Butter, some whole Pepper, Mace, and Salt; cover them close, and stew them a Quarter of an Hour over a Stove-Fire; when cold put them

into

into a Pot, cover them as above, and they will keep a Quarter of a Year, to use as you please.

To roast Chickens a-la-Smithergall.
Poulets à la Smithergall roti.

TAKE some fat Bacon shred fine; then mince four Anchovies, with some Parsley Chives, and a little Lemon Peel; mix all together, with the Yolk of an Egg, and a Spoonful of Cream; loosen the Skin off the Breasts of your Chickens, and put some of this Force into each Chicken's Breast; butter some Paper, and tie over them; put some minc'd Parsley, Butter, and Salt, into their Bellies; spit and roast them; dish them, and let the Sauce be Lemon, Butter and Gravey, or Gravey by itself.

To make Cullis of Craw-Fish.

TAKE out the Tails, and take out the Bleb that is betwixt the Tail and the Body, for it is bitter; then pound the Shells in a Marble Mortar, with some blanch'd Almonds; then slice Half a Parsnip, two Onions, Half a Carrot; put these into a Stewpan, with a good Piece of Butter, cover them down close, set them on a Charcoal Fire that is slow; let them simmer till they begin to stick to the Bottom; put in some Fish Broth, with the Crust of a French Roll; season it with Pepper, Salt, and Nutmeg, some Parsley and a little Thyme; let them simmer till you can break the Bread to Pieces with a Ladle, put in the Shells, with some minc'd Mushrooms; let them simmer a little longer, with a minc'd Anchovey; strain it through a Sieve, and keep it for any Thing in Meagre, as Vegetables, Soops, &c.

To stew Craw-Fish for a Dish, and how to dish them.
Des Ecrevices etuvée.

WASH them, and put them into a Kettle, with Salt, White Wine Vinegar, Thyme, Parsley, and

and some Slices of Lemon; cover them close and stew them on a slow Fire till they be all very red; then strain them, and spread them to cool; then dish them in a Dish, the Size of that you design to send them up in; then lay them all round the Inside of your Dish, next the Rim, on their Backs, with their Tails next the Rim; so fill the Bottom of your Dish, then begin at the Edge again, and lay one betwixt them again as before, with all their Tails even; so continue till you have laid in as many as you would have; then pick some Fennel, and lay all over them as they lie on their Backs; then lay on the Dish that you design them to go in; turn them Upside down, and they will look very well; if you have laid them even, so send them up.

To make a Cullis of Mushrooms.
Coulis des Champignons.

TAKE some of the finest red Mushrooms, take off the outside Skins, break them to Pieces, put to them some Salt, Pepper, Mace, a slic'd Onion, a little Parsley and Thyme, with a Piece of Butter; put all into a Stew-pan, covered down close, set it on a slow Fire Half an Hour; strain and squeeze them out of the Liquor, then put the Liquor into the Stew-pan, with the Crust of a Roll, soak it till tender, rub all through a Sieve; keep it for Use.

How to order and keep Lobsters a Month for Fish Sauce.
Pour garder des Ecrevices fair une Sause.

TAKE the Spawn or Berries of the Lobsters that are boil'd, pound them in a Mortar, with some Vinegar; take a Quart of Water, put in it six Anchovies, some whole Pepper and Mace, a Stick of Horse-Raddish slic'd, two Lemons par'd and slic'd; let it boil till one-third be wasted, then put in your Lobster-Spawn, with a Pint of White Wine; let it but boil up, then strain it; take the Tails and Claws of your
Lob-

Lobsters, and cut them an Inch long; then cut them long-ways like a Wheat Straw; put your Stock into your Stew-pan again, and put in your Lobster; if your Anchovies have not made it salt enough, put in some to your Taste. At any Time, when you have any Lobster left, cut it as above, make it hot in Salt and Water, and put it to the rest; put it into a Jar, tie it down with Leather, set it in a cold Place; when you would use any, take it out with a small Wooden Ladle; put it into a Stew-pan, with a little good Gravey (if for Fish-Days, call'd Fasts, put in some Fish Broth) with a little Onion and Anchovey shred fine, squeeze in a little Lemon to brisken the Taste, grate in a little Nutmeg, put in your Butter, dust in a little Flour, draw it up thick; keep this Order, and you will never want good Lobster Sauce upon all Occasions. You may order Crabs the same Way.

To farce Veal Cutlets.

Cotelets de Veau farcie.

TAKE the best End of a Neck of Veal, and boil it in strong Broth a Quarter of an Hour; let it cool, cut it Bone by Bone, take off the Skin, mince the Flesh, save the Bones, take six Morels, blanch them, take off their Stalks, and mince them with a few preserved Mushrooms, a few Chives or Onion; then mince some Marrow or Beef Suet, shred it fine, mix all together, season it with Pepper, Salt, Nutmeg, and a little Lemon Peel shred fine; pound it in a Mortar, with some Bread Crumbs, and three or four Yolks of raw Eggs; cut some Bards of Bacon, like a Cutlet in Shape, lay on some of the Forcing, lay on a Boce of the Veal, rub it all over with the Yolk of an Egg, lay more Forcing on that, rub it with Egg, dridge them with fine Bread Crumbs, and brown them in an Oven; let the Sauce be Seville Orange, and a Cullis of Veal and Ham, or Gravey and Lemon.

To farce Mutton Cutlets.
Cotelets de Mouton farcie.

YOU may do Mutton the same Way, or cut the Flesh off it when par-boil'd, but skewer it first to keep it streight; order it as you did the Veal, but leave the Bones whole, and the Skin betwixt the Bones; rub them with Yolks of Eggs, lay on your Forcing all over, rub it over with Yolks of Eggs, dridge it with Bread Crumbs, brown it in the Oven; let the Sauce be Gravey, Butter, and Capers.

Ducks a-la-Braise with Turnips.
Canards à la Braise.

LARD them, or one, and let the other go plain, and season them with Pepper, Salt, and sweet Herbs; lay some Bards in the Bottom, with Slices of Beef season'd as the Ducks; lay them in, with Bacon and Beef, season'd as under, on the Top of them; put to them a Pint of Red or White Wine; set it on a slow Fire, cover'd down close; make a Fire on the Lid, that is, take a few live Coals out of the Stove, and put them on the Lid, let them stew for two Hours; when they are ready, having your Turnips prepar'd in the Manner following, pare and scoop them, cut them the Length of an Olive, round them at the Ends, and put them into Salt and Vinegar colour'd with Saffron; let them lie till they have taken the Colour, dry them in a Cloth, and fry them in clarified Butter; then make a Frown, with a Piece of Butter and a little Flour; put in some Gravey, take up your Ducks, let them drain, lay them in the Dish, strain the Liquor that comes from them, skim off the Fat, put it to your Brown; put in the Turnips, skim it, and pour it over your Ducks.

If I was to be particular about every Sort of Braise, of Flesh, Fowls, and Fish, it would take up too much of the Book; as I have mention'd several already, I shall give the ingenious Practiser, a full Account of the several Ways, in a Place by itself; and likewise of the different Ways of making Cullis, with several other Things worth Notice.

Eggs in Crampine.
Oeufs au Crampine.

TAKE four Veal Sweet-breads, blanch them; take a Piece of Ham, cut both in Dice, toss up the Ham in some clarified Butter, dridge in some Flour, moisten it with good Gravey; do the same by the Sweet-breads, then shred some Morels and Mushrooms, put them to the Sweet-breads; then mince some Parsley and Chives, let them be scalded first, and put them in with a minc'd Anchovey, two or three Spoonfuls of White Wine, grate in some Nutmeg, put in a little Pepper, then skim the Fat off your Ham, and put it in; then beat the Yolks of ten Eggs, mix them with a little Cullis, and strain them in first; take your Stew-pan off the Fire, toss all up together, then beat the Whites, and strain them in; squeeze in some Lemon, stir all together, and set it on the Fire again, keep it stirring till it is thicken'd a little; then take a Pulpatoon Pan, butter it, take the Kell of a Veal, warm it before the Fire, and put it into your Pulpatoon Pan; then put in your Campine, when it is cold, press it down with a Ladle; rub it all over with the Yolks of Eggs, lay on the Top some of the Kell, cut it close to your Pan, wash it all over with Eggs, dridge on some Bread Crumbs, bake it three Quarters of an Hour, loosen it round the Edges with a sharp Knife, turn it into your Dish; garnish with Orange and fried Parsley.

To make a Salmon Pye.
Paté de Saumon.

TAKE a double Joul of Salmon, scale and clean it, season it with Pepper, Salt, Nutmeg, Parsley, and Chives; let it lie till you have made your Paste; take a Pound of Butter, put it into a Sauce-pan, with a Quart of Water, set on the Fire to boil; lay on your Dresser Half a Peck of Flour, make a Hole in the Middle, skim off the Butter; put it in, and as much of the Water as will make it into a stiff Paste; spread it, and lay a Cloth over it to sweat it, then work it up, and take a Piece, and roll it out big enough to hold your Salmon; take two Sheets of Paper, lay on it your Sheet of Paste, lay on it your Salmon; then roll out another Piece long enough to go round the Salmon; wet and close it close to the Bottom; cut it all round, to stand an Inch above your Salmon; then fill up the Sides with Slices of Salmon, and lay your Butter over, season the Slices as you did the other, roll out your other Paste large enough to cover all, wet it all over, and lay on the Cover; close it tight at the Bottom, and close it at the Top, as you do another rais'd Pye; then take a streight Stick, the Thickness of your Finger, and rib it all round; cut it even at the Top, so that the Closing may be an Inch and a Half above your Pye, and it will look like another rais'd Pye; cut it all round the Bottom of the Pye, within an Inch of the Side, and turn it up as you do a Pasty; make a Vent Hole in the Middle of the Pye, put in a Wheat Sheaf or a Pine Apple, as we call them, made of Paste; wash it all over with the Yolks of Eggs; butter a Paper, put it all round the Pye, and bake it two Hours; you may cut open the Lid, take off as much of the Fat as you can, then make a Lare of Oysters, Lobsters, or a plain Sauce, see Fish-Sauce, put it all over; you may send this Pye for a Remove, without the Lid; if you would make a middle Dish of it, send it with the Lid on; and, if you please, you may ornament it more, by taking a small Fish, and make it in the Manner as you are directed for a Fish Pye, like a Fish; lay it on the Top, and bake it on the Pye; garnish it round, as you will find by the Draught hereafter.

To

To make Lobster Patty.
Paté d'Ecrevises.

BOIL your Lobsters in Salt and Water, take the Meat out of their Tails and Claws, pound their Bodies and small Claws in a Mortar; moisten them with some Gravey, if they have any Spawn; put it in likewise, soak the Crust of a French Roll in strong Broth, pound it, and rub it through a Cullinder; season your Lobsters with Pepper, Salt, and Nutmeg; sheet your Dish with Puff-Paste, lay in the Lobster, cut as you like, mix your Liquor that comes from the Shells, &c. when strain'd, minc'd with an Anchovey and a little Onion, squeeze in some Lemon, mix it with melted Butter, put in a Spoonful of White Wine, put Half of it into the Pye, lid it, and wash it with Egg; bake it, when bak'd cut off the Lid, warm the rest of the Lare, and put it in; cut the Lid in two, lay it on each Side to shew what is in it, and send it up.

Pigeons a-la-Basilic.
Pigeons à la Basilique.

PICK, draw, singe, and truss them, as for boiling; make a Stuffing of their Livers, Parsley, Marrow, Bread Crumbs, Pepper, Salt, and Nutmeg, shred and mince all together, work it up with the Yolks of two Eggs, and a little Cream; put a Piece of this into each Pigeon, then season them with Pepper and Salt; dip them in the Yolks of beaten Eggs, dridge them very thick with Bread Crumbs; cut Bards of Bacon to lay under each Pigeon, lay them in a convenient Thing to bake, drip them with Butter, bake them three Quarters of an Hour; dish them, and send them with a Cullis of Veal and Ham.

To make Pigeon Dumplings.
Pigeons à la Guinguet.

PICK, draw, and singe them; cut off their Wings and Legs, bone them, tie up their Vents, make some

some Water boil through them till they be plump; take them out, drain them, and take out the Strings; let them lie to cool, season them with Pepper and Salt, put a Bit of Butter work'd in Parsley into each Belly; then having some Puff-paste made, roll some Pieces out, put in your Pigeons, make them up as you do Apple-Dumplings; tie them up in Cloths, boil them an Hour, dish them; let the Sauce be Lemon, Butter, and Gravey, or plain Butter.

Ducks and stew'd Cellery.

Canards au Celery etuvée.

STEW your Ducks a-la-braise; and stew your Cellery as directed. See stew'd Cellery.

Ducks and Morels, Mushrooms and Oysters.

Canards au Morills, Champignons & Huitres.

DUCKS and Oysters are done the same Way. See stew'd Oysters, adding some Mushrooms and Morels.

Eggs and stew'd Cucumbers.

Oeufs aux Concumbres etuvé.

TAKE some, pare and cut them in two, take out the Seeds, and slice them fine; put them into an Earthen Dish, salt them, and let them lie two Hours; drain them from their Liquor, fry them in clarified Butter till they turn brown; take them out to drain, then slice an Onion, and fry it also, put it to your Cucumbers, make a Brown, put in some Gravey, put in a little Pepper and Vinegar, with your Cucumbers and Onion; stew them till tender, then potch as many Eggs as you think will do; lay them in your Dish, pour over your Cucumbers; garnish with Rashers of Bacon.

You may poach your Eggs in clarified Butter, which is the best Way for Eggs sent up with any of these Vegetables; you may send them up with stew'd Cellery, Lettice, Spinage, Colliflowers, &c.

You

You must observe to give all these Things that you send up with Eggs a tart Taste, put in some Pepper, and garnish with Bacon.

To make an Amulet of Sweet-meats.
Omelet aux Douceurs.

BEAT twelve Eggs very well, put in Half a Pint of Cream, with a little Salt; strain all through a Sieve, set them on a Fire, and stir them with a Whisk till they begin to be thicken'd; then take them off, and take a Pancake Pan, put in a Piece of Butter; then put in Half your Eggs, and strew in some minc'd Citron and Lemon Peel, with some Sugar; put on the rest of the Eggs, turn it, and fry it on the other Side; dish it, put on it Sugar, Butter, and Sack.

To make a Patty of Cockles or Muscles.
Tourte de Limacon de Mer ou de Moules.

WASH them clean, put them into a Pot, and set them on a slow Fire, cover'd close, till they are open'd; take them out, take the Beards off the Muscles, make a Brown, put in some good Gravey, put in some Vinegar, an Anchovey shred fine, with a little Onion, just toss them up, let them cool, sheet your Dish with Puff-paste, put in your Cockles or Muscles; you may put in some Forc'd-meat Balls made of Fish, close it and bake it; wash it over with the Yolk of an Egg; it is enough when the Paste is bak'd.

To order and stew Giblets.
Gigiés de l'Oye etuvé.

SCALD and clean the Wings, skin the Feet, cut off the Nails, singe the Wings, cut them into Pieces as you like, clean the Gizards cut off the inside Skin, and the blue Skin on the Out-side; put all into an Earthen Pot, season them with Pepper and Salt, put in a large Onion, with a Faggot of sweet Herbs, lay over them a thick Slice of coarse Beef, put to them some Water, tie them down close, and bake them two Hours; you may keep them, thus order'd, three or four Days. You may make them into a Pye, or stew them as follows: Make a Brown with a Piece of Butter, put in some Gravey, skim off the Fat from the Giblets, put them in, and stew them till they be tender; put some Sippets into the Bottom of your Dish, season them to your Taste; take out the Onion and the Faggot of Herbs, and dish them up; take out the Beef also.

To make Mackroney for present Use.

Macaroni.

TAKE some Flour, and make it into Paste with two Eggs, roll it out thin, and cut it like Wheat Straws, about an Inch and a Half long; set on a Pint of Milk and a Pint of Cream to boil in a Stew-pan on a Charcoal Fire; put in the Paste first, let it be parted Bit from Bit, or it will stick together; let it boil till it is the Thickness of a Cream, stir it sometimes or it will stick to the Bottom; sweeten it with Sugar to your Taste; dish it, and strew on some Cinnamon beat fine and sifted; garnish it with Seville Orange.

To dress Pigeons like Cypress Birds.

Pigeons à la Cipres des Oiseaux.

PICK them very clean, leave the Skins of the Necks very long, take out the Crops, and draw them very carefully, make the Vent as small as you can, cut off their Wings to the last Joint, and cut off one Leg; take out the Bones at the Neck, leaving the Wing and Leg Bones, singe them, make a Stuffing of their Livers, a good Piece of Parsley, the Marrow of one Marrow-bone, a few Chives or Shallot, some Bread Crumbs; season with Pepper, Salt, Nutmeg, and Lemon Peel; put in four Yolks of Eggs, pound all in a Mortar very fine, stuff their Bellies with it,

truss

truss them as you do a Chicken, for boiling; let the whole Leg come out at the Vent; skewer them with two fine Skewers, tie them close at the Vents, stew them a-la-braise, as you do Fowls; let them be tender, but not too much, let them stand in the Braise till cold, make a Pickle for them of Bran, Salt, Vinegar, and Water; boil it Half an Hour, strain it, and let it stand to cool; put in some Mace, whole Pepper, and White Wine; take out the Pigeons, take the Fat clean off, strain the Liquor they were in, put all into the Pickle; when you send any to the Table, garnish them with raw Parsley; mind to take off the Strings; boil the Pickle once a Week.

To make Black Puddings.

Boudins noir.

TAKE some whole Groats, pick them clean, and wash them in Water, boil them in Milk and Water till they be tender, take Care don't to the Bottom; if there be too much Liquor to them, strain them through a Sieve; put them into a Pot or Bowl, strew on them some Salt, stir them, and set them to cool; then take a clean Thing, put in it some Salt, and catch the Blood from the Swine when it is kill'd, keep it stirring till it is near cold, mix it with your Groats, season them with Pepper, Thyme, Penny-rial, and a little Jamaica Pepper; then shred some Beef Suet very fine, and mix all together; take a little of it, and put it into a Sauce-pan, set it on the Fire, and taste it as to Salt or any other Spice or Herbs, if it wants add more; you may put in Mace, Nutmeg, or what you like; then take some of the Leaf of the Hog, cut it into square Bits, put it into an Earthen Pot, and salt it; let it lie three or four Hours, or put it into Salt and Water, which is the best Way; lay something on it to keep it under the Water; it does not only favour the Fat, but hardens it and makes it eat better in the Puddings; strain and mix it with

the

the reſt of your Ingredients, your Skins being prepar'd and made very clean, turn them the Outſide inwards, fill them in what Length you pleaſe, and put the Fat equally in each Pudding, don't fill them too full, tie them tight at each End; when you boil them put ſome Hay or Wheat Straw in the Bottom of your Kettle to keep them from breaking; let them boil ſoftly, when they are boil'd put ſome Straw in a Sieve, and lay your Puddings on it to cool; when you would uſe any make them hot in Water, and boil them on a Gridiron; eat them with Muſtard; before you ſend them to the Table, cut off the Strings.

To make White Puddings.
Boudins blanc.

TAKE ſome ſtale Bread, and rub it through a Cullinder, put it into an Earthen Pot, ſet on ſome Milk and Cream, and make it boil, put it to the Bread, cover it down; then to the Quantity add ſo many Yolks of Eggs; to a Pint of Bread Crumbs take Half a Pint of Milk and Half a Pint of Cream, the Yolks of five Eggs beat and ſtrain'd; take two Ounces of Beef Suet finely ſhred, three Ounces of Butter melted, a Quarter of a Pound of Currants waſh'd and dried before the Fire; ſeaſon with Salt, Cinnamon, Mace, and Nutmeg; put in as much Sugar as will ſweeten it to your Taſte; put in a little Lemon Peel ſhred fine, candied or plain; mix all together, and fill your Skins order'd as before; tie, boil, and order them as you did the Black Puddings; you may put into the Mixture a Glaſs of Sack, Wine, or Brandy, as you like; you may add ſome Almonds blanch'd and ſhred fine, and put in a Roſe or Orange Flower Water; ſome chuſe Naple Biſcuit inſtead of Bread; ſome chuſe creed Rice; if ſo, you muſt uſe more Eggs, and what Sweet-meats you pleaſe; ſome make them without Fruit.

To make Black Puddings another Way.

Boudins noir d'une autre façon.

TAKE some cut Groats call'd by some Chimins, soak them in Milk all Night, and mix it with the Ingredients as before; some chop the Fat, or cut it fine, and leave out the Suet; some put in Mint dried or green, shred fine, and Chives, Leek, Shallot, or Onions; all the rest order'd as before.

To make a Woodcock Pye.

Tourte de Beçasses.

WHEN they are pick'd, drawn, and sing'd, cut off their Legs and Heads, season them with Pepper and Salt, truss them like Chickens for boiling, sheet your Dish with Puff-paste, lay in your Woodcocks, take the Entrails from them; lay them betwixt each Woodcock, and the Yolk of an Egg boil'd hard, then blanch some Morels, shred them fine, and lay them in with some Butter over all; moisten them with Gravey, roll out the Lid, wet it, and close your Pye, rub it over with the Yolk of an Egg, stick in some Bills, and bake it an Hour and a Half; when bak'd, put in some good Gravey, and send it up.

To dress Veal a-la-Hastereaux.

Veau à la Hastereaux.

TAKE a Leg of Veal, take off the Fat and Skin, take Care of the Udder; cut the Veal longways in thin Slices, flat it with a Cleaver; then make a Forc'd-meat of some of the Veal, some Beef-Suet, and fat Bacon, sweet Herbs, Bread Crumbs, Pepper, Salt, Nutmeg, and some minc'd Lemon Peel; make it up with the Yolks of Eggs, pound it fine in a Mortar, hack the Veal with the Back of a Knife, rub it over with Egg, season it as you did the Forc'd-meat; lay a Piece of Forc'd-meat in each Collop, make them up round, and the Udder likewise, tie them with
Pack-

Packthread, stew them a la braise; make a Ragoo for them of Mushrooms, a Couple of Veal Sweet-breads, &c. See Sweet-breads ragoo'd. Strain the Liquor that comes from them, take off the Fat, and put the Gravey to your Ragoo, take off the Strings; dish them with the Udder in the Middle, put the Ragoo over them; garnish with Seville Orange and Barberries.

To make a Pigeon Pye the French Way.
Tourte de Pigeous à la Francoise.

WHEN they are clean'd, truss them as for boiling; wash them clean, dry them with a Cloth, stuff them with Forc'd-meat, made as above, adding more Parsley, flour them, and brown them with Eggs laid in a Stew-pan; put in some blanch'd Artichoke Bottoms and Sweet-breads cut in Dice, Mushrooms cut in two, toss all up together, moisten it with strong Broth; let them stew a little, season all with Pepper, Salt, and Nutmeg, skim off the Fat, let it stand to cool; then raise a Pye in the Dish, a little higher than a Custard, cut out a Piece of the Bottom, lay in your Pigeons, with a whole Artichoke Bottom in the Middle, fill'd with Forc'd-meat, and lay the rest of the Ingredients betwixt the Pigeons, with the Yolk of an hard Egg betwixt; likewise lid your Pye, and lay a Border of Puff-paste on the Rim of the Dish, wash it all over with an Egg, beat with a little Cream; stick on the Top some of the Feet, bake it an Hour and a Half; put in a little Gravey and Butter, with the Juice of a Lemon; shake all together in the Pye, and send it up.

Lobsters, Crow-Fish, or Shrimps, in Jelly.
Ecrevice en Gellé.

TAKE what Sort of Fish you can get, boil it in Water, sweet Herbs, Spices, and Salt, strain it off, let it stand to cool, take the Sim off the Top and the Sediment from the Bottom; take some Isinglass, beat with a Hammer, and pull'd to Pieces; put it it to your Stock, and boil it till it comes to a strong Jelly; then run it through a Jelly Bag; first put in four Whites of Eggs, beat with some Juice of Lemon; let all boil till it breaks, then run it through your Bag till it be as clear as Water, then put a little into the Bottom of your Pot, let it stand to cool; keep the other warm, so as it will run; then take your Lobster out of the Shell, cut it into what Form you please, and lay it into the Pot, with some slic'd Lemon and pick'd Fennel; keep this Order till your Pot be full, then fill it quite full with your other Jelly, let it stand till the next Day; then dip the Pot in hot Water, and turn it out in the Dish you design to send it in, that is, you must lay the Dish on the Pot, and turn it upside down; garnish it with flour'd Fennel and Lemon.

Crow-Fish in Jelly.
Ecrevise de Reviere en Gellé.

YOU may send Prawns, Shrimps or Crow-Fish, the same Way; first pick them out of their Shells.

Shrimps in Jelly.
Guernetts en Gellé.

YOU may send Oysters in Jelly the same Way as before; open and blanch them, wash them clean from their Liquor, and stick them with Lemon Peel and pickled Barberries; run some Jelly in the Pot as you did before, let it cool, then lay in your Oysters, with some pretty Leaves of Flowers, Lemon, and small Sprigs of Fennel; fill the Pot with Jelly, and order it as you did your Lobsters.

To make a Slic'd Pudding with Dates.
Boudin de Pain en Tranchs.

SHEET your Pudding-Dish with Puff-paste, cut a Piece out of the Bottom, then lay in some French Bread cut very thin, then lay over it some

Raisins

Raisins ston'd and cut, then some Dates cut also, then some Marrow cut in Slices, then lay on more Bread, and the same on it as before, till you have fill'd your Dish; then boil half Milk and half Cream, beat six Eggs, and strain them in; then put in a little Salt, sweeten it with fine Sugar to your Taste, grate in some Nutmeg, stir all together, and fill up your Dish; wash over the Rim of the Dish with the Yolk of an Egg and a little Cream; bake it an Hour, when bak'd, stick the Top with Dates cut thin, and candied Citron cut also; bake it an Hour; you may send up Sugar, Wine, and melted Butter in a Bason or Boat.

You make a Pudding in this Manner: Use Almonds instead of Dates; you may cut a Cover, and put over it; put it on when your Pudding is half-bak'd; you may ice it, and stick the open Places in the Cover with candied Orange Peel, Lemon, Citron, and Almonds blanch'd and cut in four long-ways.

To make a Patty of Lamb Stones.

Tourte de Couillons d'Agneau.

CUT them down the Middle, and slip them out of their Skins, blanch them in scalding Water, then make a Brown for them, put in a Pint of Gravey, with an Anchovey shred fine, with an Onion, grate in some Nutmeg; season them with Pepper, Salt, and shred Parsley, shred three or four Morels, with some Mushrooms, two or three Artichoke Bottoms blanch'd and slic'd; toss all up together, squeeze in some Juice of Lemon; let it stand to cool; then prepare eight Yolks of Eggs boil'd hard, make some Forc'd-meat Balls, sheet your Dish with Puff-paste, put in your Ingredients, lay on the Top the Eggs and Forc'd-meat Balls; close your Pye, rub over your Pye with the Yolk of Egg and Cream, bake it an Hour; when bak'd, put in Gravey and Butter, and send it up.

To make a Pye of Larks, Sparrows, or any small Birds.
Tourte des Alouettes ou d'autre Oiseaux.

PICK and draw them, cut off their Heads and Legs, spit them on a small Spit, singe them, make a Forc'd-meat for them of a Piece of tender Veal and Marrow, shred it fine, then shred some Parsley, a little Lemon Peel, with Half an Anchovey; season them with Nutmeg, Pepper, and Salt; mix all together, with some Bread Crumbs, and the Yolks of three or four Eggs, beat it in a Mortar, and put a Bit of this into each Bird's Belly; then raise a Pye in a Dish very low, cut out a Piece of the Bottom, lay in the Larks with a fine thin Bit of interlar'd Bacon betwixt each Bird; fill up the interval Places with Forc'd-meat, sprinkle over all some shred Parsley and some pickled Barberries pull'd off their Stalks; lay over all some thin Slices of Veal, hack'd with the Back of a Knife, seasons'd with Pepper and Salt; lay Butter over all, lid the Pye, lay a Border of Puff-paste round the Rim of the Dish, wash it over as before, bake it; when bak'd, put in some melted Butter and Gravey.

To make a Quaking Pudding.
Boudin tremblant.

TAKE a Pint of Cream, and Half a Pint of Milk, boil it with Cinnamon, a Piece of Ginger, and slic'd Nutmeg; let it stand to cool, then beat ten Eggs, leave out four Whites, blanch and beat a Quarter of a Pound of Almonds, with a little Cream; mix all together, and strain it through a coarse Napkin, wring it hard; then take three Spoonfuls of fine Flour, put a little of your strain'd Liquor to it, and mix it well; then add more till you have got it all mix'd, and beat it very well; sweeten it with Loaf Sugar, pounded and sifted; butter a fine Cloth, and flour it, put in your Pudding, and tie it up tight, put it into a Pot of boiling Water, let it boil an Hour; when
boiling

boiling turn it about fometimes ; then take it up into a Sieve or Bafon that will conveniently hold it, untie the String, turn the Cloth over the Bafon, and turn it upfide down into the Difh ; ftick it with any candied Peel you like, or blanch'd Almonds cut in four long-ways ;. melt your Butter with White Wine, fweeten it with fine Sugar, and garnifh with Seville Orange.

NOVEMBER.

To dress Soop in Balneo Moria.
Potage Balneo maria.

TAKE three Pounds of Beef, two Pound of Mutton, a Knuckle of Veal; put all into a large Earthen Jug, with a Carrot, two large Onions, four Heads of Cellery, two or three Turnips, a Faggot of Sweet-Herbs, a little whole Pepper and Mace, some Salt; let your Meat be cut small before you put it in, and wash it in warm Water; put as much Water to it as will scarce cover it, cork it close, or stop it with a coarse Cloth, put it into a Kettle of Water, or into a Copper; if the Copper be large, you may hang it in a String with the Neck above the Water, so that no Liquor can get in; let it stew in this Manner five or six Hours, keep your Pot or Copper fill'd up, that is, to the Neck of the Pitcher; then having some Herbs prepar'd as for Soop Sante, strain it and put it to your Herbs, make it very hot, skim off the Fat; put into your Soop Dish some Crusts of French Bread cut and dry'd before the Fire, with a boil'd Fowl in the Middle; dish your Soop; garnish with Spinage and Rashers of Bacon.

To make a Peacock Pye.
Paté de Paon.

PICK it, and leave the Feathers on the Neck, cut the Neck off close to the Body, skin the Neck close to the Head, and cut it off; put a Stick tight into the Skin up to the Head, dry it in an Oven; cut off the Legs, and keep them, then draw it and singe it; keep some of the short Feathers of the Tail; truss it as for boiling, break down the Breast Bone, season it with Pepper and Salt, skewer it, put a Piece of Butter into the Belly of it, roast it about half enough, and let it cool; raise a Pye for it, or make it as you do a Ham Pye; put in the Belly of the Peacock ten Yolks of Eggs boil'd hard, blanch half a Dozen Sweet-breads, cut them in Dice, lay them round the Bird so as to make it even at Top, lay over that some thin Slices of interlar'd Bacon, and Butter over all; close your Pye, and make a Funnel in the Middle; garnish it as you'll see in the garnishing of some of the other Pies, which will direct you how to place the Head and Feet; you must make a Piece of Paste like the Rump, stick five or six Feathers in it after the Pye is bak'd, place the Head at the Head of the Pye, and carve the Outsides; when it is bak'd, fill the Pye up with clarified Butter, and keep it for a standing Dish to ornament the Middle of your Table, or set it on a Side Table.

To roast a Ham.
Jambon roti.

TAKE a Ham about half a Year old, soak it all Night in Water, then pare it clean on the Inside, pare off the Skin, cut off the Shank, spit it, and lay it down to roast, baste it with a Pint of Rhenish Wine put into the Dripping Pan, and baste it often; if the Ham weigh 14 lb. it will take three Hours and a Half to roast; you must lay it at a good Distance, and roast it leisurely; send what Roots or Greens you like in a bye Dish, or Beans in Saucers, or in hot butter'd Paste bak'd in Patty-Pans; if there is any left off the Basting, mix it with Gravey, skim off the Fat, and put it under the Ham.

To dress a Breast of Veal a-la-Smithergall.
Poitrine de Veau à-la-Smithergal.

TAKE a Breast of Veal, raise the Flesh from the Bones and a good Way under the Skin at the thin End, make a Forc'd-Meat as in the Receipt for a Lark Pye, wash the Veal within where you have made the Incision, and fill it with Forc'd-Meat, skewer it all along with short Skewers, and tie it down with Packthread, that is, cross the Packthread round the first Skewer, then cross it again and bring it round the next, so to the Bottom and fasten it; let the Skewers be pretty thick or the Forc'd-Meat will get out; take a strong Skewer and skewer it down the Middle, then lay it into an Oval Stew-Pan, put to it some strong Broth, with a Faggot of Sweet-Herbs, some whole Pepper, Mace, a Carrot, and two or three Onions, with a Blanch of Cellery, cover it close, and let it stew two Hours; take it up, and brown a Pan with a Piece of Butter, dust in some Flour, strain in some of the strong Broth, skim off the Fat, put in two blanch'd Sweet-breads cut in Dice, some Forc'd-Meat Balls and Mushrooms, squeeze in some Lemon, put in a Glass of White Wine, put in the Veal, let it stew a little, dish it, and garnish with Lemon and Rashers of Bacon.

To dress a Fillet of Beef in Ragoo.
Fillets de Beuf en ragoût.

TAKE the Inside of a Surloin, take off the Suet, lard it with Bacon, and stew it a-la-brase; make a Ragoo for it of small Onions, peel them, and put them into Salt and Water for two Hours, drain them, and dry them with a Cloth, flour and fry them in clarified Butter, keep them stirring till they be brown, drain them in a Cullinder, make a Brown for them, put in some Gravey, or the Gravey that comes from the Brase, skim off the Fat, put in the Onions, with some pickled Girkins or Kidney-beans; put in your Fillet of Beef, let all stew together, skim off the Fat, dish it up; garnish with Horse-raddish scrap'd and set before the Fire till it grows red; lay Pickles betwixt the Raddish.

To dress Pullets with Mushrooms.
Poulets aux Champignons.

DRAW, singe, and truss them for roasting, force their Crops, put a Piece of Butter work'd in Salt into their Bellies, spit them, rub their Breasts over with Butter, strinkle them over with Salt, lay on the Breasts a Piece of Veal Kell, Butter, and a double Paper, tie it over them, roast them softly, make a Ragoo of Mushrooms; if they be pickled, put them into warm Water for an Hour to take out some of the Tartness; make a Brown, put in some Gravey, let them simmer in it a while, put in a little Anchovey and Onion shred fine, grate in a little Nutmeg, put in a Glass of White Wine, put in a Ladleful of drawn Butter, draw all up together, dish your Fowls, and put the Sauce to them; garnish with Barberries and Lemon.

To make a Crow Fish Soop.
Potage d'Ecrevise.

YOUR Crow Fish being boil'd, pick the Shells off the Tails of them, and leave the Bodies and Legs together; prepare two Dozen in this Manner to garnish your Dish; if your Dish be large you ought to have an hundred Crow Fish; pick the Tails out of the rest from the Shells, put them into a Sauce-Pan, then you'll find a little Bag at the End next the Claws which is Bitter like Gall, that you must take Care to throw away, likewise you must take Care to throw away any Thing that is white and woolly in the Belly; then put the Shells in a Marble or Wooden Mortar, and pound them to a Paste; while your Shells are thus pounding, put in a large Stew-Pan three Quarters of a Pound of Butter, the Crust of two French Rolls, three or four sliced Onions, some whole Pepper Corns, half a Dozen Cloves, a Sprig of Thyme, and a Handful of Parsley; stew these Ingredients slowly over the Fire half an Hour, fry some French Bread in Butter, at the same Time take Care to prepare your Fish for the

Stock;

Stock; what fresh Fish you can conveniently get, four or five Pound Weight, put it to your above-mentioned Ingredients; let them stew half an Hour, stir them now and then that they burn not; when the Rawness is taken off the Fish, then pour in four Quarts of boiling Water, let it boil half an Hour, skim off the Fat, put in your fry'd Bread with two Quarts of Fish Broth, let it simmer all together, strain it through a fine Strainer to keep your Soop from tasting gritty, but if you let it stand some Time after it will prevent that; your Stock being thus got ready, take five or six Yolks of hard Eggs, the Crumb of a French Roll soak'd in Cream, four Onions boil'd tender, a little Parsley boil'd and shred fine, a little Pepper and Salt, grate in half a Nutmeg, put in a Piece of good Butter, squeeze in the Juice of a Lemon, pound all those together in a Mortar, mix it with some of your Stock; cut some Slices of Bread, dry them before the Fire, put them into your Soop Dish, with a forc'd Carp, or any other Fish you chuse, mix all your Ingredients and Soop together, put in the Tails of your Crow Fish, put a Ladleful or two of the Soop to your Bread, make it thoroughly hot, dish it up, round your Fish that is in the Middle of your Dish; your Dish being rim'd, and the Bodies of the Crow Fish being stuff'd with Forc'd-Meat, and gently baked in an Oven, or boil'd a little in some of your strong Broth; garnish the Dish with them.

There is a Receipt before given how to farce your Fish. The Fish that is to be in the Middle of your Soop is to be done the same Way; take Care to drain it from the Fat, and skim the Fat off your Soop before you send it up; after you have mix'd all your Ingredients together for your Soop; take Care it don't boil for fear it should curdle.

To make Lisbon Biscuits.
Biscuit de Lisbon.

TAKE four Eggs, or according to the Quantity you design to make, beat them very well, strain them through a Sieve to take out the Treads, put to them some double-refin'd Sugar pounded and sifted, with four or five Spoonfuls of fine Flour dried in an Oven, put in a little candied Lemon Peel shred very fine, beat it with a wooden Spoon, for a Quarter of an Hour, lay a Sheet of Wafer Paper upon a Tin Plate, drop the Biscuit upon it, or spread it all over it, rub it over with the White of an Egg beat to a Froth, dridge it with fine Sugar, sprinkle over it some Rose Water, let it be bak'd in a moderate Oven; whilst it is warm, cut it into what Shape you please, put it into a paper'd Box, keep it in a dry Place for Use.

To make a Lyng Pye.
Paté de Lyng.

SKIN it, cut it in Slices, season it with Pepper and Salt, sheet a Dish with Puff Paste, lay in your Lyng, with Force-Meat made of Fish (as you are directed in the Receipt for Fish dress'd in the French Way) lay in with it some Yolks of Eggs boil'd hard, throw over it some minc'd Capers and pick'd Barberries; put in half a Gill of White Wine, with the Juice of a Lemon; lay Butter over all, lid it, brush it over with the Yolk of an Egg and a little Cream, bake it an Hour and a Half.

To make a Moor Game Pye.

PICK, draw, singe, and truss them as for boiling, season with Pepper and Salt; take what Number you please, as to what Bigness you would have your Pye, sheet a Dish with Puff Paste, lay them in with their Rumps to meet in the Middle, lay betwixt them

them some Force-Meat and Yolks of Eggs boil'd hard, lay Butter over all; lid it and bake it as you did the Pye before mentioned; cut open the Lid, and throw over it a Ragoo of Sweet-breads, lay on the Lid again, and send it up; you may raise your Pye with Paste, as directed for raising Pies made with the same Ingredients; but if to be eaten cold, only season it with Pepper and Salt, and put in hard Eggs and Butter; when baked, fill it with clarified Butter.

To make a Beef-Stake Pye.
Paté de Beuf en filets.

CUT them off a Rump, hack them with the Back of a large Knife, season them with Pepper and Salt, sheet your Dish with Patty Paste, lay in your Beef-stakes, lay over them some good large Oysters, strinkle them over with a little shred Parsley and Thyme, shred some Capers with a little Onion, strew that over all, lay Butter on that, lid it, and bake it; when baked, put in some good Gravey, shake it to mix it with the Ingredients in the Inside, and send it up.

To make Marmalade of Currants.
De Corinth en Marmalade.

TAKE the largest you can get, pick them from the Stalks, put them into your Preserving-pan, with their Weight of Sugar, bruize them and the Sugar together, set them on the Fire, let them boil till clear, and of the strong Jelly, and put them into Pots: This is for Red Currants; if you would make some of White ones, you must bruize them well, and rub them through a coarse Sieve; use the same Quantity of Sugar pounded, the finer the better; you may put it into small Glasses, and dry it; or put it into Pots, and cut it out.

ART of COOKERY. 285

To pickle Cucumbers like Mangos.
Concombres à la Maniere de Mangoes.

TAKE large ones that are ftreight, and as green as you can get them, cut off the Yellow End, fkoup out the Seeds, make as ftrong a Brine of Salt and Water, as will bear an Egg, fhift them every other Day for nine Days; then put them into a Brafs-Pan, with fome frefh Salt and Water enough to cover them, cover them clofe with the Lid of the Pan, and fet them on a flow Fire to green; then take them up, dry them, and fill them with Muftard Seed, flic'd Ginger, white Pepper, and Shallot; faften on the Bit you cut off, clean your Pan, and put them in again, with as much White Wine Vinegar as will cover them, put on the Lid, and fet them on the Fire to fimmer a little, but not to boil; put them into your Jar, let them ftand to cool, and tie them down with a Bladder and Leather; you may put on fome Dill.

To pickle Sampher.
Samphire confervé au Vinaigre.

TAKE the largeft Bunches, cut off the Root Ends, make a Brine for it as before, and keep the fame Order for nine Days; boil the laft Brine and put to it, and it will turn yellow; then drain it well from the Brine, and take as much White Wine Vinegar as will cover it, and put it into a Brafs-pan; put on the Lid, and clofe it tight, fet it on a flow Fire to fimmer, but not to boil; when it is green, put it into a Jar, with whole Pepper, Ginger, and Mace; tie it down when cold as before. I fhall give you a general Receipt how to order all Fickles.

To pickle Walnuts.
Des Noix au Vinaigre.

GATHER them about Midfummer, when you can eafily run a Pin through them, fcald them and put them into Salt and Water, fhift them every other

other Day for fourteen Days; boil your Brine, and let it ſtand to cool before you put it to them; then take a coarſe Cloth, and rub them, to take of the black Skin, and put them into freſh Salt and Water; put them into a Braſs-pan, and ſet them over a ſlow Fire to ſimmer, but not to boil; ſtrain them, and make a Pickle for them of White Wine Vinegar, whole Pepper, Mace, ſlic'd Ginger, ſome Muſtard-ſeed, ſlic'd Horſe-Raddiſh, and three or four Cloves of Garlic, boil all together, let it ſtand to cool, dry your Walnuts and put them into a Jar; put the Pickle to them, and let them ſtand a Week; then ſtrain the Pickle from them, add a little freſh Vinegar to the Pickle, boil and ſkim it, let it ſtand to cool, and clean out your Jar; put the Walnuts and Spices into it, pour off the Clear of the Pickle to them, tie them down with a Bladder and Leather, and keep them in a cold Place.

A Biſque of Fiſh.

Biſque de Poiſſon.

I Shall give you a Biſque of Fiſh, ſo that the inginious Practiſers may dreſs any Thing in the Way: You muſt provide a Stock, as directed for Fiſh or Meagre Soop; take what Sort of Fiſh you can moſt conveniently get, take off the Fleſh and mince it ſmall with Muſhrooms; put it into a Stew-pan, with a good Piece of Butter, a Faggot of ſweet Herbs, a whole Onion, Pepper, Salt, and a minc'd Anchovey; when it is ſtew'd a little, put in ſome Fiſh Broth; then cut a French Roll in Slices, and taſte them, or dry them in an Oven or before the Fire; lay them in the Bottom of your Diſh, put a Forc'd-Fiſh, turn'd round in the Middle, as you will find in the Index, for Fiſh the French Way; ſome make a Ragoo of Lobſters, Crow-Fiſh, &c. to throw over the Fiſh, or put in a Baſon, and ſet in the Middle of the Fiſh, and the Diſh fill'd up with Fiſh-broth; ſend it up hot, that is, with the ſtew'd Fiſh in it.

To make Almond Cheese.

Fromage aux Amandes.

TAKE Half a Pound of blanch'd Almonds, beat them fine, with a little Orange Flour Water; take a Quart of Cream, and boil it with a Stick of Cinnamon, the Rind of a Lemon; take out these, when boil'd, and put in Half a Pint of Sack; let it boil till it is turn'd to a Curd; put the Curd into a Marble Mortar, when ſtrain'd, put in some powder'd Loaf Sugar, with a Slice of good Butter, and the Almonds beat all together; then put it into a Mould of what Fashion you please, let it ſtand till the next Day, preſs'd down hard; then dip the Mould in ſealding Water, and turn it out into your Diſh; ſift on ſome fine Sugar; garniſh it with Seville Orange, cut in Slices; ſend it up for a ſecond Courſe.

Almond Torte for a ſmall China Diſh.

Tourte aux Amandes.

SHEET your Diſh with Puff-paſte, take an Ounce of blanch'd Almonds, and beat them very well, moiſten'd with a little Cream; then take a Pint of Cream, and boil it; beat eight Yolks of Eggs, mix your Cream with them, put in a little Juice of Spinage as will colour it green, ſweeten it with Loaf Sugar to your Taſte, ſtrain it through a Sieve, put it into a Stew-pan, and ſtir it till it begins to thicken; let it ſtand to cool, ſqueeze in Half a Lemon, ſtir it well to mix it, put it into your Diſh, lay all over it thin Slices of Citron, rub it all over with a beaten White of an Egg, ſift on fine Sugar, ſprinkle on ſome Roſe Water, and bake it, but not too much.

N. B. Mix your Almonds with it, after it is thicken'd put in a Piece of Butter.

To make Apple Cream.
Crême aux Pommes.

TAKE ten or twelve Apples, that are pretty ripe, Codlins, at this Time are as good as any; core and pare them, flice them thin, put them into a Stew-pan, with Half a Pint of Water, Half a Pint of White Wine, and Half a Pound of double-refin'd Sugar, grate in the Rind of a Lemon, cover them down clofe, and ftew them till they be all in a Pulp on a flow Fire; let them ftand to cool; then boil what Quantity of Cream you chufe, with a Stick of Cinnamon, fweeten it, and let it cool; then mix Apples and Cream together the Thicknefs you would have it, and put it into Glaffes.

Beef drefs'd to be eat cold, call'd a-la-Vinaigrette.
Beuf accommodé à manger froid.

TAKE a Piece of the Brifket, Sur-Loin, or thin Part of the Ribs, and falt it with common Salt and Salt-petre, very well; turn it and rub it twice a-day for four Days; then wafh it and boil it in a Pot with hard Water, Pepper, Half a Pint of Vinegar, Mace, a Piece of lean Ham or Bacon, Half a Dozen Onions, Thyme, Parfley, a Carrot, a flic'd Lemon, and a Bay-Leaf or two; let it boil till tender, let it ftand in the Liquor till cold, then difh it with raw Parfley; ftrain the Liquor, and put it into an Earthen Pot that will hold it and the Beef and keep it in; it is eat with Muftard, hard Eggs, Oil, and Vinegar.

Bifques and Olios.

BIfques and Olios were much in Fafhion formerly, but are not fo now: I fhall give you the Method firft of an Olio, having fome Gravey and ftrong Broth provided, as directed in the Beginning of the Book, proceed as follows; take Pigeons, Partridges, or Chickens, what Quantity you pleafe, pick, draw, and

and finge them; trufs them as for boiling, lay them to foak in warm Water, take the Cruft of two or three French Rolls, foak them in Gravey, then boil them, and rub them through a Cullinder with a wooden Ladle; put to it a Quart of ftrong Broth; take out your Birds, and tofs them up in melted Butter till they turn a little brown; then put them into a Stew-pan, with your Bread, Gravey, and ftrong Broth; let all ftew together till the Birds be tender; then prepare a Ragoo of dic'd Sweet-breads, Cocks-combs, dic'd Ham, that have been boil'd; Colliflowers, frefh Mufhrooms, if you can get them; if not, fome pickled; tofs all together, with a little fhred Parfley and Onion, and the Juice of a Lemon, the ftrong Broth, Gravey, and Bread, muft fimmer till it is the Thicknefs of a Cream; then Rim your Difh, as you are directed for, the Soop Difh, in the Beginning of the Book; put in the Bread, Gravey, &c. lay in the Birds, with their Breafts next the Rim of the Difh, then their Rumps will meet all in the Middle; then lay a Toaft of White Bread betwixt each Bird; pour on the hot Ragoo over all. See how the Ragoos are made, in their proper Places. So fend it up hot; fometimes you leave out the Ham, and add more Gravey and ftrong Broth, and fend it for the firft Difh, like a Soop; garnifh the Rim of the Difh with potch'd Eggs, Spinage, and Rafhers of Bacon.

To preferve Kidney Beans in Salt.

Des Haricot confervé dans Sel.

TAKE the young ones, take a Jar or Pitcher that will hold the Quantity you would keep; lay in fome Salt, then fome Beans prefs'd down hard, then Salt on them again, and fo continue till you have fill'd the Veffel; then butter a Paper, and lay on the Top, cut the Edges in Nicks to make it fix faft to the Pitcher; then render fome Mutton Suet, and let it be almoft cold before you put it on, to prevent it from

running

running down amongſt the Beans, and ſpread it on with the Back of a Spoon; let it cover the Beans two Inches; put over the Top of the Veſſel a wet Bladder, tie over that a Leather, and keep them in a Place not too damp nor too hot; when you uſe any, ſoak them in warm Water for twenty-four Hours; then cut and uſe them as you would freſh ones.

To keep green Peas all the Year.
Des Pois à garder tous l'Année.

SHELL them, and order them as you did the French Beans; or thus: Take the middle-grown ones (that is to ſay not too young nor too old) ſhell them, and put them into a Stew-pan, with a Piece of Butter and a little Salt; toſs them now and then on a gentle Fire, till they turn a little; then put in a little Water, with ſome powder'd Sugar, let them ſtew a little, take them off, and put them into Bottles whilſt they are warm, and the Butter will riſe to the Top; let them ſtand till they be cold, cork them down, cut off the Ends of the Corks, and Roſin them as you do Gooſberries; when you would uſe them draw the Cork, and take the Butter off from the Top, ſtrain them from the Liquor, ſet them on hard Water, make it boil, put in the Peas, boil them tender, toſs them up with Butter as you would freſh Peas.

To make Chicken Pye the French Way.
Paté de Poulets à la Fraucoiſe.

DRAW, crop, ſinge, and truſs them, as for boiling; ſeaſon them with Pepper and Salt, with a Piece of Butter in their Bellies; then raiſe a Coffin for them in the Form following, or round, as you like beſt; make your Paſte as directed in No. 2; if you would make it in a Diſh, ſee Paſty-paſte in the ſame Number; when your Pye is rais'd lay in your Chickens, with their Breaſts up, lay between them Forc'd-meat Balls and the Yolks of hard Eggs and Butter over
all

all; close your Pye, garnish it, and bake it two Hours; if you would have it to be eat cold, you must fill it up with clarified Butter; if to be eat hot, you may put in a Ragoo of Sweet-breads, or of Asparagus Tops, or stew'd Oysters, as you like, or only put in some good hot Gravey. You may make a Pigeon Pye the same Way; some set them off first, that is, break down their Breast Bones, and put a good Piece of Butter into a Stew-pan, lay them in with their Breasts down, put in a Faggot of sweet Herbs, and lay all over them, some lean Beef Stakes, with some Rashers or Bacon; cover them down close, and set them on a slow Fire till they are set; you may lay in some Stakes first to keep their Breasts from scorching or browning; let them stand to cool before you put them into your Pye.

Sausages stew'd a-la-braise.
Saucisses etuvé à la braise.

TAKE two Pounds of a Leg of Pork, Half a Pound of fat Pork, Half a Pound of Beef Suet, shred them very fine, season it with Pepper and Salt; put in the Crumb of a Penny Roll, and a little Sage shred fine, with a small Matter of Thyme, pound all together in a Marble Mortar; then having some of the small Guts of your Swine or of a Sheep wash'd, turn'd, scrap'd, and scour'd with Salt, and wash'd in several Waters till they feel rough; fill them and cut them into what Lengths you please, smooth them with your Hand that they may be fill'd all alike, tie their Ends with Thread, and fry, boil, or broil them, as you like; you may roast them with a Turkey, Fowls, Capon, &c. you may fill some of the large Guts with it, and tie it in short Lengths, and stew them a-la-braise, and send them up for a Dish on Sippets of White Bread; put to them some of the Gravey that they were stew'd in, taking off the Fat; and you may potch some Eggs, and lay one between each Sausage, and garnish them with stew'd Spinage.

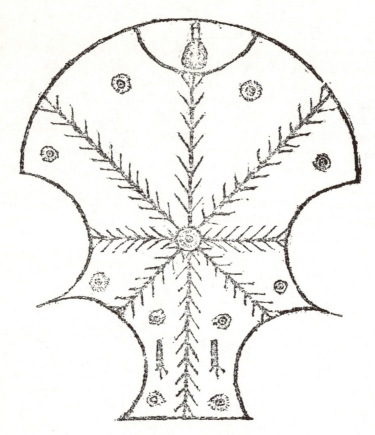

To make a Goose Pye.

Paté d'Oye.

BONE and par-boil it, first tie up the Vents, and if you cut it down the Back, sew it up again; singe it well before you put it into your boiling Water; when it is quite plump'd up, take it out, and let it lie to cool; take out the Threads, season it with Pepper and Salt, and lay it into your Pye made in the above Form; you may fill up the Corners with two Ducks bon'd and cut to Pieces, and season'd as before; lay on a good deal of Butter, lid it, and bake it two Hours and a Half, and fill it up with clarified Butter.

ART of COOKERY. 293

Butter, if you defign to keep it till cold. You may make a Duck Pye the fame Way.

To make a Giblet Pye.
Paté de Gigiés.

TAKE two Pair of Goofe-Giblets, fcald and clean them well; fheet a Difh, and lay in the Giblets, with a Pound of Saufages, cut into Lengths as long as your Finger; feafon your Giblets with Pepper and Salt, put in Half a Pint of Water, lay on fome Butter, and lid it; wafh it over with an Egg, and bake it two Hours and a Half; when bak'd, put in fome good Gravey; fome put in fome fhred Parfley and Onion before it is bak'd.

To preferve Golden Pippins, Nonparels, or Green Genitons.
Pommes d'Or confervé.

SEE Green Codlins.

To roaft Larks.
Aloüettes roti.

PICK them clean, draw them, leave on their Heads, fpit them a-crofs, and put betwixt every Lark a thin Bit of interlar'd Bacon, and a Sage Leaf; finge them, and tie your fmall Spit to a larger one; then beat two or three Yolks of Eggs, mix them with a little melted Butter, and wafh them all over with it, and dridge them with fome Bread Crumbs, Flour, and a little Salt; lay them a good Diftance from the Fire till the Coat is hardened on them; then bafte them with Butter, and dridge them with the fame as before; take Care you don't roaft them too much; difh them in Rows; the Sauce is Butter and Gravey, with a little Lemon.

To drefs Hog's Feet and Ears a-la-grandvell.
Pieds de Cochon et Oreilles à la Grandvall.

WHEN they are clean'd, take a deep Stew-pan, and lay fome Bards of Bacon in the Bottom; then

then some Slices of Veal and Beef, season'd with Pepper, Salt, sweet Herbs, and Onions; lay in your Hog's Feet slit in two; season the Ears, &c. with Veal and Beef, season'd as below; put to them a Pint of Water, a Pint of Vinegar, a Pint of White Wine; set them over a slow Fire, cover'd close down, let them stew till they be tender; let them stand to cool, then take one of the Ears, and cut it into thin shreds; put a Piece of Butter into a Stew pan, and make a Brown with Flour; put in some slic'd Onion, with a Pint of Gravey, some Mustard and Vinegar, a little Nutmeg; let all stew together till it is the Thickness of a Cream; then having the Feet broil'd, put the ragoo'd Ears into the Dish, and lay on the Feet at Top. How to broil the Feet; dry them well with a Cloth; wash them over with melted Butter, and the Yolks of Eggs; dridge them with Bread Crumbs, and broil them before the Fire, or brown them in an Oven.

To broil Herrings.
Harangues grillé.

SCALE them rub them dry, take out the Guts, with the Gills, nick them on the Sides, and dip them in melted Butter; dridge them with Bread Crumbs, broil them on a Gridiron, over a slow Fire; make the Sauce of Mustard, Butter, and Vinegar, put into a Cup, or Bason set in the Middle of the Dish; dish your Herrings round it.

To bake Herrings.
Harangues cuit au Four.

CLEAN them as before, lay some in the Bottom of an Earthen Pot, then some whole Pepper Corns, a little Mace, a little Thyme and Parsley, a little slic'd Onion, strinkle on some Salt, then lay in some more Herrings, then some more Spice and Herbs; pack them in as close as you can; keep this Order
till

till the Pot be full, then fill it up with Vinegar; tie it down with brown Paper, bake it two Hours, let it ſtand till they be cold; eat them with ſome of their Pickle.

To dreſs Kid.

KID is a Thing ſeldom uſed now at the beſt Tables: It is dreſs'd as you do Lamb; ſo I need mention no more of it.

To bake Roach and Dare.
Rougets et Suiffes cuit au Four.

YOU may dreſs them as you do Trouts; the ſmall Fry dreſs'd, as you do a Smelt or Gudgeon, will eat very well; the larger ones, bak'd as you do Herrings, eat very well.

To pickle Bleaks like Anchovies.
Ables confit à la Maniere des Anchoyes.

BLEAKS are a freſh Water Fiſh, they are greeniſh on their Backs, and like Silver on their Sides and Bellies; we dreſs them like Smelts, and they eat very well; I have ſalted them with Bay-Salt and Salt-Petre, and ſent them up like Anchovies; they are a very tender Fiſh, and come up to an Anchovey the nigheſt of any Fiſh I know.

Turkey Figs in Jelly.
Figues de Turqeie en Gellé.

ORDER your Figs as directed for Turkey Figs in Syrrup; make a ſtrong Jelly of Hartſhorn and Icinglaſs, or Calf's Feet and Icinglaſs, ſtrain it and order it as you do other Jelly; when run through a Jelly Bag, put to it ſome of the Syrrup they are preſerved in; put ſome of the Jelly into the Baſon you deſign to put them in, or any other Thing that will look pretty; let it cool, then lay in your Peaches with their fair Sides downwards; fill up the Thing quite full with Jelly, let it ſtand till the next Day, and dip the Baſon in warm Water; lay your Diſh on it, and

and turn it upside down into your Dish; you may lay any Sweet-meat betwixt the Peaches that will look pretty, as candied Lemon, Orange, or Citron Peel; or dried Cherries, Currants, &c.

To roast a Black Heath-Cock.
Coc de Bruyere roti.

ROAST him as you do a Pheasant; the Sauce the same; with two or three of his Tail Feathers stuck upright in his Rump when you send him up.

To roast Teal.
Cercelles roti.

TEALS are roasted as you do wild Ducks; all the rest that is mention'd in the Bill of Fare you'll find in their proper Places.

To stew Pigeons.

THE best Way is to stew them a-la-braise, and send them with a Ragoo of Sweet-breads, Morels, Mushrooms, Cocks' Combs, with Forc'd-meat Balls, Colliflowers, &c. garnish with Rashers of Bacon. Chickens may be done the same Way.

To make a Hare Pye the French Way.
Paté de Lievre.

LARD and truss it, as for roasting; tie it two or three Times a-cross with Packthread, give it two or three Leaps in boiling Water, to keep the Legs from starting; set it to cool, then make a Pudding for the Belly, as directed. See roast Hare. Then raise a Pye, as you will see by the Figure, Page 122; lay in the Hare first, pull out the Skewers, untie the Legs, and crack the Bones, fill the Belly with the Pudding; if you have more Pudding than the Belly will hold, lay it round the Hare, with Forc'd-meat Balls, Sweetbreads dic'd, and some dic'd Ham made into a Ragoo; let all stand to cool, and lay it

round

ART of COOKERY. 297

round and over the Hare; lid it and garnish it as you will see in the Figure; wash it over with Egg, and bake it; then put in some good Gravey, and shake it; then send it up.

To jug Hare.
Lievre etuvé.

SKIN and rub it dry with a wet Cloth, cut it in Pieces, put it into a Jug, season it with Pepper and Salt, a large Onion stuck with four or five Cloves, a Bunch of Herbs; put in a Pint of Red Wine, and a Pint of Gravey, a Quarter of a Pound of Butter, with a Piece of interlar'd Bacon; stop up the Mouth of the Jug, and set it to stew in a Kettle of Water for four or five Hours; take Care none of the Water goes into the Jug, then make a Brown for it, put it all in, let it simmer a little, squeeze in a Lemon; if it be not season'd enough, season it to your Taste; dish it with the Bacon in the Middle, take out the Onion and the Herbs; garnish it with Seville Orange and Barberries; send it up hot.

To stuff and roast a Leg of Pork.
Jigot de Porc farcie et roti.

TAKE off the Skin about half Way, that is, the Half from the Shank End to the thick End; leave the Skin on the Shank End, and score it; make a Stuffing of a little Veal, some Suet, Bread Crumbs, Parsley, some Sage, and a little Thyme shred fine; mix it with the Yolks of Eggs, season it with Pepper and Salt; make Incisions in the thick End to hold the Stuffing; spit it, and tie the Kell of a Veal over it to keep in the Stuffing; roast it leisurely, when ready dish it; send Gravey in the Dish, and Apple-Sauce in a Boat.

To make a Pork Pye.
Paté de Porc.

TAKE a Neck of Pork, cut it into Stakes, cut off the Skin, season it with Pepper, Salt, and a little Sage; make it in a Dish, or raise it, as you like; fill your Pye, and lid it, first lay Butter all over the Top, wash it over with the Yolk of an Egg, bake it two Hours; when bak'd, put in some Gravey; if you would eat it cold, put nothing in after it is bak'd.

To dress a Pike in Jelly.
Brochet en Gellée.

SCALE and clean your Pike, turn it round with the Tail in its Mouth, indent it on each Side with a sharp-pointed Knife; rub it all over with some melted Butter, the Yolk of an Egg, strinkle it over with Bread Crumbs, Salt, and some sweet Herbs minc'd fine; put it into a convenient Thing to bake in a moderate Oven; when bak'd, set it by to cool; then make a strong Jelly, as you are directed, see Lobsters in Jelly; put your Pike into a Thing that is deep enough for the Jelly to go over it; lay it on its Back, lay in Sprigs of Fennel, and Slices of Lemon all round; fill the Pot with Jelly, let it stand till the next Day, dip it into boiling Water, lay the Dish on the Top of the Pot, and turn it upside down into it, and the Fish will lie on its Belly in the Dish; garnish it with Fennel and Seville Orange.

A gallanted Goose.
Oye en Galantine.

WHEN your Goose is pick'd clean, sing'd, and drawn, bone it, season it with Pepper, Salt, Mace, and sweet Herbs; lay on it Yolks of Eggs boil'd hard; before you season it, rub the Goose over with Yolks of raw Eggs, then season it, then lay on your hard Eggs with some Pistacho Nut Kernels; then having a Forc'd-meat made, with Veal and fat Bacon, season'd as you did the Goose; beat it very fine in a Mortar, lay it all over the Eggs, &c. then stick more Eggs, and Nut Kernels as before, lay more Forc'd-meat on that again; roll it up, and tie it tight in a

Cloth,

Cloth, put it into a Pot of Water with Spice, Vinegar, Salt, Lemon Peel, a Pound of Butter, and some fat Bacon; let it boil softly while it is tender, then take it up, tie it tight at the Ends, and wrap it smooth with Incle; put it into the Pot again, lay on it a Thing to keep it under the Liquor; let it stand to cool, take the Fat off the Pot, drain it from the Liquor, put it into a Bowl, and beat till it is like a Cream; take the Goose out of the Cloth, lay it in the Dish, and rub or lay on the Fat smoothly; garnish with Flowers or any pretty Greens, &c.

DECEMBER.

To make Plumb Broth.
Potage de Noël à faire.

TAKE a Leg of Beef, a Knuckle of Veal, the Scrag End of a Neck of Mutton, lay them to soak in a good Deal of Water when cut in Pieces; let them lie to soak two Hours, wash them out very clean, put all into a Pot that will conveniently hold them, the Beef being boil'd two Hours before the rest is put in, keep filling of it up with Water as it boils away, and skimming of it; when your Meat is all in, and your Pot is well skim'd, put in a large Faggot of Sweet-Herbs, five or six Turnips, six Heads of Cellery, a Couple of Carrots, a Parsnip, some whole Pepper, Mace, and Salt; let it boil till it is almost boil'd to Rags, strain it, let it stand to cool (if you have Time) take the Fat off the Top, leave the Seddiment at the Bottom; to two Gallons of this, put in two Bottles of Wine, the one White and the other Red; put in two Pounds of Currants well wash'd and pick'd; a Pound of Raisins, and a Pound of Prunes wash'd and pick'd; also put in some whole Mace, and a Stick of Cinnamon; grate in two Nutmegs, put in 1 lb. and a half of Sugar, with the Crumb of two Penny Loaves rubb'd thro' a Cullinder, squeeze in the Juice of four Lemons, put in the Peel of two; let all boil together till the Fruit is plump; salt it to your Taste, and dish it up hot.

To order a Swan for a Pye.
Paté de Signe.

WHEN it is pick'd, sing'd, and drawn, bone it, take off the Head and Legs first, season it within with Pepper and Salt, let it lie two Days, tie or sew up the Vents where you took out the Bones, make a Kettle of Water boil, put in your Swan till it is plump'd up, take out all the Threads when cold, make a Coffin for it as directed for a Peacock Pye, ornament it as there directed; as to fixing the Head and Feet, and as to the other Garniture, I shall give a Description of; the Pye is to be filled up with a Goose boned and cut into Pieces, season all well with Pepper and Salt; lay a good Deal of Butter on the Top, lid it, and bake it three Hours; when baked, fill it with clarified Butter. This is a proper Standing Pye for Chriftmas.

A Breaft of Veal fricafy'd.
Poitrine de Veau eu fricaffée.

TAKE the griftly Part of a Breaft of Veal cut in fquare Pieces, blanch it, pafs it in a Sauce-Pan with Tops of Afparagus, Artichoke Bottoms blanch'd, fome Butter, a Faggot of Sweet-Herbs, a whole Onion, a Bit of Bacon ftuck with Cloves, a Slice of Ham, Pepper and Salt; let it take two or three Turns, moiften with Veal Broth, and cover it; let it fimmer till tender; prepare a Lare of three or four Yolks of Eggs, fome Cream, minc'd Parfley, and the Juice of a Lemon; when the Liquor is fufficiently diminifhed, pour your Cream and Eggs in, and keep it ftirring till thicken'd; difh your Veal, and pour your Sauce over it. You may drefs it with green Peas, but then ufe no Parfley.

To make a green Sauce.
Saufe Vert.

TAKE Spinage and Sorrel, blanch it, and fqueeze it from the Water, pound it with fome Shallot, then pafs it thro' a Sieve with Veal Gravey or Broth, which put into a Sauce-Pan and thicken it with a Lump of Butter rubb'd in Flour; when of a due Thicknefs, fqueeze in fome Lemon, add thereto Salt, Pepper, and Hnchovy, with Capers. This Sauce is good for boil'd or broil'd Chickens, or with Mutton.

Mutton

Mutton cuebob'd.
Mouton accommodé l'Indien.

TAKE a Loin or a Neck of Mutton, fkin it, and chop it into Cutlets, but do not feparate them, that they may ftick together; fteep it in Elder Vinegar, Oil, fome Garlic, Indian Pepper, whole Spice, and Saffron, with Slices of Spanifh Onions, fix or eight Anchovies flipt in two; let your Mutton marinade therein about two Hours, then put it over a very gentle Fire, let it fimmer juft to parboil, then take it out; when cold, put between each Cutlet a little Seafoning, and a Slip of Anchovey, a Slice of Onion, fome Indian Pepper, Salt, fome cut Parfley, Sweet-Bafil, and a Lump of Butter, fo clofe each Cutlet together as if the Loin was entire, wrap it up in a Sheep's Kell, foak'd in luke-warm Water, fpit it on a Lark Spit, tie it to another Spit, roaft it thoroughly; but when it is about three Parts ready, take off the Kell, and bafte it with the marinade Liquor and thick drawn Butter fcalding hot, faving it as you bafte it; then dridge with grated Bread and Flour, bring it to a fine Colour; ferve it with a Sauce thus, take your marinade Liquor, put it in a Sauce-pan, fet it over the Stove, fkim off the Fat, ftrain it thro' a Sieve, pouring therein fome good Gravey, and a Lump of Butter rub'd in Flour, which put under your Mutton; garnifh your Difh with Cutlets marinaded; dip them in melted Butter, dridge them with grated Bread, Salt, Pepper, Parfley, Thyme, and Shallot; broil them, and place round your Mutton.

Chickens Chiringras.
Poulets aux Chiringras.

CUT off the Feet of your Chickens, lard them with Bacon and Ham, roaft them and bring them to a fine Colour, make a good ragoo'd Sauce, and fet the Chickens a ftewing therein; when almoft ready, dy, put to them handsome Slices of boil'd Ham, let them simmer a little together, serve up your Chickens with the Slices of Ham round them, pouring your ragoo'd Sauce over them; or you may dress them in a Braise, with Slices of Ham and some cut small, with a Cullis of Veal and Ham, so serve them up.

Orange Tart.
Tourte d'Orange.

TAKE eight golden Pippins, pound them with the Rind of an Orange boil'd tender, half a Pound of Butter, eight Yolks of Eggs well beat together, two Whites whipt to a Froth, with Loaf Sugar, Nutmeg and Cinnamon pounded, thicken it over the Stove, put it on Puff Paste, cross-bar it, and bake it.

A Water Tart.
Tourte d'C'eau.

TAKE a Pint of Spring Water, the Rind of a Lemon, half the Rind of an Orange, squeeze in the Juice of three Oranges and three Lemons, with fine Sugar, a Spoonful of Honey and Rose-water, beat the Yolks of eight Eggs, the Whites beat to a Froth, strain it, mix with it half a Pound of clarified Butter, strain your Water and Juice through a Sieve, stir it over the Stove with a Blade of Mace and a Stick of Cinnamon; when thoroughly warm'd, whisk in your Eggs and clarified Butter; take Care it does not curdle when it is thick; bake it on a fine Paste, cross-bar it, and serve it up.

To stew Peas.
Pois Etuvée.

TAKE Spinage and Lettice, three or four Onions cut small, some Butter and Slices of Bacon, season with Pepper and Salt; when it is a little stew'd, put in your Peas, put to them some good Broth, stew them easily till tender; serve them up with a Piece of broil'd

Bacon in the Middle, and dridge them with grated brown'd Bread before the Fire.

Eggs with Sorrel.
Oeufs a l'Ozéille.

POACH your Eggs, get some Sorrel and Spinage Juice, put it in a Sauce-pan with a Lump of Butter rub'd in Flour, some Sugar, and two or three Yolks of Eggs; when thicken'd, squeeze an Orange or half a Lemon therein, with some Nutmeg; when your Eggs are poach'd and drain'd, put your Sauce in the Dish and the Eggs upon it, with Sippets round.

Sturgeon roasted.
Esturgeon roti.

TAKE a handsome Piece of the middle Part, steep it in half Vinegar and half White Wine, with whole Pepper and Spices, Slices of Onion, Bay Leaves, a Faggot of Sweet-Herbs, Anchovies cut small, and Salt; let it marinade twenty-four Hours, spit your Sturgeon, and baste it with the Marinade till just ready; then baste it with Butter, and dridge it with Bread Crumbs; let it be brought to a fine Colour, and serve it with the Marinade strain'd and thicken'd with Butter and scalded White Wine.

Sturgeon broil'd.
Esturgeon grillée.

CUT your Sturgeon in Slices the Thickness of your Finger, put in a Sauce-pan with melted Butter, Pepper, Salt, Sweet-Herbs, Onions, and the Juice of Lemon; let it lie therein two Hours to give it a Relish, afterwards dip them in melted Butter, bread them and broil them, serve them on a Napkin with plain Butter Sauce, Capers, fry'd Parsley, and Slices of Onion.

A Breast of Veal collar'd.
Poitrine de Veau en ruel.

BONE it, lay a Napkin over the Dresser, lay your Breast of Veal over it : boil half a Dozen Eggs hard, and mince them a-part, season with Pepper, Salt, Cloves, and Mace ; cut long Slips of Bacon and the Lean of Ham as thick as your little Finger ; make Rows cross over your Breast of Veal ; mince a Quantity of Parsley, Thyme, and Sweet-Basil ; then lay a Row of Yolks and Whites of Egg between the Rows of Bacon and Ham alternately ; then season with your Spices, Pepper, Salt, and Sweet-Herbs, a Dust of Flour over all ; roll it up tight with Tape, boil it in a well-season'd Liquor, or a-la-Braise, serve it up in Slices, with Parsley and Slices of Lemon.

Mutton Rumps farc'd.
Cu de Mouton farcie.

WHEN they are stew'd a-la braise, wrap them up in fine Forc'd Meat, dip them in beaten Eggs, dridge them with Bread Crumb, and fry them of a fine Colour ; dish them, and serve them with fry'd Parsley on a Napkin. Mutton Cutlets may be dress'd the same Way, or marinaded and fry'd in a thin Batter, with Gravey thicken'd, and the Juice of a Lemon.

A Leg of Mutton accommodé.
Gigot de Mouton accommodé.

PARE off all the Skin and marinade it in Vinegar, White Wine, Onions, whole Pepper, Spices, and a Clove of Garlic bruis'd ; lard with Slips of Bacon well season'd, doing the same to a Piece of Beef of the Buttock ; flour them, and give them a Brown, put them in a Pot with Bards of Bacon and Slices of Onions ; put at the Bottom Slices of Beef, Mutton, Veal, also on the Top ; cover your Pot close, and set it a-la-braise ; when ready, drain your Meat, pour to your

your Mutton and Beef the Marinade, with some strong Broth or Gravey, let it stew some Time, skim off the Fat, strain it through a Sieve, make a Brown, pour your Liquor thereto, put your Mutton and Beef therein to imbibe; let there be ready prepar'd, a good thick Gravey Sauce, with a good Garniture, as Sweet-Breads, Morels, and Truffles, or any other that is in Season; dish your Leg, cut your Beef in Slices, round it, and pour Sauce over it.

A Poupeton of a Leg of Lamb a la Cream.
Poupeton d'un Jigot d'agneau a la Cream.

WITH the Flesh of a Leg of Lamb make a delicious Forc'd-Meat, wash the inside with Eggs, and afterwards farce it about half an Inch thick, having ready a Ragoo of Sweet-breads in large Dice, Cocks-combs, Mushrooms, Asparagus Tops, Artichoke Bottoms in Dice, well season'd and cold, fill your Dish therewith; then place on your Forc'd meat that none of your Ragoo may come out, in the same Manner as a Pulpatoon, wash it with beaten Yolks of Eggs, dridge it with grated Bread, either set it a la Braise, or by baking it in the Oven on a Tourtiere; when ready, dish your Lamb, garnish with Sweet Breads larded, and Bottoms of Artichokes ragoo'd, or marinaded and fried; put on round Slices of Orange or Lemon; you may stick in your Leg, Hatlets of Sweet breads: Your Lamb may be diversified by filling it with a Ragoo of Larks and Capons Livers, with Chickens marinaded round it.

A Hotch Potch of Fowls.
Hoche Pot de Volailes.

MAKE a very good well-season'd Stock of Broth; take two Ducks or Teals, two Turkey Pouts or Chickens, a Leveret, a Rabbit, two Partridges, two Woodcocks being properly trust and sing'd; blanch them,

them, feafon, flour, and fry them to a brown Colour, juft to fettle the Gravey in them, put them in a Soop Pot, with a Piece of Ham, a Faggot of Herbs, whole Onions, a Piece of Bacon ftuck with Cloves; cover them with Broth, cover your Pot clofe; after having fkim'd it well, keep it fimmering; then take fome Carrots and Turnips cut long-ways, Cabbage Savoys cut in Quarters, with Cellery, Endive, Lettice blanch'd and ty'd in Bundles, dridge them with Flour, give them a Frying in Butter to give a Relifh, all which put into a Pot with a Piece of Ham, and a Faggot of Herbs, an Onion ftuck with Cloves; fo cover your Pot as you did your Fowls with Broth; alfo prepare Artichoke Bottoms, Tops of Afparagus, with about a Dozen and a Half of fmall whole Onions; fry them in Butter, as alfo Chefnuts roafted, place them a-part in a Sauce-pan, cover them in the aforefaid Manner, and let them fimmer; likewife tofs up fome Mufhrooms and green Peas a part; when all is ready and fkim'd, make a Rim two or three Inches high round a large Soop Difh, and place up to the Rim each Sort of Fowl, &c. againft each other, placing properly between your Roots and your Onions, Chefnuts, Mufhrooms, and Peas, with a handfome Fowl or Capon in the Middle; pour your Potage over the whole, with Carrots and Turnips cut round, with whole fmall Onions in your Potage, fo ferve it up.

An Oyfter Pye the Dutch Way.
Tourte aux Huitres à l'Hollandoife.

PUT upon your Abefs Butter and Rafpings of Bread, Parfley cut fmall; put over that a Lare of Oyfters, over that Bits of Butter, Rafpings, and cut Parfley; fo on of Oyfters, Rafpings, Parfley, and Butter; when bak'd, pour in thicken'd Gravey, Oyfter Liquor, and the Juice of a Lemon.

To

To make an Oatmeal Pudding.
Boudin de farine d' Avoine à faire.

TAKE the largest Oatmeal, put it to soak in Milk all Night, strain it from the Milk, shred the Marrow of two Marrow-Bones, put it to a Pint of this steep'd Oatmeal, with ten Eggs, leave out four of the Whites, put in half a Pound of Raisins ston'd and chop'd, with half a Pound of Currants well wash'd, dry'd, and pick'd; put in some fine Sugar, with some Cinnamon and Nutmeg beat fine, the Crumb of two French Rolls rub'd thro' a Cullinder; put in a little Salt, mix all very well together, butter a Cloth, tie it up pretty tight, and boil it for three Hours; dish it, let the Sauce be the Juice of a Seville Orange, a little White Wine, some Sugar and Butter drawn up thick and poured over it.

To stew Rabbits the French Way.
Lapins etuvée à la Francoise.

SKIN them, cut them in Quarters, lard them with Bacon, dridge them with Flour, fry them in clarified Butter; take a Stew-pan, put in a Piece of Butter, dridge in some Flour, put in a Pint and a Half of good Gravey, with a Faggot of Sweet-Herbs, whole Pepper and Mace, some Artichoke Bottoms cut in Dice, some Asparagus Tops blanch'd, three or four Morels blanch'd and shred fine, with an Anchovey, an Onion stuck with three or four Cloves; let all stew till the Rabbits are tender; but you must observe to let the Rabbits be almost enough before you put in the rest of the Ingredients, skim off the Fat; dish them up; garnish your Dish with Barberries and Lemon.

To make a Biscuit, call'd the Queen's Biscuit.

TAKE twelve Ounces of Flour, dry it well, a Pound of double-refined Sugar pounded and sift-

sifted; take twelve Eggs, leave out four of the Yolks; beat them very well, and strain them through a Sieve into your Sugar and Flour; take a few Anniseeds bruise them, put them to the rest, and beat them very well together; the more you beat them, the lighter all will be; then lay some Wafer Paper upon a Tin Plate, and drop them upon that; dridge them over with fine Sugar, sprinkle them with Rose Water, and bake them in a moderate Oven; when baked, cut them asunder, and keep them in a dry Place in a paper'd Box.

To make Wafer Paper.

I Have mentioned this as it was given to me in a Receipt as follows: Take Wheat Flour very fine, mix it with the Whites of Eggs, Icing-glass, and a little Yest; mix them together, beat them well, make them thin with Gum Water, spread the Batter on even Tin Plates, and dry them in a slow Oven or in a drying Stove.

To make a Dish of Soles a-la-Sante Menehart.

SCRAPE and wash your Fish clean, take off the black Skin, cut off all the Fins; put three Pints of skim'd Milk into a Stew-pan, strain it through a Sieve into another Stew-pan, and put the Soles into it with a good Piece of Butter; season it with Salt, Pepper, and some Slices of Onions; put in a Sprig of Thyme with some Parsley tied together, let them stew gently till they are enough, set them to cool in that Liquor, take them up carefully, first take the Fat off the Top, lay it on the Back of the Sieve to drain; dry your Soles with a Cloth, melt the Fat in a Stew-pan that you took off the Liquor in, rub it over your Soles, dridge them with fine Bread Crumbs and minc'd Parsley, brown them before a Fire or in an Oven, lay a good Quantity of Parsley wash'd and pick'd in the

Bot-

Bottom of your Dish, lay the Soles upon it, and send it up with a Rammolade made as follows; it is composed of Parsley, Chives, Capers, and Anchovies, shred all very small; put in some Salt, Pepper, and Nutmeg; then take some Oil and incorporate it with the Yolk of an Egg, some White Wine Vinegar, and the Juice of a Lemon, mix all very well together, put it into a Bason or a Boat, set it in the Middle of your Fish.

N. B. We send this Rammolade with any Fish that is pickled, or marinaded, or collar'd, to be eaten cold.

To make Salmon like Ham.

Saumon à la Maniere de Jambon.

SCALE and gut it, and wash it clean; skin it, take the Flesh off the Bones, and mince it fine with savory Herbs; season it with Pepper, Salt, and Nutmeg; salt it very well, then pound it in a Mortar, with a Pound of good Butter, four Anchovies, and the Yolks of ten Eggs; beat it till it is like a Paste, then spread the Skin, and lay on the Fish, shape it in the Fashion of a Ham, then sew it up in a fine Cloth, lay it on a Fish Drainer; then make your Fish Kettle boil with hard Water, and a Pint of Vinegar; put in the Fish, and let it boil an Hour; let it stand to cool in the Liquor, then take it out of the Cloth, and dish it with raw Parsley; it will slice and look like a Ham.

A Pulpatoon of Quails.

Cailles en Poupeton.

DRAW, singe, and truss them, as for boiling, fill their Bellies with a good Forc'd-meat, put a good Piece of Butter into a Stew-pan, put them in with their Breasts downwards, keep them moving over a Charcoal Fire till they are of a light Brown; take off the Pan, take them out, and dridge in a little Flour; put in a Pint of good Gravey, grate in a little Nutmeg, put in some Pepper and Salt, put in a Spoonful or two of White Wine, with an Anchovey mix'd with a little Onion, half a Dozen Morels
blanch'd

blanch'd and cut in Quarters, a few Chesnuts roasted and peel'd, two Spoonfuls of pickl'd Mushrooms, a little Parsley boil'd and minc'd fine, tofs all up together, set it by to cool, take your Pulpotoon-pan, butter it, lay a round Slice of Lemon in the Bottom, lay in some Rashers of Bacon alternately, with Parsley scalded, and lay it between each Rasher of Bacon, and round the Slice of Lemon that is in the Middle, so that none of your Pulpotoon-pan may be seen; then prepare a Sheet of Forc'd-meat, and lay it carefully over that, to fill the Pan up to the Edge; press it all round with your Hand, then lay in the Quails into the Pan, with their Breasts downwards; then lay in some Yolks of Eggs, boil'd hard, between every Bird, with some Forc'd-meat Balls; then put in Half of your Ragoo, lay in some more Yolks of Eggs upon that, and Forc'd-meat Balls, put in the rest of your Ragoo over them, then lay on a Sheet of Forc'd-meat Balls over the Top, and close it down with some Yolks of raw Eggs; bake it an Hour and a Half, loosen it with a sharp-pointed Knife round the Edges; when bak'd, lay the Dish upon it which you design to send it in, turn'd upside down; garnish it with fried Parsley and Seville Orange.

Pulpotoon of Partridges and Chickens.
Perdrix et Poulets en Poupeton.

YOU may make a Pulpotoon of Partridges, Pigeons, and Chickens, the same Way.

Pulpotoon of Woodcocks.
Becasses eu Poupeton.

FOR a Change you may garnish your Pulpotoon-pan with Ringlets of Vermicelly and Slices of Lemon cut in two, between the Rashers of Bacon; we likewise make Pulpotoons of Sweet-breads, Lamb-stones, made into Ragoos as before directed; sometimes with a Partridge in the Middle, Chicken, Woodcock, or Bottoms of Artichokes forced, &c.

Piſtacho Ammulet.

Piſtacho en Omelet.

BEAT twelve Eggs, put them into a Stew-pan, with a good Slice of Butter, and Half a Pint of Cream, ſhred three Anchovies fine, beat two Ounces of Piſtacho Kernels, add it to the Eggs, with a Quarter of a Pint of good Gravey; ſet it on the Fire, ſtir it till pretty thick, put it in your Diſh, and brown it with a Salamander, or a red-hot Fire-ſhovel; the Sauce Lemon, Butter, and White Wine; garniſh with Seville Orange.

Rabbits a la-braiſe.

Lapins à la Braiſe.

TRUSS them as you do a Leveret for roaſting, lard them with Bacon, cover the Bottom of a Stew-pan with Bards of Bacon, lay over that ſome Slices of Beef cut thin, hack them with the Back of a Knife; ſeaſon them with Pepper, Salt, Thyme, Parſley, Slices of Onion; tie your Rabbits round with Packthread, to keep them from ſtarting; lay over them ſome Bards of Bacon and ſome below, with Beef order'd in the ſame Manner; lay in a Faggot of Herbs, with a Carrot ſliced, and a Parſnip, four Heads of Cellery waſh'd clean and cut; ſtrinkle ſome Seaſoning over all, cover it with a Cover, ſet it on a ſlow Charcoal Fire, both above and under; look at it ſometimes that it does burn; when it is brown'd at the Bottom, put in three Quarters of a Pint of good ſtrong Broth, let it ſimmer till the Rabbits are pretty tender, ſtrain the Liquor from them, ſkim off the Fat, make a Ragoo of Sweet-breads, cut into ſmall Dice, add thereto ſome Forc'd-meat Ball, with ſome Parſley boil'd and ſhred fine, ſqueeze in the Juice of a Lemon, your Rabbits being kept hot; take out the Skewers, and take the Packthread off them; diſh them, and throw the Ragoo over them; garniſh with Barberries and Lemon.

Hare

ART of COOKERY.

Hare or Leveret a-la-braise.
Lievres ou Leverete à la Braise.

A Leveret or Hare may be done the same Way, adding a little Red Wine.

Pigeon Surtout.
Pigeons en Surtout.

TAKE the largest Pigeons you can get, make a Farce of fat Bacon, the lean of a Ham, some Macaroons and Truffles, some Parsley and Chives, two Veal Sweat-breads blanch'd; season with Pepper, Salt, and Nutmeg, shred all very fine together, mix it with the Yolks of two raw Eggs, force their Bellies with this Force, truss them as for roasting, wash each Breast with some melted Butter, lay on their Breasts a thin Slice of Veal larded with Bacon, and season'd with sweet Herbs and Spices, with a little Lemon Peel shred very fine, bind it on with Packthread, lay them down to roast, baste them with Butter; take off the Packthread when they are enough, and dish them with Veal upon them; the Sauce is Butter, Gravey, and the Juice of a Lemon.

To preserve Oranges whole.
Oranges conservè entirè.

TAKE your Oranges and make a Hole in the End where the Stalk grew, take out all the Seeds, but not any Palp, squeeze out the Juice, which must be saved, to put to them; take Care you do not loosen the Pulp; put them into an Earthen Pot, with fair Water, boil them till the Water be bitter, shifting them three Times, and in the last Water put a little Salt, and boil them till they are very tender, but not to break, take them out and drain them; then take two Pounds of Sugar, a Quart of Pippin Jelly, boil it to a Syrup, skim it very clear, then put in your Oranges, set them over a gentle Fire, let them boil till you see them very tender and clear; then put to them the

Juice

Juice that you took from them, prick them with a Knife, that the Sirrup may go in; if you cut them in Halves, lay the Skin Side upwards, so put them up and cover them well with Sirrup. Lemons, and Citrons may be done the same Way.

To candy Cowslips or any Flowers or Greens in Bunches.
Primeveres confit et autres Fleurs en Bouquets.

STEEP Gum-arabec in Water, and wet the Flowers; shake them in a Cloath that they may not be wet; then dip them in fine sifted Sugar, and hang them on a String to dry; they must hang two or three Days.

To make Orange Cakes.
Gateaux d' Oranges à faire.

TAKE three great Oranges and pare them, rub them with Salt, and boil them tender, cut them in Halves, and take out the Seeds; then stamp the Oranges, rub them through a Hair Sieve, till you have a Pound; then put to them a Pound and a Quarter of double refin'd Sugar, boil'd to Sugar again; put in a Pint of strong Juice of Pippins, and the Juice of a Lemon; keep it stirring on the Fire, till all the Sugar is melted.

To preserve green Apricots.
Apricots conservée vert.

TAKE Apricots before the Stone is hard, wet them, lay them upon a course Cloath, and put to them two or three Handfuls of Salt, rub them till the Roughness is off, then put them in scalding Water, and set them over a Fire, till almost cold; do so two or three Times, let them be close covered, and when they begin to be green, let them boil till they are tender, weigh them, and make a Sirrup with their Weight of Sugar, and to a Pound of Sugar, put half a Pint of Water, make a Sirrup, let it be almost cold; before you put in the Apricots; then boil them fast,
till

till they are clear, heat them every Day till the Sirrup is thick; you may put them in Codlin Jelly, or dry as you use them, or put them in Hartshorn Jelly.

To preserve Gooseberries.
Des Groseilles conservée.

STONE your Gooseberries, and as you stone them put them into Water, then weigh them, and put to half a Pound of Gooseberries, put three Quarters of a Pound of double refin'd Sugar, to as much Water as will make it a pretty thick Sirrup; when it is boiled and skimmed, let it cool a little; then put the Gooseberries into the Sirrup, and let them boil very quickly, till they look clear; take them out one by one, and put them into the Glasses they are to be kept in; then heat the Sirrup and strain it through Muslin, and put it to your Gooseberries, and it will jelly when it is cold.

To make Chocolate Almonds.
Des Amandes en Chocolat.

TAKE two Pounds of fine Sugar sifted, half a Pound of Chocolate, grated and sifted, a Grain of Musk, a Grain of Ambergreece, two Spoonfuls of Yest; make this up to a stiff Paste, with Gumdragon well steeped in Orange Flower Water, beat it well in a Mortar, and make it in a Mould like Almonds, lay them to dry on Papers, but not in a Stove

Te make Orange Marmalade.
Marmalade d' Oranges à faire.

RASP the Oranges and cut out the Meat; boil the Rinds tender, and beat them fine; take three Pounds of Sugar, and a Pint of Water, boil and skim it well; then put in a Pound of the Rind, boil it fast, till the Sugar is thick; then put in a Pint of the Meat of the Orange, and a Pint of strong Pippin Jelly, boil all together very fast, till it jellies; you may boil it half an Hour, then put it in Pots.

To make white Quince Marmalade.
Marmalade d' Oranges blanche à faire.

PARE the Quinces and quarter them, put as much Water to them as will cover them, boil all to Pieces, to make Jelly of, and run it through a Jelly Bag; then take a Pound of Quinces and quarter them; cut all the Hard out of them and pare them, to a Pound of Quinces, put a Pound and Half of Sugar, and half a Pint of Water; let it boil till it is clear, keep stirring it, and it will break as much as it should be; when the Sugar is boiled almost to a Candy, put in half a Pint of Jelly, and let it boil very fast till it jellies; when you take it off, put in the Juice of a Lemon, and skim it; put it in Pots or Glasses; it is better for having Lumps in it.

To make Raspberry Paste.
Pate de Framboises à faire.

TAKE a Quart of stripped Currants, and a Pint and a half of Water, and boil it; then strain it and put it into a bason; then take a Pound of sifted Sugar, wet it a little, and boil it till it looks glazed; take a Pint of the Jelly, and a Pint of Raspberries, and boil it till it looks clear, then put it to the Sugar; rub it well together, and then put it into Pots.

To make a Marmalade of Cherries.
Marmalade de Cerises à faire.

TAKE a Pound of Sugar and boil it, then take a Pint of stoned Cherries, and boil it with the Sugar; then take a Pint and a half of Jelly of Currants, and put to it; then boil it a considerable while, and put it into Glasses.

To make clear Cake of Currants or Raspberries.

TAKE a Pound of Sugar and wet it a little, boil it till it looks glazed; then take a Pint of the Jelly

Jelly of Currants, and put it to it; then rub it well together, and put it into Pots, if it is Raspberries; you must put in some Currants, when you make the Jelly.

To make white Marmalade of Quinces.
Marmalade de Coins blanche.

TAKE three Pounds of Quinces, and three Pound and three Quarters of fine Sugar, and boil it together; Then take two Pints of Pippin Jelly, and put to it; boil it till it is clear, then put it into Glasses; you must coddle your Quinces.

To make Apricot Paste.
Pate de Apricots a faire.

TAKE two Pound of par'd and ston'd Apricots, put to them a Pound and a Quarter of fine sifted Sugar; then take a Pint of the Jelly of Pippins; boil the Apricots and Sugar; then put the Jelly to it, and boil it till it looks very clear; then take a Pound of sifted Sugar, wet it a little, and boil it till it is glazed; then put the Apricots to it mix it well together, and put it into Pots.

To make red Marmalade of Quinces.
Marmalade de Coins rouge.

TAKE nine Pounds of Quinces, and four Pounds of Sugar; put to it three Quarts of Pippin Jelly; then half boil it, take three Pounds of Sugar and put to it, and boil it till it looks of a good Colour, put a Quart of the Juice of Barberries to it, so put it into Glasses.

To dry Damsins,
Prunes de Damas à Seché.

TAKE five Pounds of Damsins, and two Pounds of Sugar, then warm them, two or three Days together, so dry them.

To preserve Jelly of Grapes.
Des Raisins conservè en Géleé

FIRST peel and stone them, and pour all the Juice from them; then put as much Codlin Jelly to them as you think fit; then boil it up very fast, take them off the Fire, and let them stand till they be cold; then let them boil again till they be green; then measure it, and put a Pound of fine Sugar to every Pint of Grapes; let them boil fast till they Jelly, so put them into Glasses.

To make red Quince clear Cake
Gateaux de Coins rouge transparante

MAKE a good strong Jelly of Apples, and run it through a Jelly Bag; then pare a good many Quinces to your Jelly; that it may taste strong of the Quinces; then set it on the Fire, and let it boil till the Quinces are pretty well melted; then run it through a Jelly Bag, take some Barberries and draw them with a little Water, and run them through a Strainer; put to a Quarter of a Pint of Juice, a Pound of fine Sugar; then set it on the Fire and give it a Scald; then draw some Damsins with a pretty deal of Water, and run them through a Strainer; put in as much of the Barberry Juice as you think will make your clear Cake of a brisk Colour, and make it deep enough with the Damsin Juice; measure the Juice, and to a Pint, put in a Pound of double refined Sugar, then set it on the Fire, and make it scalding hot; skim it, fill your Pots, and let it stand five Days before you turn it out.

To make Orange clear Cake.
Gateaux de Oranges transparante.

MAKE a very strong Jelly of Apples, the whitest you can get, when your Jelly is made, take as much as you design to make, and to every Pint of Jelly, put in an Orange, peel off the Rind as much as
you

you can; then give it a boil or two, and run it through your Jelly Bag; meafure it, and to every Pint put a Pound of double refined Sugar, good Weight; fet it on the Fire and make it fcalding hot; then pafs it through a Strainer to clear it from the Skim; take fome Orange Peel, boiled very tender, fhred it very fmall, and put into it, fo give them one fcald in it, and fill it out. You may make Lemon clear Cake the fame Way; but you muft put as much Orange Juice as you put Oranges, and give it a Scald before the Sugar goes in.

To make Lemon Puffs.
Gateaux de Lemons.

TAKE half a Pound of blanch'd Almonds and beat them fine; then take a Pound and a Half of Loaf Sugar, finely fifted, beat it by little and little into the Almonds; you muft be beating it in for two Hours; put in two Spoonfuls of Flour, the White of an Egg beat to a Froth, fome Juice of Lemon, fome Lemon Peel, beaten to Powder, mix'd with it; drop them on Wafers or Papers; fift Sugar and Flour over them, and bake them off in a quick Oven.

To make Orange Puffs.
Gateauxt de Oranges.

TAKE Seville Oranges, and pare them very thin, boil the Peel till they are tender, then take the Peel out and pound them in a Mortar very well; then take the Juice of a Lemon and put to it, thicken it with double refined Sugar, beat very fine and fifted, enough to make it candy; then fet it over the Fire, but it muft not boil, when it juft begins to candy; drop it on Glaffes or Wafers, dry them on a Stove or in an Oven.

To make Fruit Biscuits.
Biscuits de Fonit a faire.

SCALD the Fruit, dry it from the Water, and rub it through a Hair Seive; then set it on a slow Fire, stir it till it be pretty thick, the stiffer it is the better, then take two Pounds of fine sifted Sugar, and a Spoonful of Gumdragon well steep'd and strained; put in a Quarter of a Pound of Fruit and beat it well; then take the Whites of twelve Eggs, beat up to a Stiff Froth; put in a little at a Time; keep beating it till all is in, and look as white as Snow, and is thick; then drop it on Papers, and bake them in a warm Oven; the Oven must be shut up to make them rise. The Lemon is made the same way, instead of Fruit put in Juice of Lemon; three Lemons will make two Pound; it must have Juice enough to make it to a Paste, and the Rind of two Lemons grated; when it is beat enough, put in a little Musk or Amber, and drop it on Papers.

To preserve Quinces whole.
Coins a Conserve entire.

A POUND of Quinces par'd and quarter'd, a pound of Sugar and half a Pint of Water, let them boil, and break it very well, till it is of a good Jelly; then take fine Muslin and tie it up; this Quantity will make three Quinces; set them in Pots or China Dishes, that will hold a Quince, cut off the Stalk End of a Quinces, and put in a Pot or Cup to make a Dent in the Quince, that it may be like a whole Quince; let it stand two or three Days that it may be stiff; take it out of the Muslin, and make a strong Jelly of Apples and Quinces; take two Pints of Jelly, and two Pounds of Sugar, boil them fast till they jelly well; then put in the Quinces, and let them have two or three boils to make them hot, put them in Pots close cover'd.

To preserve white Plumbs.
Des Prunes blanche à conservé

FIRST scald them, in Water till they are tender; to a Pound of Plumbs, put three Quarters of a Pound of fine Sugar very thick; then put in the Plumbs, and let them boil till they are clear, let them stand a Day or two to take the Sirrup, and a Quarter of a Pound of Sugar; let it boil till it jellies; then put in the Plumbs, and let them boil up, then put them into Glasses.

To make Rock Candy.
Roche en sucre Confit.

TAKE a Pint of Orange Flower Water, and a Pint of Spring Water, the White of an Egg; beat this together, then put to it, four Pounds of double refined Sugar; stir it all together, and put it on the Fire, make it boil very fast; when it is boiled, take off the Skim, skim it often and let it boil to a drawing Candy; then take a Pot and heat it very hot; put some small Twigs into it, and a good Handful of Orange Flowers, then take the Candy boiling off the Fire, and put it into the hot Pot, and twist a Paper over it, and set over a very hot Stove; keep the Stove very hot to it two Days, and let it be as hot as for clear; let it stand in the Stove a Fortnight, just dip the Rock into hot Water, and lay it upon a Plate, let it lie in the Stove a little While, and it will be dry.

Velvet Cream.
Une Cream Velouté.

TAKE a Pint of Cream, put it with some Sugar into a Stew-pan over the Fire; take a Couple of Gizzards of either Fowls or Chickens, open them and take out the Skin, wash it well, and cut it very small; put it into a Cup or other Vessel, put to it

some

some of your boil'd Cream luke-warm, put it near Cinders till it takes; then put it to your Cream and strain it off two or three Times; put a Stew-pan full of Water upon the Fire, put the Dish upon a Level upon the Water, put your Cream in it, covering it with another Dish, with a few Charcoals over it; it being taken, put it into a cool Place.

A Cream Velouté with Pistachos.

TAKE a Quart of Cream and some Sugar, let it boil as aforesaid; take a Quarter of a Pound of scalded and well-pounded Pistachos, and reserve a Dozen of whole ones to put round your Dish; take a Couple of Gizzards and order them as before; put the Pistachos into the Cream and the Skin of your Gizzards, as you have done with the Cream before; strain off your Cream two or three Times, pour it into the Dish you serve it in, and cover it with another Dish, with Charcoal over it; it will take presently; put it in a cool Place, and when you serve it up, garnish your Dish with the reserv'd Pistachos; it may be put in Ice as the aforesaid Cream; the Way of congealing these Creams is better than to make Use of Rennet or Thistle. If your Cream is not green enough, blanch some Spinage, pound, squeeze, and put it into your Cream, and it will be green enough: If you will make it red, use Cochineal or some Juice of bak'd Beets.

F I N I S.

A SET OF BILLS OF FARE FOR THE RESIDENCE IN THE COLLEGE OF DURHAM, BEGUN SEPT. 29th. 1753

[This section has been reset as the original printing is hard to read. The original spelling has been kept]

N° 1. First Course—Per Day.

A
Dish of
Fish.

Roast
Goose

A
Mutton
Stake Pye.

A
Leg of Pork
Boil'd.

A
Large Plumb
Pudding.

Veal
Collops.

Roast
Beef.

Second Day.

Roast
Partridges.

Rasberry
Cream.

Stew'd
Pears.

Sillibubs.

Apples

Custards.

Roast
Hare.

BILLS of FARE.

Nº. II. Per Day.

First Course.

Fish.

Mutton Cutlets.

Pig.

Boil'd Rabbits.

Goose.

A Slic'd Pudding.

A Round of Beef boil'd.

Second Course.

Roast Turkey.

Apple Pye cream'd

Preserv'd Damsins.

Sillabubs.

Stew'd Pears.

Cheese-cakes.

Roast Ducks.

BILLS of FARE.

N° III. FIRST COURSE.

	Fish.	
Pudding.		Fricasy'd Rabbits
	Boil'd Pork.	
Beef Stakes	Loin of Veal.	Fry'd Tripe.

SECOND COURSE.

	Partridges.	
Cheese-Cakes.		Wallnuts.
	Sillabubs.	
Apples.		Custards.
	Wild-Fowl.	

N⁰ IV. FIRST COURSE.

	Fish.	
Tongue.		Chickens.
	Pudding.	
Goose.		Veal Collops.
	Surloin of Beef.	

SECOND COURSE.

	Roast Turkey.	
Cheese-Cakes.		Stew'd Pears
	Jellies and Possets.	
Apple-Pye.		Custards.
	Roast Ducks.	

BILLS of FARE.

N⁰ V. FIRST COURSE.

	Boil'd Rabbits.	
Pye.		Breast of Veal.
	Pig.	
Hare Roasted.		Pudding.
	Chine of Mutton Roasted.	

SECOND COURSE.

	Pigeons.	
Custards.		Apple-Pye
	Sillabubs	
A Dish of Pippins.		Cheese Cakes.
	Pullets.	

N⁰ VI. FIRST COURSE

	Calves Head Hash.	
Pigeon Pye.		Chickens and Tongue boil'd.
	Brawn.	
Roast Pork.		Pudding.
	Leg of Mutton.	

SECOND COURSE.

	Fricasy'd Chickens.	
Custards.		Nuts.
	Jellies.	
Apples.		Stew'd Pears.
	Ducks.	

N⁰ VII.

Veal Collops.

Ham and
Chickens.

Goose.

Pudding.

Brawn.

Fricasy'd
Rabbits.

Pigeon
 Pye.

Pork.

Roast Beef.

Patridges

Apple
Pye.

Castards.

Stew'd Pears.

Jellies.

Nuts.

Walnuts.

Apples.

Turkey.

N.º VII. First Course.

	A Soop Hance of Venison	
Tongues.		Minc'd Pye.
	Hare.	
Sweet Breads.		Boil'd Chickens.
	Ham.	
Rabbits Spruc'd		Feet and Ears.
	Daub'd Veal.	
Fry'd Smelts.		Marrow Bones with Toast.
	Brawn.	
Forc'd Pallets		Scallop'd Oysters.
	Goose.	
Small Pig.		Collar'd Calf's-head.
	Pork cue-bob'd.	
Mutton Cutlets.		Lobsters.
	Venison Pasty.	
Pudding.		Turkey boil'd with Cellery.
	Soop Roast Beef.	

BILLS of FARE.

Second Course.

	Wood-Cocks.	
Quinces.		Stew'd Pears.
	Jellies.	
Golden Pippins.		Walnuts in their Shells.
	Walnuts in Sack.	
Flummery		Wet sweet Meats
	Small Pyramid, of wet sweet Meats	
Dried sweet Meats.		Custards.
	Sillabubs A large Pyramid, and dried sweet Meats.	
Cheese Cakes.		Dried Sweet Meats.
	A small Pyramid of Sillabubs.	
Wet sweet Meats.		Flummery.
	Walnuts in Sack.	
Walnuts in their Shells.		Golden Fippins.
	Jellies.	
Stew'd Pears.		Quinces.
	Roast Capons.	

N⁰ IX. First Course.

                Fish.
Pudding.   Breast of Veal.
                Brawn.
Fried Tripe..   Pye.
                Chine of
                Mutton.

Second Course

                Ducks.
Stew'd   Almonds and
Pears.   Raisins.
                Lemon Jelly
                and Possets.
Nuts.   Apples.
                Rabbits.

N⁰ X. First Course.

                Fish.
Pudding.   Pork cuebob'd.
                Brawn.
Beef-Stakes   Pye.
                Loin of Veal.

Second Course

                Partridges.
Custards.   Pippins.
                Possets and
                Jellies.
Stew'd   Apple
Pears   Pye.
                Hot Turkey.

BILLS of FARE.

Nº XI. FIRST COURSE.

Fish.

Pudding.   A Loin of
                                              Veal roasted.

Goose
Roasted.

Ham and
Chickens.   Florentaine.

Surloin of
Beef.

SECOND COURSE.

Partridges.

Stew'd   Cheese-
Pears.   cakes.

Jellies.

Cust-
ards.   Apples.

Turkey.

BILLS of FARE.

Nº XII. FIRST COURSE.

<table>
<tr><td>Minc'd Pyes</td><td>Soop.
Fish, Woodcocks.</td><td>Roast Sweet Breads.</td></tr>
<tr><td>Roast Hare.</td><td>Hanch
of Venison.</td><td>Tongue.</td></tr>
<tr><td>Pallets
ragoos'd</td><td>Boil'd
Turkey and
Oysters.</td><td>Feet and
Ears.</td></tr>
<tr><td>Pigeons broil'd
Whole.</td><td>Brawn.</td><td>Pork
cuebob'd.</td></tr>
<tr><td>Broil'd
Chickens.</td><td>Roast
Goose.</td><td>Marinaded
Rabbits.</td></tr>
<tr><td>Calf Head
Hash.</td><td>Ham.</td><td>Lemon
Pudding.</td></tr>
<tr><td></td><td>Roast Beef and
Partridges.</td><td></td></tr>
</table>

Second Course.

Jellies.

Preserv'd Quinces		Flummery.
	Walnuts and Sack.	
Cheese Cakes		Pippins.
Walnuts.	A little Pyramid of sweet Meats.	Jarr- Raisins and Almonds.
Wet sweet Meats.		Dried sweet Meats.
	Sillabubs a large Pyramid	
Dried sweet Meats		Wet sweet Meats.
	Sillabubs, a little Pyramid.	
Pistasia Nuts.		Filberts.
	Walnuts and Sack.	
Pears.		Custards.
Rasberrys and Cream.		Preserv'd Quinces.

Jellies.

BILLS of FARE.

Nº XIII. First Course.

	Soop, Fish, Woodcocks.	
Tongue and Udder.		Minc'd Pyes.
	Venison Pasty.	
Fricasy'd Rabbits.		Boil'd Ducks and Onions.
	Ragoo'd Veal	
Mutton cuebob'd		Pig.
	Brawn.	
Hogs Feet and Ears		Pulpotoon of Pigeons.
	Goose.	
Boil'd Turkey and Oysters.		Roast sweet Breads.
	Ham.	
Orange Pudding.		Boil'd Chickens.
	Roast Beef, two Capons	

Second Course.

Preserv'd Quinces.	Jellies.	Rasberry-Cream.
Cheese-cakes.	Walnuts and Sack.	Wet Sweet-meats.
Pears.	Sillabubs.	Dry Sweet-meats.
Walnuts.	A large Pyramid of Sweet-meats.	Filberts.
Dry Sweet-meats		Pippins.
Wet Sweet-meats	Sillabubs.	Custards.
Flummery	Walnuts and Sack.	Preserv'd Quinces
	Jellies.	

BILLS of FARE

N⁰ X1V. First Course.   Second Course.

Fish.   Ducks.

Veal Collops.   Apple Pye.

Pork.   Walnuts.

Pudding.   Stew'd Pears.

Chine of
Mutton.   Possets.

Giblet
Pye.   Custards.

Pig.   Apples.

Pudding.   Tarts.

Boil'd Beef.   Rabbits.

BILLS of FARE.

Nº XV. FIRST COURSE.

Fry'd Smelts.	Soope, boil'd Turkey.	Venison Pasty.
Tongue and Chickens.	Brawn.	Goose.
Boil'd and bak'd Pudding	Chine of Mutton	Veal Collops.

SECOND COURSE.

Tarts.	Woodcocks.	Stew'd Pears.
Sweet Meats.	Jellies and Possets.	Sweet Meats.
Pippins.		Walnuts.
	Capons.	

Nº XVI. FIRST COURSE.

Pig.	Veal Collops.	Pudding.
Fry'd Tripe.	Brawn.	Boil'd Partridges and Stew'd Cellery.
	Leg of Mutton roasted.	

SECOND COURSE.

	Chickens.	
Flummery.	Sillabubs and Jellies.	Apple-Pye.
Pippins.		Walnuts.
	Ducks.	

BILLS of FARE.

Nº XVII. FIRST COURSE.

	Fish.	
Roast Pork.		Beef Stakes.
	Brawn.	
Pudding.		Hare.
	Loin of Veal	

SECOND COURSE.

	Partridges.	
Tarts.		Walnuts.
	Jellies and Possets.	
Pears and Apples.		Flummery.
	Capons.	

Nº XVIII. FIRST COURSE.

	Ham and Chickens.	
Minc'd Pyes.		Smelts.
	Brawn.	
Pig.		Hare.
Rabbits	Roast Beef.	Pudding.

SECOND COURSE.

	Patridges.	
Rasp Cream.		Pears.
	Almonds and Raisins.	
Sweet-meats.	Jellies.	Sweet-meats.
	Nuts.	
Apples.		Whip'd Possets.
	Capons.	

BILLS of FARE.

Nº XIX. First Course.

	Soop.	
	Veal Collops.	
	Wood-cocks.	
Minc'd pyes		Boil'd Chickens.
	Ham.	
Pig.		Leveret.
	Brawn.	
Mutton carabinated		Tongue and Udder.
	Turky and Oysters.	
Fricasy of Rabbits, white.		Small Pudding.
	Roast Beef, Wild-ducks.	

Second Course.

	Jellies.	
Sweet-meats.		Sweet-meats.
	White Syllabubs.	
Almond Cheese-cakes.		Pippins.
	A large Pyramid.	
Burgany Pears.		Walnuts.
	Red Syllabubs.	
Sweet-meats		Sweet-meats.
	Jellies.	

BILLS of FARE.

Nº XX. First Course.

	Leg of Pork boil'd.	
Pudding.		Calf's Head Hash.
	Strugeon.	
Goose.		Pigeons and Bacon.
	Chine of Mutton.	

Second Course.

	Partridges.	
Walnuts.		Pears.
	Jellies.	
Apples.		Apple-pye.
	Chickens.	

Nº XXI. First Course.

	Boil'd Rabbits and Onions.	
Pork cubob'd		Pudding.
	Brawn.	
Patty of Pigeons.		Veal Cutlets.
	Roast Beef.	

Second Course.

	Turkey.	
Pippins.		Jellies.
	Strugeon.	
Possets.		Stew'd Pears.
	Apple Pye.	

BILLS of FARE.

FIRST COURSE.

An Orange Pudding	Soop. Remove, Fish	Boil'd Fowls and Oysters.
Roast Sweet-breads with Asparagus.	A Ham.	A Ragoo of Lamb-stones, &c.
A small Pig Roasted.	A Chine of Lamb, and stew'd cucumbers	Pickled Salmon.
Coller'd Beef.	Boil'd Tongue, Udder, &c.	A Pulpotoon.
Cutlets a-la-main-tenoy	Venison Pasty, or Pigeon Pye.	Potted Moor Game.
Lobsters.	A Boil'd Goose.	A Dish of Brochlets.
A Ragoo of Ox Palates.	A Fillet of Veal daub'd	Stew'd Soles.
Boil'd Rabbits	A Dish of Beans and Bacon.	A Florentine
	A Haunch of Venison, or Roast Beef.	

BILLS of FARE.

Second Course.

	Six Moor Game.	
A White Fricasay of Mushrooms		Moulded Fritters.
	A Raised Custard.	
Three Ducks		Six Quails roasted.
	A Dish of Sturgeon.	
Green Pease		Artichokes.
	Ten Pigeons roasted.	
A. Hamblite Shambone.		Mackroney.
	A Crowcant.	
A Tanzey.		Asparagus.
	Six small Chickens roasted.	
Marrow Pasties		Scorch'd Cream.
	Coller'd Eels.	
Six Land Rales roasted.		Three Turkey Pouts roasted.
	Cheese Cakes.	
Fry'd Toasts.		Fricasey of Eggs.
	A Leveret roasted.	

The DESERT.

	Jellies of different Colours.	
Nectarines.		Apricots.
	Sillabubs, &c.	
Grapes.		Cherries.
	A Pyramid of Sweet-meats.	
Gooseberries.		White Strawberries.
	A Pyramid of Sweet-meats.	
A Melon		Preserv'd Girkins.
	A Large Pyramid of dry Sweet-meats.	
Preserv'd Angelica.		A Pine Apple.
	A Pyramid of Sweet-meats.	
A Citron		Plumbs.
	A Pyramid of Sweet-meats.	
Turkey Figs in jelly		Currants.
	Sillabubs, &c.	
Peaches.		Pears.
	Jellies as at Top.	

BILLS of FARE

A Dinner for the Grand Jury, when there was no Residence.

Fish.	Turkey.
Ham.	Apple Pye.
Fowls.	Custards.
Pig.	White Possets.
Venison Pasty.	Jellies.
Veal Collops.	Red Possets.
Pudding.	Flummery.
A Leg of Pork boil'd	Cheese-cakes.
Roast Beef.	Roast Pigeons.

BILLS of FARE.
The Justices' Dinner.

	Soop. Salmon,	
Puddings of	Hanch of Venison,	Rabbits a la
several Sorts	Wild Ducks.	Cream.
Roast Tongues.	Veal Olives	Hogs Feet and Ears.
Roast Sweet-breads	A Herrico of Mutton	Lobsters.
Scollop'd Oysters.	Roast Lamb.	Pigeons Camport.
Colour'd Palates.	Boil'd Turkey and Cellery.	Marrow-bones.
Boil'd Chickens,	Ham.	Florentine.
	Soop, Salmon, Roast Beef, Capons.	
Preserv'd Quinces	Jellies.	Curds and Cream.
Pears.	A small Pyramid.	Filberts.
Citron	Sillabubs.	Wet sweet Meats.
Almond Cakes	Lemon Cream.	Rasp Puffs.
	A large Pyramid.	
Tarts.	Orange Cream.	Wafers.
Wet Sweet-meats.	Sillabubs.	Citron.
Walnuts.	A small Pyramid.	Golden Pippins.
Curds and Cream	Jellies.	Preserv'd Quinces.

BILLS of FARE.

Dr Sterne's first Dinner for the Prebendaries at Durham.

	Soop. Remove, Hanch of Venison.	
Pudding.		Stew'd Soles.
	Daub'd Ducks.	
A Pulpotoon with Brochlets round.		French Peas.
	Sturgeon.	
Crab Loves		Turkey and stew'd Cellery.
	Friecandox of Veal.	
A Leveret.		Lamb's-fry.
	A roasted Pigeon Pye.	
Italian Artichokes.		Mackaroney Parmasan.
	Roast Tongue and Claret Sauce.	
Pig.		Stew'd or scollop'd Oysters.
	Potted Moor-game.	
Eggs in Crampine.		Boil'd Chickens and Collyflowers.
	Ham with Patties of Greens.	
Mutton Cutlets marinaded. Desert.		Spinage Tart.
	Soop. Beef, Tromblance removes.	Ruffs and reserv'd Wildfowls.

BILLS of FARE.

A Dinner at Newcastle.

Soop.
Wild-fowl, Fish.

Boil'd Chickens.	Fruit.	Fruit.	Hanch of Venison.
Fruit.	A Pyramid of Sweet-meats.		Fruit.
Ham.	Fruit.	Fruit.	White Veal Collops.
Turkey.	Tarts with Crowcant Covers.		Pigeons comport.
Ragoo of Sweetbreads, &c.	Blammange.		Boil'd and bak'd Pudding.
	Dried Tongue and Butter.		
A Chump of Beef roasted.	Fruit.	Fruit.	Lamb and stew'd Cucumbers.
Fruit.	A Pyramid, ditto.		Fruit.
Apple Pye Cream'd	Fruit.	Fruit.	Peas.
Goose.			Roast Ducks.
Fried Soles, Wild-fowl.	Sturgeon. Cheese-cakes.		Venison Pasty.
Pulpotoon.	Lobsters.		Fricandox of Veal.
Fruit.	Fruit.	Fruit.	Fruit.
	Pyramid, ditto.		

BILLS of FARE.

The Dinner at Newcastle, continued.

	Fruit. Fruit.	
	Lobsters.	
Fricandoux of Veal.		Pulpotoon.
	Cheese-cakes.	
Venison Pasty.		Fried Soles, Wild-fowls.
	Sturgeon.	
Roast Ducks.		Goose.
	Fruit. Fruit.	
Peas.	Pyramid, ditto.	A Codlin Pye cream'd.
	Fruit. Fruit.	
Fruit.		Fruit.
	Dried Tongue and Butter.	
Lamb and stew'd Cucumbers.		A Chump of Beef roasted.
	Blammange.	
Boil'd and back'd Pudding.		Ragoo of Sweet-breads.
	Tarts with Crowcant Covers.	
Ragoo of Lamb Stones.		Turkey.
	Fruit. Fruit.	
White Veal Collops.		Ham.
Fruit.	Pyramid of, ditto.	Fruit.
Hanch of Venison.	Fruit. Fruit.	Boil'd Chickens.
	Fish, Wild-fowls.	

A Bill of FARE for January.

Puddings of Sorts	Soop. Remove Fish.	Calf's Head Hash.
Boil'd Turkey and Oysters.	A Ham with Patties of Roots and greens round it	Boil'd Fowls and Sprouts.
Mutton Cutlets	A Surloin of Beef roasted.	A Florentine, or minc'd Pyes.

SECOND COURSE.

Stew'd Pears	Four Woodcock	Blancmanger.
Dry'd Tongues.	A Hare or Jellies, &c.	Lobsters.
Rasberry Cream	Two Wild-Ducks roasted	Apples in Jelly.

A Bill of FARE for February.

Veal Collops.	Peas Soop, Fish.	Roast Neats Tongue and a Marrow-bone
Roast Pig	Pigeon Pye. A Leg of Lamb boil'd, the Loin fried, laid round.	Stew'd Hare.

SECOND COURSE.

Apple Pye.	Four Partridges roasted.	Jellies.
Sillabubs	A Pyramid of Sweet-meats. A Hen, Turkey, with Eggs.	Marrow-Pudding-

A Bill of FARE for March.

A Herricos.	Vermicelly Soup, Remove a Breast of Veal stew'd white	A bak'd Plumb-pudding.
Stew'd Soles.	A Leg of Lamb Forc'd and Cutlets.	Fried Tripe.
A Patty Devo.	A Round of Beef stuff'd and boil'd	Coller'd Pig hot.

SECOND COURSE.

Mackaroney.	Roast Chickens.	Asparagus.
Lemon Jelly.	Chocolate-Cream.	Hartshorn Jelly.
Tanzy.	Pigeons stuff'd and roasted	Custards.

A Bill of FARE for April.

	Soop de-sante the French Way, Salmon and Smelts.	
A Herb Pudding	Fish Sauce on a Plate	Neck of Veal daub'd.
A dress'd Sallet.	A Quarter of Lamb roasted.	Pickles
A Fowl a-la-Braise	A Plate with Greens Tongue & Udder boil'd.	A Pupton of Lobsters.

SECOND COURSE.

Rice Cream in Rasp-jelly	Young Ducklins with green Sauce.	Welch Flummery.
Asparagus.	A Pyramid of Sweet-meats.	Rosasolis of Spinach.
Almond Snow.	Young Rabbits roasted.	Cream, call'd Foul Cream.

A Bill of FARE for May.

A Green
Puree Soop,
Turbet or Brit.

Farc'd Chickens.   Tongue and Greens.

A Rice
Pudding with or
without Currants.

Lambs Trotters marinaded, split and fried   Ramkins.

Veal Olives.   Four young Rabbits boil'd with Asparagus a-la-Cream.

A Chine of
Mutton.

SECOND COURSE.

Young Turkey
roasted.

Gooseberry Cream.   China Oranges ic'd

Peas.   Desert.   A Green Appricot Tart.

Turkey Figs in Syrrop.   Almond Custards.

Ducklins.

A Bill of FARE for June.

Soop,
Au Bourgeois.
First remove, Roast
Pike, or what other
Fish you can get,
Second Remove,
Four Moorgame,
by some called,
Heath Pouts.

Hare Collops, &c.		Chickens and Rice.
Patte of Sweetbreads.	A Wesphalia Ham, with Windsor Beans.	Potatoe Pudding.
Two Ducks and Onion Sauce.		Forc'd Veal.
	A Hanch of Venison roasted, Three Turkey Pouts.	

SECOND COURSE.

Jellies.

Straw Berries.		Preserv'd Codling.
	Pyramid of wet Sweet-meats	
Clouted Cream.		Cherries.
	Pyramid of dried Sweet-meats.	
Cherries.		Clouted Cream.
	Pyramid of wet Sweet-meats.	
Preserv'd Cucumbers.		Strawberries.

A Bill of FARE for July.

Chickens the Barbary way.	A Soop Puree of Artichokes. Remove Ling, Skate or Thorn Backs	Rabbits a-la-Saingaraz.
Farc'd Cucumbers	Venison Pasty.	Ragoo'd Cabbage.
Veal Cutlets & Mushrooms.	A Jigget of Mutton A-la-Royal.	A boil'd Flour Pudding.

SECOND COURSE.

Cherries.	Six Quails roasted.	Appricots.
Kidney Beans.	A Currant Tart.	Green Peas.
White Plumbs.	Six Pigeons farc'd and roasted.	Raspberries and Cream.

A Bill of FARE for August.

A White Fricasey of Pigeons.	Cray-fish Soop, Beef, a-la-Mode, remove, roast Pike	Pullets-a-la-Smithergall with Oysters.
Sturgeon.	Umble Pye.	Coller'd Beef.
Rabbits boil'd the French way.	A Hanch of Venison boil'd.	A Carbanado of Mutton.

SECOND COURSE.

Cherries.	Two Pheasants roasted.	Peaches.
White Raspberries and Cream.	A Pyramid of Sweetmeats wet and dry.	White Currants.
Pears.	Six grey Plovers roasted.	Red Plumbs.

A Bill of FARE for September.

A Pye of Mutton Olives.	Jacobine Soop, the Italian way. Remove a Mackarel.	A Hare in Puree.
Boil'd Turkey and Oyster Sauce.	A Goose roasted. A Leg of Veal stuff'd with forc'd Meat, and daub'd.	A Danish Pudding.

SECOND COURSE.

Grapes.	Weet Ears, or Teals.	Black caps.
Jellies.	Mulberry Cream.	Possets.
Stew'd Pears white	Ruffs and Reeves, or Land Raels.	Green gages.

A Bill of FARE for October.

A Patty of Oysters, a-la-Cream	Cockle Soop, with broil'd Cod. Remove, the Hanch of a Doe.	A brown Fricasey of Rabbits.
Chitkens with Colli-Flowers and Bacon.	Partridge Pye.	Ducks a-la-Braise with Capons.
Grill'd Pork Stakes.	A Chine of Veal, a-la-Smithergall.	A Compote of Mushrooms.

SECOND COURSE.

A Mellon	Wood-cocks, &c.	Peaches.
Fried Smelts.	A Tart of different Sorts of Fruit.	Broil'd Sweet-breads.
Pears.	Roast Pigeons.	China Oranges.

A Bill of FARE for November.

Mutton a-la-force.	Soop dress'd in Balneomarie. Remove Stew'd Carp	A Breast of Veal a-la-Smithergall.
Ragoo'd Colliflowers.	A Peacock Pye.	Stew'd Cucumbers.
Fowls boil'd with Mushrooms.	A Ham roasted.	Fillets of Beef in Ragoo.

SECOND COURSE.

Raspberry Cream.	A Black Moorcock roasted.	Turkey Figs in Jelly.
Fruit.	Jellies, &c.	Fruit.
Peaches in Jelly.	Six Teals roasted.	Flummery.

A Bill of FARE for December.

Tongue & Chickens.	Plumb Broth. Remove Roast Ling.	Minc'd Pyes.
	Plain Butter. Fish sauce.	
Coller'd Brawn.	A Swan Pye.	Sturgeons.
	Pickles. Sallet.	
A Boil'd Plumb Pudding, with bak'd ditto	Ribs of Beef roasted.	A Quarter of Lamb roasted.

SECOND COURSE.

Two Wild Ducks roasted.

Pears.		Jellies.
Oysters in Jelly.	Pyramid of Sweet-meats	Dish of Cray Fish.
Syllabubs.	A Turkey larded.	Golden Pippins.

GLOSSARY

Abess *A round of puff pastry at the bottom of a dish*
Ambergris *a wax-like secretion of the sperm whale used as a flavouring in cookery and as a perfume*
Amulet *omelette*
Balance Skewer *skewer on which a weight could be hung to enable meat to turn evenly on a spit.*
Berry Lobster *lobster with spawn*
Bleaks *sometimes blay, small silver fish of the carp family*
Bleb *a small swelling containing the remains of entrails of the crayfish between the tail and body*
Brotch Lights *small pieces of offal for roasting*
Chimins *groats*
Chiringras, Chiringrate *in gipsy style*
Coller *collar, to bone, roll and tie meat for cooking*
Collops *thin slices of meat*
Cowfish *crawfish, crayfish*
Cram *force feed*
Crampine *a fowl*
Creed Rice *rice cooked into mush*
Crocaunt, Crocan *a china or pastry cover with cut out holes in decorative lozenge shapes*
Cruddle *curdle*
Cuebob'd *kebabbed*
Curranberry Leaves *blackcurrant leaves*
Dare *dace*
Esturgeon Seeds *caviare*
Gallipot *small tall cooking pot, glazed*
Gum Arabic *gum from* Acacia

Gumdragon *gum tragacanth from shrubs of the genus* Astragalus *found in the Middle East*
Hartshorn *the antlers of a stag, rasped or sliced, to make jelly*
Hastereaux *literally a ball of liver wrapped in caul but used by Thacker as stuffed slices of leg of veal or kidney etc. roasted on a skewer, in this case sweetbreads.*
Hoop *wooden ring in which cakes baked*
Inckle *tape*
Jennetons, Juneatings, Joaneatings. *An ancient early ripening desert apple*
Jigget *gigot*
Kell *caul*
Kiley *kyloe, small Northumbrian longhaired cattle*
Knockle *knuckle*
Lare *layer*
Mallagay Mountain *Malaga wine from mountain grapes*
Massereen, Mazerine, *a deep plate usually of metal, placed as a strainer inside a serving dish*
Morel *edible cup fungi of the genus* Morchella
Penny-rial *pennyroyal*
Pouts *young turkeys, chickens pheasants etc.*
Pulpatoon Pan *deep cylindrical copper pan resembling a charlotte mould, with a handle. Used in French court cookery.*
Quey Calf *a heifer*
Rammolade, Rémoulade, *sauce made with oil and mustard*
Sack *white wine from Spain*
Tereins *tureens*
Thropples *windpipes, gullets*

Southover's reprints of Cookery classics

Titles in print

THE ENGLISH BREAD BOOK by Eliza Acton (1857). Acton's ideas on healthy eating are relevant now and her directions to a novice breadmaker have still to be bettered. Introduction by Elizabeth Ray.   ISBN 1 870962 0 4   Price £14.95

MODERN COOKERY FOR PRIVATE FAMILIES by Eliza Acton (first published in 1845). Cookery classic of the 19th century. This is an unabridged reprint of the second edition of 1855 enlarged by the author to include British and foreign cookery. An introduction by Elizabeth Ray unearths some fresh information about the shadowy Miss Acton.
ISBN 1 870962 08 7   Price £25.00

THE COOKERY BOOK OF LADY CLARK OF TILLYPRONIE. Recipes collected by the author throughout her life. Unique culinary reportage from the second half of the 19th century, first published in 1909. Introduction by Geraldene Holt.
ISBN 1 870962 10 9   Price £22.00

A CULINARY CAMPAIGN by Alexis Soyer. Memoir of the great chef's time in the Crimea and his reorganisation of Army and hospital food, first published in 1857. With introductions by Michael Barthorp and Elizabeth Ray.
ISBN 1 870962 11 7   Price £22.00

THE GOOD HOUSEWIFE'S JEWEL by Thomas Dawson (1596/7). Written for the growing middle classes in Elizabethan England, contemporary with Shakespeare's *Much Ado* and *Merry Wives*. A sophisticated cookery book. Introduction by Maggie Black.   ISBN 1 870962 12 5   Price £14.95

THE EXPERIENCED ENGLISH HOUSEKEEPER by Elizabeth Raffald (1769). Elizabeth Raffald was an unusual woman entrepreneur ò housekeeper, author, shopkeeper, caterer and owner of an employment exchange, who compiled the first street directory and servants' register. Her cookery book became a bestseller. Introduction by Roy Shipperbottom.
ISBN 1 870962 13 3   Price £18.95

BEETON'S BOOK OF HOUSEHOLD MANAGEMENT. The original Mrs Beeton: a handsome facsimile of the very rare first impression of the first edition of 1861, with its splendid colour plates   ISBN 1 870962 15 X   Price £29.99

WILLIAM VERRALL'S COOKERY BOOK (1759). Written by the celebrated chef of the White Hart at Lewes, Verrall's book is lively and amusing, with a collection of sophisticated and cookable recipes.   ISBN 1 870962 00 1   Price £14.95

THE LIEBIG COMPANY'S PRACTICAL COOKERY BOOK compiled by Hannah M. Young. A facsimile of a charming hardback of 1894, promoting a product that later became Oxo.
ISBN 1 870962 16 8   Price £12.50

THE COMPLETE SERVANT by Samuel & Sarah Adams (1825) deals not only with the kitchen but also with the house, stables and garden. Pamela Horn, an authority on servant life of the period, writes an introduction.
ISBN 1 870962 09 5   Paperback £13.00

THE FRENCH COOK by François Pierre La Varenne. Translated by I.D.G. in 1653 from the 2nd edition of 1652. The foundation of classic French cuisine, changing European cookery for centuries to come. With an introduction by Philip and Mary Hyman.
ISBN 1 870962 17 6   Price £22.00

THE BOOK OF KERUYNGE (Book of Carving) (1508) printed by Wynkyn de Worde. Manual for arranging feasts and grand dinners, rituals of table-laying, saucing, servants' duties. Introduction and drawings by Peter Brears.
ISBN 1 870962 19 2   Price £13.50

SOUTHOVER PRESS

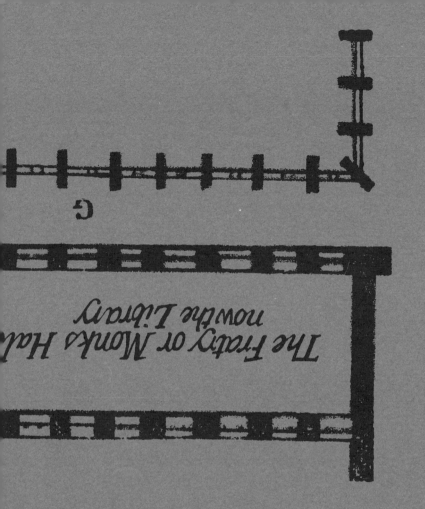